GERMAN
ENGLISH
ILLUSTRATED DICTIONARY

FREE
AUDIO APP

Author

Thomas Booth worked for 10 years as an English teacher in Poland, Romania, and Russia. He now lives in England, where he works as an editor and English-language materials writer. He has contributed to a number of books in the *English for Everyone* series.

GERMAN
ENGLISH
ILLUSTRATED DICTIONARY

PRODUCED BY
Author / Editor Thomas Booth
Senior Art Editor Sunita Gahir
Art Editors Ali Jayne Scrivens, Samantha Richiardi
Illustrators Edward Byrne, Gus Scott
Project Manager Sunita Gahir / bigmetalfish design

DK UK
Senior Editors Amelia Peterson, Christine Stroyan
Senior Designers Clare Shedden, Vicky Read
Managing Art Editor Anna Hall
Managing Editor Carine Tracanelli
Jacket Editors Stephanie Cheng Hui Tan, Juhi Sheth
Jacket Development Manager Sophia MTT
Production Editors Gillian Reid, Robert Dunn, Jacqueline Street
Production Controller Sian Cheung
Publisher Andrew Macintyre
Art Director Karen Self
Publishing Director Jonathan Metcalf

Translation Andiamo! Language Services Ltd

DK INDIA
Desk Editors Joicy John, Tanya Lohan
DTP Designers Anurag Trivedi, Satish Gaur,
Jaypal Chauhan, Bimlesh Tiwary, Rakesh Kumar
DTP Coordinator Pushpak Tyagi
Jacket Designer Vidushi Chaudhry
Senior Jackets Coordinator Priyanka Sharma Saddi
Managing Editor Saloni Talwar
Creative Head Malavika Talukder

First published in Great Britain in 2023 by
Dorling Kindersley Limited
20 Vauxhall Bridge Road, London, SW1V 2SA

The authorized representative in the EEA is
Dorling Kindersley Verlag GmbH. Arnulfstr. 124,
80636 Munich, Germany

Copyright © 2023 Dorling Kindersley Limited
A Penguin Random House Company
10 9 8 7 6 5 4 3
004–334030–Jun/2023

A CIP catalogue record for this book is available from the British Library
ISBN 978-0-2416-0148-8

Printed and bound in China

www.dk.com

Contents

DIE INFORMATIONEN REFERENCE

Komm, wir lernen ein paar Insektennamen!
Let's learn some words for bugs!

Ich habe mehr als 10.000 Wörter gelesen!
I have read more than 10,000 words!

How to use this book

This *German English Illustrated Dictionary* will help you to understand and remember more than 10,000 of the most useful words and phrases in German. Each of the 180 units in the dictionary covers a practical or everyday topic (such as health, food, or the natural world), and words are shown in a visual context to fix them in your memory along with their English equivalent. Using the audio app that accompanies the dictionary will help you learn and remember the new vocabulary.

Unit number The book is divided into units. The unit number helps you to find the unit easily when searching through the contents page.

Illustrated scenes Many units include illustrated scenes that make vocabulary easy to understand and remember.

English words The English translation is provided for each word.

Module numbers Most units are broken down into modules. Every module is identified with a unique number, so you can locate the audio on the app.

Illustrations All the entries in the dictionary are illustrated, helping you to understand and memorize new vocabulary.

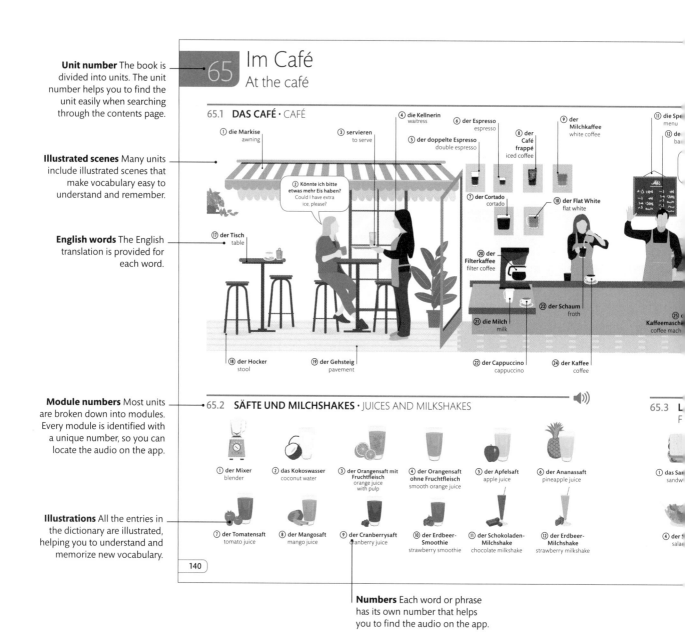

65 Im Café
At the café

65.1 DAS CAFÉ · CAFÉ

① die Markise — awning
② Könnte ich bitte etwas mehr Eis haben? Could I have extra ice, please?
③ servieren — to serve
④ die Kellnerin — waitress
⑤ der doppelte Espresso — double espresso
⑥ der Espresso — espresso
⑦ der Cortado — cortado
⑧ der Café frappé — iced coffee
⑨ der Milchkaffee — white coffee
⑩ der Flat White — flat white
⑪ die Spe... — menu
⑫ de... — ba...
⑰ der Tisch — table
⑱ der Hocker — stool
⑲ der Gehsteig — pavement
⑳ der Filterkaffee — filter coffee
㉑ die Milch — milk
㉒ der Cappuccino — cappuccino
㉓ der Schaum — froth
㉔ der Kaffee — coffee
㉕ ... Kaffeemaschi... coffee mach...

65.2 SÄFTE UND MILCHSHAKES · JUICES AND MILKSHAKES

① der Mixer — blender
② das Kokoswasser — coconut water
③ der Orangensaft mit Fruchtfleisch — orange juice with pulp
④ der Orangensaft ohne Fruchtfleisch — smooth orange juice
⑤ der Apfelsaft — apple juice
⑥ der Ananassaft — pineapple juice
⑦ der Tomatensaft — tomato juice
⑧ der Mangosaft — mango juice
⑨ der Cranberrysaft — cranberry juice
⑩ der Erdbeer-Smoothie — strawberry smoothie
⑪ der Schokoladen-Milchshake — chocolate milkshake
⑫ der Erdbeer-Milchshake — strawberry milkshake

65.3 L... F...
① das Sa... sandw...
④ der S... sala...

140

Numbers Each word or phrase has its own number that helps you to find the audio on the app.

Gender and articles

All nouns in the dictionary are preceded by the definite article ("the"). In German, nouns are masculine, feminine or neuter. "Der" is used before masculine nouns, "die" is used with feminine and plural nouns, and "das" is used before the neuter. Where "die" is used with a plural, the gender is indicated with *m, f* or *n*.

der Spielzeugladen
toy shop

die Wanderschuhe
m, pl
hiking boots

die Schwester
sister

die Käsesorten *f, pl*
cheeses

das Doppelbett
double bed

die Bücher *n, pl*
books

Word lists

The German and English word lists at the back of the book contain every entry from the dictionary. All the vocabulary is listed in alphabetical order, and each entry is followed by the unit number or numbers in which it is found, enabling you to look up any word in either German or English. The German words are listed without the articles, so that you can search for words alphabetically. The English word list also provides information about the part of speech (for example noun, verb, or adjective) of each word.

Audio app

The *German English Illustrated Dictionary* is supported by a free audio app containing every German word and phrase in the book. Listen to the audio and repeat the words and phrases out loud, until you are confident you understand and can pronounce what has been said. The app can be found by searching for "DK Illustrated Dictionary" in the App Store or Google Play.

FREE
AUDIO APP

See also Each unit has a "see also" box that directs you to other units with useful or related vocabulary.

See also
27 Die Küche und das Geschirr • Kitchen and tableware 52 Trinken und
essen • Drinking and eating 66 Im Café (Fortsetzung) • At the café continued
70 Fastfood • Fast food 72 Das Mittagessen und das Abendessen • Lunch and dinner

⑭ das **Kakaopulver**
cocoa powder

die **Barista** *f*

⑮ der **Irish Coffee**
Irish coffee

⑯ der **Sonnenschirm**
patio umbrella / parasol

…, ich hätte
…en Espresso
…tnehmen.
… to go, please.

㉖ der **Gast** *m* / die **Gästin** *f*
customer

㉗ der **schwarze Kaffee**
black coffee

㉘ die **Terrasse**
terrace

㉙ das **Geländer**
railing

SMITTEL UND SNACKS
AND SNACKS

② der **Pfannkuchen**
pancake

③ die **Waffel**
waffle

⑤ das **Eis in der Waffel**
ice cream cone

⑥ das **Eis im Becher**
ice cream scoop

⑩ Es tut mir leid, Sandwiches
sind leider aus.
Sorry, we've run out of sandwiches.

⑨ das **Getränk**
beverages

⑧ der **Snack**
snacks

⑦ die **Snackbar**
snack bar

141

Speech bubbles Useful expressions and examples of real-life German appear in speech bubbles throughout the book.

1.1   DER MENSCHLICHE KÖRPER · THE HUMAN BODY

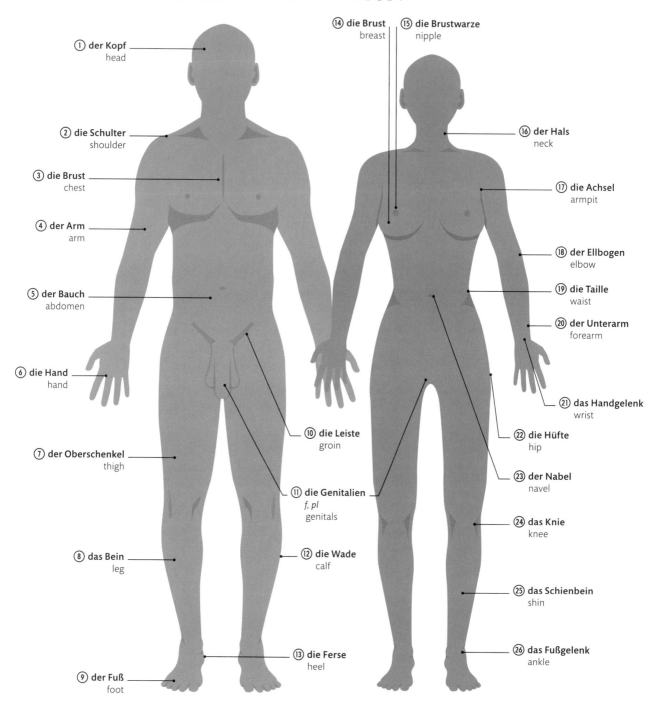

1 **der Kopf**
head

2 **die Schulter**
shoulder

3 **die Brust**
chest

4 **der Arm**
arm

5 **der Bauch**
abdomen

6 **die Hand**
hand

7 **der Oberschenkel**
thigh

8 **das Bein**
leg

9 **der Fuß**
foot

10 **die Leiste**
groin

11 **die Genitalien**
f, pl
genitals

12 **die Wade**
calf

13 **die Ferse**
heel

14 **die Brust**
breast

15 **die Brustwarze**
nipple

16 **der Hals**
neck

17 **die Achsel**
armpit

18 **der Ellbogen**
elbow

19 **die Taille**
waist

20 **der Unterarm**
forearm

21 **das Handgelenk**
wrist

22 **die Hüfte**
hip

23 **der Nabel**
navel

24 **das Knie**
knee

25 **das Schienbein**
shin

26 **das Fußgelenk**
ankle

See also
02 Hände und Füße · Hands and feet **03** Muskeln und Skelett · Muscles and skeleton
04 Innere Organe · Internal organs **19** Krankheiten und Verletzungen · Illness and injury
20 Beim Arzt · Visiting the doctor **22** Der Zahnarzt und der Optiker · The dentist and optician

1.2 DAS GESICHT · FACE

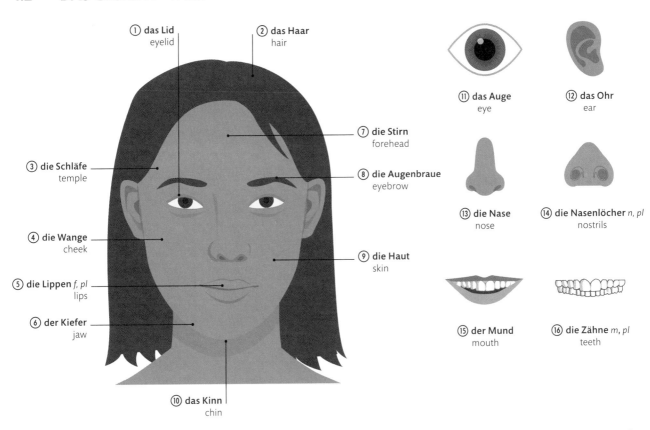

① das Lid
eyelid

② das Haar
hair

⑦ die Stirn
forehead

③ die Schläfe
temple

⑧ die Augenbraue
eyebrow

④ die Wange
cheek

⑤ die Lippen *f, pl*
lips

⑥ der Kiefer
jaw

⑨ die Haut
skin

⑩ das Kinn
chin

⑪ das Auge
eye

⑫ das Ohr
ear

⑬ die Nase
nose

⑭ die Nasenlöcher *n, pl*
nostrils

⑮ der Mund
mouth

⑯ die Zähne *m, pl*
teeth

1.3 DIE AUGEN · EYES

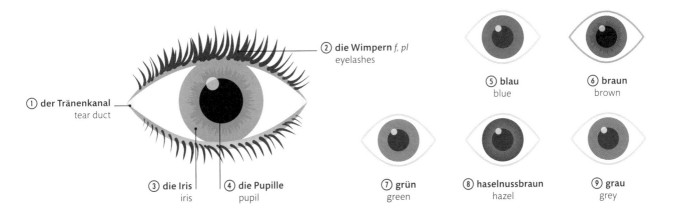

② die Wimpern *f, pl*
eyelashes

① der Tränenkanal
tear duct

③ die Iris
iris

④ die Pupille
pupil

⑤ blau
blue

⑥ braun
brown

⑦ grün
green

⑧ haselnussbraun
hazel

⑨ grau
grey

2.1 DIE HÄNDE · HANDS

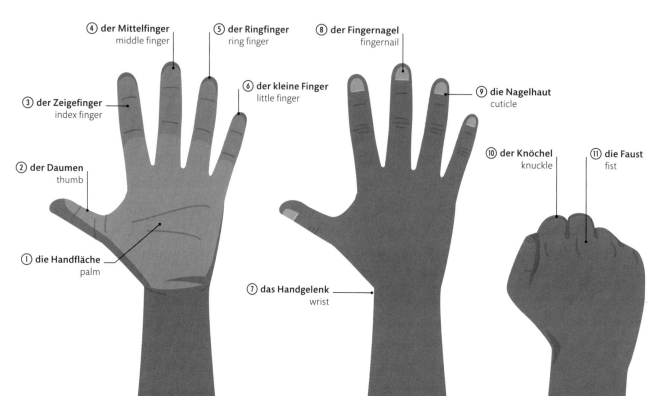

④ **der Mittelfinger**
middle finger

⑤ **der Ringfinger**
ring finger

⑧ **der Fingernagel**
fingernail

③ **der Zeigefinger**
index finger

⑥ **der kleine Finger**
little finger

⑨ **die Nagelhaut**
cuticle

② **der Daumen**
thumb

⑩ **der Knöchel**
knuckle

⑪ **die Faust**
fist

① **die Handfläche**
palm

⑦ **das Handgelenk**
wrist

2.2 KÖRPERVERBEN · BODY VERBS

① **lächeln**
to smile

② **grinsen**
to grin

③ **die Stirn runzeln**
to frown

④ **zwinkern**
to wink

⑤ **blinzeln**
to blink

⑥ **rot werden**
to blush

⑦ **gähnen**
to yawn

⑧ **schnarchen**
to snore

⑨ **lecken**
to lick

⑩ **saugen**
to suck

⑪ **atmen**
to breathe

⑫ **den Atem anhalten**
to hold your breath

See also
01 Körperteile • Parts of the body **03** Muskeln und Skelett • Muscles and skeleton
19 Krankheiten und Verletzungen • Illness and injury **20** Beim Arzt • Visiting the doctor
21 Das Krankenhaus • The hospital

2.3 DIE FÜSSE · FEET

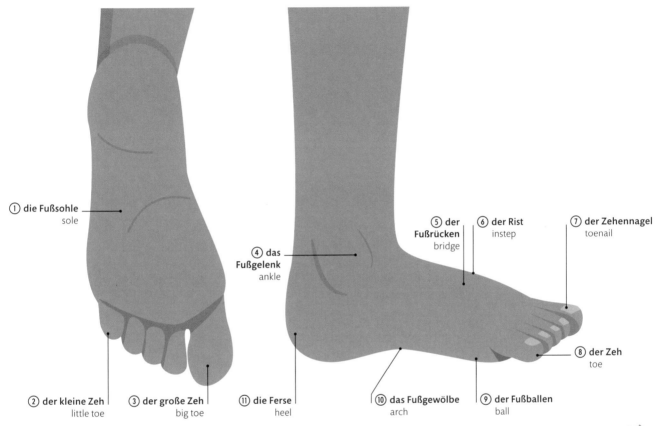

① **die Fußsohle**
sole

④ **das Fußgelenk**
ankle

⑤ **der Fußrücken**
bridge

⑥ **der Rist**
instep

⑦ **der Zehennagel**
toenail

⑧ **der Zeh**
toe

② **der kleine Zeh**
little toe

③ **der große Zeh**
big toe

⑪ **die Ferse**
heel

⑩ **das Fußgewölbe**
arch

⑨ **der Fußballen**
ball

"Ha ha!"

⑬ **lachen**
to laugh

⑭ **weinen**
to cry

⑮ **seufzen**
to sigh

⑯ **winken**
to wave

⑰ **mit den Schultern zucken**
to shrug

⑱ **sich verbeugen**
to bow

⑲ **klatschen**
to clap

⑳ **schwitzen**
to sweat /
to perspire

㉑ **zittern**
to shiver

㉒ **niesen**
to sneeze

㉓ **den Kopf schütteln**
to shake your head

㉔ **nicken**
to nod

3.1 DIE MUSKELN
MUSCLES

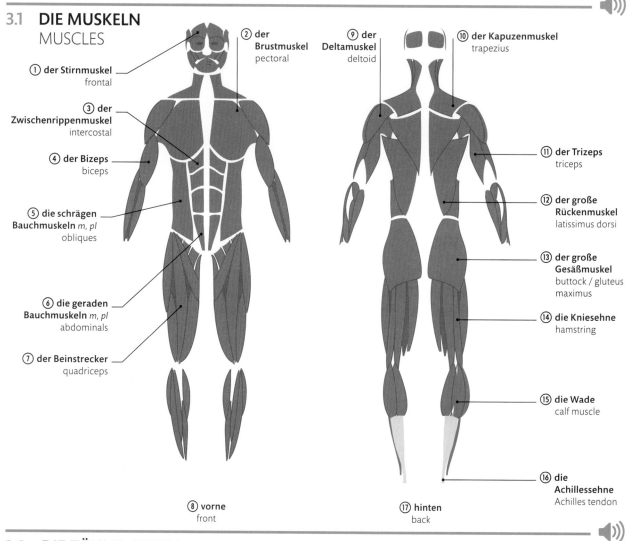

① der Stirnmuskel
frontal

② der Brustmuskel
pectoral

③ der Zwischenrippenmuskel
intercostal

④ der Bizeps
biceps

⑤ die schrägen Bauchmuskeln m, pl
obliques

⑥ die geraden Bauchmuskeln m, pl
abdominals

⑦ der Beinstrecker
quadriceps

⑧ vorne
front

⑨ der Deltamuskel
deltoid

⑩ der Kapuzenmuskel
trapezius

⑪ der Trizeps
triceps

⑫ der große Rückenmuskel
latissimus dorsi

⑬ der große Gesäßmuskel
buttock / gluteus maximus

⑭ die Kniesehne
hamstring

⑮ die Wade
calf muscle

⑯ die Achillessehne
Achilles tendon

⑰ hinten
back

3.2 DIE ZÄHNE · TEETH

① die Schneidezähne m, pl
incisors

② die Eckzähne m, pl
canines

③ die Backenzähne m, pl
molars

④ die vorderen Backenzähne m, pl
premolars

⑤ das Zahnfleisch
gum

⑥ das Zahnmark
pulp

⑦ der Nerv
nerve

⑧ der Zahnschmelz
enamel

⑨ der Knochen
bone

⑩ die Wurzel
root

⑪ der Zahn
tooth

See also
01 Körperteile • Parts of the body **02** Hände und Füße • Hands and feet
04 Innere Organe • Internal organs **19** Krankheiten und Verletzungen • Illness
and injury **20** Beim Arzt • Visiting the doctor **21** Das Krankenhaus • The hospital

3.3 DAS SKELETT · SKELETON

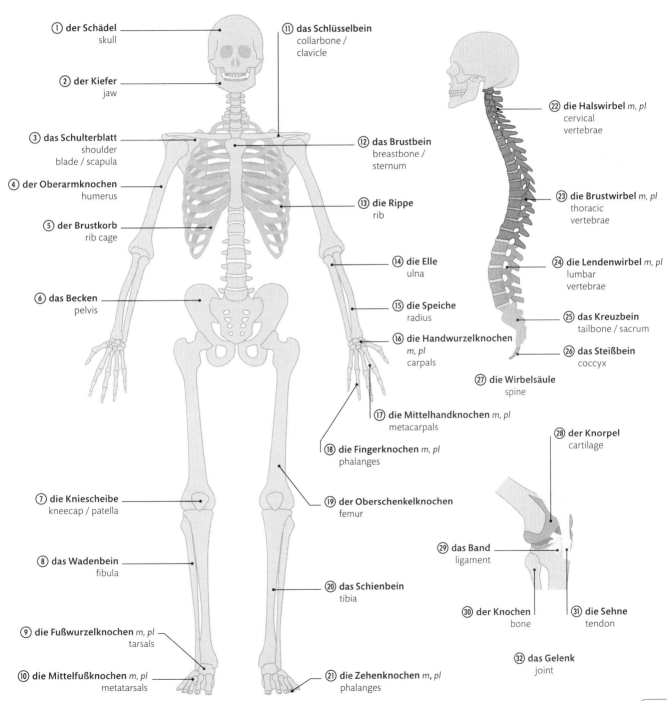

① **der Schädel**
skull

② **der Kiefer**
jaw

③ **das Schulterblatt**
shoulder
blade / scapula

④ **der Oberarmknochen**
humerus

⑤ **der Brustkorb**
rib cage

⑥ **das Becken**
pelvis

⑦ **die Kniescheibe**
kneecap / patella

⑧ **das Wadenbein**
fibula

⑨ **die Fußwurzelknochen** *m, pl*
tarsals

⑩ **die Mittelfußknochen** *m, pl*
metatarsals

⑪ **das Schlüsselbein**
collarbone /
clavicle

⑫ **das Brustbein**
breastbone /
sternum

⑬ **die Rippe**
rib

⑭ **die Elle**
ulna

⑮ **die Speiche**
radius

⑯ **die Handwurzelknochen**
m, pl
carpals

⑰ **die Mittelhandknochen** *m, pl*
metacarpals

⑱ **die Fingerknochen** *m, pl*
phalanges

⑲ **der Oberschenkelknochen**
femur

⑳ **das Schienbein**
tibia

㉑ **die Zehenknochen** *m, pl*
phalanges

㉒ **die Halswirbel** *m, pl*
cervical
vertebrae

㉓ **die Brustwirbel** *m, pl*
thoracic
vertebrae

㉔ **die Lendenwirbel** *m, pl*
lumbar
vertebrae

㉕ **das Kreuzbein**
tailbone / sacrum

㉖ **das Steißbein**
coccyx

㉗ **die Wirbelsäule**
spine

㉘ **der Knorpel**
cartilage

㉙ **das Band**
ligament

㉚ **der Knochen**
bone

㉛ **die Sehne**
tendon

㉜ **das Gelenk**
joint

4.1 INNERE ORGANE · INTERNAL ORGANS

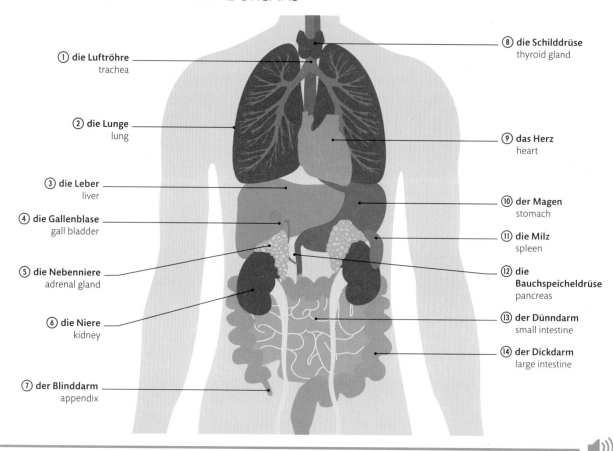

① **die Luftröhre**
trachea

② **die Lunge**
lung

③ **die Leber**
liver

④ **die Gallenblase**
gall bladder

⑤ **die Nebenniere**
adrenal gland

⑥ **die Niere**
kidney

⑦ **der Blinddarm**
appendix

⑧ **die Schilddrüse**
thyroid gland

⑨ **das Herz**
heart

⑩ **der Magen**
stomach

⑪ **die Milz**
spleen

⑫ **die Bauchspeicheldrüse**
pancreas

⑬ **der Dünndarm**
small intestine

⑭ **der Dickdarm**
large intestine

4.2 KÖRPERSYSTEME · BODY SYSTEMS

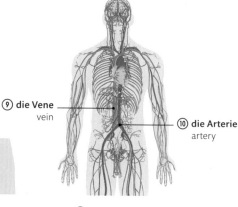

① **die Atemwege** *m, pl*
respiratory

② **der Verdauungstrakt**
digestive

③ **das Nervensystem**
nervous

④ **der Harntrakt**
urinary

⑤ **das endokrine System**
endocrine

⑥ **das Lymphsystem**
lymphatic

⑦ **das Fortpflanzungssystem**
reproductive

⑧ **der Blutkreislauf**
cardiovascular

⑨ **die Vene**
vein

⑩ **die Arterie**
artery

See also
01 Körperteile • Parts of the body **03** Muskeln und Skelett • Muscles and skeleton
19 Krankheiten und Verletzungen • Illness and injury **20** Beim Arzt • Visiting the doctor
21 Das Krankenhaus • The hospital

4.3 **DER KOPF** · HEAD

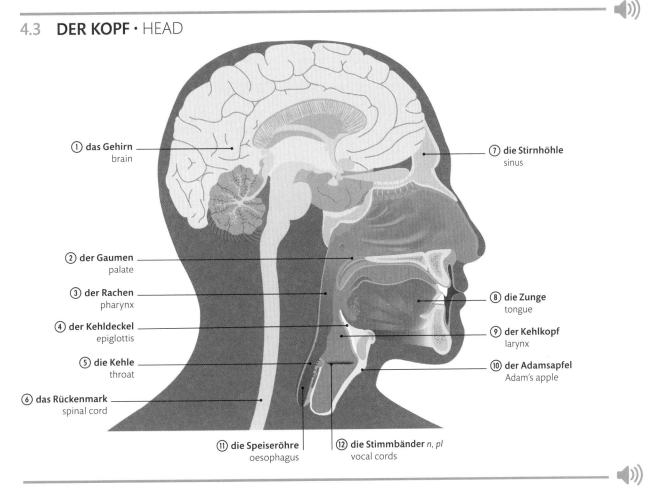

① das Gehirn
brain

⑦ die Stirnhöhle
sinus

② der Gaumen
palate

⑧ die Zunge
tongue

③ der Rachen
pharynx

④ der Kehldeckel
epiglottis

⑨ der Kehlkopf
larynx

⑤ die Kehle
throat

⑩ der Adamsapfel
Adam's apple

⑥ das Rückenmark
spinal cord

⑪ die Speiseröhre
oesophagus

⑫ die Stimmbänder *n, pl*
vocal cords

4.4 **DIE FORTPFLANZUNGSORGANE** · REPRODUCTIVE ORGANS

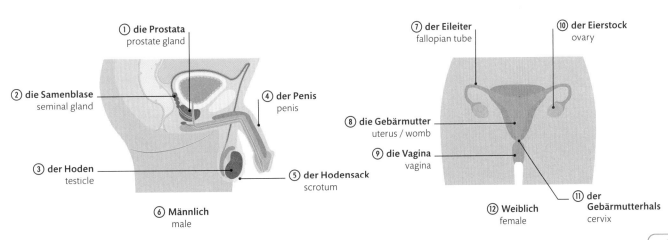

① die Prostata
prostate gland

⑦ der Eileiter
fallopian tube

⑩ der Eierstock
ovary

② die Samenblase
seminal gland

④ der Penis
penis

⑧ die Gebärmutter
uterus / womb

③ der Hoden
testicle

⑤ der Hodensack
scrotum

⑨ die Vagina
vagina

⑥ Männlich
male

⑫ Weiblich
female

⑪ der Gebärmutterhals
cervix

5.1 CARLOS FAMILIE · CARLOS'S FAMILY

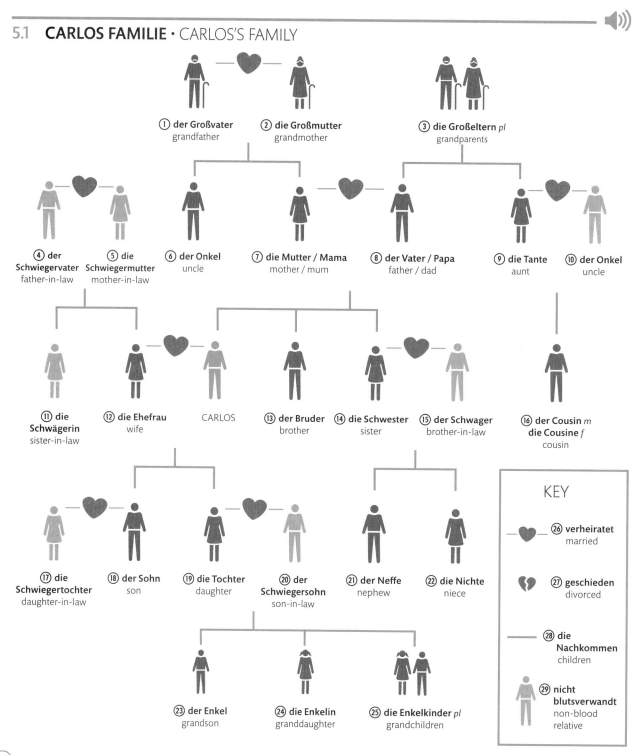

① **der Großvater** grandfather

② **die Großmutter** grandmother

③ **die Großeltern** *pl* grandparents

④ **der Schwiegervater** father-in-law

⑤ **die Schwiegermutter** mother-in-law

⑥ **der Onkel** uncle

⑦ **die Mutter / Mama** mother / mum

⑧ **der Vater / Papa** father / dad

⑨ **die Tante** aunt

⑩ **der Onkel** uncle

⑪ **die Schwägerin** sister-in-law

⑫ **die Ehefrau** wife

CARLOS

⑬ **der Bruder** brother

⑭ **die Schwester** sister

⑮ **der Schwager** brother-in-law

⑯ **der Cousin** *m* **die Cousine** *f* cousin

⑰ **die Schwiegertochter** daughter-in-law

⑱ **der Sohn** son

⑲ **die Tochter** daughter

⑳ **der Schwiegersohn** son-in-law

㉑ **der Neffe** nephew

㉒ **die Nichte** niece

㉓ **der Enkel** grandson

㉔ **die Enkelin** granddaughter

㉕ **die Enkelkinder** *pl* grandchildren

KEY

㉖ **verheiratet** married

㉗ **geschieden** divorced

㉘ **die Nachkommen** children

㉙ **nicht blutsverwandt** non-blood relative

See also
07 Lebensereignisse · Life events
08 Schwangerschaft und Kindheit · Pregnancy and childhood

5.2 SARAHS FAMILIE
SARAH'S FAMILY

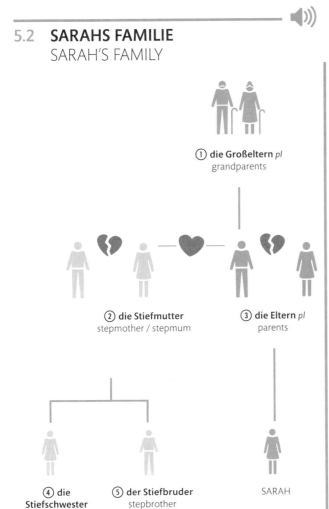

① **die Großeltern** *pl*
grandparents

② **die Stiefmutter**
stepmother / stepmum

③ **die Eltern** *pl*
parents

④ **die Stiefschwester**
stepsister

⑤ **der Stiefbruder**
stepbrother

SARAH

5.3 BEZIEHUNGEN · RELATIONSHIPS

① **der (feste) Freund** *m*
die (feste) Freundin *f*
boyfriend / girlfriend

② **der Partner** *m*
die Partnerin *f*
partner

③ **der Alleinerziehende** *m*
die Alleinerziehende *f*
single parent

④ **die Witwe**
widow

⑥ **der Ehemann**
husband

⑦ **die Ehefrau**
wife

⑤ **verheiratet**
married

⑨ **die Ex-Frau**
ex-wife

⑩ **der Ex-Mann**
ex-husband

⑧ **geschieden**
divorced

⑪ **die Geschwister** *pl*
siblings

⑫ **die Zwillinge** *m, pl*
twins

⑬ **die Drillinge** *m, pl*
triplets

⑭ **das Einzelkind**
only child

5.4 AUFWACHSEN · GROWING UP

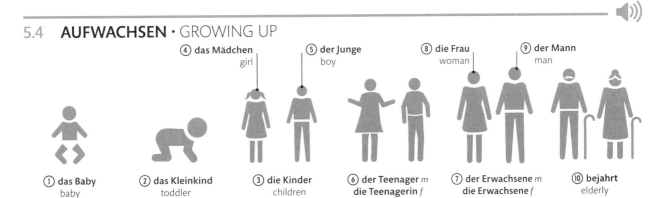

④ **das Mädchen**
girl

⑤ **der Junge**
boy

⑧ **die Frau**
woman

⑨ **der Mann**
man

① **das Baby**
baby

② **das Kleinkind**
toddler

③ **die Kinder**
children

⑥ **der Teenager** *m*
die Teenagerin *f*
teenagers

⑦ **der Erwachsene** *m*
die Erwachsene *f*
adults

⑩ **bejahrt**
elderly

06 Gefühle und Stimmung
Feelings and moods

6.1 GEFÜHLE UND STIMMUNG · FEELINGS AND MOODS

① **zufrieden**
pleased

② **fröhlich**
cheerful

③ **glücklich**
happy

④ **erfreut**
delighted

⑤ **verzückt**
ecstatic

⑥ **amüsiert**
amused

⑦ **dankbar**
grateful

⑧ **glücklich**
lucky

⑨ **interessiert**
interested

⑩ **neugierig**
curious

⑪ **fasziniert**
intrigued

⑫ **erstaunt**
amazed

⑬ **überrascht**
surprised

⑭ **stolz**
proud

⑮ **aufgeregt**
excited

⑯ **begeistert**
thrilled

⑰ **ruhig**
calm

⑱ **entspannt**
relaxed

⑳ **Danke. Das Essen war hervorragend.**
Thank you. I really enjoyed the meal.

⑲ **wertschätzend**
appreciative

㉑ **selbstbewusst**
confident

㉒ **hoffnungsvoll**
hopeful

㉓ **mitfühlend**
sympathetic

㉔ **genervt**
annoyed

㉕ **eifersüchtig**
jealous

㉖ **peinlich berührt**
embarrassed

See also
10 Eigenschaften • Personality traits **24** Gesunder Körper, gesunder Geist • Healthy body, healthy mind **93** Nützliche Fähigkeiten für den Arbeitsplatz • Workplace skills

㉘ **Ich habe schon wieder nicht bestanden. Ich bin sehr enttäuscht.**
I failed the exam again. I'm very disappointed.

㉗ **enttäuscht**
disappointed

㉙ **besorgt**
worried

㉚ **ängstlich**
anxious

㉛ **nervös**
nervous

㉜ **erschrocken**
frightened

㉝ **verängstigt**
scared

㉞ **in Schrecken versetzt**
terrified

㉟ **traurig**
sad

㊱ **unglücklich**
unhappy

㊲ **den Tränen nah**
tearful

㊳ **elend**
miserable

㊴ **depressiv**
depressed

㊵ **einsam**
lonely

㊶ **verärgert**
irritated

㊷ **frustriert**
frustrated

㊸ **sauer**
angry

㊹ **wütend**
furious

㊺ **angeekelt**
disgusted

㊻ **lustlos**
unenthusiastic

㊼ **müde**
tired

㊽ **erschöpft**
exhausted

㊾ **verwirrt**
confused

㊿ **gelangweilt**
bored

(51) **abgelenkt**
distracted

(52) **ernst**
serious

(53) **gleichgültig**
indifferent

(54) **gestresst**
stressed

(55) **schuldbewusst**
guilty

(56) **unbeeindruckt**
unimpressed

(57) **aufgelöst**
upset

(58) **schockiert**
shocked

7.1 BEZIEHUNGEN · RELATIONSHIPS

① **der Nachbar** *m*
die Nachbarin *f*
neighbour

② **der Freund** *m*
die Freundin *f*
friend

③ **der Bekannte** *m*
die Bekannte *f*
acquaintance

④ **der Kollege** *m*
die Kollegin *f*
colleague

⑤ **der Brieffreund** *m*
die Brieffreundin *f*
pen pal

⑥ **das Paar**
couple

⑦ **der beste Freund** *m*
die beste Freundin *f*
best friend

⑧ **der Partner** *m*
die Partnerin *f*
partner

⑨ **Willst du mich heiraten?**
Will you marry me?

⑩ **die Verlobte**
fiancée

⑪ **der Verlobte**
fiancé

⑫ **die Verlobten** *pl*
engaged couple

⑬ **die Braut**
bride

⑭ **der Bräutigam**
groom

⑮ **das Ehepaar** *pl*
married couple

7.2 LEBENSEREIGNISSE · LIFE EVENTS

① **geboren werden**
to be born

② **die Geburtsurkunde**
birth certificate

③ **in den Kindergarten gehen**
to go to nursery

④ **eingeschult werden**
to start school

⑤ **Freunde finden**
to make friends

⑥ **einen Preis gewinnen**
to win a prize

⑦ **einen Abschluss machen**
to graduate

⑧ **auswandern**
to emigrate

⑨ **einen Job annehmen**
to get a job

⑩ **sich verlieben**
to fall in love

⑪ **heiraten**
to get married

See also
05 Die Familie · Family **08** Schwangerschaft und Kindheit · Pregnancy and childhood **19** Krankheiten und Verletzungen · Illness and injury **73** In der Schule · At school **80** An der Universität · At college **92** Bewerbungen · Applying for a job **131** Reise und Unterkunft · Travel and accommodation

7.3 FESTE UND FEIERLICHKEITEN · FESTIVALS AND CELEBRATIONS

① **der Geburtstag**
birthday

② **das Geschenk**
present

③ **die Geburtstagskarte**
birthday card

④ **Weihnachten** n
Christmas

⑤ **Silvester** n
New Year

⑥ **Fasching** m
carnival

⑦ **Erntedank** m
Thanksgiving

⑧ **Ostern** n
Easter

⑨ **Halloween** n
Halloween

⑩ **Kwanzaa** n
Kwanzaa

⑪ **das Passahfest**
Passover

⑫ **Diwali** n
Diwali

⑬ **der Tag der Toten**
Day of the Dead

⑭ **das Fest des Fastenbrechens**
Eid al-Fitr

⑮ **das Holi-Fest**
Holi

⑯ **Chanukka** n
Hanukkah

⑰ **Vaisakhi** n
Baisakhi / Vaisakhi

⑫ **die Hochzeit**
wedding

⑬ **die Hochzeitsreise**
honeymoon

⑭ **der Jahrestag**
anniversary

⑮ **ein Kind bekommen**
to have a baby

⑰ **das Weihwasser**
holy water

⑯ **die Taufe**
christening / baptism

⑱ **der Bar Mitzwa die Bat Mitzwa**
bar mitzvah / bat mitzvah

⑲ **den Hadsch machen**
to go on Hajj

⑳ **in Rente gehen**
to retire

㉑ **sich scheiden lassen**
divorce

㉒ **ein Testament aufsetzen**
to make a will

㉓ **sterben**
to die

㉔ **die Beerdigung**
funeral

8.1 SCHWANGERSCHAFT UND GEBURT · PREGNANCY AND CHILDBIRTH

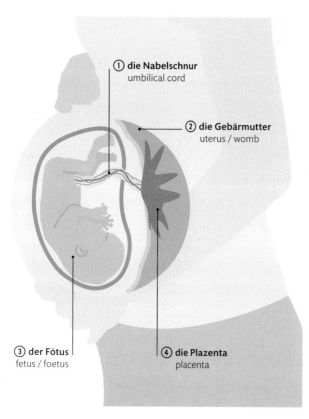

① **die Nabelschnur**
umbilical cord

② **die Gebärmutter**
uterus / womb

③ **der Fötus**
fetus / foetus

④ **die Plazenta**
placenta

⑤ **der Schwangerschaftstest**
pregnancy test

⑥ **schwanger**
pregnant

⑧ **der Embryo**
embryo

⑦ **der Ultraschall**
ultrasound

⑨ **der Geburtstermin**
due date

⑩ **der Geburtshelfer** *m*
die Hebamme *f*
midwife

⑪ **der Entbindungsarzt** *m*
die Entbindungsärztin *f*
obstetrician

⑫ **die Geburt**
birth

⑬ **das Neugeborene**
newborn baby

⑭ **die Impfung**
vaccination

⑮ **der Brutkasten**
incubator

8.2 SPIELE UND SPIELZEUGE · TOYS AND GAMES

① **die Puppe**
doll

② **das Puppenhaus**
doll's house

③ **das Stofftier**
soft toy

④ **das Brettspiel**
board game

⑤ **die Bauklötze** *m, pl*
building blocks /
building bricks

⑥ **der Ball**
ball

⑦ **der Kreisel**
spinning top

⑧ **das Jo-Jo**
yo-yo

⑨ **das Springseil**
skipping rope

⑩ **das Trampolin**
trampoline

⑪ **das Puzzle**
jigsaw puzzle

⑫ **die Spielzeugeisenbahn**
train set

See also
05 Die Familie · Family **13** Kleidung · Clothes **20** Beim Arzt · Visiting the doctor
21 Das Krankenhaus · The hospital **30** Das Schlafzimmerr · Bedroom

8.3 DIE KINDHEIT · CHILDHOOD

① **der Buggy**
buggy

② **der Kinderwagen**
pram

③ **der Hochstuhl**
high chair

④ **der Schnuller**
dummy

⑤ **die Rassel**
rattle

⑥ **das Babyfon**
baby monitor

⑦ **das Treppengitter**
stair gate

⑧ **das Babykörbchen**
Moses basket

⑨ **die Babybadewanne**
baby bath

⑩ **das Töpfchen**
potty

⑪ **das Feuchttuch**
wet wipe

⑫ **das Kleinkind**
toddler

⑬ **die Wundschutzcreme**
nappy rash cream

⑭ **die Windel**
nappy

⑮ **die Windeltasche**
changing bag

⑯ **der Laufstall**
playpen

⑱ **der Sauger**
teat

⑰ **das Fläschchen**
bottle

⑲ **die Milchnahrung**
baby formula

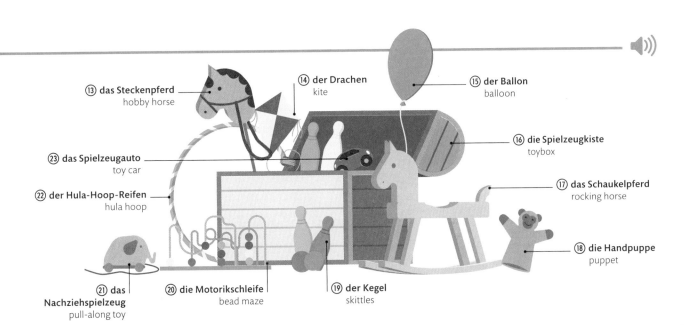

⑬ **das Steckenpferd**
hobby horse

⑭ **der Drachen**
kite

⑮ **der Ballon**
balloon

⑯ **die Spielzeugkiste**
toybox

㉓ **das Spielzeugauto**
toy car

⑰ **das Schaukelpferd**
rocking horse

㉒ **der Hula-Hoop-Reifen**
hula hoop

⑱ **die Handpuppe**
puppet

㉑ **das Nachziehspielzeug**
pull-along toy

⑳ **die Motorikschleife**
bead maze

⑲ **der Kegel**
skittles

Die Alltagsroutine
Daily routines

9.1 VORMITTAG UND NACHMITTAG · MORNING AND AFTERNOON

① **der Wecker klingelt**
alarm goes off

② **aufwachen**
to wake up

③ **aufstehen**
to get up

④ **sich duschen**
to take (or have) a shower

⑤ **sich baden**
to take (or have) a bath

⑥ **sich schminken**
to put on makeup

⑦ **sich rasieren**
to shave

⑧ **sich die Haare waschen**
to wash your hair

⑨ **sich die Haare föhnen**
to dry your hair

⑩ **ein Hemd bügeln**
to iron a shirt

⑪ **sich anziehen**
to get dressed

⑫ **sich die Zähne putzen**
to brush your teeth

⑬ **sich das Gesicht waschen**
to wash your face

⑭ **sich die Haare bürsten**
to brush your hair

⑮ **das Bett machen**
to make the bed

⑯ **frühstücken**
to have (or eat) breakfast

⑰ **das Mittagessen einpacken**
to pack your lunch

⑱ **das Haus verlassen**
to leave the house

⑲ **zur Arbeit gehen**
to go to work

⑳ **in die Schule gehen**
to go to school

㉑ **fahren**
to drive

㉒ **mit dem Bus fahren**
to catch the bus

㉓ **mit dem Zug fahren**
to catch the train

㉔ **die Zeitung lesen**
to read a newspaper

㉕ **ankommen**
to arrive

㉖ **früh ankommen**
to arrive early

㉗ **pünktlich ankommen**
to arrive on time

㉜ **Es tut mir leid, dass ich schon wieder zu spät gekommen bin.**
I'm sorry I'm late again.

㉛ **zu spät kommen**
to arrive late / to be late

㉘ **zu Mittag essen**
to have (or eat) lunch

㉙ **die E-Mails checken**
to check your emails

㉚ **eine Pause machen**
to have a break

See also
11 Fähigkeiten und Handlungen · Abilities and actions **29** Kochen · Cooking
81 Auf der Arbeit · At work **82** Im Büro · In the office **171** Die Zeit · Time
178 Geläufige Verben · Common phrasal verbs

9.2 DER ABEND · EVENING

④ **Am schönsten ist es zu Hause!**
There's no place like home!

① **die Arbeit beenden**
to finish work

② **die Arbeit verlassen**
to leave work

③ **Überstunden machen**
to work overtime

⑤ **nach Hause kommen**
to arrive home

⑥ **das Abendessen kochen**
to cook dinner

⑦ **zu Abend essen**
to have (or eat) dinner

⑧ **den Tisch abräumen**
to clear the table

⑨ **abspülen**
to wash up

⑩ **Radio hören**
to listen to the radio

⑪ **fernsehen**
to watch TV

⑫ **Tee oder Kaffee trinken**
to drink tea or coffee

⑬ **den Müll hinausbringen**
to take out the rubbish

⑭ **die Kinder ins Bett bringen**
to put the children to bed

⑮ **ins Bett gehen**
to go to bed

⑯ **den Wecker stellen**
to set the alarm

⑰ **einschlafen**
to go to sleep

9.3 ANDERE AKTIVITÄTEN OTHER ACTIVITIES

① **Hausaufgaben machen**
to do homework

② **Gassi gehen**
to walk the dog

③ **den Hund / die Katze füttern**
to feed the dog / cat

④ **Lebensmittel einkaufen**
to buy groceries

⑤ **sich mit Freunden treffen**
to go out with friends

⑥ **in ein Café gehen**
to go to a café

⑦ **Freunde anrufen die Familie anrufen**
to call a friend /
to call your family

⑧ **den Rasen mähen**
to mow the lawn

⑨ **Sport machen**
to exercise

⑩ **mit den Kindern spielen**
to play with your kids

⑪ **Rechnungen bezahlen**
to pay the bills

⑫ **ein Nickerchen machen**
to take a nap

⑬ **das Auto putzen**
to clean the car

⑭ **ein Instrument spielen**
to play a musical instrument

⑮ **sich mit Freunden unterhalten**
to chat with friends

⑯ **online chatten**
to chat online

⑰ **die Blumen gießen**
to water the plants

⑱ **ein Paket verschicken**
to send a package / parcel

10 Eigenschaften
Personality traits

10.1 PERSONEN BESCHREIBEN · DESCRIBING PERSONALITIES

① nett
friendly

② unfreundlich
unfriendly

③ gesprächig
talkative

④ enthusiastisch
enthusiastic

⑤ ernst
serious

⑥ bestimmt
assertive

⑦ kritisch
critical

⑧ fürsorglich
caring

⑨ empfindlich
sensitive

⑩ unsensibel
insensitive

⑪ vernünftig
reasonable

⑫ unvernünftig
unreasonable

⑬ freundlich
kind

⑭ unfreundlich
unkind

⑮ geheimniskrämerisch
secretive

⑯ erwachsen
mature

⑰ kindisch
immature

⑱ vorsichtig
cautious

⑲ großzügig
generous

⑳ mutig
brave

㉑ witzig
funny

㉒ gemein
mean

㉓ geduldig
patient

㉔ ungeduldig
impatient

㉕ faul
lazy

㉖ optimistisch
optimistic

㉗ aufgeschlossen / extrovertiert
outgoing

㉘ leidenschaftlich
passionate

㉙ höflich
polite

㉚ unhöflich
rude

㉛ schüchtern
shy

㉜ intelligent
intelligent

㉝ nervös
nervous

㉞ selbstbewusst
confident

㉟ albern
silly

㊱ selbstsüchtig
selfish

See also
05 Die Familie • Family **06** Gefühle und Stimmung • Feelings and moods **11** Fähigkeiten und Handlungen • Abilities and actions **93** Nützliche Fähigkeiten für den Arbeitsplatz • Workplace skills

㊳ **Die Arbeit kann warten.**
My work can wait until later.

㊲ **entspannt**
laid-back

㊴ **ehrgeizig**
ambitious

㊵ **spontan**
spontaneous

㊶ **romantisch**
romantic

㊷ **ruhig**
calm

㊸ **exzentrisch**
eccentric

㊹ **ehrlich**
honest

㊺ **unehrlich**
dishonest

㊻ **hilfsbereit**
supportive

㊼ **impulsiv**
impulsive

㊽ **zuverlässig**
reliable

㊾ **unzuverlässig**
unreliable

㊿ **talentiert**
talented

(51) **arrogant**
arrogant

(52) **rücksichtsvoll**
considerate

(53) **abenteuerlustig**
adventurous

(54) **nahbar**
approachable

(55) **unnahbar**
unapproachable

(56) **entscheidungsfreudig**
decisive

(57) **akkurat**
meticulous

(58) **ungeschickt**
clumsy

(59) **gedankenlos**
thoughtless

11 Fähigkeiten und Handlungen
Abilities and actions

11.1 FÄHIGKEITEN UND HANDLUNGEN BESCHREIBEN
DESCRIBING ABILITIES AND ACTIONS

(10) **Tanzen macht mir Spaß!**
I love to dance.

(11) **Mir auch!**
Me too!

① **sehen**
to see

② **schmecken**
to taste

③ **riechen**
to smell

④ **kriechen**
to crawl

⑤ **schlagen**
to hit

⑥ **spielen**
to play

⑦ **treten**
to kick

⑧ **werfen**
to throw

⑨ **tanzen**
to dance

⑫ **fangen**
to catch

⑬ **laufen**
to run

⑭ **hüpfen**
to hop

⑮ **springen**
to jump

⑯ **schleichen**
to creep

⑰ **schütteln**
to shake

⑱ **arbeiten**
to work

⑲ **blasen**
to blow

⑳ **(einen Schneemann) bauen**
to make (a snowman)

㉑ **buchstabieren**
to spell

㉒ **(die Hausaufgaben) machen**
to do (homework)

㉓ **abschreiben**
to copy

㉔ **bauen**
to build

㉕ **graben**
to dig

㉖ **reparieren**
to repair

㉗ **richten**
to fix

㉘ **sich hinsetzen**
to sit down

㉙ **aufstehen**
to stand up

㉚ **verstehen**
to understand

㉛ **hinfallen**
to fall

㉜ **heben**
to lift

㉝ **addieren**
to add

㉞ **subtrahieren**
to subtract

㉟ **zählen**
to count

See also
09 Die Alltagsroutine • Daily routines **93** Nützliche Fähigkeiten für den Arbeitsplatz • Workplace skills **178** Geläufige Verben • Common phrasal verbs

㊱ **zuhören**
to listen

㊲ **reden**
to talk

㊳ **sprechen**
to speak

㊴ **schreien**
to shout

㊵ **singen**
to sing

㊶ **schauspielern**
to act

㊷ **flüstern**
to whisper

㊸ **denken**
to think

㊹ **entscheiden**
to decide

㊺ **sich erinnern**
to remember

㊻ **vergessen**
to forget

㊼ **helfen**
to help

㊽ **auf etwas deuten**
to point

㊾ **packen**
to pack

㊿ **auspacken**
to unpack

(51) **fliegen**
to fly

(52) **fahren**
to ride

(53) **klettern**
to climb

(54) **lecken**
to lick

(55) **nehmen**
to take

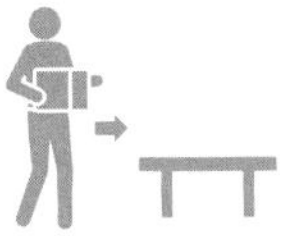

(56) **bringen**
to bring

(57) **mitnehmen**
to pick up / to collect

(58) **eintreten**
to enter

(59) **verlassen**
to exit

(60) **gewinnen**
to win

(61) **heben**
to raise

(62) **tragen**
to carry

(63) **jonglieren**
to juggle

(64) **festhalten**
to hold

(65) **umziehen**
to move

(66) **schieben**
to push

(67) **ziehen**
to pull

12 Aussehen und Haar
Appearance and hair

12.1 ALLGEMEINES AUSSEHEN
GENERAL APPEARANCE

① **mittelgroß**
medium height

② **groß**
tall

③ **klein**
short

④ **schön**
beautiful

⑤ **gutaussehend**
handsome

⑥ **jung**
young

⑦ **mittleren Alters**
middle-aged

⑧ **alt**
old

⑨ **die Poren** *f, pl*
pores

⑩ **die Sommersprossen** *f, pl*
freckles

⑪ **die Falten** *f, pl*
wrinkles

⑫ **die Grübchen** *f, pl*
dimples

⑬ **das Muttermal**
mole

12.2 DAS HAAR · HAIR

① **das Haar stylen**
to style your hair

② **die Haare waschen**
to wash your hair

③ **die Haare schneiden lassen**
to have (or get) your hair cut

④ **die Haare hochbinden**
to tie your hair back

⑤ **die Haare wachsen lassen**
to grow your hair

⑥ **sich rasieren**
to shave

⑦ **langes Haar**
long hair

⑧ **kurzes Haar**
short hair

⑨ **schulterlanges Haar**
shoulder-length hair

⑩ **der Seitenscheitel**
side parting

⑪ **der Mittelscheitel**
centre parting

⑫ **der Schnurrbart**
moustache

⑬ **der Kinnbart**
goatee

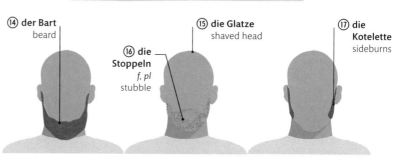

⑭ **der Bart**
beard

⑯ **die Stoppeln** *f, pl*
stubble

⑮ **die Glatze**
shaved head

⑰ **die Kotelette**
sideburns

⑱ **die Gesichtsbehaarung**
facial hair

See also
13-15 Kleidung • Clothes **16** Accessoires • Accessories
17 Schuhe • Shoes **18** Beauty • Beauty

⑲ **der Bürstenschnitt**
crew cut

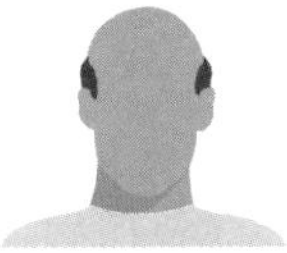
⑳ **glatzköpfig**
bald

㉑ **das glatte Haar**
straight hair

㉒ **das wellige Haar**
wavy hair

㉓ **das lockige Haar**
curly hair

㉔ **das gekräuselte Haar**
frizzy hair

㉕ **der Pferdeschwanz**
ponytail

㉖ **der Flechtzopf**
plait

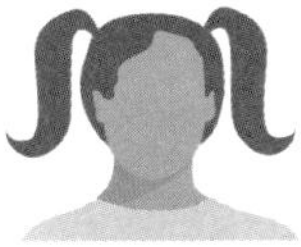
㉗ **die Rattenschwänze**
pigtails

㉘ **der Bob**
bob

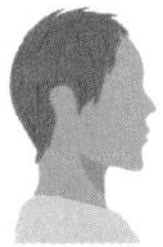
㉙ **sehr kurzes Haar**
crop

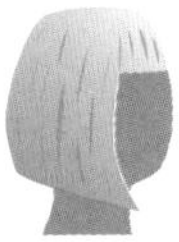
㉚ **die Perücke**
wig

㉛ **der Französische Zopf**
French plait

㉜ **der Dutt**
bun

㉝ **die Strähnchen**
n, pl
highlights

㉞ **der Afro**
Afro

㉟ **die Rastazöpfe**
m, pl
braids

㊱ **die Cornrows**
f, pl
cornrows

㊲ **das normale Haar**
normal hair

㊳ **das fettige Haar**
greasy hair

㊴ **das trockene Haar**
dry hair

㊵ **die Schuppen**
f, pl
dandruff

㊶ **das Haargel**
hair gel

㊷ **das Haarspray**
hair spray

㊸ **das schwarze Haar**
black hair

㊹ **das braune Haar**
brown hair

㊺ **das blonde Haar**
blond / blonde hair

㊻ **das rote Haar**
red hair

㊼ **das kastanienbraune Haar**
auburn hair

㊽ **das graue Haar**
grey hair

㊾ **das Glätteisen**
hair straightener

㊿ **der Lockenstab**
hair curler

(51) **die Haarbürste**
hairbrush

(52) **der Kamm**
comb

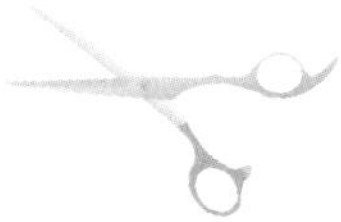
(53) **die Haarschere**
hair scissors

(54) **der Haarföhn**
hair dryer

13 Kleidung
Clothes

13.1 KLEIDUNG BESCHREIBEN · DESCRIBING CLOTHES

① **das Leder**
leather

② **die Baumwolle**
cotton

③ **aus Wolle**
woollen

④ **die Seide**
silk

⑤ **die Synthetikfaser**
synthetic

⑥ **der Jeansstoff**
denim

⑦ **einfarbig**
plain

⑧ **gestreift**
striped

⑨ **kariert**
checked

⑩ **gepunktet**
spotted

⑪ **das Paisleymuster**
paisley

⑫ **das Schottenkaro**
plaid

⑬ **locker**
loose / baggy

⑭ **figurbetont**
fitted

⑮ **eng**
tight

⑯ **faltig**
crumpled

⑰ **kurz**
cropped

⑱ **klassisch**
vintage

13.2 ARBEITSBEKLEIDUNG UND UNIFORMEN · WORK CLOTHES AND UNIFORMS

① **die Kochmütze**
chef's hat

② **die Kochjacke**
chef's coat

③ **die Kochuniform**
chef's uniform

④ **die Schürze**
apron

⑤ **der Laborkittel**
lab coat

⑥ **die Feuerwehruniform**
firefighter's uniform

⑦ **der Overall**
overalls

See also
12 Aussehen und haar · Appearance and hair **14-15** Kleidung (Fortsetzung)
Clothes continued **16** Accessoires · Accessories **17** Schuhe · Shoes

13.3 BABYKLEIDUNG UND KINDERKLEIDUNG · KIDS' AND BABIES' CLOTHES

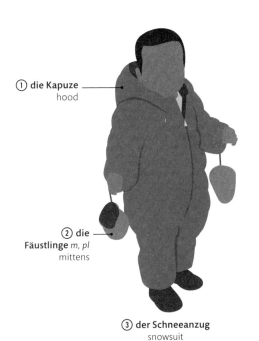

① die Kapuze
hood

② die Fäustlinge *m, pl*
mittens

③ der Schneeanzug
snowsuit

④ der Latz
bib

⑤ die Latzhose
dungarees

⑥ der Body
babygro

⑦ der Druckknopf
popper

⑧ der Schlafanzug
sleepsuit

⑨ der Strampler
play suit

⑩ der Strampler
romper suit

⑪ der Strampler
onesie

⑫ das Kostüm
costume

⑬ die Babystiefel *m, pl*
booties

⑧ die Militäruniform
military uniform

⑨ die OP-Kleidung
scrubs

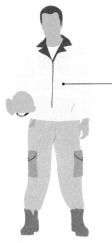

⑩ die Cargohose
cargo trousers

⑪ die Warnweste
high-visibility jacket

⑫ der Überwurf
tabard

⑭ das Schulhemd
school shirt

⑮ die Schulkrawatte
school tie

⑬ die Schuluniform
school uniform

14.1 FREIZEITKLEIDUNG · CASUAL CLOTHES

① **Ich trage meine Freizeitkleidung lieber als meine Arbeitskleidung.**
I prefer this casual outfit to my formal work clothes.

⑦ **Nach der Arbeit trage ich gerne Jeans und ein T-Shirt.**
After work, I like to change into jeans and a T-shirt.

② **die Bluse**
blouse

③ **der Pullover**
sweater / jumper

④ **der Rock**
pajamas

⑤ **die Falte**
pleat

⑥ **der Saum**
hem

⑧ **das T-Shirt**
T-shirt

⑨ **die Streifen** *m, pl*
stripes

⑩ **die Jeans**
jeans

⑪ **das Sweatshirt**
sweatshirt

⑫ **die Short**
shorts

⑬ **die Bermudashort**
bermuda shorts

⑭ **die Strickjacke**
cardigan

⑮ **das Trägerhemd**
tank top

⑯ **das Kleid**
dress

⑰ **die Leggings**
leggings

⑱ **das kurzärmelige Hemd**
short-sleeved shirt

⑲ **das Polohemd**
polo shirt

⑳ **der Sonnenhut**
sun hat

㉑ **der V-Ausschnitt**
V-neck

㉒ **der Rundhals**
round neck

See also
12 Aussehen und haar · Appearance and hair **15** Kleidung (Fortsetzung)
Clothes continued **16** Accessoires · Accessories **17** Schuhe · Shoes

14.2 SCHLAFBEKLEIDUNG · NIGHTWEAR

① **das Leibchen**
camisole

② **die Pantoffeln** *m, pl*
slippers

③ **die Schlafmaske**
eye mask

④ **der Schlafanzug**
pyjamas

⑤ **das Nachthemd**
nightgown / nightie

⑥ **der Bademantel**
dressing gown

14.3 UNTERWÄSCHE · UNDERWEAR

① **die Unterhose**
knickers

② **der Slip**
pants

③ **die Boxershorts**
boxer shorts *f, pl*

④ **die Socken** *f, pl*
socks

⑤ **der BH**
bra

⑥ **das Unterkleid**
slip dress

⑦ **das Unterhemd**
vest

⑧ **die Strumpfhose**
tights

⑨ **die Strümpfe** *m, pl*
stockings

⑩ **das Mieder**
basque

⑪ **das Strumpfband**
garter

⑫ **der Strumpfhalter**
suspenders

14.4 KLEIDUNGSVERBEN · VERBS FOR CLOTHES

① **tragen**
to wear

② **anprobieren**
to fit

③ **anziehen**
to put on

④ **ausziehen**
to take off

⑤ **binden**
to fasten

⑥ **lockern**
to unfasten

⑦ **(jemandem)
stehen**
to suit (someone)

⑧ **sich umziehen**
to change /
to get changed

⑨ **aufhängen**
to hang up

⑩ **zusammenlegen**
to fold

⑪ **aufkrempeln**
to turn up

⑫ **etwas
anprobieren**
to try something on

15 Kleidung (Fortsetzung)
Clothes continued

15.1 FORMELLE KLEIDUNG · FORMAL WEAR

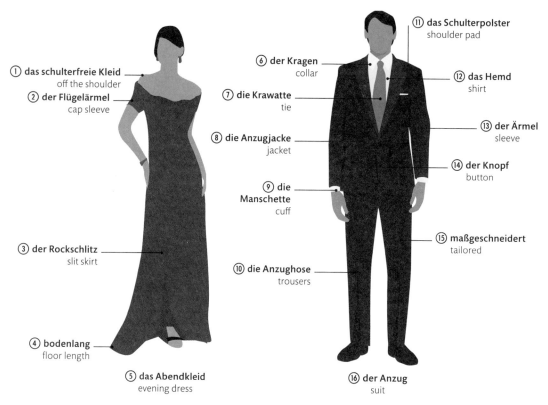

① das schulterfreie Kleid
off the shoulder

② der Flügelärmel
cap sleeve

③ der Rockschlitz
slit skirt

④ bodenlang
floor length

⑤ das Abendkleid
evening dress

⑪ das Schulterpolster
shoulder pad

⑥ der Kragen
collar

⑦ die Krawatte
tie

⑧ die Anzugjacke
jacket

⑨ die Manschette
cuff

⑩ die Anzughose
trousers

⑫ das Hemd
shirt

⑬ der Ärmel
sleeve

⑭ der Knopf
button

⑮ maßgeschneidert
tailored

⑯ der Anzug
suit

⑰ ärmellos
sleeveless

⑱ das Brautjungfernkleid
bridesmaid's dress

⑲ der Blumenstrauß
bouquet

⑳ der Schleier
veil

㉑ trägerlos
strapless

㉒ die Schleppe
train

㉓ das Hochzeitskleid
wedding dress

㉔ der Smoking
tuxedo

㉕ das Sportsakko
sports jacket

㉖ das Neckholder-Kleid
halter neck

㉗ der Hosenbund
waistband

㉘ die Weste
waistcoat

See also
12 Aussehen und haar · Appearance and hair
16 Accessoires · Accessories **17** Schuhe · Shoes

15.2 JACKEN · COATS

② **die Kapuze**
hood

⑪ **das Futter**
lining

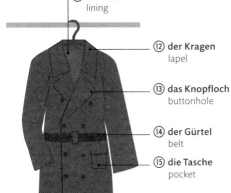

① **die Regenjacke**
raincoat

③ **der Anorak**
anorak

④ **der Dufflecoat**
duffle coat

⑤ **der Poncho**
poncho

⑫ **der Kragen**
lapel

⑬ **das Knopfloch**
buttonhole

⑭ **der Gürtel**
belt

⑮ **die Tasche**
pocket

⑥ **die Jeansjacke**
denim jacket

⑦ **die Steppjacke**
quilted jacket

⑧ **die Bomberjacke**
bomber jacket

⑨ **der Umhang**
cloak

⑩ **der Trenchcoat**
trench coat

15.3 SPORTKLEIDUNG · SPORTSWEAR

① **der Trainingsanzug**
tracksuit

② **der Sport-BH**
sports bra

③ **die Jogginghose**
sweatpants

⑥ **der Schnorchel und die Taucherbrille**
snorkel and mask

⑨ **die Schwimmbrille**
goggles

④ **der Gymnastikanzug**
leotard

⑦ **die Flossen**
f, pl
fins / flippers

⑤ **das Trikot**
football shirt

⑧ **der Badeanzug**
swimsuit

⑩ **die Badehose**
swimming trunks

15.4 TRADITIONELLE KLEIDUNG
TRADITIONAL CLOTHES

① **die Agbada**
agbada

② **das Flamenco-Kleid**
flamenco dress

③ **die Lederhose**
lederhosen

④ **der Kimono**
kimono

⑤ **der Thawb**
thawb

⑥ **der Sari**
sari

⑦ **der Kilt**
kilt

⑧ **der Sarong**
sarong

⑨ **die Folklorebluse**
folk blouse

16 Accessoires
Accessories

16.1 MODEACCESSOIRES · FASHION ACCESSORIES

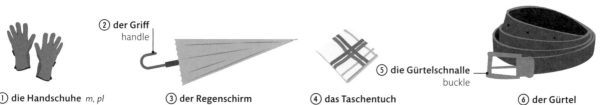

① **die Handschuhe** *m, pl*
gloves

② **der Griff**
handle

③ **der Regenschirm**
umbrella

④ **das Taschentuch**
handkerchief

⑤ **die Gürtelschnalle**
buckle

⑥ **der Gürtel**
belt

⑦ **der Schal**
scarf

⑧ **die Krawatte**
tie

⑨ **die Krawattennadel**
tie-pin

⑩ **die Fliege**
bow tie

⑪ **die Anstecknadel**
badge

⑫ **der Haarreif**
Alice band

16.2 SCHMUCK · JEWELLERY

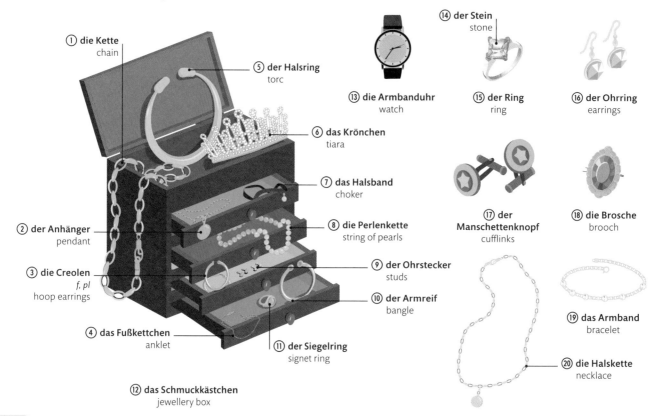

① **die Kette**
chain

② **der Anhänger**
pendant

③ **die Creolen**
f, pl
hoop earrings

④ **das Fußkettchen**
anklet

⑤ **der Halsring**
torc

⑥ **das Krönchen**
tiara

⑦ **das Halsband**
choker

⑧ **die Perlenkette**
string of pearls

⑨ **der Ohrstecker**
studs

⑩ **der Armreif**
bangle

⑪ **der Siegelring**
signet ring

⑫ **das Schmuckkästchen**
jewellery box

⑬ **die Armbanduhr**
watch

⑭ **der Stein**
stone

⑮ **der Ring**
ring

⑯ **der Ohrring**
earrings

⑰ **der Manschettenknopf**
cufflinks

⑱ **die Brosche**
brooch

⑲ **das Armband**
bracelet

⑳ **die Halskette**
necklace

See also
12 Aussehen und haar · Appearance and hair
13-15 Kleidung · Clothes **17** Schuhe · Shoes

16.3 KOPFBEDECKUNGEN · HEADWEAR

① die Schiebermütze
flat cap

② die Baseballkappe
baseball cap

③ die Bommelmütze
bobble hat

④ der Hidschab
hijab

⑤ die Jarmulke
yarmulke

⑥ der Turban
turban

⑦ das Barett
beret

⑧ der Fedora
fedora

⑨ die Sherlock-Holmes-Mütze
deerstalker

⑩ der Fes
fez

⑪ der Cowboy-Hut
cowboy hat

⑫ der Sombrero
sombrero

⑬ der Sonnenhut
sun hat

⑭ die Ballonmütze
newsboy cap

⑮ der Panamahut
panama

⑯ der Strohhut
boater

⑰ die Mütze
beanie

⑱ der Glockenhut
cloche

16.4 TASCHEN · BAGS

① die Aktentasche
briefcase

② der Rucksack
backpack / rucksack

③ der Geldbeutel
purse

⑥ der Koffer
suitcase

④ die Reisetasche
holdall

⑤ die Handtasche
handbag

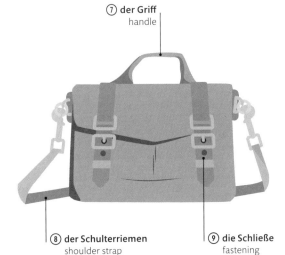
⑦ der Griff
handle

⑧ der Schulterriemen
shoulder strap

⑨ die Schließe
fastening

⑩ die Umhängetasche
shoulder bag

17.1 SCHUHE UND ZUBEHÖR · SHOES AND ACCESSORIES

① die Stöckelschuhe *m, pl*
high-heeled shoes

② die flachen Schuhe *m, pl*
flats

③ die Flipflops *m, pl*
flip-flops

④ die Espandrillen *f, pl*
espadrilles

⑤ die Kitten-Heel-Schuhe *m, pl*
kitten heels

⑥ die Stilettos *m, pl*
stilettos

⑦ die Sandalen *f, pl*
sandals

⑧ die Gummisandalen *f, pl*
jelly sandals

⑨ die Römersandalen *f, pl*
gladiator sandals

⑩ die Keilabsatz-Sandalen *f, pl*
wedge sandals

⑪ die T-Strap-Pumps *m, pl*
T-strap heels

⑫ die Plateauschuhe *m, pl*
platforms

⑬ die Schuhe mit Fesselriemen *m, pl*
ankle strap heels

⑭ die Peep-Toes *m, pl*
peep toes

⑮ die Schuhe mit Fersenriemen *m, pl*
slingback heels

⑯ die Ballerinas *m, pl*
ballet flats

⑰ die Pantoffeln *m, pl*
mules

⑱ die Spangenschuhe *m, pl*
Mary Janes

17.2 STIEFEL · BOOTS

⑥ der Reißverschluss
zip

① die Arbeitsschuhe *m, pl*
work boots

② die Chelsea-Boots *m, pl*
Chelsea boots

③ die Wanderschuhe *m, pl*
hiking boots

④ die Stiefeletten *f, pl*
ankle boots

⑤ der oberschenkellange Stiefel
thigh-high boot

⑦ die Desert-Boots *m, pl*
chukka boots
desert boots

⑧ das Schuhband
lace

⑩ die Öse
eyelet

⑨ die Sohle
sole

⑪ der Absatz
heel

⑫ die Schnürstiefel *m, pl*
lace-up boots

⑬ die kniehohen Stiefel *m, pl*
knee-high boots

⑭ die Regenstiefel *m, pl*
wellington boots

⑮ die Cowboy-Stiefel *m, pl*
cowboy boots

See also
12 Aussehen und haar • Appearance and hair **13-15** Kleidung • Clothes
16 Accessoires • Accessories **40** Gartengeräte • Garden tools

⑲ die Oxford-
Schuhe
Oxfords

⑳ die Derbys
Derby shoes

㉑ die Slipper
slip-ons

㉒ die Mokassins
moccasins

㉓ der Schaftformer
boot shapers

㉔ der
Schuhspanner
shoe trees

㉕ die Clogs
m, pl
clogs

㉖ die Schnallenschuhe
m, pl
buckled shoes

㉗ die Schlappen
m, pl
slides

㉘ die Schlappen
m, pl
slippers

㉙ die Schnürsenkel
m, pl
shoelaces

㉚ die Einlagen
f, pl
insoles

㉛ die Slipper
m, pl
loafers

㉜ die Bootsschuhe
m, pl
boat shoes

㉝ die Kinderschuhe
m, pl
kids' shoes

㉞ die
Herrenhalbschuhe *m, pl*
brogues

㉟ die Schuhcreme
shoe polish

㊱ die Schuhbürste
shoe brush

17.3 **SPORTSCHUHE** · SPORTS SHOES

⑦ die Zunge
tongue

① die Laufschuhe
(mit Spikes) *m, pl*
running spikes

② die Stollenschuhe
m, pl
baseball cleats

③ die Laufschuhe
m, pl
running shoes

④ die Knöchelturnschuhe
m, pl
high-tops

⑤ die Golfschuhe
m, pl
golf shoes

⑥ der Turnschuh
trainer

⑧ der Radschuh
cycling shoe

⑨ der Skischuh
ski boot

⑩ die
Wasserschuhe
m, pl
water shoes

⑪ die Reitstiefel
m, pl
riding boots

⑫ die Tabi-Schuhe
m, pl
tabi boots

⑬ die Stollenschuhe
m, pl
football boots

18.1 **MAKE-UP** · MAKEUP

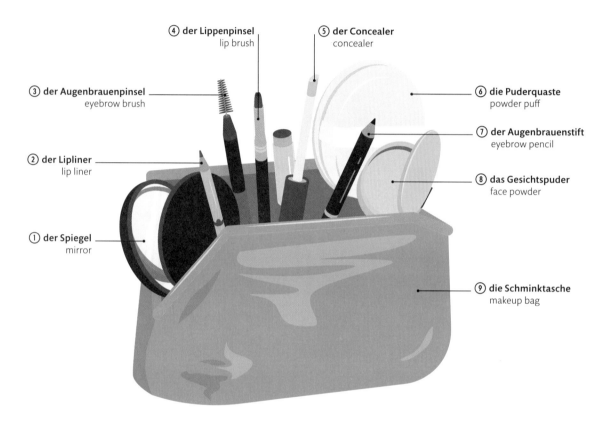

④ **der Lippenpinsel**
lip brush

⑤ **der Concealer**
concealer

③ **der Augenbrauenpinsel**
eyebrow brush

⑥ **die Puderquaste**
powder puff

⑦ **der Augenbrauenstift**
eyebrow pencil

② **der Lipliner**
lip liner

⑧ **das Gesichtspuder**
face powder

① **der Spiegel**
mirror

⑨ **die Schminktasche**
makeup bag

⑩ **das Rouge**
blusher

⑪ **der Eyeliner**
eyeliner

⑫ **der Lidschatten**
eyeshadow

⑬ **die Foundation**
foundation

⑭ **die Wimperntusche**
mascara

⑮ **der Lippenstift**
lipstick

18.2 **HAUTTYPEN** · SKIN TYPE

① **normal**
normal

② **trocken**
dry

③ **fettig**
oily

④ **empfindlich**
sensitive

⑤ **der Mischtyp**
combination

See also
12 Aussehen und haar · Appearance and hair **13-15** Kleidung · Clothes
16 Accessoires · Accessories **17** Schuhe · Shoes **31** Das Badezimmer · Bathroom

18.3 **MANIKÜRE** · MANICURE

① **die Nagelschere**
nail scissors

② **der Nagelknipser**
nail clippers

③ **der Nagellack**
nail polish /
nail varnish

④ **der Nagellackentferner**
nail polish remover

⑤ **die Nagelfeile**
nail file

⑥ **die Handcreme**
hand cream

18.4 **TOILETTENARTIKEL UND SCHÖNHEITSKUREN**
TOILETRIES AND BEAUTY TREATMENTS

① **die Feuchtigkeitscreme**
moisturizer

② **das Gesichtswasser**
toner

③ **der Gesichtsreiniger**
face wash

④ **der Gesichtsreiniger**
cleanser

⑤ **das Parfüm**
perfume

⑥ **das Aftershave**
aftershave

⑦ **der Lippenbalsam**
lip balm

⑧ **das Schaumbad**
bubble bath

⑨ **der Wattebausch**
cotton balls

⑩ **das Haarfärbemittel**
hair dye

⑪ **die Pinzette**
tweezers

⑫ **das Wachs**
wax

⑮ **der Applikationshandschuh**
tanning mitt

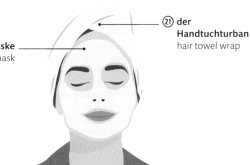

㉑ **der Handtuchturban**
hair towel wrap

⑬ **die Pediküre**
pedicure

⑭ **der Selbstbräuner**
self-tanning lotion

⑳ **die Gesichtsmaske**
face mask

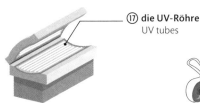

⑰ **die UV-Röhre**
UV tubes

⑯ **die Sonnenbank**
sun bed

⑱ **die Schutzbrille**
tanning goggles

⑲ **die Gesichtsbehandlung**
facial

Krankheiten und Verletzungen
Illness and injury

19.1 KRANKHEITEN · ILLNESS

① **die Grippe**
flu

② **die Erkältung**
cold

③ **der Husten**
cough

④ **die laufende Nase**
runny nose

⑤ **das Virus**
virus

⑥ **das Fieber**
fever

⑦ **der Schüttelfrost**
chill

⑧ **die Halsschmerzen** *m, pl*
sore throat

⑨ **die Mandelentzündung**
tonsillitis

⑩ **die Kopfschmerzen** *m, pl*
headache

⑪ **die Migräne**
migraine

⑫ **der Schwindel**
dizzy

⑬ **die Lebensmittelvergiftung**
food poisoning

⑭ **die Vergiftung**
poisoning

⑮ **der Ausschlag**
rash

⑯ **die Windpocken**
chickenpox

⑰ **die Masern**
measles

⑱ **der Mumps**
mumps

⑲ **das Ekzem**
eczema

⑳ **das Asthma**
asthma

㉑ **die Allergie**
allergy

㉒ **der Heuschnupfen**
hay fever

㉓ **die Infektion**
infection

㉔ **der Diabetes**
diabetes

㉕ **der Stress**
stress

㉖ **das Nasenbluten**
nosebleed

㉗ **die Übelkeit**
nausea

㉘ **die Blinddarmentzündung**
appendicitis

㉙ **der Bluthochdruck**
high blood pressure

㉚ **die Symptome** *n, pl*
symptoms

㉛ **der Krampf**
cramp

㉜ **die Rückenschmerzen** *m, pl*
backache

㉝ **der Schmerz**
pain

㉞ **die Bauchschmerzen** *m, pl*
stomach ache

㉟ **die Schlaflosigkeit**
insomnia

㊱ **der Durchfall**
diarrhoea

See also
01 Körperteile • Parts of the body **03** Muskeln und Skelett • Muscles and skeleton
04 Innere Organe • Internal organs **20** Beim Arzt • Visiting the doctor
21 Das Krankenhaus • The hospital

19.2 VERLETZUNGEN · INJURY

③ **das Röntgenbild**
X-ray

④ **der Bruch**
fracture

① **Auf dem Röntgenbild ist zu sehen, dass Ihr Knöchel gebrochen ist.**
Your X-ray shows that you have broken your ankle.

② **der Patient** m
die Patientin f
patient

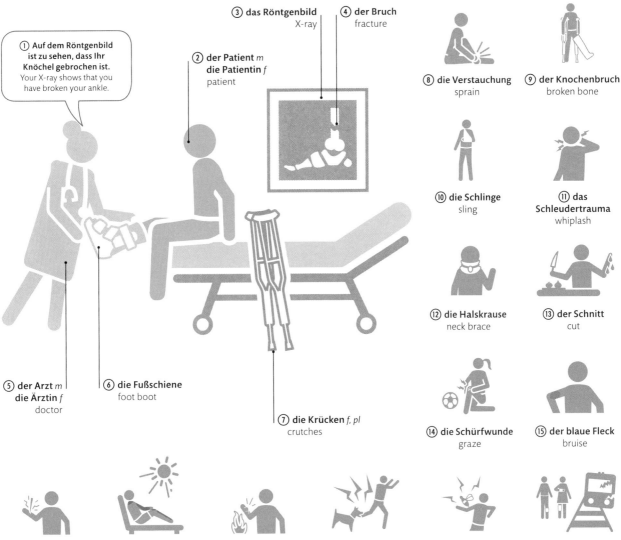

⑤ **der Arzt** m
die Ärztin f
doctor

⑥ **die Fußschiene**
foot boot

⑦ **die Krücken** f, pl
crutches

⑧ **die Verstauchung**
sprain

⑨ **der Knochenbruch**
broken bone

⑩ **die Schlinge**
sling

⑪ **das Schleudertrauma**
whiplash

⑫ **die Halskrause**
neck brace

⑬ **der Schnitt**
cut

⑭ **die Schürfwunde**
graze

⑮ **der blaue Fleck**
bruise

⑯ **der Splitter**
splinter

⑰ **der Sonnenbrand**
sunburn

⑱ **die Verbrennung**
burn

⑲ **der Biss**
bite

⑳ **der Stich**
sting

㉑ **der Unfall**
accident

㉒ **die Wunde**
wound

㉓ **die Blutung**
haemorrhage

㉔ **die Blase**
blister

㉕ **die Gehirnerschütterung**
concussion

㉖ **die Kopfverletzung**
head injury

㉗ **der elektrische Schlag**
electric shock

20.1 DIE BEHANDLUNG · TREATMENT

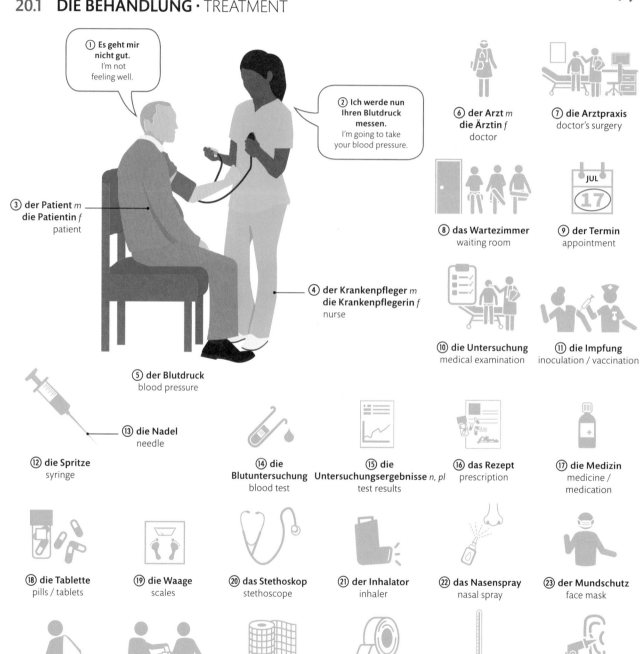

① **Es geht mir nicht gut.**
I'm not feeling well.

② **Ich werde nun Ihren Blutdruck messen.**
I'm going to take your blood pressure.

③ **der Patient** *m*
die Patientin *f*
patient

④ **der Krankenpfleger** *m*
die Krankenpflegerin *f*
nurse

⑤ **der Blutdruck**
blood pressure

⑥ **der Arzt** *m*
die Ärztin *f*
doctor

⑦ **die Arztpraxis**
doctor's surgery

⑧ **das Wartezimmer**
waiting room

⑨ **der Termin**
appointment

⑩ **die Untersuchung**
medical examination

⑪ **die Impfung**
inoculation / vaccination

⑫ **die Spritze**
syringe

⑬ **die Nadel**
needle

⑭ **die Blutuntersuchung**
blood test

⑮ **die Untersuchungsergebnisse** *n, pl*
test results

⑯ **das Rezept**
prescription

⑰ **die Medizin**
medicine / medication

⑱ **die Tablette**
pills / tablets

⑲ **die Waage**
scales

⑳ **das Stethoskop**
stethoscope

㉑ **der Inhalator**
inhaler

㉒ **das Nasenspray**
nasal spray

㉓ **der Mundschutz**
face mask

㉔ **die Schlinge**
sling

㉕ **der Verband**
dressing

㉖ **der Mull**
gauze

㉗ **das Heftpflaster**
tape

㉘ **das Thermometer**
thermometer

㉙ **das Ohrthermometer**
ear thermometer

See also
01 Körperteile · Parts of the body **02** Hände und Füße · Hands and feet
03 Muskeln und Skelett · Muscles and skeleton **04** Innere Organe · Internal organs
19 Krankheiten und Verletzungen · Illness and injury **21** Das Krankenhaus · The hospital

20.2 DER ERSTE-HILFE-KASTEN · FIRST-AID KIT

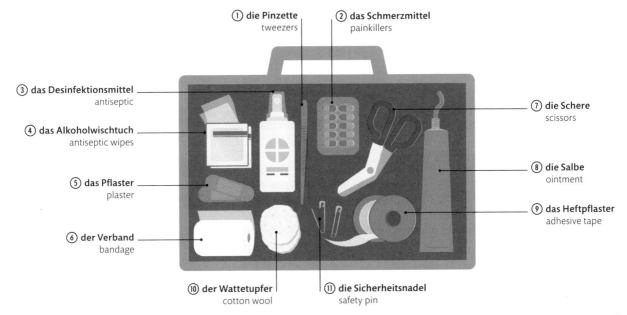

① **die Pinzette** tweezers

② **das Schmerzmittel** painkillers

③ **das Desinfektionsmittel** antiseptic

④ **das Alkoholwischtuch** antiseptic wipes

⑤ **das Pflaster** plaster

⑥ **der Verband** bandage

⑦ **die Schere** scissors

⑧ **die Salbe** ointment

⑨ **das Heftpflaster** adhesive tape

⑩ **der Wattetupfer** cotton wool

⑪ **die Sicherheitsnadel** safety pin

20.3 KRANKHEITSVERBEN · VERBS TO DESCRIBE ILLNESS

① **sich übergeben** to vomit

② **niesen** to sneeze

③ **husten** to cough

④ **schmerzen** to hurt / to ache

⑤ **bluten** to bleed

⑥ **in Ohnmacht fallen** to faint

⑦ **sich hinlegen** to lie down

⑧ **sich ausruhen** to rest

⑨ **abnehmen** to lose weight

⑩ **zunehmen** to gain weight

⑪ **Wasser trinken** to drink water

⑰ **die Herzdruckmassage** chest compressions

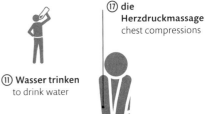

⑫ **Sport machen** to exercise

⑬ **heilen** to heal

⑭ **sich erholen** to recover

⑮ **sich besser fühlen** to feel better

⑯ **wiederbeleben** to resuscitate

21.1 IM KRANKENHAUS · AT THE HOSPITAL

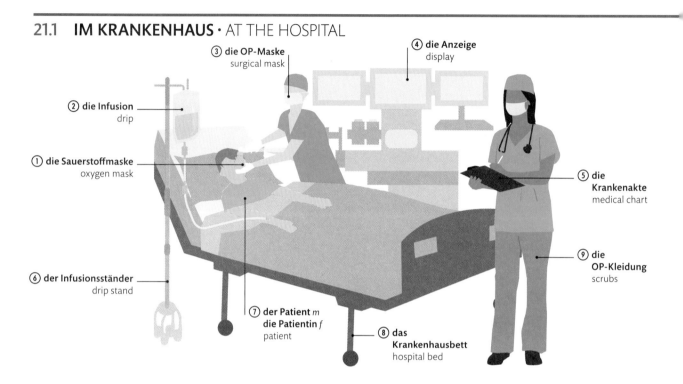

③ die OP-Maske
surgical mask

④ die Anzeige
display

② die Infusion
drip

① die Sauerstoffmaske
oxygen mask

⑤ die Krankenakte
medical chart

⑨ die OP-Kleidung
scrubs

⑥ der Infusionsständer
drip stand

⑦ der Patient m
die Patientin f
patient

⑧ das Krankenhausbett
hospital bed

⑩ das Krankenhaus
hospital

⑪ der Krankenwagen
ambulance

⑫ der Rettungssanitäter m
die Rettungssanitäterin f
paramedic

⑬ die Trage
stretcher

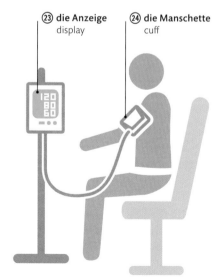

㉓ die Anzeige
display

㉔ die Manschette
cuff

⑭ der Chirurg m
die Chirurgin f
surgeon

⑮ der Arzt m
die Ärztin f
doctor

⑯ der Krankenpfleger m
die Krankenpflegerin f
nurse

⑰ die Stationshilfskraft
porter

⑱ der Rollstuhl
wheelchair

⑲ die Aufnahme
scan

⑳ das Röntgen
X-ray

㉑ die Blutuntersuchung
blood test

㉒ das Blutdruckmessgerät
blood pressure monitor

See also
01 Körperteile • Parts of the body **03** Muskeln und Skelett • Muscles and skeleton
04 Innere Organe • Internal organs **19** Krankheiten und Verletzungen • Illness
and injury **20** Beim Arzt • Visiting the doctor

21.2 ABTEILUNGEN · DEPARTMENTS

㉕ **das Skalpell**
scalpel

㉖ **die Naht**
stitches

㉗ **der Schönheitseingriff**
plastic surgery

① **HNO (Hals, Nase, Ohren)**
ENT (ear, nose, and throat)

② **die Kardiologie**
cardiology

③ **die Orthopädie**
orthopaedics

㉘ **die Behandlung**
treatment

㉙ **die Operation**
operation

㉚ **der OP-Tisch**
operating table

④ **die Neurologie**
neurology

⑤ **die Radiologie**
radiology

⑥ **die Pathologie**
pathology

㉛ **der OP-Saal**
operating theatre

㉜ **die Notaufnahme**
A&E

⑦ **die Pädiatrie**
paediatrics

⑧ **die Dermatologie**
dermatology

⑨ **die Gynäkologie**
gynaecology

㉝ **die Intensivstation**
intensive care unit

㉞ **der Aufwachraum**
recovery room

㉟ **das Einzelzimmer**
private room

⑩ **die Chirurgie**
surgery

⑪ **die Physiotherapie**
physiotherapy

⑫ **die Urologie**
urology

㊱ **die Station**
ward

㊲ **die Kinderstation**
children's ward

㊳ **die Entbindungsstation**
maternity ward

⑬ **die Geburtshilfe**
maternity

⑭ **die Psychiatrie**
psychiatry

㊴ **einweisen**
to admit

㊵ **entlassen**
to discharge

㊶ **ambulant**
outpatient

⑯ **die Endokrinologie**
endocrinology

⑰ **die Onkologie**
oncology

⑮ **die Augenheilkunde**
ophthalmology

⑱ **die Gastroenterologie**
gastroenterology

22.1 BEIM ZAHNARZT · DENTAL SURGERY

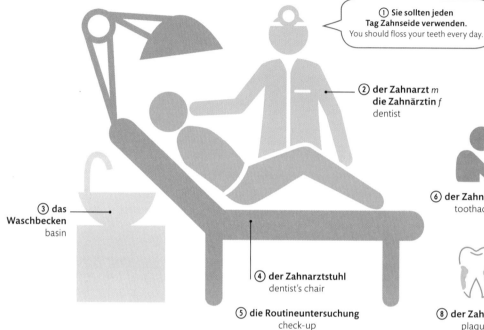

① Sie sollten jeden Tag **Zahnseide verwenden.**
You should floss your teeth every day.

② **der Zahnarzt** *m*
die Zahnärztin *f*
dentist

③ **das Waschbecken**
basin

④ **der Zahnarztstuhl**
dentist's chair

⑤ **die Routineuntersuchung**
check-up

⑥ **der Zahnschmerz**
toothache

⑦ **die Füllung**
filling

⑧ **der Zahnbelag**
plaque

⑨ **der Karies**
decay

⑩ **das Loch**
cavity

⑪ **die Krone**
crown

⑫ **einen Zahn ziehen**
extraction

⑬ **die Milchzähne** *m, pl*
milk teeth

⑭ **die Zahnspange**
braces

⑮ **das künstliche Gebiss**
dentures / false teeth

⑯ **die Zahnröntgenaufnahme**
dental X-ray

⑰ **die zahnärztliche Krankengeschichte**
dental history

⑱ **der Bohrer**
drill

⑲ **der Spiegel**
dental mirror

⑳ **die Sonde**
probe

㉑ **die Zahnzwischenraumbürste**
interdental brush

㉒ **das Bleichen**
whitening

㉓ **der Zahnpfleger** *m*
die Zahnpflegerin *f*
dental hygienist

㉔ **die Zahnseide**
dental floss

㉕ **Zahnseide benutzen**
to floss

㉖ **die Zähne putzen**
to brush

㉗ **ausspülen**
to rinse

See also
01 Körperteile · Parts of the body **03** Muskeln und Skelett · Muscles and skeleton
20 Beim Arzt · Visiting the doctor **21** Das Krankenhaus · The hospital
31 Das Badezimmer · Bathroom

22.2 BEIM OPTIKER · OPTICIAN

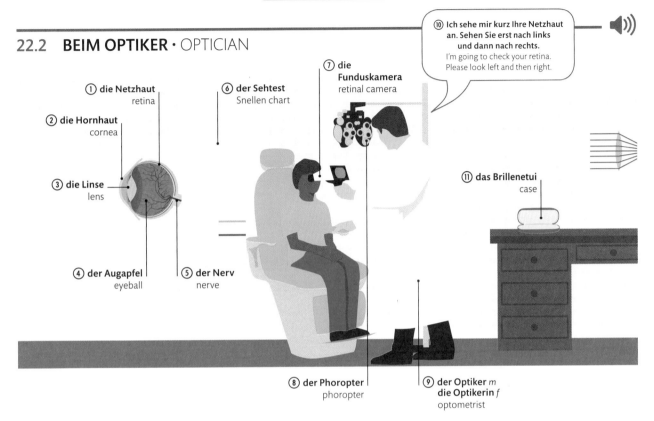

⑩ Ich sehe mir kurz Ihre Netzhaut an. Sehen Sie erst nach links und dann nach rechts.
I'm going to check your retina. Please look left and then right.

① **die Netzhaut**
retina

② **die Hornhaut**
cornea

③ **die Linse**
lens

④ **der Augapfel**
eyeball

⑤ **der Nerv**
nerve

⑥ **der Sehtest**
Snellen chart

⑦ **die Funduskamera**
retinal camera

⑧ **der Phoropter**
phoropter

⑨ **der Optiker** *m*
die Optikerin *f*
optometrist

⑪ **das Brillenetui**
case

⑫ **die Sehkraft**
vision

⑬ **weitsichtig**
long-sighted

⑭ **kurzsichtig**
short-sighted

⑮ **die Träne**
tear

⑯ **der graue Star**
cataract

⑰ **die Hornhautverkrümmung**
astigmatism

⑱ **die Lesebrille**
reading glasses

⑲ **die Gleitsichtbrille**
bifocal

⑳ **das Monokel**
monocle

㉑ **das Opernglas**
opera glasses

㉒ **die Brille**
glasses

㉓ **das Brillenglas**
lens

㉔ **die Sonnenbrille**
sunglasses

㉕ **das Brillenputztuch**
lens cleaning cloth

㉖ **die Kontaktlinse**
contact lenses

㉗ **die Kontaktlinsenflüssigkeit**
contact lens solution

㉘ **die Kontaktlinsendose**
lens case

㉙ **die Augentropfen**
m, pl
eye drops

23.1 EIN GESUNDER LEBENSSTIL · HEALTHY LIVING

① **das Eiweiß**
protein

② **die Kohlenhydrate** *n, pl*
carbohydrates

③ **die Ballaststoffe** *m, pl*
fibre

④ **das Milchprodukt**
dairy

⑤ **die Hülsenfrüchte** *f, pl*
pulses

⑥ **der Zucker**
sugar

⑦ **das Salz**
salt

⑧ **die gesättigten Fettsäuren** *f, pl*
saturated fat

⑨ **die ungesättigten Fettsäuren** *f, pl*
unsaturated fat

⑩ **die Kalorien** *f, pl*
calories / energy

⑪ **die Vitamine** *n, pl*
vitamins

⑫ **die Mineralstoffe** *m, pl*
minerals

⑬ **das Kalzium**
calcium

⑭ **das Eisen**
iron

⑮ **das Cholesterin**
cholesterol

⑯ **der Detox**
detox

⑰ **die ausgewogene Ernährung**
balanced diet

⑱ **die kalorienbewusste Ernährung**
calorie-controlled diet

HEALTH FOOD

⑲ **der Bioladen**
health food shop

⑳ **die Bioabteilung**
organic food section

㉑ **die lokalen Erzeugnisse** *n, pl*
local produce

㉒ **Ich kaufe gerne Bioobst und -gemüse.**
I like to buy organic fruit and vegetables.

㉓ **der Wochenmarkt**
farmers' market

See also
03 Muskeln und Skelett • Muscles and skeleton **19** Krankheiten und Verletzungen • Illness and injury
24 Gesunder Körper, gesunder Geist • Healthy body, healthy mind **29** Kochen • Cooking
48 Der Supermarkt • The supermarket **52-72** Lebensmittel und Nahrungsmittel • Food

23.2 LEBENSMITTELALLERGIEN
FOOD ALLERGIES

㉔ **das industriell verarbeitete Lebensmittel**
processed food

㉕ **die Superfoods**
superfoods

㉖ **Bio-**
organic

① **die Nussallergie**
nut allergy

② **die Erdnussallergie**
peanut allergy

③ **die Meeresfrüchteallergie**
seafood allergy

㉗ **das Nahrungsergänzungsmittel**
supplement

㉘ **die Zusatzstoffe**
m, pl
additives

㉙ **ohne Milchprodukte** *n, pl*
dairy-free

④ **die Laktoseintoleranz**
lactose intolerant

⑤ **die Glutenunverträglichkeit**
gluten intolerant

⑥ **die Milchallergie**
dairy allergy

㉚ **vegetarisch**
vegetarian

㉛ **vegan**
vegan

㉜ **pescetarisch**
pescatarian

⑦ **die Weizenallergie**
wheat allergy

⑧ **die Eiallergie**
egg allergy

⑨ **die Sesamallergie**
sesame allergy

㉝ **glutenfrei**
gluten-free

㉞ **abnehmen**
to lose weight

㉟ **die Fertignahrung**
convenience food

⑩ **die Sojaallergie**
soya allergy

⑪ **die Sellerieallergie**
celery allergy

⑫ **die Sulfitallergie**
sulphite allergy

㊱ **energiereich**
high-calorie

㊲ **kalorienarm**
low-calorie

㊳ **sich bei etwas einschränken**
to cut down on

⑭ **die Senfallergie**
mustard allergy

㊴ **auf etwas verzichten**
to give up

㊵ **eine Diät machen**
to go on a diet

㊶ **zu viel essen**
to overeat

⑬ **allergisch**
allergic

⑮ **intolerant**
intolerant

24.1 **YOGA** · YOGA

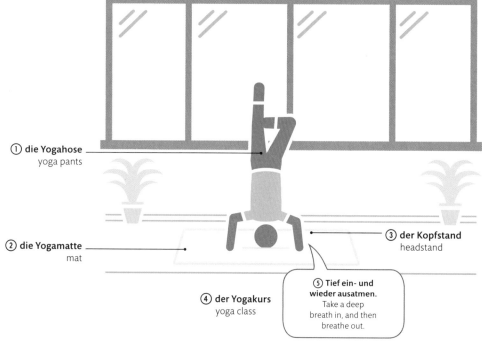

① die Yogahose
yoga pants

② die Yogamatte
mat

③ der Kopfstand
headstand

④ der Yogakurs
yoga class

⑤ Tief ein- und wieder ausatmen.
Take a deep breath in, and then breathe out.

⑥ das Kind
child's pose

⑦ die Kobra
cobra pose

⑧ der Krieger
warrior pose

⑨ der Drehsitz
seated twist

⑩ das Dreieck
triangle pose

⑪ die sitzende Vorbeuge
seated forward fold

⑫ die Totenhaltung
corpse pose

⑬ die Krähe
crow pose

⑭ der Stuhl
chair pose

⑮ die Berghaltung
mountain pose

⑯ die Brücke
bridge pose

⑰ die Bretthaltung
plank pose

⑱ der Bogen
bow pose

⑲ die Taube
pigeon pose

⑳ der Baum
tree pose

㉑ der herabschauende Hund
downward dog

㉒ die geschlossene Winkelhaltung im Sitz mit Fußsohlen aneinander
bound ankle pose

㉓ das Kamel
camel pose

㉔ das Rad
wheel pose

㉕ der Halbmond
half moon pose

㉖ der Delfin
dolphin pose

See also
03 Muskeln und Skelett · Muscles and skeleton **04** Innere Organe · Internal organs
19 Krankheiten und Verletzungen · Illness and injury **20** Beim Arzt · Visiting the doctor
21 Das Krankenhaus · The hospital **23** Die Ernährung · Diet and nutrition **29** Kochen · Cooking

24.2 BEHANDLUNGEN UND THERAPIEN · TREATMENTS AND THERAPY

① **die Massage**
massage

② **das Shiatsu**
shiatsu

③ **die Chiropraktik**
chiropractic

④ **die Osteopathie**
osteopathy

⑤ **die Reflexzonenmassage**
reflexology

⑥ **die Meditation**
meditation

⑦ **das Reiki**
reiki

⑧ **die Akupunktur**
acupuncture

⑨ **das Ayurveda**
ayurveda

⑩ **die Hypnosetherapie**
hypnotherapy

⑪ **die Hydrotherapie**
hydrotherapy

⑫ **die Aromatherapie**
aromatherapy

⑬ **die Kräuterheilkunde**
herbalism

⑭ **die ätherischen Öle** *n, pl*
essential oils

⑮ **die Homöopathie**
homeopathy

⑯ **die Akupressur**
acupressure

⑰ **die Heilsteinbehandlung**
crystal healing

⑱ **die natürliche Behandlung**
naturopathy

⑲ **das Fengshui**
feng shui

⑳ **die Dichtungstherapie**
poetry therapy

㉑ **die Gestaltungstherapie**
art therapy

㉒ **die Tiertherapie**
pet therapy

㉓ **die Naturtherapie**
nature therapy

㉔ **die Musiktherapie**
music therapy

㉕ **die Entspannung**
relaxation

㉖ **die Achtsamkeit**
mindfulness

㉗ **der Berater** *m*
die Beraterin *f*
counsellor

㉘ **die Psychotherapie**
psychotherapy

㉚ **Heute wollen wir uns über Stress bei der Arbeit unterhalten.**
Today, we're talking about stress at work.

㉙ **die Gruppentherapie**
group therapy

25 Ein Ort zum Leben
A place to live

25.1 HÄUSER · HOUSES

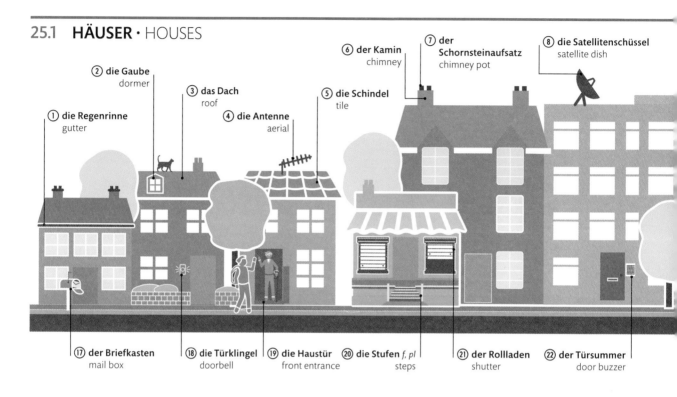

① die Regenrinne
gutter

② die Gaube
dormer

③ das Dach
roof

④ die Antenne
aerial

⑤ die Schindel
tile

⑥ der Kamin
chimney

⑦ der Schornsteinaufsatz
chimney pot

⑧ die Satellitenschüssel
satellite dish

⑰ der Briefkasten
mail box

⑱ die Türklingel
doorbell

⑲ die Haustür
front entrance

⑳ die Stufen f, pl
steps

㉑ der Rollladen
shutter

㉒ der Türsummer
door buzzer

㉚ die Treppe
staircase / stairs

㉛ unten
downstairs

㉜ oben
upstairs

㉝ der Keller
basement

㉞ das Erdgeschoss
ground floor

㉟ der erste Stock
first floor

㊶ die Wohnung
flat

㊱ die Terrasse
patio / terrace

㊲ die Terrassentür
patio doors /
French doors

㊳ der Balkon
balcony

㊴ der Hof
courtyard

㊵ die Gegensprechanlage
intercom

㊷ der Aufzug
lift

㊸ das Planschbecken
paddling pool

㊹ der Whirlpool
jacuzzi

㊺ die Hütte
shed

㊻ die Tonne
wheelie bin

See also
32 Haus und Heim · House and home **34** Hausarbeit · Household chores
37 Wohnraumverschönerung · Decorating **42-43** In der Stadt · In town
44 Gebäude und Architektur · Buildings and architecture

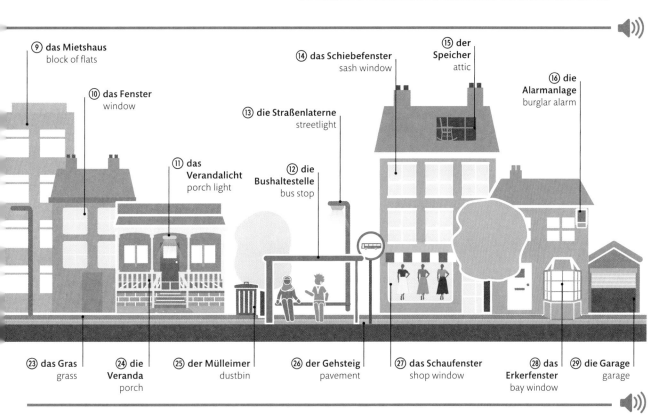

⑨ **das Mietshaus**
block of flats

⑩ **das Fenster**
window

⑪ **das Verandalicht**
porch light

⑭ **das Schiebefenster**
sash window

⑮ **der Speicher**
attic

⑯ **die Alarmanlage**
burglar alarm

⑬ **die Straßenlaterne**
streetlight

⑫ **die Bushaltestelle**
bus stop

㉓ **das Gras**
grass

㉔ **die Veranda**
porch

㉕ **der Mülleimer**
dustbin

㉖ **der Gehsteig**
pavement

㉗ **das Schaufenster**
shop window

㉘ **das Erkerfenster**
bay window

㉙ **die Garage**
garage

25.2 **DER GANG** · HALLWAY

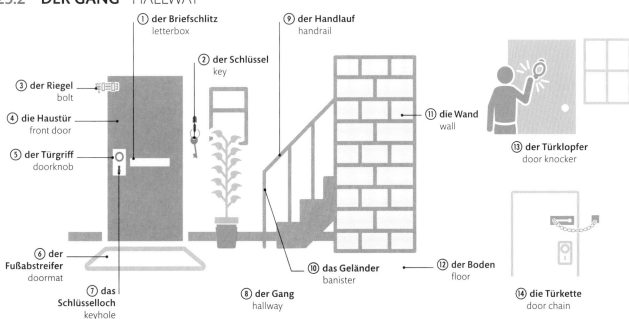

① **der Briefschlitz**
letterbox

⑨ **der Handlauf**
handrail

② **der Schlüssel**
key

③ **der Riegel**
bolt

④ **die Haustür**
front door

⑤ **der Türgriff**
doorknob

⑪ **die Wand**
wall

⑬ **der Türklopfer**
door knocker

⑥ **der Fußabstreifer**
doormat

⑦ **das Schlüsselloch**
keyhole

⑩ **das Geländer**
banister

⑧ **der Gang**
hallway

⑫ **der Boden**
floor

⑭ **die Türkette**
door chain

26.1 DAS WOHNZIMMER · LIVING ROOM

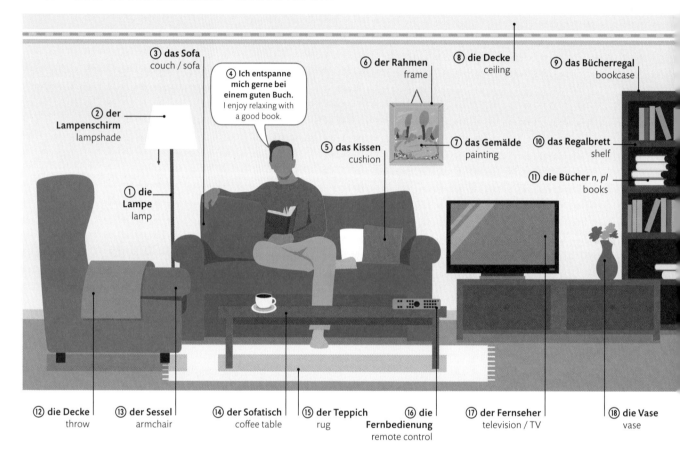

③ **das Sofa**
couch / sofa

④ **Ich entspanne mich gerne bei einem guten Buch.**
I enjoy relaxing with a good book.

⑥ **der Rahmen**
frame

⑧ **die Decke**
ceiling

⑨ **das Bücherregal**
bookcase

② **der Lampenschirm**
lampshade

⑤ **das Kissen**
cushion

⑦ **das Gemälde**
painting

⑩ **das Regalbrett**
shelf

⑪ **die Bücher** n, pl
books

① **die Lampe**
lamp

⑫ **die Decke**
throw

⑬ **der Sessel**
armchair

⑭ **der Sofatisch**
coffee table

⑮ **der Teppich**
rug

⑯ **die Fernbedienung**
remote control

⑰ **der Fernseher**
television / TV

⑱ **die Vase**
vase

⑲ **der Kamin**
fireplace

⑳ **der Kaminsims**
mantlepiece

㉑ **die Jalousie**
Venetian blinds

㉒ **der Rollladen**
roller blind

㉓ **die Tüllgardine**
curtains

㉔ **der Netzvorhang**
net curtain

㉕ **das Ausziehsofa**
sofa bed

㉖ **der Schaukelstuhl**
rocking chair

㉗ **der Schemel**
foot stool

㉘ **die Wandleuchte**
wall light

㉙ **das Arbeitszimmer**
study

See also
25 Ein Ort zum Leben · A place to live **27** Die Küche und das Geschirr · Kitchen and tableware **34** Hausarbeit · Household chores **71** Das Frühstück · Breakfast **72** Das Mittagessen und das Abendessen · Lunch and dinner **136** Unterhaltung zu Hause · Home entertainment

26.2 DAS ESSZIMMER · DINING ROOM

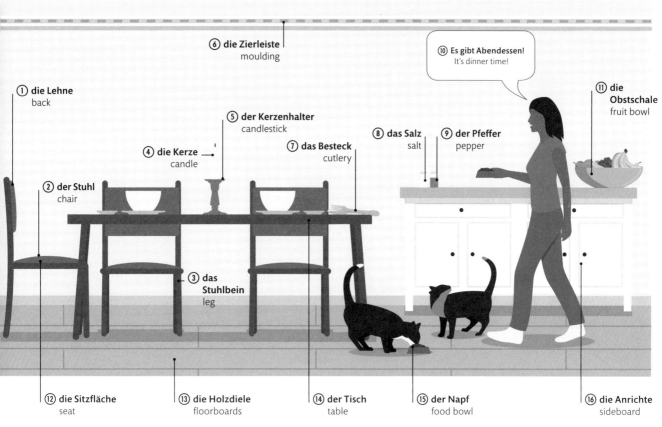

⑥ **die Zierleiste** moulding

⑩ **Es gibt Abendessen!** It's dinner time!

① **die Lehne** back

⑪ **die Obstschale** fruit bowl

⑤ **der Kerzenhalter** candlestick

⑧ **das Salz** salt

⑨ **der Pfeffer** pepper

④ **die Kerze** candle

⑦ **das Besteck** cutlery

② **der Stuhl** chair

③ **das Stuhlbein** leg

⑫ **die Sitzfläche** seat

⑬ **die Holzdiele** floorboards

⑭ **der Tisch** table

⑮ **der Napf** food bowl

⑯ **die Anrichte** sideboard

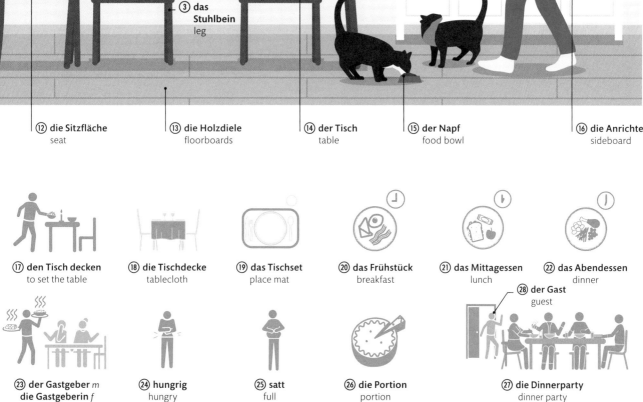

⑰ **den Tisch decken** to set the table

⑱ **die Tischdecke** tablecloth

⑲ **das Tischset** place mat

⑳ **das Frühstück** breakfast

㉑ **das Mittagessen** lunch

㉒ **das Abendessen** dinner

㉓ **der Gastgeber** m **die Gastgeberin** f host / hostess

㉔ **hungrig** hungry

㉕ **satt** full

㉖ **die Portion** portion

㉘ **der Gast** guest

㉗ **die Dinnerparty** dinner party

27.1 KÜCHENGERÄTE · KITCHEN APPLIANCES

① das Rührgerät
mixer

② der Toaster
toaster

③ der Mixer
blender / food processor

⑦ das Gefrierfach
freezer

⑧ die Kühlbox
ice maker

④ die Spülmaschine
dishwasher

⑤ der Wasserkocher
electric kettle

⑥ der Reiskocher
rice cooker

⑨ das Fach
shelf

⑩ das Salatfach
salad drawer

⑪ der Kühlschrank
fridge / refrigerator

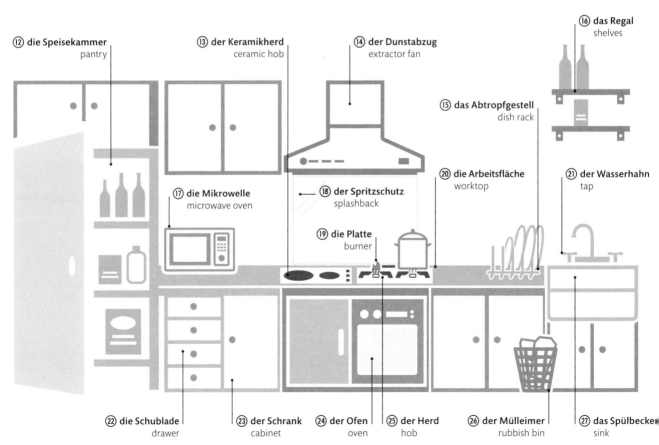

⑫ die Speisekammer
pantry

⑬ der Keramikherd
ceramic hob

⑭ der Dunstabzug
extractor fan

⑯ das Regal
shelves

⑮ das Abtropfgestell
dish rack

⑰ die Mikrowelle
microwave oven

⑱ der Spritzschutz
splashback

⑳ die Arbeitsfläche
worktop

㉑ der Wasserhahn
tap

⑲ die Platte
burner

㉒ die Schublade
drawer

㉓ der Schrank
cabinet

㉔ der Ofen
oven

㉕ der Herd
hob

㉖ der Mülleimer
rubbish bin

㉗ das Spülbecken
sink

See also
28 Küchenutensilien · Kitchenware **29** Kochen · Cooking **59** Kräuter und Gewürze · Herbs and spices **60** In der Vorratskammer · In the pantry **71** Das Frühstück · Breakfast **72** Das Mittagessen und das Abendessen · Lunch and dinner

27.2 DAS GESCHIRR · TABLEWARE

① **die Gabel**
fork

② **das Messer**
knife

③ **der Esslöffel**
tablespoon

④ **der Teelöffel**
teaspoon

⑤ **der Suppenlöffel**
soup spoon

⑥ **der Servierlöffel**
serving spoon

⑦ **das Besteck**
cutlery

⑧ **das Buttermesser**
butter knife

⑨ **die Essstäbchen** *n, pl*
chopsticks

⑩ **die Kelle**
ladle

⑪ **der Essteller**
dinner plate

⑫ **der Beilagenteller**
side plate

⑬ **das Geschirr**
crockery

⑭ **die Kaffeetasse**
coffee cup

⑮ **die Teetasse**
teacup

⑯ **die Tasse**
mug

⑰ **der Espressokocher**
espresso maker

⑱ **die Teekanne**
teapot

⑲ **das Gedeck**
place setting

⑳ **die Serviette**
napkin

㉑ **der Serviettenring**
napkin ring

㉒ **die Schüssel**
bowl

㉓ **die Suppenschüssel**
soup bowl

㉔ **die Reisschüssel**
rice bowl

㉕ **der Eierbecher**
egg cup

㉖ **das Sushi-Set**
sushi set

㉗ **der Messbecher**
measuring jug

㉘ **das Becherglas**
tumbler

㉙ **das Weinglas**
wineglass

㉚ **das Pint-Glas**
pint glass

㉛ **die Stielgläser** *n, pl*
stemware

㉜ **die Gläser** *n, pl*
glasses / glassware

㉝ **das Einmachglas**
jar

㉞ **der Becher**
beaker

㉟ **der Sake-Becher**
sake cup

㊱ **der Untersetzer**
coaster

28.1 DIE KÜCHENAUSSTATTUNG · KITCHEN EQUIPMENT

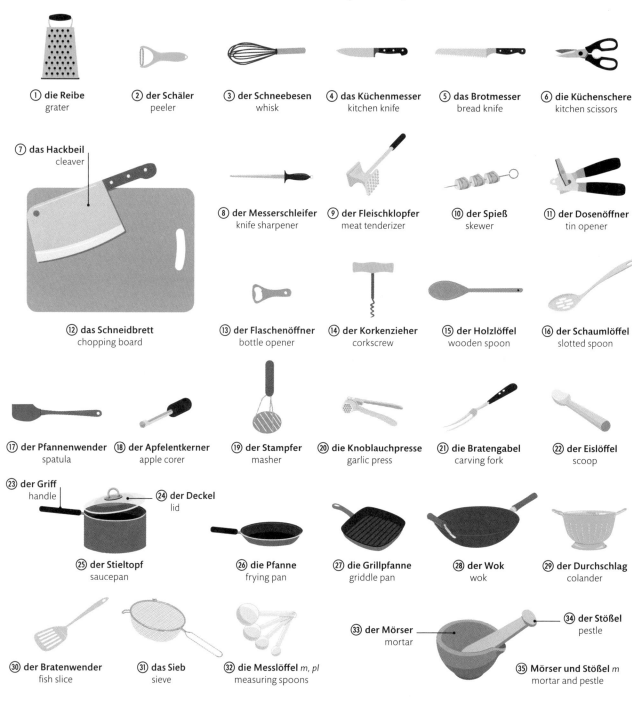

① **die Reibe**
grater

② **der Schäler**
peeler

③ **der Schneebesen**
whisk

④ **das Küchenmesser**
kitchen knife

⑤ **das Brotmesser**
bread knife

⑥ **die Küchenschere**
kitchen scissors

⑦ **das Hackbeil**
cleaver

⑧ **der Messerschleifer**
knife sharpener

⑨ **der Fleischklopfer**
meat tenderizer

⑩ **der Spieß**
skewer

⑪ **der Dosenöffner**
tin opener

⑫ **das Schneidbrett**
chopping board

⑬ **der Flaschenöffner**
bottle opener

⑭ **der Korkenzieher**
corkscrew

⑮ **der Holzlöffel**
wooden spoon

⑯ **der Schaumlöffel**
slotted spoon

⑰ **der Pfannenwender**
spatula

⑱ **der Apfelentkerner**
apple corer

⑲ **der Stampfer**
masher

⑳ **die Knoblauchpresse**
garlic press

㉑ **die Bratengabel**
carving fork

㉒ **der Eislöffel**
scoop

㉓ **der Griff**
handle

㉔ **der Deckel**
lid

㉕ **der Stieltopf**
saucepan

㉖ **die Pfanne**
frying pan

㉗ **die Grillpfanne**
griddle pan

㉘ **der Wok**
wok

㉙ **der Durchschlag**
colander

㉚ **der Bratenwender**
fish slice

㉛ **das Sieb**
sieve

㉜ **die Messlöffel** m, pl
measuring spoons

㉝ **der Mörser**
mortar

㉞ **der Stößel**
pestle

㉟ **Mörser und Stößel** m
mortar and pestle

See also
27 Küche und Geschirr • Kitchen and tableware **29** Kochen • Cooking
59 Kräuter und Gewürze • Herbs and spices **60** In der Vorratskammer • In the pantry
71 Das Frühstück • Breakfast **72** Das Mittagessen und das Abendessen • Lunch and dinner

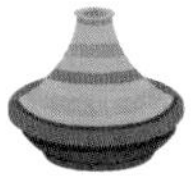

㊱ **die Tajine**
tagine

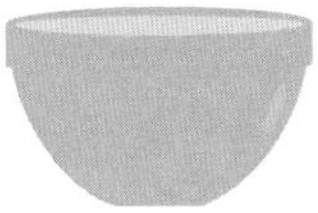

㊲ **die Rührschüssel**
mixing bowl

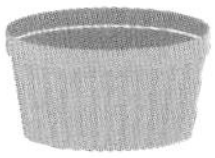

㊳ **die Souffléform**
soufflé dish

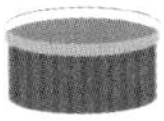

㊴ **das Auflaufförmchen**
ramekin

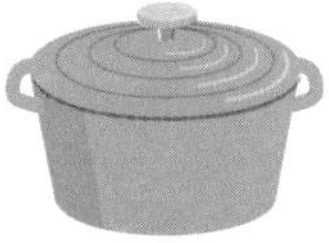

㊵ **die Kasserole**
casserole dish

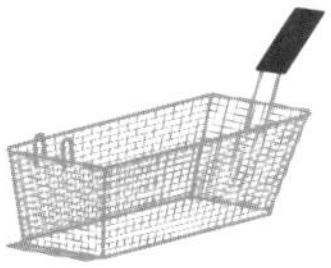

㊶ **der Frittierkorb**
frying basket

㊷ **die Butterschale**
butter dish

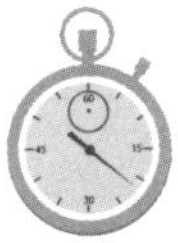

㊸ **der Wecker**
timer

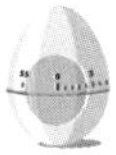

㊹ **die Eieruhr**
egg timer

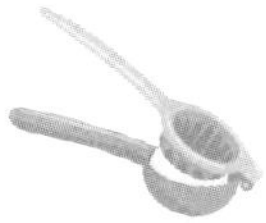

㊺ **die Zitronenpresse**
lemon squeezer

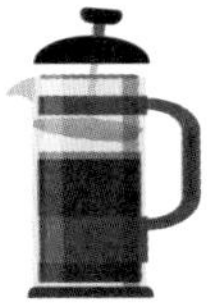

㊻ **die French Press**
coffee press / cafetière

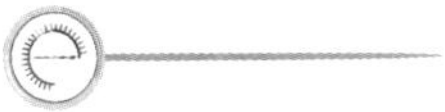

㊼ **das Bratenthermometer**
meat thermometer

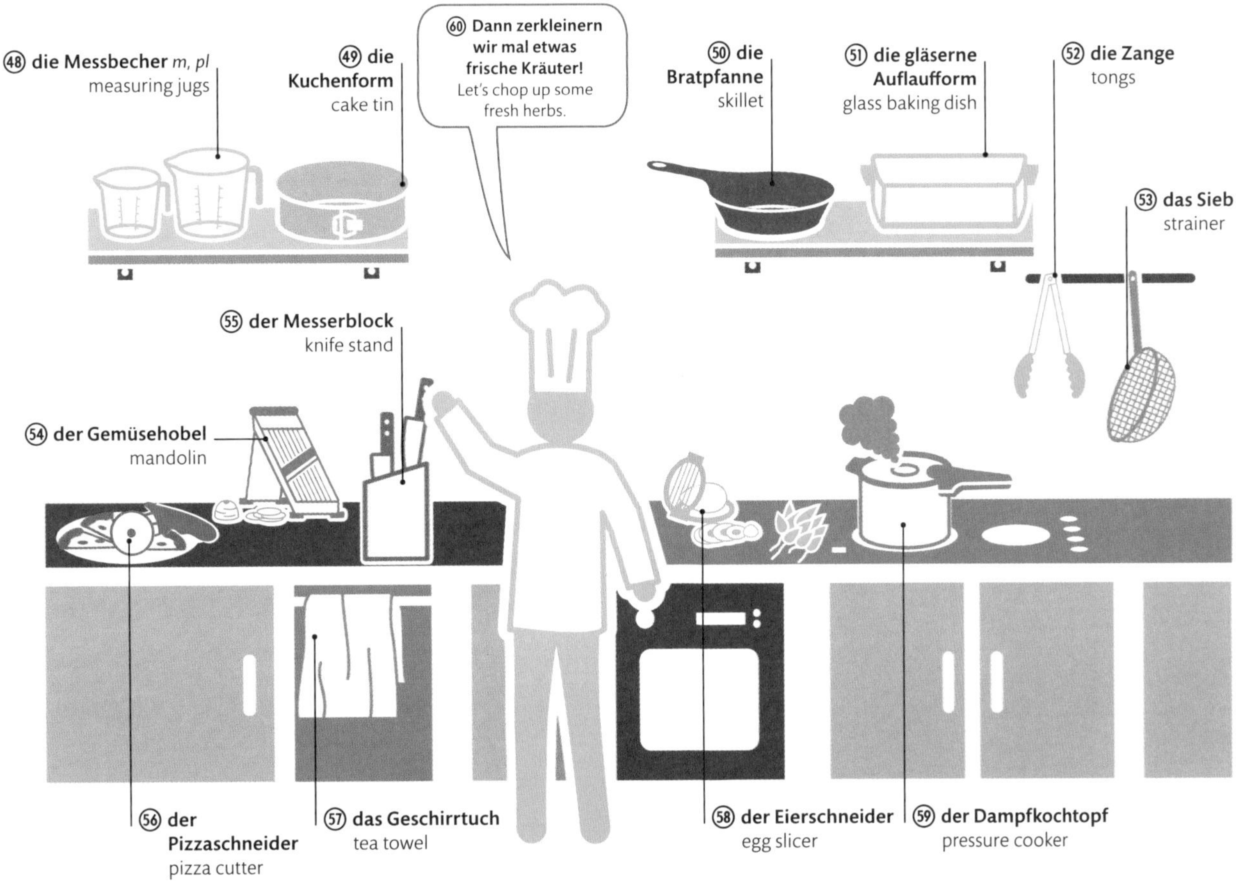
㊽ **die Messbecher** *m, pl*
measuring jugs
㊾ **die Kuchenform**
cake tin
(60) **Dann zerkleinern wir mal etwas frische Kräuter!**
Let's chop up some fresh herbs.
㊿ **die Bratpfanne**
skillet
(51) **die gläserne Auflaufform**
glass baking dish
(52) **die Zange**
tongs
(53) **das Sieb**
strainer
(55) **der Messerblock**
knife stand
(54) **der Gemüsehobel**
mandolin
(56) **der Pizzaschneider**
pizza cutter
(57) **das Geschirrtuch**
tea towel
(58) **der Eierschneider**
egg slicer
(59) **der Dampfkochtopf**
pressure cooker

29.1 KOCHVERBEN · COOKING VERBS

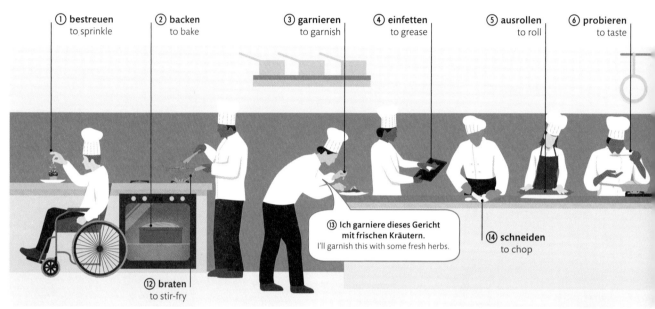

① **bestreuen**
to sprinkle

② **backen**
to bake

③ **garnieren**
to garnish

④ **einfetten**
to grease

⑤ **ausrollen**
to roll

⑥ **probieren**
to taste

⑬ Ich garniere dieses Gericht mit frischen Kräutern.
I'll garnish this with some fresh herbs.

⑭ **schneiden**
to chop

⑫ **braten**
to stir-fry

⑳ **grillen**
to grill

㉑ **rösten**
to roast

㉒ **braten**
to fry

㉓ **pochieren**
to poach

㉔ **köcheln**
to simmer

㉕ **kochen**
to boil

㉖ **einfrieren**
to freeze

㉗ **hinzugeben**
to add

㉘ **mischen**
to mix

㉙ **umrühren**
to stir

㉚ **verrühren**
to whisk

㉛ **zerstampfen**
to mash

㉜ **in Scheiben schneiden**
to slice

㉝ **eine Prise**
a pinch

㉞ **ein Schuss**
a dash

㉟ **eine Handvoll**
a handful

㊱ **zerhacken**
to mince

㊲ **schälen**
to peel

㊳ **schneiden**
to cut

㊴ **reiben**
to grate

㊵ **gießen**
to pour

See also
27 Die Küche und das Geschirr • Kitchen and tableware **28** Küchenutensilien • Kitchenware **59** Kräuter und Gewürze • Herbs and spices **60** In der Vorratskammer • In the pantry **62-63** Die Bäckerei • The bakery **71** Das Frühstück • Breakfast **72** Das Mittagessen und das Abendessen • Lunch and dinner

⑦ **dünsten**
to steam

⑧ **Kannst du mir bitte eine Karotte in Würfel schneiden?**
Can you dice a carrot for me, please?

⑨ **Eier schlagen**
to beat eggs

⑩ **Mir sind die Zwiebeln angebrannt. Sie sind ruiniert!**
I've burned the onions. They are ruined!

⑪ **in der Mikrowelle erwärmen**
to microwave

⑮ **Butter schmelzen**
to melt butter

⑯ **zerlegen**
to carve

⑰ **würfeln**
to dice

⑱ **anbrennen**
to burn

⑲ **anschwitzen**
to sauté

29.2 **BACKEN** · BAKING

① **die Schürze**
apron

② **der Ofenhandschuh**
oven glove

③ **die Kuchenform**
cake tin

④ **die Pastetenform**
flan tin

⑤ **die Pie-Form**
pie dish

⑥ **der Backpinsel**
pastry brush

⑦ **das Nudelholz**
rolling pin

⑧ **das Backblech**
baking tray

⑨ **die Muffinform**
muffin tray

⑩ **das Kuchengitter**
cooling rack

⑪ **die Glasur**
icing

② **der Spritzbeutel**
piping bag

⑬ **die Waage**
scales

⑭ **der Messbecher**
measuring jug

⑮ **dekorieren**
to decorate

30.1 DAS SCHLAFZIMMER · BEDROOM

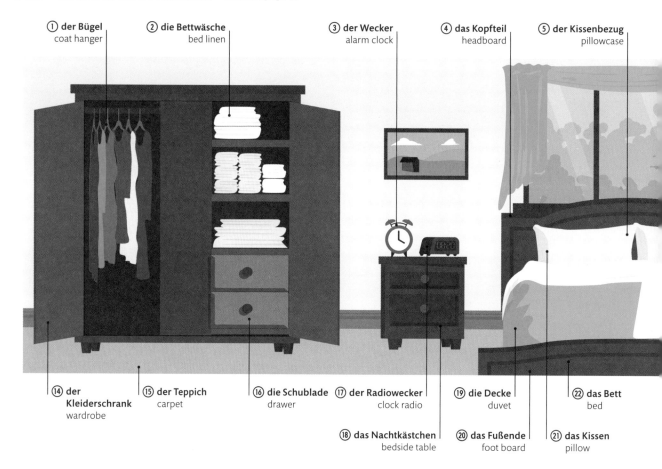

① der Bügel
coat hanger

② die Bettwäsche
bed linen

③ der Wecker
alarm clock

④ das Kopfteil
headboard

⑤ der Kissenbezug
pillowcase

⑭ der Kleiderschrank
wardrobe

⑮ der Teppich
carpet

⑯ die Schublade
drawer

⑰ der Radiowecker
clock radio

⑲ die Decke
duvet

㉒ das Bett
bed

⑱ das Nachtkästchen
bedside table

⑳ das Fußende
foot board

㉑ das Kissen
pillow

㉗ das Einzelbett
single bed

㉘ das Doppelbett
double bed

㉙ die Boxspring-Matratze
bedspring

㉚ der Polsterhocker
Ottoman

㉛ die Wäschetruhe
linen chest

㉜ der Überwurf
throw

㉝ die Steppdecke
quilt

㉞ die Decke
blanket

㉟ die Heizdecke
electric blanket

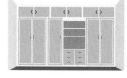

㊱ der Einbauschrank
built-in wardrobe

㊲ die Wärmflasche
hot-water bottle

See also
08 Schwangerschaft und Kindheit • Pregnancy and childhood **13-15** Kleidung • Clothes
25 Ein Ort zum Leben • A place to live **32** Haus und Heim • House and home

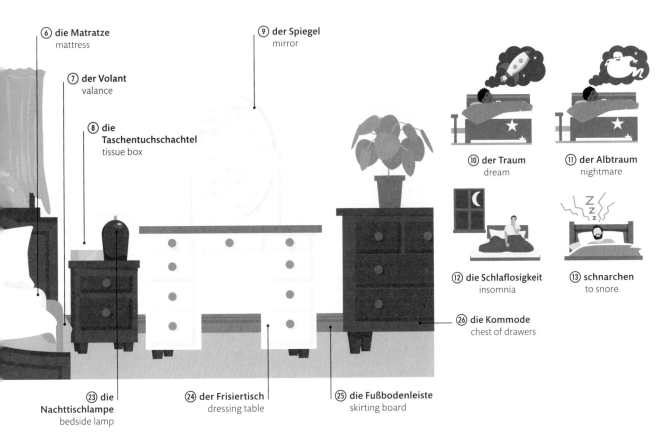

⑥ **die Matratze**
mattress

⑨ **der Spiegel**
mirror

⑦ **der Volant**
valance

⑧ **die Taschentuchschachtel**
tissue box

⑩ **der Traum**
dream

⑪ **der Albtraum**
nightmare

⑫ **die Schlaflosigkeit**
insomnia

⑬ **schnarchen**
to snore

㉖ **die Kommode**
chest of drawers

㉓ **die Nachttischlampe**
bedside lamp

㉔ **der Frisiertisch**
dressing table

㉕ **die Fußbodenleiste**
skirting board

30.2 **DAS KINDERZIMMER** · NURSERY

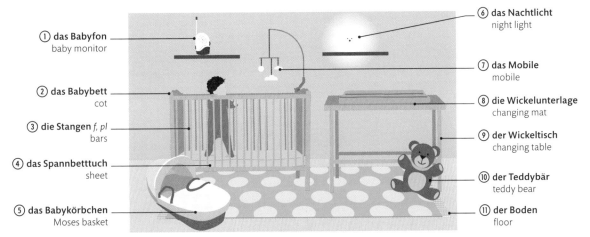

① **das Babyfon**
baby monitor

② **das Babybett**
cot

③ **die Stangen** *f, pl*
bars

④ **das Spannbetttuch**
sheet

⑤ **das Babykörbchen**
Moses basket

⑥ **das Nachtlicht**
night light

⑦ **das Mobile**
mobile

⑧ **die Wickelunterlage**
changing mat

⑨ **der Wickeltisch**
changing table

⑩ **der Teddybär**
teddy bear

⑪ **der Boden**
floor

31.1 IM BADEZIMMER · IN THE BATHROOM

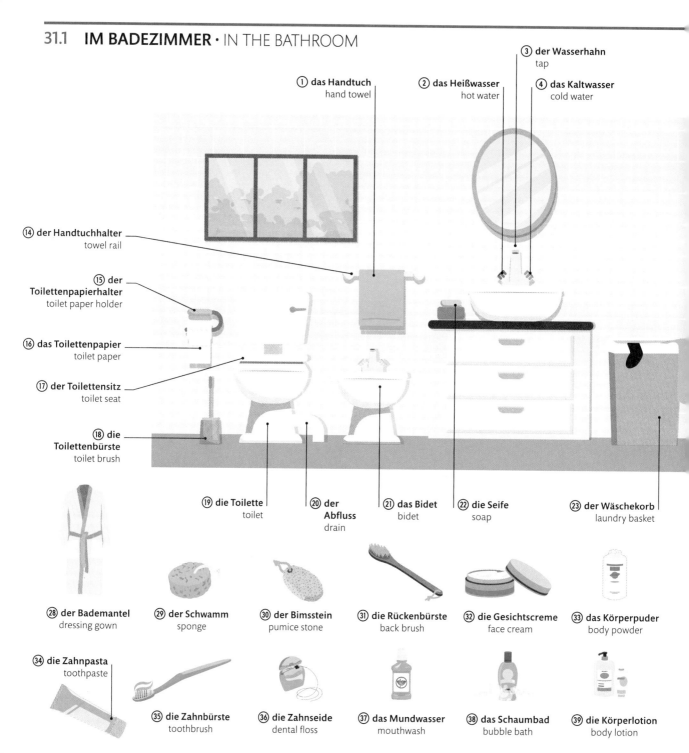

③ der Wasserhahn
tap

① das Handtuch
hand towel

② das Heißwasser
hot water

④ das Kaltwasser
cold water

⑭ der Handtuchhalter
towel rail

⑮ der
Toilettenpapierhalter
toilet paper holder

⑯ das Toilettenpapier
toilet paper

⑰ der Toilettensitz
toilet seat

⑱ die
Toilettenbürste
toilet brush

⑲ die Toilette
toilet

⑳ der
Abfluss
drain

㉑ das Bidet
bidet

㉒ die Seife
soap

㉓ der Wäschekorb
laundry basket

㉘ der Bademantel
dressing gown

㉙ der Schwamm
sponge

㉚ der Bimsstein
pumice stone

㉛ die Rückenbürste
back brush

㉜ die Gesichtscreme
face cream

㉝ das Körperpuder
body powder

㉞ die Zahnpasta
toothpaste

㉟ die Zahnbürste
toothbrush

㊱ die Zahnseide
dental floss

㊲ das Mundwasser
mouthwash

㊳ das Schaumbad
bubble bath

㊴ die Körperlotion
body lotion

See also
18 Beauty • Beauty **25** Ein Ort zum Leben • A place to live **32** Haus und Heim • House and home
33 Elektrizität und Sanitärtechnik • Electrics and plumbing

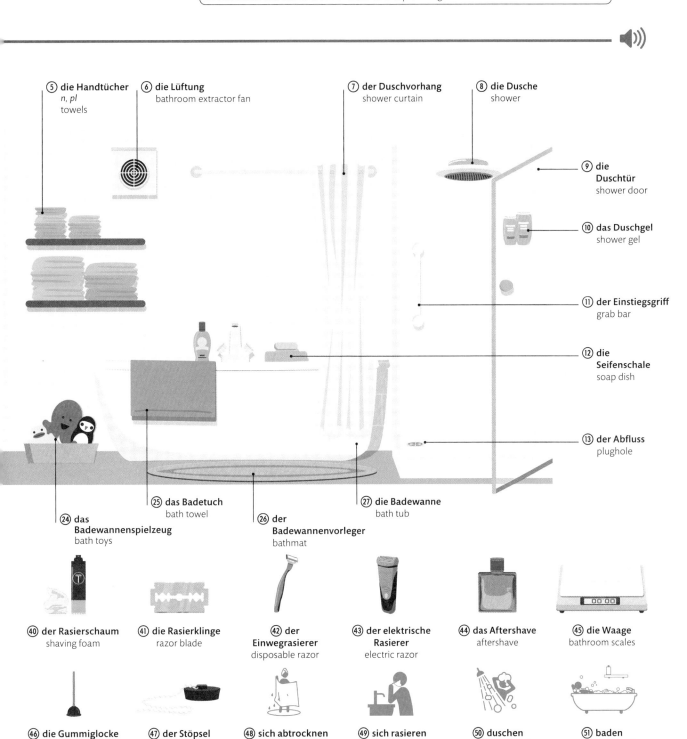

⑤ **die Handtücher**
n, pl
towels

⑥ **die Lüftung**
bathroom extractor fan

⑦ **der Duschvorhang**
shower curtain

⑧ **die Dusche**
shower

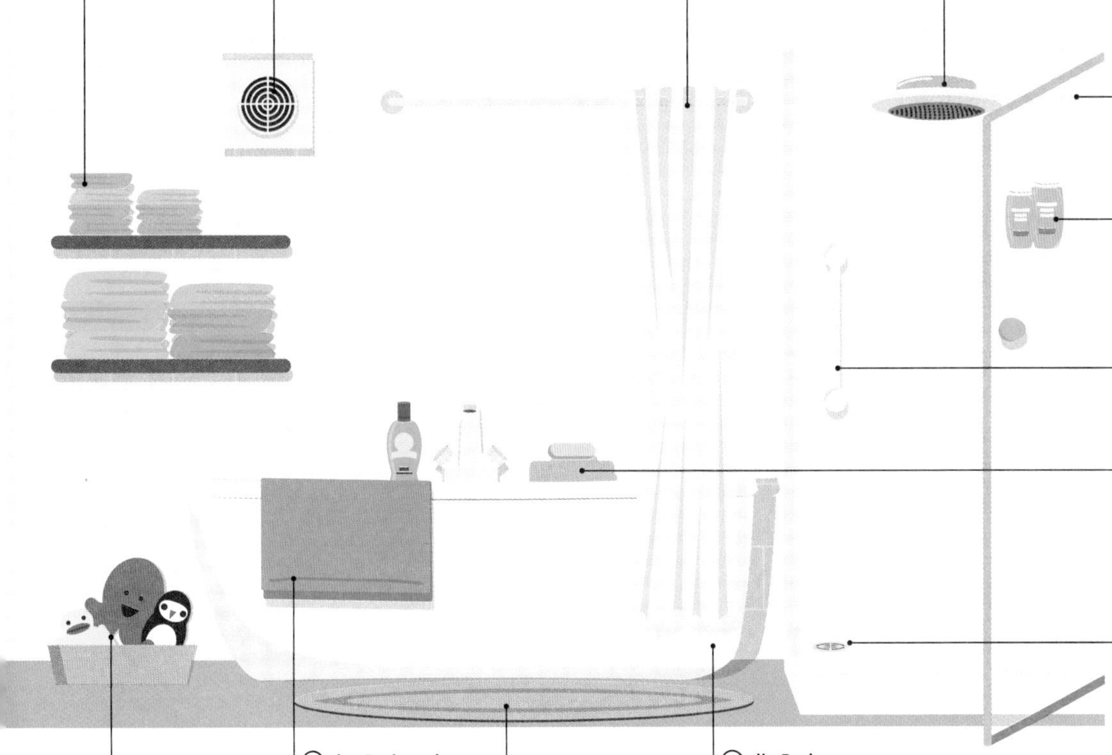

⑨ **die Duschtür**
shower door

⑩ **das Duschgel**
shower gel

⑪ **der Einstiegsgriff**
grab bar

⑫ **die Seifenschale**
soap dish

⑬ **der Abfluss**
plughole

㉔ **das Badewannenspielzeug**
bath toys

㉕ **das Badetuch**
bath towel

㉖ **der Badewannenvorleger**
bathmat

㉗ **die Badewanne**
bath tub

㊵ **der Rasierschaum**
shaving foam

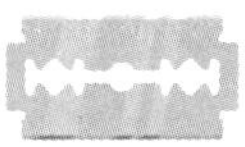

㊶ **die Rasierklinge**
razor blade

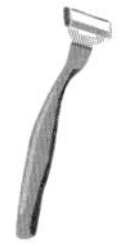

㊷ **der Einwegrasierer**
disposable razor

㊸ **der elektrische Rasierer**
electric razor

㊹ **das Aftershave**
aftershave

㊺ **die Waage**
bathroom scales

㊻ **die Gummiglocke**
plunger

㊼ **der Stöpsel**
plug

㊽ **sich abtrocknen**
to dry yourself

㊾ **sich rasieren**
to shave

㊿ **duschen**
to take (or have) a shower

(51) **baden**
to take (or have) a bath

32 Haus und Heim
House and home

32.1 HAUSARTEN · TYPES OF HOUSES

① **das Einfamilienhaus**
detached house

② **die Doppelhaushälfte**
semi-detached

③ **das Reihenhaus**
terraced house

④ **das Stadthaus**
town house

⑤ **das Cottage**
cottage

⑥ **die Villa**
villa

⑦ **der Bungalow**
bungalow

⑧ **das Anwesen**
mansion

⑨ **der Wohnwagen**
caravan

⑩ **die Blockhütte**
cabin

⑪ **das Baumhaus**
tree house

⑫ **die Berghütte**
chalet

⑬ **die Jurte**
yurt

⑭ **die Hütte**
hut

⑮ **der Wigwam**
wigwam

⑯ **das Iglu**
igloo

⑰ **das Tipi**
teepee

⑱ **das Hausboot**
houseboat

⑲ **das Fertighaus**
prefab house

⑳ **das Pfahlhaus**
stilt house

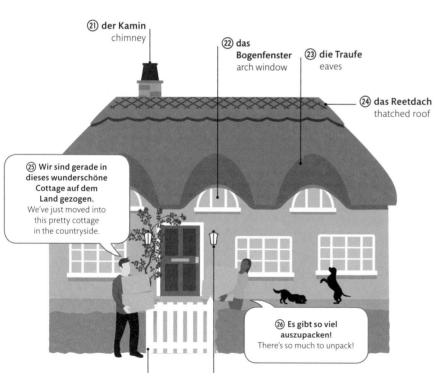

㉑ **der Kamin**
chimney

㉒ **das Bogenfenster**
arch window

㉓ **die Traufe**
eaves

㉔ **das Reetdach**
thatched roof

㉕ **Wir sind gerade in dieses wunderschöne Cottage auf dem Land gezogen.**
We've just moved into this pretty cottage in the countryside.

㉖ **Es gibt so viel auszupacken!**
There's so much to unpack!

㉘ **das Tor**
gate

㉗ **die Lampe**
light

㉙ **das Cottage mit Reetdach**
thatched cottage

See also
25 Ein Ort zum Leben · A place to live **33** Elektrizität und Sanitärtechnik · Electrics and plumbing **35** Heimwerken · Home improvements **37** Wohnraumverschönerung · Decorating **42-43** In der Stadt · In town **44** Gebäude und Architektur · Buildings and architecture

32.2 EIN HAUS KAUFEN ODER MIETEN · BUYING AND RENTING A HOUSE

① **der Makler** m
die Maklerin f
estate agent

② **die Immobilie**
property

③ **ein Haus besichtigen**
to view a house

④ **möbliert**
furnished

⑤ **unmöbliert**
unfurnished

⑥ **der offene Wohnbereich**
open-plan

⑦ **der Parkplatz**
parking space

⑧ **der Lagerraum**
storage

⑨ **sparen**
to save up

⑩ **kaufen**
to buy

⑪ **besitzen**
to own

⑫ **die Kartons** m, pl
boxes

⑬ **das Klebeband**
tape

⑭ **die Schlüssel** m, pl
keys

⑮ **packen**
to pack

⑯ **das Umzugsauto**
removal van

⑰ **ausziehen**
to move out

⑱ **einziehen**
to move in

⑲ **auspacken**
to unpack

⑳ **vermieten**
to rent out

㉑ **mieten**
to rent

㉒ **der Mietvertrag**
lease / tenancy
agreement

㉓ **der Mieter** m
die Mieterin f
tenant

㉔ **der Vermieter** m
die Vermieterin f
landlord

㉕ **die Kaution**
deposit

㉖ **den Mietvertrag kündigen**
to give notice

㉗ **der Kredit**
mortgage

㉘ **die Rechnungen**
f, pl
bills

㉙ **der Untermieter** m
die Untermieterin f
lodger

㉚ **der Mitbewohner** m
die Mitbewohnerin f
housemate

㉛ **das Wohngebiet**
residential area

33.1 DIE ELEKTRIZITÄT · ELECTRICITY

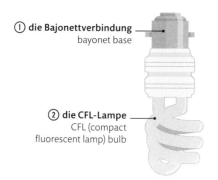

① **die Bajonettverbindung**
bayonet base

② **die CFL-Lampe**
CFL (compact fluorescent lamp) bulb

③ **die Glühbirne**
incandescent bulb

④ **die Schraubverbindung**
screw base

⑤ **die LED-Lampe**
LED (light emitting diode) bulb

⑥ **das Leuchtmittel**
light bulbs

⑦ **die Steckdose**
socket

⑧ **der Lichtschalter**
light switch

⑨ **der Gleichstrom**
direct current

⑩ **der Wechselstrom**
alternating current

⑪ **der Generator**
generator

⑫ **die Gasheizung**
gas space heater

⑬ **die Ölheizung**
oil-filled radiator

⑭ **das Heizgebläse**
fan space heater

⑯ **der Ventilatorflügel**
blade

⑮ **der Deckenventilator**
ceiling fan

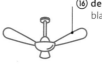

⑰ **der Ventilator**
fan

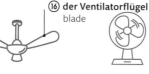

⑱ **die Klimaanlage**
air conditioning

⑲ **der Strom**
power

② **der Sicherungskasten**
fuse box

㉑ **der Schutzschalter**
trip switch

㉒ **das Ampere**
amp

㉓ **die Phase**
live

㉔ **der Nullleiter**
neutral

㉕ **die Drähte** *m, pl*
wires

㉖ **die Erdung**
earthing

㉗ **die Spannung**
voltage

㉘ **der Stecker**
plug

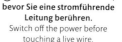

㉙ **der Kontakt**
pin

㉟ **Schalten Sie den Strom ab, bevor Sie eine stromführende Leitung berühren.**
Switch off the power before touching a live wire.

㉚ **der Stromzähler**
electricity meter

㉛ **der Transformator**
transformer

㉜ **der Stromausfall**
power cut

㉝ **der Netzstrom**
mains supply

㉞ **die Verdrahtung**
wiring

See also
31 Das Badezimmer • Bathroom **35** Heimwerken • Home improvements **36** Werkzeuge • Tools
37 Wohnraumverschönerung • Decorating **87** Der Bau • Construction

33.2 SANITÄRTECHNIK · PLUMBING

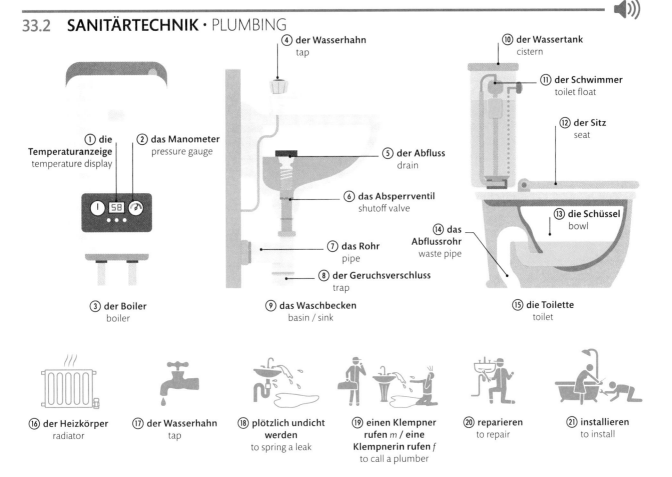

④ **der Wasserhahn**
tap

⑩ **der Wassertank**
cistern

⑪ **der Schwimmer**
toilet float

① **die Temperaturanzeige**
temperature display

② **das Manometer**
pressure gauge

⑫ **der Sitz**
seat

⑤ **der Abfluss**
drain

⑥ **das Absperrventil**
shutoff valve

⑬ **die Schüssel**
bowl

⑦ **das Rohr**
pipe

⑭ **das Abflussrohr**
waste pipe

⑧ **der Geruchsverschluss**
trap

③ **der Boiler**
boiler

⑨ **das Waschbecken**
basin / sink

⑮ **die Toilette**
toilet

⑯ **der Heizkörper**
radiator

⑰ **der Wasserhahn**
tap

⑱ **plötzlich undicht werden**
to spring a leak

⑲ **einen Klempner rufen** *m* / **eine Klempnerin rufen** *f*
to call a plumber

⑳ **reparieren**
to repair

㉑ **installieren**
to install

33.3 ABFALL · WASTE

① **der Abfalleimer**
rubbish bin

② **die Recycling-Tonne**
recycling bin

③ **der Recyclinghof**
sorting unit

④ **der Kompost**
food compost bin

⑤ **der Müllbeutel**
bin liner

⑥ **der Biomüll**
biodegradable waste

⑦ **der Sondermüll**
hazardous waste

⑧ **der Elektroschrott**
electrical waste

⑨ **der Bauschutt**
construction waste

34 Hausarbeit
Household chores

34.1 AUFGABEN IM HAUSHALT · HOUSEHOLD TASKS

① **das Bett beziehen**
to change
the sheets

② **das Bett machen**
to make
the bed

③ **das Haustier füttern**
to feed the pets

④ **die Blumen gießen**
to water the plants

⑤ **das Auto putzen**
to wash the car

⑥ **den Boden kehren**
to sweep the floor

⑦ **den Boden schrubben**
to scrub the floor

⑧ **den Ofen putzen**
to clean the oven

⑨ **die Fenster putzen**
to clean the windows

⑩ **das Gefrierfach abtauen**
to defrost the freezer

⑪ **den Teppich saugen**
to vacuum the carpet

⑫ **abstauben**
to dust

⑬ **das Bad putzen**
to clean the bathroom

⑭ **aufräumen**
to tidy

⑮ **Lebensmittel einkaufen**
to buy groceries

⑯ **die Wäsche machen**
to do the laundry

⑰ **die Wäsche aufhängen**
to hang out clothes

⑱ **die Kleidung bügeln**
to do the ironing

⑲ **den Boden wischen**
to mop the floor

⑳ Normalerweise erledige ich die Hausarbeit abends.
I usually do the housework in the evening.

㉑ **die Wäsche zusammenlegen**
to fold clothes

㉒ **den Tisch decken**
to set the table

㉓ **den Tisch abräumen**
to clear the table

㉔ **die Spülmaschine einräumen**
to load the dishwasher

㉕ **die Spülmaschine ausräumen**
to unload
the dishwasher

㉖ **die Oberflächen abwischen**
to wipe the surfaces

㉗ **das Geschirr spülen**
to do the dishes

㉘ **das Geschirr abtrocknen**
to dry the dishes

㉙ **den Müll hinausbringen**
to take out the
rubbish

See also
09 Die Alltagsroutine • Daily routines **25** Ein Ort zum Leben • A place to live **33** Elektrizität und Sanitärtechnik • Electrics and plumbing **35** Heimwerken • Home improvements **37** Wohnraumverschönerung • Decorating **39** Gartenarbeit • Practical gardening

34.2 WÄSCHE UND PUTZEN · LAUNDRY AND CLEANING

① **der Scheuerschwamm**
scouring pad

② **der Schwamm**
sponge

③ **das Tuch**
cloth

④ **das Staubtuch**
duster

⑤ **der Staubwedel**
feather duster

⑥ **der Abzieher**
squeegee

⑦ **der Eimer**
bucket

⑧ **der Mopp**
mop

⑨ **die Scheuerbürste**
scrubbing brush

⑩ **die Kehrschaufel**
dustpan

⑪ **der Kehrbesen**
brush

⑫ **der Besen**
broom

⑬ **der Recyclingmüll**
recycling bin

⑭ **der Müllbeutel**
bin liner

⑮ **das Putzmittel**
polish

⑯ **der Oberflächenreiniger**
surface cleaner

⑰ **der WC-Reiniger**
toilet cleaner

⑱ **der WC-Stein**
toilet block

⑳ **das Saugrohr**
suction hose

⑲ **der Staubsauger**
vacuum cleaner

㉑ **die Gummihandschuhe** *m, pl*
rubber gloves

㉒ **der klare Essig**
white vinegar

㉓ **die schmutzige Wäsche**
dirty washing

㉔ **der Wäschekorb**
laundry basket

㉕ **die Waschmaschine**
washing machine

㉖ **der Trockner**
tumble dryer

㉗ **das Bügeleisen**
iron

㉘ **das Bügelbrett**
ironing board

㉙ **die Wäscheklammer**
clothes peg

㉚ **die Wäscheleine**
clothesline / washing line

㉛ **das Waschmittel**
laundry detergent

㉜ **der Weichspüler**
fabric softener

㉝ **die Spülmaschine**
dishwasher

㉞ **das Geschirrspültab**
dishwasher tablets

㉟ **das Geschirrspülmittel**
washing-up liquid

㊱ **die Bleiche**
bleach

Heimwerken
Home improvements

35.1 WERKZEUG UND HEIMWERKERZUBEHÖR · TOOLS AND DIY EQUIPMENT

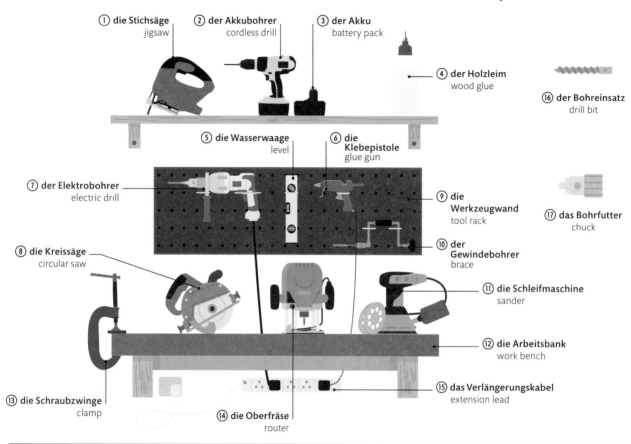

① die Stichsäge
jigsaw

② der Akkubohrer
cordless drill

③ der Akku
battery pack

④ der Holzleim
wood glue

⑯ der Bohreinsatz
drill bit

⑤ die Wasserwaage
level

⑥ die Klebepistole
glue gun

⑦ der Elektrobohrer
electric drill

⑨ die Werkzeugwand
tool rack

⑰ das Bohrfutter
chuck

⑩ der Gewindebohrer
brace

⑧ die Kreissäge
circular saw

⑪ die Schleifmaschine
sander

⑫ die Arbeitsbank
work bench

⑬ die Schraubzwinge
clamp

⑭ die Oberfräse
router

⑮ das Verlängerungskabel
extension lead

35.2 HEIMWERKERVERBEN · DIY VERBS

① schneiden
to cut

② sägen
to saw

③ bohren
to drill

④ hämmern
to hammer

⑤ hobeln
to plane

⑥ drehen
to turn

⑦ schnitzen
to carve

⑧ fliesen
to tile

⑨ löten
to solder

⑩ das Lot
solder

⑪ der Lötkolben
soldering iron

See also
33 Elektrizität und Sanitärtechnik • Electrics and plumbing **36** Werkzeuge
Tools **37** Wohnraumverschönerung • Decorating **87** Der Bau • Construction

35.3 **WERKSTOFFE** · MATERIALS

① **das Holz**
wood

② **das Hartholz**
hardwood

③ **das Weichholz**
softwood

④ **die Hartfaserplatte**
hardboard

⑤ **die Spanplatte**
chipboard

⑥ **das Sperrholz**
plywood

⑦ **die MDF-Platte**
MDF

⑧ **die Fliese**
tiles

⑨ **der Beton**
concrete

⑩ **das Metall**
metal

⑪ **der Draht**
wire

⑫ **die Steinplatte**
flagstone

⑬ **das Isoliermaterial**
insulation

⑭ **der Sand**
sand

⑮ **der Kies**
gravel

⑰ **Ich arbeite an einem Anbau.**
I'm building a new extension.

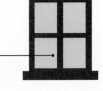

⑱ **das Glas**
glass

⑯ **die Ziegel** *m, pl*
bricks

⑲ **der Mörtel**
mortar

⑫ **einen Teppich verlegen**
to fit a carpet

⑬ **den Abfluss (des Waschbeckens) frei machen**
to unblock the sink

⑭ **das Haus neu verkabeln**
to rewire the house

⑮ **mauern**
to lay bricks

⑯ **das Dachgeschoss umbauen**
to convert the attic / loft

⑰ **einen Vorhang nähen**
to make curtains

⑱ **ein Regal aufhängen**
to put up shelves

⑲ **eine Glühbirne wechseln**
to change a light bulb

⑳ **den Abfluss (der Toilette) frei machen**
to unblock the toilet

㉑ **eine Wand einreißen**
to knock down a wall

㉒ **eine Wand streichen**
to paint a wall

㉓ **einen Zaun reparieren**
to fix a fence

36 Werkzeuge
Tools

36.1 DER WERKZEUGKASTEN · TOOLBOX

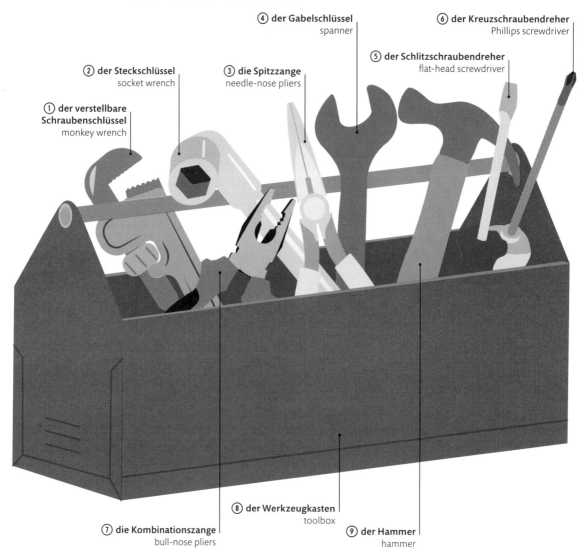

④ **der Gabelschlüssel**
spanner

⑥ **der Kreuzschraubendreher**
Phillips screwdriver

⑤ **der Schlitzschraubendreher**
flat-head screwdriver

② **der Steckschlüssel**
socket wrench

③ **die Spitzzange**
needle-nose pliers

① **der verstellbare Schraubenschlüssel**
monkey wrench

⑧ **der Werkzeugkasten**
toolbox

⑦ **die Kombinationszange**
bull-nose pliers

⑨ **der Hammer**
hammer

36.2 BOHREINSÄTZE · DRILL BITS

① **der Metallbohrer**
metal bit

② **der Steinbohrer**
masonry bit

③ **der Holzbohrer**
carpentry bit

④ **der Flachfräsbohrer**
flat wood bit

⑤ **der Torxeinsatz**
security bit

⑥ **die Reibahle**
reamer

See also
33 Elektrizität und Sanitärtechnik · Electrics and plumbing **35** Heimwerken · Home improvements **37** Wohnraumverschönerung · Decorating **87** Der Bau · Construction

36.3 WERKZEUGE · TOOLS

① der Werkzeuggürtel
tool belt

② der Nagel
nail

③ die Schraube
screw

④ die Schraube
bolt

⑤ die Unterlegscheibe
washer

⑥ die Mutter
nut

⑦ der Inbusschlüssel
hex keys / Allen keys

⑧ das Maßband
tape measure

⑨ das Teppichmesser
utility knife

⑩ die Bügelsäge
hacksaw

⑪ der Fuchsschwanz
tenon saw

⑫ die Handsäge
handsaw

⑬ der Hobel
plane

⑭ der Handbohrer
hand drill

⑮ der Schraubenschlüssel
spanner

⑯ der Meißel
chisel

⑰ die Feile
file

⑱ der Wetzstein
sharpening stone

⑳ die Sprosse
rung

㉑ die Abisolierzange
wire strippers

㉒ der Seitenschneider
wire cutters

㉓ das Isolierband
insulating tape

㉔ der Rohrschneider
pipe cutter

㉕ die Gummiglocke
plunger

㉖ der Gummihammer
mallet

㉗ die Axt
axe

㉘ die Stahlwolle
wire wool

㉙ das Schleifpapier
sandpaper

㉚ die Schutzbrille
safety goggles

⑲ die Leiter
ladder

㉛ der Lötkolben
soldering iron

㉜ das Lot
solder

㉝ die Libelle
vial

㉞ die Wasserwaage
spirit level

37.1 RENOVIERUNG · HOUSEHOLD RENOVATION

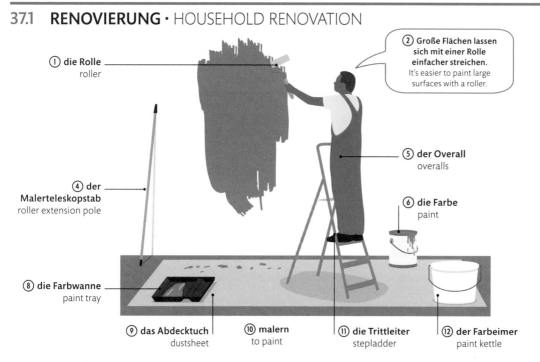

① **die Rolle**
roller

② **Große Flächen lassen sich mit einer Rolle einfacher streichen.**
It's easier to paint large surfaces with a roller.

④ **der Malerteleskopstab**
roller extension pole

⑤ **der Overall**
overalls

⑥ **die Farbe**
paint

⑧ **die Farbwanne**
paint tray

⑨ **das Abdecktuch**
dustsheet

⑩ **malern**
to paint

⑪ **die Trittleiter**
stepladder

⑫ **der Farbeimer**
paint kettle

③ **der Pinsel**
paintbrush

⑦ **der Schwamm**
sponge

⑬ **der Malerkrepp**
masking tape

⑭ **das Teppichmesser**
craft knife

⑮ **das Lot**
plumb line

⑯ **das Schleifpapier**
sandpaper

⑰ **die Füllmasse**
filler

⑱ **der Terpentinersatz**
white spirit

⑲ **das Abbeizmittel**
paint stripper

⑳ **der Putz**
plaster

㉑ **die Grundierung**
sealer / primer

㉒ **der Voranstrich**
undercoat

㉓ **die Dispersionsfarbe**
paint / emulsion

㉔ **die matte Farbe**
matte

㉕ **die glänzende Farbe**
gloss

㉖ **die Schablone**
stencil

㉗ **das Lösungsmittel**
solvent

㉘ **die Dichtmasse**
sealant / caulk

㉙ **der Fugenmörtel**
grout

㉚ **das Holzschutzmittel**
wood preserver

㉛ **der Lack**
varnish

See also
32 Haus und Heim · House and home **33** Elektrizität und Sanitärtechnik · Electrics and plumbing **34** Hausarbeit · Household chores **35** Heimwerken · Home improvements

32 die Schere
scissors

33 das Schrankpapier
lining paper

34 der Tapetenlöser
wallpaper stripper

35 der Spachtel
scraper

36 die Tapetenrolle
wallpaper roll

37 die Tapetenbordüre
wallpaper border

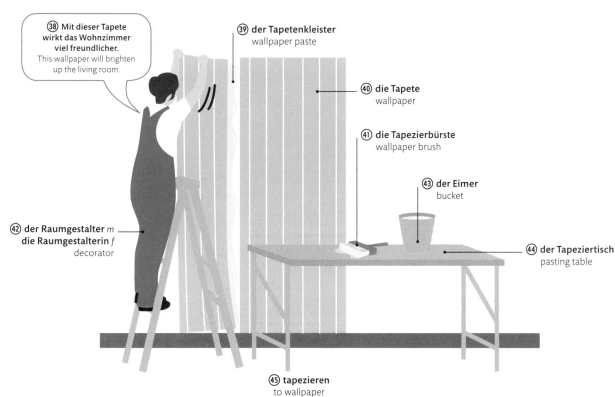

38 Mit dieser Tapete wirkt das Wohnzimmer viel freundlicher.
This wallpaper will brighten up the living room.

39 der Tapetenkleister
wallpaper paste

40 die Tapete
wallpaper

41 die Tapezierbürste
wallpaper brush

43 der Eimer
bucket

42 der Raumgestalter *m*
die Raumgestalterin *f*
decorator

44 der Tapeziertisch
pasting table

45 tapezieren
to wallpaper

37.2 GESTALTUNGSVERBEN · VERBS FOR DECORATING

1 entfernen
to strip

2 verspachteln
to fill

3 schleifen
to sand

4 verputzen
to plaster

5 aufhängen
to hang

6 fliesen
to tile

38.1 BLUMEN UND PFLANZEN IM GARTEN · GARDEN PLANTS AND FLOWERS

① **der Löwenzahn**
dandelion

② **die Nachtkerze**
evening primrose

③ **die Distel**
thistle

④ **die Tulpe**
tulip

⑤ **das Maiglöckchen**
lily of the valley

⑥ **die Nelke**
carnation

⑧ **das Gänseblümchen**
daisy

⑨ **die Butterblume**
buttercup

⑩ **der Mohn**
poppy

⑪ **das Stiefmütterchen**
pansy

⑫ **die Geranie**
geranium

⑬ **der Fingerhut**
foxglove

⑮ **die Lupine**
lupin

⑯ **die Rose**
rose

⑰ **die Sonnenblume**
sunflower

⑱ **die Orchidee**
orchid

⑲ **die Begonie**
begonia

⑳ **die Lilie**
lily

㉒ **das Veilchen**
violet

㉓ **der Krokus**
crocus

㉔ **die Narzisse**
daffodil

㉕ **der Flieder**
lilac

㉖ **die Gardenie**
gardenia

㉗ **der Lavendel**
lavender

㉙ **die Ringelblume**
marigold

㉚ **die Azalee**
azalea

㉛ **die Chrysantheme**
chrysanthemum

㉜ **der Rhododendron**
rhododendron

㉝ **der Hibiskus**
rose of Sharon / hibiscus

㉟ **das Geißblatt**
honeysuckle

㊱ **die Iris**
iris

㊲ **der Lotus**
lotus

㊳ **die Glyzine**
wisteria

㊴ **das Kapkörbchen**
African daisy

㊵ **die Hortensie**
hydrangea

See also
39 Gartenarbeit • Practical gardening **40** Gartengeräte • Garden tools **41** Gartenelemente
Garden features **167-169** Pflanzen und Bäume • Plants and trees

38.2 ZIMMERPFLANZEN · HOUSEPLANTS

⑦ **das Heidekraut**
heather

① **das Einblatt**
peace lily

② **der Bogenhanf**
snake plant

③ **die Grünlilie**
spider plant

④ **die Palmlilie**
yucca

⑤ **der Drachenbaum**
dragon tree

⑭ **die Kamelie**
camellia

⑥ **der Bonsai**
bonsai tree

⑦ **das Köstliche Fensterblatt**
Swiss cheese plant

⑧ **die Sukkulenten** *f, pl*
succulents

⑨ **der Chinesische Geldbaum**
Chinese money plant

㉑ **das Pampasgras**
pampas grass

⑩ **der Gummibaum**
rubber plant

⑪ **das Schildblatt**
umbrella plant

⑫ **die Punktblume**
polka dot plant

⑬ **die Efeutute**
marble queen

⑭ **die Efeutute**
jade pothos

㉘ **die Protea**
protea

㉞ **der Rosmarin**
rosemary

㊶ **der Lorbeerbaum**
bay tree

38.3 DER BLÜTENAUFBAU
FLOWER ANATOMY

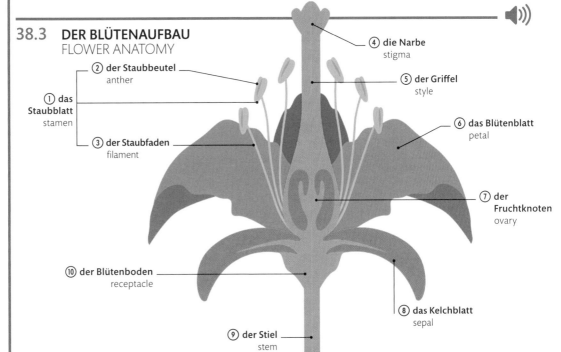

④ **die Narbe**
stigma

② **der Staubbeutel**
anther

① **das Staubblatt**
stamen

③ **der Staubfaden**
filament

⑤ **der Griffel**
style

⑥ **das Blütenblatt**
petal

⑦ **der Fruchtknoten**
ovary

⑩ **der Blütenboden**
receptacle

⑧ **das Kelchblatt**
sepal

⑨ **der Stiel**
stem

39.1 VERBEN FÜR DIE GARTENARBEIT · GARDENING VERBS

① Meine Familie und ich arbeiten im Sommer gerne im Garten.
My family and I enjoy gardening in the summer.

② **hochbinden**
to stake

③ **säen**
to sow

⑥ **zurückschneiden**
to deadhead

⑦ **gießen**
to water

⑧ **ernten**
to harvest

⑮ **den Rasen mähen**
to mow the lawn

⑯ **Gras verlegen**
to lay turf

⑰ **rechen**
to rake (soil)

⑱ **zusammenrechen**
to rake (leaves)

⑲ **belüften**
to aerate

⑳ **das Frühbeet**
cold frame

㉔ **aufpfropfen**
to graft

㉕ **vermehren**
to propagate

㉖ **anpflanzen**
to plant

㉗ **mulchen**
to mulch

㉘ **das Unkraut jäten**
to do the weeding

㉙ **umsetzen**
to transplant

㉞ **kultivieren**
to cultivate

㉟ **zuschneiden**
to trim

㊱ **stutzen**
to prune

㊲ **fällen**
to chop

㊳ **sieben**
to sieve

㊴ **den Garten gestalten**
to landscape

See also
38 Gartenpflanzen und Zimmerpflanzen · Garden plants and houseplants **40** Gartengeräte
Garden tools **41** Gartenelemente · Garden features **167-69** Pflanzen und Bäume · Plants and trees

④ **der Gartenschuppen**
potting shed

⑤ **graben**
to dig

⑪ **der Ableger**
plant cutting

⑫ **das Gewächshaus**
greenhouse

⑬ **der Schuppen**
shed

⑭ **die Entwässerung**
drainage

⑨ **umtopfen**
to pot up

⑩ **das Knochenmehl**
bone meal

㉑ **oberflächlich düngen**
to top dress

㉒ **pflegen**
to tend

㉓ **am Spalier aufziehen**
to train

㉚ **einsprühen**
to spray

㉛ **der Flüssigdünger**
plant food

㉜ **Bio-**
organic

㉝ **die Rankhilfe**
training / support cane

⑩ **der Dünger**
fertilizer

㊶ **düngen**
to fertilize

㊷ **der Unkrautvernichter**
weedkiller

39.2 **BODENARTEN**
TYPES OF SOIL

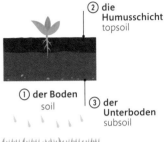

② **die Humusschicht**
topsoil

① **der Boden**
soil

③ **der Unterboden**
subsoil

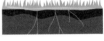

④ **die Versickerung**
leaching

⑤ **die Oberfläche**
surface

⑥ **der Lehm**
loam

⑦ **der Torf**
peat

⑧ **der Kalk**
chalk

⑨ **der Sand**
sand

⑩ **der Schluff**
silt

⑪ **der Ton**
clay

40 Gartengeräte
Garden tools

40.1 GARTENGERÄTE · GARDENING EQUIPMENT

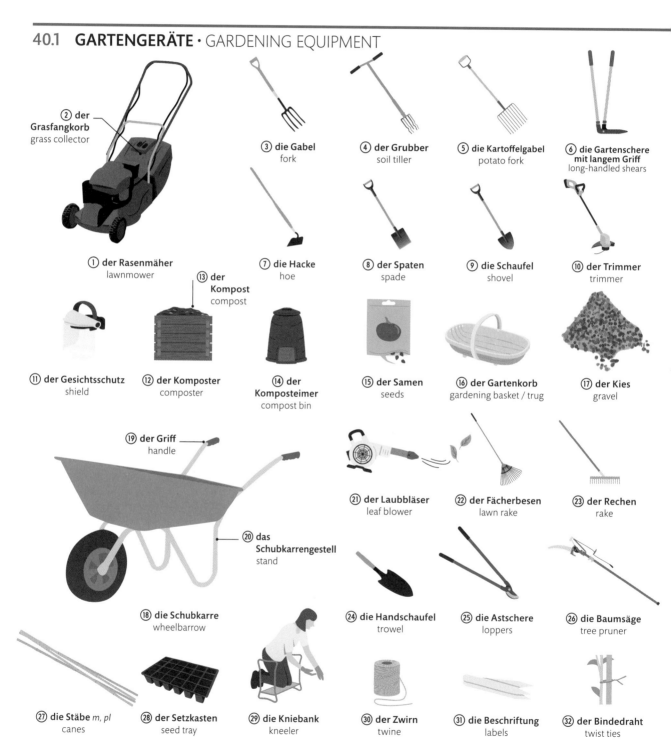

② der **Grasfangkorb**
grass collector

③ die **Gabel**
fork

④ der **Grubber**
soil tiller

⑤ die **Kartoffelgabel**
potato fork

⑥ die **Gartenschere mit langem Griff**
long-handled shears

① der **Rasenmäher**
lawnmower

⑦ die **Hacke**
hoe

⑧ der **Spaten**
spade

⑨ die **Schaufel**
shovel

⑩ der **Trimmer**
trimmer

⑪ der **Gesichtsschutz**
shield

⑬ der **Kompost**
compost

⑫ der **Komposter**
composter

⑭ der **Komposteimer**
compost bin

⑮ der **Samen**
seeds

⑯ der **Gartenkorb**
gardening basket / trug

⑰ der **Kies**
gravel

⑲ der **Griff**
handle

⑳ das **Schubkarrengestell**
stand

⑱ die **Schubkarre**
wheelbarrow

㉑ der **Laubbläser**
leaf blower

㉒ der **Fächerbesen**
lawn rake

㉓ der **Rechen**
rake

㉔ die **Handschaufel**
trowel

㉕ die **Astschere**
loppers

㉖ die **Baumsäge**
tree pruner

㉗ die **Stäbe** *m, pl*
canes

㉘ der **Setzkasten**
seed tray

㉙ die **Kniebank**
kneeler

㉚ der **Zwirn**
twine

㉛ die **Beschriftung**
labels

㉜ der **Bindedraht**
twist ties

See also
38 Gartenpflanzen und Zimmerpflanzen · Garden plants and houseplants **39** Gartenarbeit · Practical gardening **41** Gartenelemente · Garden features **167-169** Pflanzen und Bäume · Plants and trees

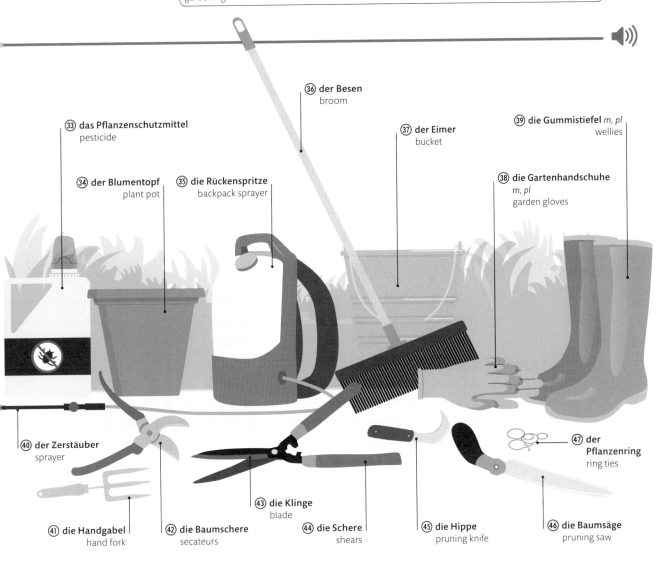

㊱ **der Besen**
broom

㊲ **der Eimer**
bucket

㊴ **die Gummistiefel** *m, pl*
wellies

㉝ **das Pflanzenschutzmittel**
pesticide

㉞ **der Blumentopf**
plant pot

㉟ **die Rückenspritze**
backpack sprayer

㊳ **die Gartenhandschuhe**
m, pl
garden gloves

㊵ **der Zerstäuber**
sprayer

㊼ **der Pflanzenring**
ring ties

㊶ **die Handgabel**
hand fork

㊷ **die Baumschere**
secateurs

㊸ **die Klinge**
blade

㊹ **die Schere**
shears

㊺ **die Hippe**
pruning knife

㊻ **die Baumsäge**
pruning saw

40.2 GIESSEN · WATERING

① **die Gießkanne**
watering can

② **der Sprühkopf**
spray nozzle

③ **der Rasensprenger**
sprinkler

④ **die Schlauchtrommel**
hose reel

⑤ **die Düse**
nozzle

⑥ **der Gartenschlauch**
garden hose

Gartenelemente
Garden features

41.1 GARTENTYPEN UND GARTENELEMENTE · GARDEN TYPES AND FEATURES

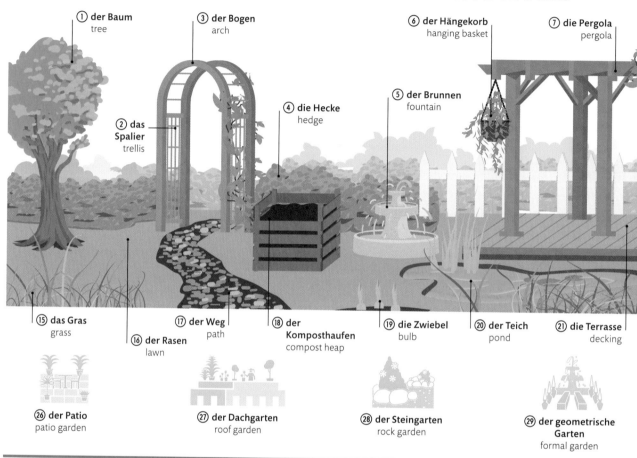

① der Baum
tree

③ der Bogen
arch

⑥ der Hängekorb
hanging basket

⑦ die Pergola
pergola

② das Spalier
trellis

④ die Hecke
hedge

⑤ der Brunnen
fountain

⑮ das Gras
grass

⑰ der Weg
path

⑱ der Komposthaufen
compost heap

⑲ die Zwiebel
bulb

⑳ der Teich
pond

㉑ die Terrasse
decking

⑯ der Rasen
lawn

㉖ der Patio
patio garden

㉗ der Dachgarten
roof garden

㉘ der Steingarten
rock garden

㉙ der geometrische Garten
formal garden

41.2 PFLANZENARTEN · TYPES OF PLANTS

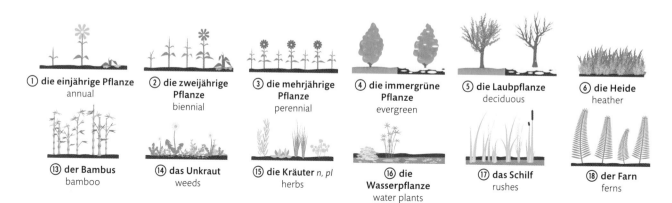

① die einjährige Pflanze
annual

② die zweijährige Pflanze
biennial

③ die mehrjährige Pflanze
perennial

④ die immergrüne Pflanze
evergreen

⑤ die Laubpflanze
deciduous

⑥ die Heide
heather

⑬ der Bambus
bamboo

⑭ das Unkraut
weeds

⑮ die Kräuter n, pl
herbs

⑯ die Wasserpflanze
water plants

⑰ das Schilf
rushes

⑱ der Farn
ferns

See also
38 Gartenpflanzen und Zimmerpflanzen · Garden plants and houseplants **39** Gartenarbeit · Practical gardening **40** Gartengeräte · Garden tools **167-169** Pflanzen und Bäume · Plants and trees

⑧ **die Kletterpflanze**
creeper

⑨ **die Topfpflanze**
potted plant

⑩ **das Blumenbeet**
flowerbed

⑪ **das Tor**
gate

⑫ **Das Gemüse muss jeden Tag gegossen werden.**
These vegetables need watering every day.

⑬ **der Gemüsegarten**
vegetable garden

⑭ **der Zaun**
fence

㉒ **das Pflaster**
paving

㉓ **die Bodenbedeckung**
ground cover

㉔ **die Blumenrabatte**
herbaceous border

㉕ **der Grill**
barbecue

㉚ **der Kräutergarten**
herb garden

㉛ **der Wassergarten**
water garden

㉜ **der Bauerngarten**
cottage garden

㉝ **der Hinterhof**
courtyard

⑦ **die Palme**
palms

⑧ **der Nadelbaum**
conifers

⑨ **der Formschnitt**
topiary

⑩ **die Kletterpflanze**
climber

⑪ **die Zierpflanze**
ornamental plants

⑫ **die Schattenpflanze**
shade plants

⑲ **die Gebirgspflanze**
alpine plants

⑳ **die Sukkulente**
succulents

㉑ **der Kaktus**
cacti

㉒ **das Gebüsch**
shrubs

㉓ **der Blütenstrauch**
flowering shrub

㉔ **die Gräser** n, pl
grasses

42.1 GEBÄUDE UND ANDERE MERKMALE
BUILDINGS AND OTHER FEATURES

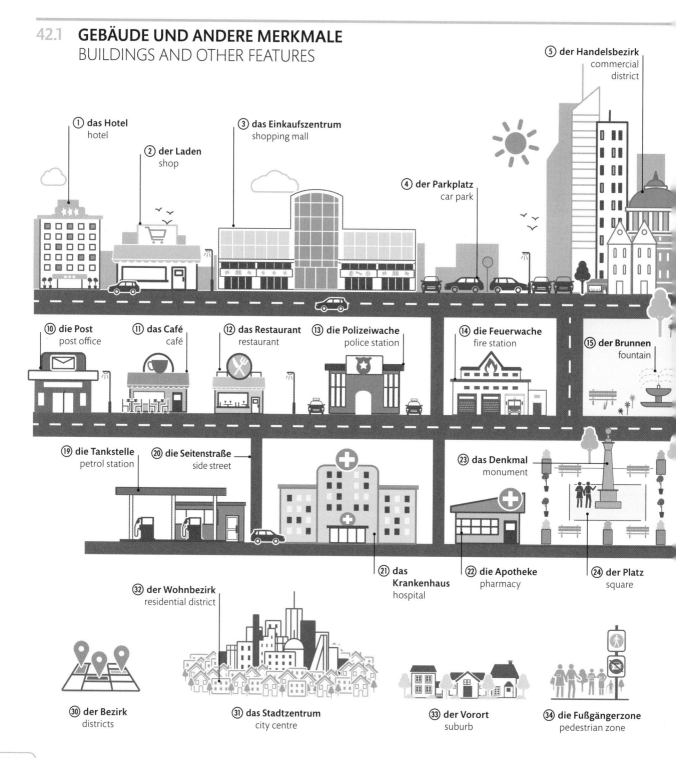

⑤ **der Handelsbezirk**
commercial district

① **das Hotel**
hotel

② **der Laden**
shop

③ **das Einkaufszentrum**
shopping mall

④ **der Parkplatz**
car park

⑩ **die Post**
post office

⑪ **das Café**
café

⑫ **das Restaurant**
restaurant

⑬ **die Polizeiwache**
police station

⑭ **die Feuerwache**
fire station

⑮ **der Brunnen**
fountain

⑲ **die Tankstelle**
petrol station

⑳ **die Seitenstraße**
side street

㉓ **das Denkmal**
monument

㉑ **das Krankenhaus**
hospital

㉒ **die Apotheke**
pharmacy

㉔ **der Platz**
square

㉜ **der Wohnbezirk**
residential district

㉚ **der Bezirk**
districts

㉛ **das Stadtzentrum**
city centre

㉝ **der Vorort**
suburb

㉞ **die Fußgängerzone**
pedestrian zone

See also
25 Ein Ort zum Leben • A place to live   **43** In der Stadt (Forsetzung) • In town continued   **44** Gebäude und Architektur • Buildings and architecture   **46** Einkaufen • Shopping   **47** Im Einkaufszentrum • The shopping mall   **102** Züge • Trains   **104** Am Flughafen • At the airport   **106** Der Hafen • The port

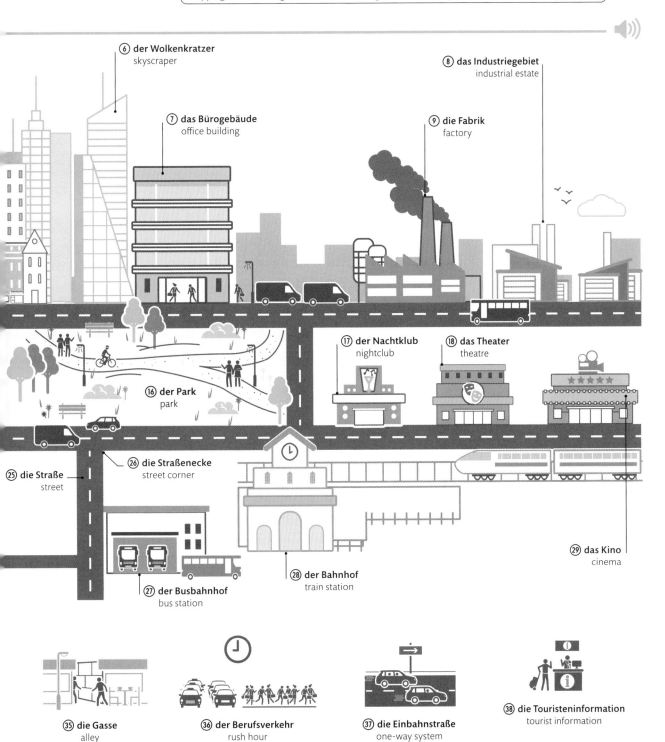

⑥ **der Wolkenkratzer**
skyscraper

⑦ **das Bürogebäude**
office building

⑧ **das Industriegebiet**
industrial estate

⑨ **die Fabrik**
factory

⑰ **der Nachtklub**
nightclub

⑱ **das Theater**
theatre

⑯ **der Park**
park

⑳ **die Straße**
street

㉖ **die Straßenecke**
street corner

㉙ **das Kino**
cinema

㉗ **der Busbahnhof**
bus station

㉘ **der Bahnhof**
train station

㉟ **die Gasse**
alley

㊱ **der Berufsverkehr**
rush hour

㊲ **die Einbahnstraße**
one-way system

㊳ **die Touristeninformation**
tourist information

95

43.1 GEBÄUDE UND ANDERE MERKMALE · BUILDINGS AND OTHER FEATURES

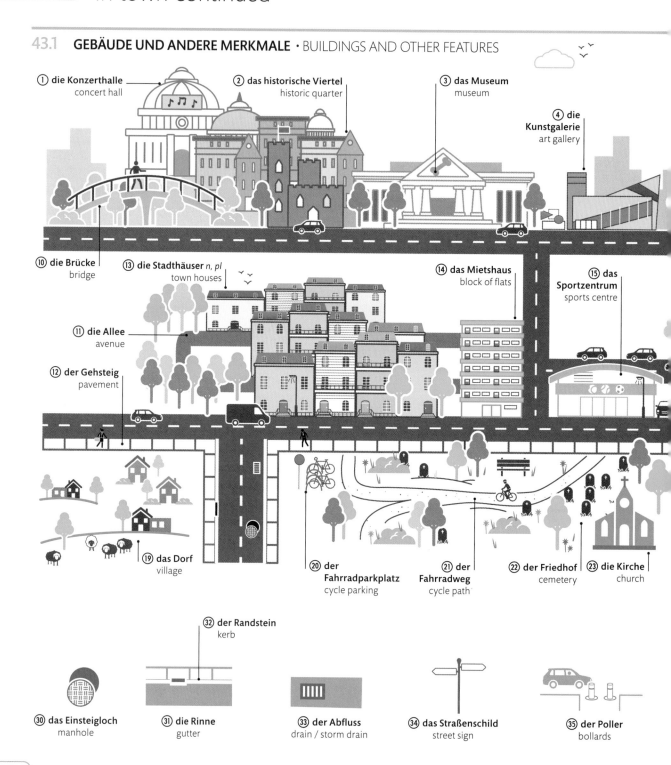

① die Konzerthalle
concert hall

② das historische Viertel
historic quarter

③ das Museum
museum

④ die Kunstgalerie
art gallery

⑩ die Brücke
bridge

⑬ die Stadthäuser n, pl
town houses

⑭ das Mietshaus
block of flats

⑮ das Sportzentrum
sports centre

⑪ die Allee
avenue

⑫ der Gehsteig
pavement

⑲ das Dorf
village

⑳ der Fahrradparkplatz
cycle parking

㉑ der Fahrradweg
cycle path

㉒ der Friedhof
cemetery

㉓ die Kirche
church

㉜ der Randstein
kerb

㉚ das Einsteigloch
manhole

㉛ die Rinne
gutter

㉝ der Abfluss
drain / storm drain

㉞ das Straßenschild
street sign

㉟ der Poller
bollards

See also
25 Ein Ort zum Leben • A place to live **44** Gebäude und Architektur • Buildings and architecture
46 Einkaufen • Shopping **47** Im Einkaufszentrum • The shopping mall **102** Züge • Trains
104 Am Flughafen • At the airport **106** Der Hafen • The port

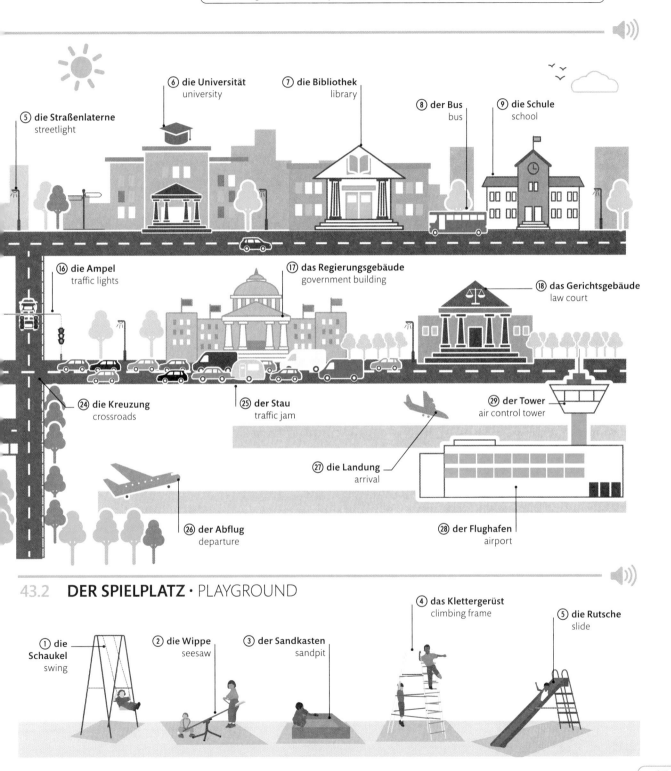

⑤ **die Straßenlaterne**
streetlight

⑥ **die Universität**
university

⑦ **die Bibliothek**
library

⑧ **der Bus**
bus

⑨ **die Schule**
school

⑯ **die Ampel**
traffic lights

⑰ **das Regierungsgebäude**
government building

⑱ **das Gerichtsgebäude**
law court

㉔ **die Kreuzung**
crossroads

㉕ **der Stau**
traffic jam

㉙ **der Tower**
air control tower

㉗ **die Landung**
arrival

㉖ **der Abflug**
departure

㉘ **der Flughafen**
airport

43.2 DER SPIELPLATZ · PLAYGROUND

① **die Schaukel**
swing

② **die Wippe**
seesaw

③ **der Sandkasten**
sandpit

④ **das Klettergerüst**
climbing frame

⑤ **die Rutsche**
slide

44.1 GEBÄUDETYPEN · TYPES OF BUILDINGS

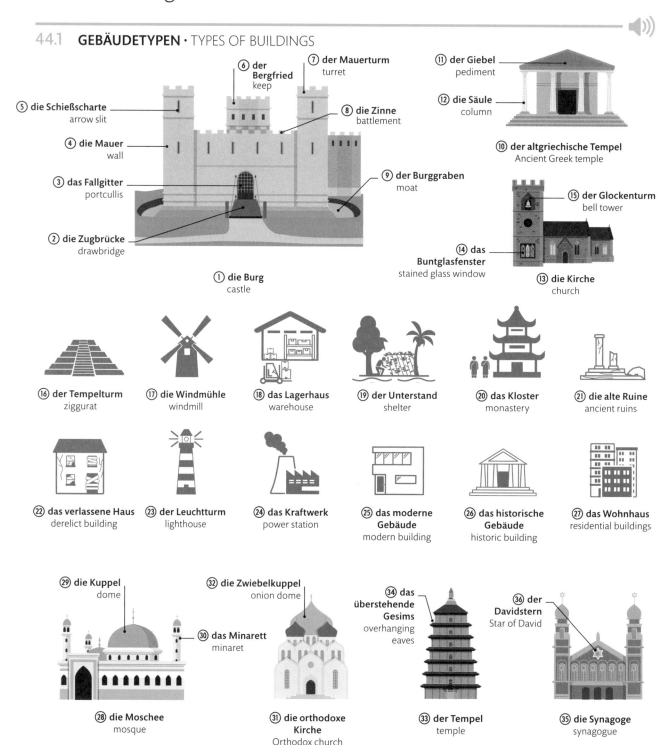

⑤ die Schießscharte
arrow slit

④ die Mauer
wall

③ das Fallgitter
portcullis

② die Zugbrücke
drawbridge

⑥ der Bergfried
keep

⑦ der Mauerturm
turret

⑧ die Zinne
battlement

⑨ der Burggraben
moat

① die Burg
castle

⑪ der Giebel
pediment

⑫ die Säule
column

⑩ der altgriechische Tempel
Ancient Greek temple

⑮ der Glockenturm
bell tower

⑭ das Buntglasfenster
stained glass window

⑬ die Kirche
church

⑯ der Tempelturm
ziggurat

⑰ die Windmühle
windmill

⑱ das Lagerhaus
warehouse

⑲ der Unterstand
shelter

⑳ das Kloster
monastery

㉑ die alte Ruine
ancient ruins

㉒ das verlassene Haus
derelict building

㉓ der Leuchtturm
lighthouse

㉔ das Kraftwerk
power station

㉕ das moderne Gebäude
modern building

㉖ das historische Gebäude
historic building

㉗ das Wohnhaus
residential buildings

㉙ die Kuppel
dome

㉜ die Zwiebelkuppel
onion dome

㉞ das überstehende Gesims
overhanging eaves

㊱ der Davidstern
Star of David

㉚ das Minarett
minaret

㉘ die Moschee
mosque

㉛ die orthodoxe Kirche
Orthodox church

㉝ der Tempel
temple

㉟ die Synagoge
synagogue

See also
25 Ein Ort zum Leben · A place to live **32** Haus und Heim · House and home **42-43** In der Stadt · In town **132** Sightseeing · Sightseeing

44.2 BERÜHMTE GEBÄUDE UND DENKMÄLER · FAMOUS BUILDINGS AND MONUMENTS

② **der Bogen**
arch

① **das Kolosseum**
the Colosseum

③ **die Pyramiden von Giseh**
the Pyramids of Giza

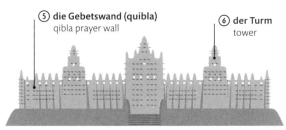

⑤ **die Gebetswand (quibla)**
qibla prayer wall

⑥ **der Turm**
tower

④ **die Große Moschee von Djenné**
the Great Mosque of Djenné

⑦ **das Weiße Haus**
the White House

⑧ **das Taj Mahal**
the Taj Mahal

⑨ **die Verbotene Stadt**
the Forbidden City

⑩ **die Basilius-Kathedrale**
St. Basil's cathedral

⑪ **das Opernhaus von Sydney**
Sydney Opera House

⑰ **die Aussichtsplattform**
viewing platform

⑭ **die Uhr**
clock

⑫ **die Burg von Himeji**
Himeji Castle

⑬ **der Big Ben**
Big Ben

⑮ **der Schiefe Turm von Pisa**
the Leaning Tower of Pisa

⑯ **der Eiffelturm**
the Eiffel Tower

⑱ **das Empire State Building**
the Empire State Building

⑲ **der Burj Khalifa**
Burj Khalifa

45.1 DIE BANK · BANK

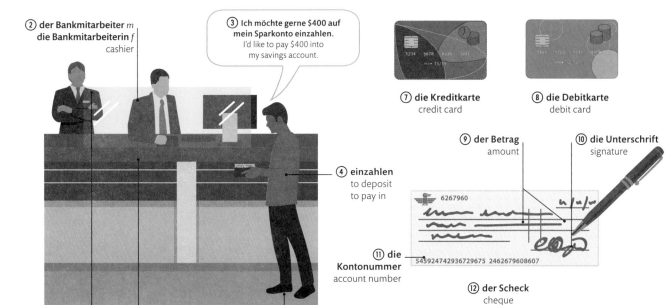

② **der Bankmitarbeiter** m
die Bankmitarbeiterin f
cashier

③ Ich möchte gerne $400 auf mein Sparkonto einzahlen.
I'd like to pay $400 into my savings account.

④ **einzahlen**
to deposit
to pay in

① **der Filialleiter** m
die Filialleiterin f
branch manager

⑤ **der Schalter**
counter

⑥ **der Kunde** m
die Kundin f
customer

⑦ **die Kreditkarte**
credit card

⑧ **die Debitkarte**
debit card

⑨ **der Betrag**
amount

⑩ **die Unterschrift**
signature

⑪ **die Kontonummer**
account number

⑫ **der Scheck**
cheque

⑬ **das Sparkonto**
savings account

⑭ **die Ersparnisse** n, pl
savings

⑮ **das Girokonto**
current account

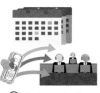
⑯ **die Lastschrift**
direct debit

⑰ **der Kontoauszug**
bank statement

⑱ **schwarze Zahlen schreiben**
in the black / in credit

⑲ **rote Zahlen schreiben / Schulden haben**
in the red / in debt

⑳ **der Dispo**
overdraft

㉑ **das Online-Banking**
online banking

㉒ **der Zinssatz**
interest rate

㉓ **das Darlehen**
bank loan

㉔ **der Immobilienkredit**
mortgage

㉕ **Geld abheben**
to withdraw money

㉖ **Geld überweisen**
to transfer money

See also
94 Geld und Finanzen · Money and finance
131 Reise und Unterkunft · Travel and accommodation

45.2 **DAS GELD** · MONEY

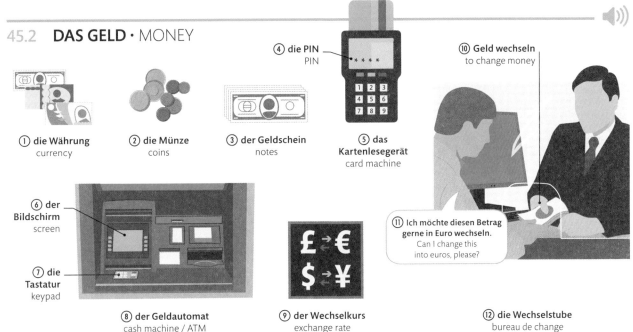

④ **die PIN**
PIN

⑩ **Geld wechseln**
to change money

① **die Währung**
currency

② **die Münze**
coins

③ **der Geldschein**
notes

⑤ **das Kartenlesegerät**
card machine

⑥ **der Bildschirm**
screen

⑦ **die Tastatur**
keypad

⑧ **der Geldautomat**
cash machine / ATM

⑨ **der Wechselkurs**
exchange rate

⑪ Ich möchte diesen Betrag gerne in Euro wechseln.
Can I change this into euros, please?

⑫ **die Wechselstube**
bureau de change

45.3 **DIE POST** · POST OFFICE

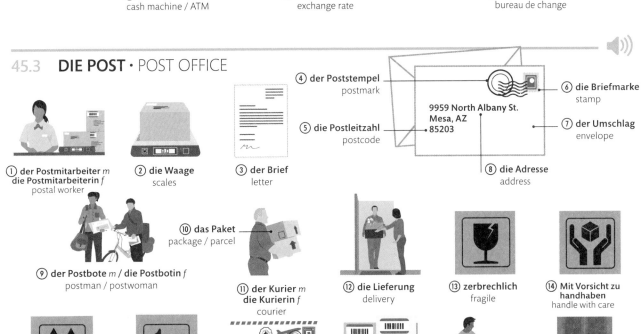

④ **der Poststempel**
postmark

⑤ **die Postleitzahl**
postcode

9959 North Albany St.
Mesa, AZ
85203

⑥ **die Briefmarke**
stamp

⑦ **der Umschlag**
envelope

⑧ **die Adresse**
address

① **der Postmitarbeiter** *m*
die Postmitarbeiterin *f*
postal worker

② **die Waage**
scales

③ **der Brief**
letter

⑨ **der Postbote** *m* / **die Postbotin** *f*
postman / postwoman

⑩ **das Paket**
package / parcel

⑪ **der Kurier** *m*
die Kurierin *f*
courier

⑫ **die Lieferung**
delivery

⑬ **zerbrechlich**
fragile

⑭ **Mit Vorsicht zu handhaben**
handle with care

⑮ **diese Seite nach oben**
this way up

⑯ **nicht biegen**
do not bend

⑰ **die Luftpost**
airmail

⑱ **das Einschreiben**
registered post

⑲ **der Briefkasten**
postbox

⑳ **der Briefschlitz**
letterbox

46 Einkaufen
Shopping

46.1 IN DER FUSSGÄNGERZONE · ON THE HIGH STREET

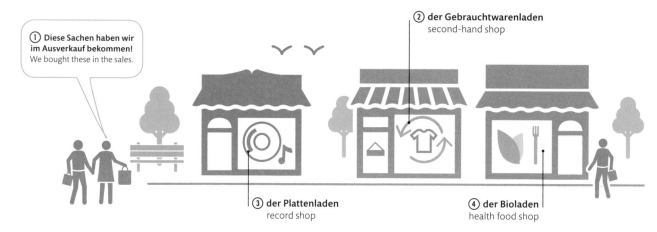

① Diese Sachen haben wir im Ausverkauf bekommen!
We bought these in the sales.

② **der Gebrauchtwarenladen**
second-hand shop

③ **der Plattenladen**
record shop

④ **der Bioladen**
health food shop

⑤ **der Geschenkladen**
gift shop

⑥ **die Boutique**
boutique

⑦ **der Juwelier**
jeweller's

⑧ **der Künstlerbedarf**
art shop

⑨ **der Antiquitätenladen**
antiques shop

⑩ **der Spielzeugladen**
toy shop

⑪ **der Optiker**
optician

⑫ **der Baumarkt**
hardware store

⑬ **die Schlosserei**
key cutting shop

⑭ **das Elektronikgeschäft**
electronics store

⑮ **der Heimtierhandel**
pet shop

⑯ **das Reisebüro**
travel agent

⑰ **der Wochenmarkt**
street market

⑱ **der Fischladen**
fishmonger

⑲ **die Metzgerei**
butcher

⑳ **die Bäckerei**
bakery

㉑ **das Lebensmittelgeschäft**
greengrocer

㉒ **das Feinkostgeschäft**
delicatessen

㉓ **die Konditorei**
cake shop

㉔ **das Café**
café / coffee shop

㉕ **der Spirituosenladen**
off licence

㉖ **der Zeitungskiosk**
newsstand / kiosk

㉗ **der Buchladen**
bookshop

㉘ **der Schuhladen**
shoe shop

See also
42-43 In der Stadt • In town   **47** Das Einkaufszentrum
The shopping mall   **48** Der Supermarkt • The supermarket

46.2   **EINKAUFSVERBEN** · SHOPPING VERBS

㉙ **das Gartencenter**
garden centre

㉚ **der Florist** *m*
die Floristin *f*
florist

① **aussuchen**
to choose

② **verkaufen**
to sell

③ **kaufen**
to buy

④ **haben wollen**
to want

㉛ **der Schneider** *m*
die Schneiderin *f*
tailor

㉜ **der Fotoautomat**
photo booth

⑤ **passen**
to fit

⑥ **bezahlen**
to pay

⑦ **anprobieren**
to try on

⑧ **verhandeln**
to haggle

㉝ **die Wäscherei**
launderette

㉞ **die Reinigung**
dry cleaner's

⑨ **sich beschweren**
to complain

⑩ **umtauschen**
to exchange

⑪ **erstatten**
to refund

⑫ **zurückgeben**
to return

㉟ **die Einkaufstour**
shopping spree

㊱ **der
Schaufensterbummel**
window shopping

46.3   **ONLINE-BESTELLUNGEN** · ORDERING ONLINE

㊲ Ich habe vergessen, Milch auf
die Einkaufsliste zu schreiben.
I forgot to put milk
on my shopping list.

㊳ **die Einkaufsliste**
shopping list

① **in den
Einkaufswagen legen**
to add to the cart

② **der Wunschliste
hinzufügen**
to add to wishlist

③ **zur Kasse gehen**
to proceed
to checkout

④ **bestellen**
to order

⑤ **die Bestellung
verfolgen**
to track your order

47.1 DAS EINKAUFSZENTRUM · SHOPPING CENTRE

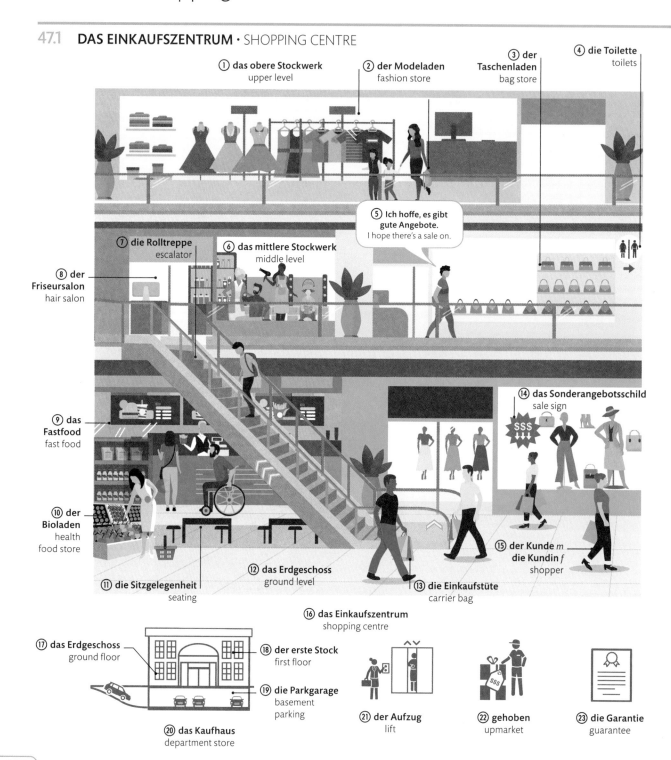

① **das obere Stockwerk**
upper level

② **der Modeladen**
fashion store

③ **der Taschenladen**
bag store

④ **die Toilette**
toilets

⑤ **Ich hoffe, es gibt gute Angebote.**
I hope there's a sale on.

⑦ **die Rolltreppe**
escalator

⑥ **das mittlere Stockwerk**
middle level

⑧ **der Friseursalon**
hair salon

⑨ **das Fastfood**
fast food

⑩ **der Bioladen**
health food store

⑭ **das Sonderangebotsschild**
sale sign

⑮ **der Kunde** *m*
die Kundin *f*
shopper

⑪ **die Sitzgelegenheit**
seating

⑫ **das Erdgeschoss**
ground level

⑬ **die Einkaufstüte**
carrier bag

⑯ **das Einkaufszentrum**
shopping centre

⑰ **das Erdgeschoss**
ground floor

⑱ **der erste Stock**
first floor

⑲ **die Parkgarage**
basement parking

⑳ **das Kaufhaus**
department store

㉑ **der Aufzug**
lift

㉒ **gehoben**
upmarket

㉓ **die Garantie**
guarantee

See also
13-15 Kleidung · Clothes **16** Accessoires · Accessories **17** Schuhe · Shoes **18** Beauty · Beauty
42-43 In der Stadt · In town **46** Einkaufen · Shopping

47.2 AM BLUMENSTAND · FLOWER STALL

24 die Umkleide
changing rooms

25 die Damenmode
womenswear

26 die Herrenmode
menswear

27 der Wickelraum
baby changing
facilities

**28 die
Kinderabteilung**
children's department

**29 das
Markenprodukt**
designer labels

30 das Sonderangebot
sale

31 die Unterwäsche
lingerie

**32 die
Einrichtungsgegenstände**
m, pl
home furnishings

33 das Preisschild
price tag

34 die Beleuchtung
lighting

35 die Elektrogeräte
n, pl
electrical appliances

36 die Treuekarte
loyalty card

**37 der
Handwerkerbedarf**
DIY (do it yourself)

**38 die Beauty-
Abteilung**
beauty

**39 der
Kundenservice**
customer service

**40 die Parfümerie-
Abteilung**
perfumery

**41 der
Gastronomiebereich**
food court

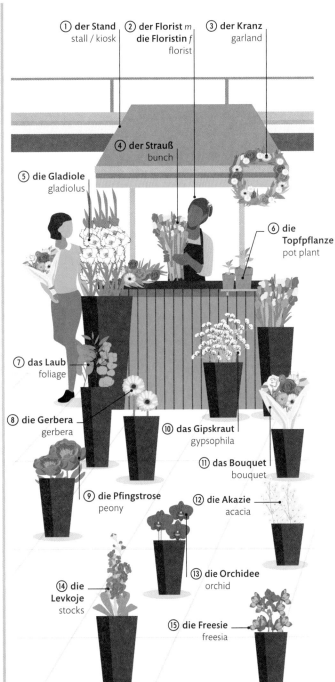

1 **der Stand**
stall / kiosk

2 **der Florist** *m*
die Floristin *f*
florist

3 **der Kranz**
garland

4 **der Strauß**
bunch

5 **die Gladiole**
gladiolus

6 **die
Topfpflanze**
pot plant

7 **das Laub**
foliage

8 **die Gerbera**
gerbera

9 **die Pfingstrose**
peony

10 **das Gipskraut**
gypsophila

11 **das Bouquet**
bouquet

12 **die Akazie**
acacia

13 **die Orchidee**
orchid

14 **die
Levkoje**
stocks

15 **die Freesie**
freesia

105

48 Der Supermarkt
The supermarket

48.1 DER SUPERMARKT · SUPERMARKET

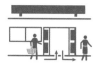
① **geöffnet**
open

② **geschlossen**
closed

③ **der Kunde** *m*
die Kundin *f*
customer

④ **der Beleg**
receipt

⑤ **das Sonderangebot**
special offer

⑥ **das Schnäppchen**
bargain

⑦ **die große Auswahl**
wide range

⑧ **die Schlange**
queue

⑨ **das Kartenlesegerät**
card machine

⑩ **das Online-Shopping**
online shopping

⑪ **der Lieferant** *m*
die Lieferantin *f*
delivery man

⑫ **die Lieferung nach Hause**
home delivery

48.2 AN DER KASSE · CHECKOUT

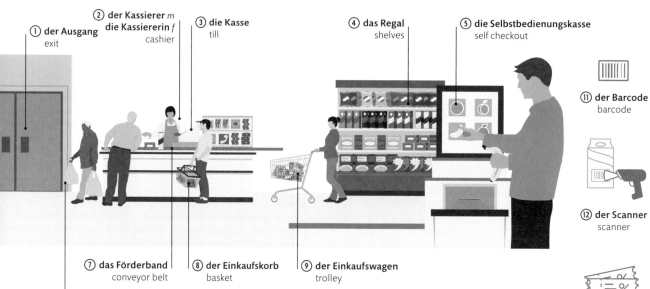

① **der Ausgang** exit
② **der Kassierer** *m* **die Kassiererin** *f* cashier
③ **die Kasse** till
④ **das Regal** shelves
⑤ **die Selbstbedienungskasse** self checkout
⑪ **der Barcode** barcode
⑫ **der Scanner** scanner
⑬ **der Gutschein** discount voucher
⑦ **das Förderband** conveyor belt
⑧ **der Einkaufskorb** basket
⑨ **der Einkaufswagen** trolley
⑥ **die Einkaufstüte** carrier bag
⑩ **die Kasse** checkout

See also
46 Einkaufen • Shopping **53** Fleisch • Meat **54** Fisch und Meeresfrüchte • Fish and seafood **55-56** Gemüse Vegetables **57** Obst • Fruit **58** Obst und Nüsse • Fruit and nuts **59** Kräuter und Gewürze • Herbs and spices **60** In der Vorratskammer • In the pantry **61** Milchprodukte • Dairy produce **62-63** Die Bäckerei • The bakery

48.3 **SUPERMARKTABTEILUNGEN** · AISLES / SECTIONS

① **das Gebäck**
bakery

② **die Milchprodukte** *n, pl*
dairy

③ **das Müsli**
breakfast cereals

④ **die Konserven** *f, pl*
tinned food

⑤ **die Süßigkeiten** *f, pl*
confectionery

⑥ **das Gemüse**
vegetables

⑦ **das Obst**
fruit

⑧ **Fleisch und Geflügel** *n, n*
meat and poultry

⑨ **der Fisch**
fish

⑩ **die Feinkostabteilung**
deli

⑪ **das Gefriergut**
frozen food

⑫ **die Fertiggerichte** *n, pl*
convenience food

⑬ **die Getränke** *n, pl*
drinks

⑭ **die Haushaltsprodukte** *n, pl*
household products

⑮ **die Hygieneartikel** *m, pl*
toiletries

⑯ **die Babyartikel** *m, pl*
baby products

⑰ **die Elektronik**
electrical goods

⑱ **die Tiernahrung**
pet food

48.4 **DER KIOSK** · NEWSSTAND / KIOSK

① **die Zeitung**
newspaper

② **die Zeitschrift**
magazine

③ **der Comic**
comic

④ **die Postkarte**
postcard

⑤ **die Karte**
tourist map

⑥ **die Briefmarke**
stamps

⑦ **die Fahrkarte**
travel card

⑧ **die SIM-Karte**
sim card

⑨ **der Riegel**
snack bar

⑩ **die Chips** *m, pl*
crisps

⑪ **das Wasser**
water

49.1 DIE APOTHEKE · PHARMACY

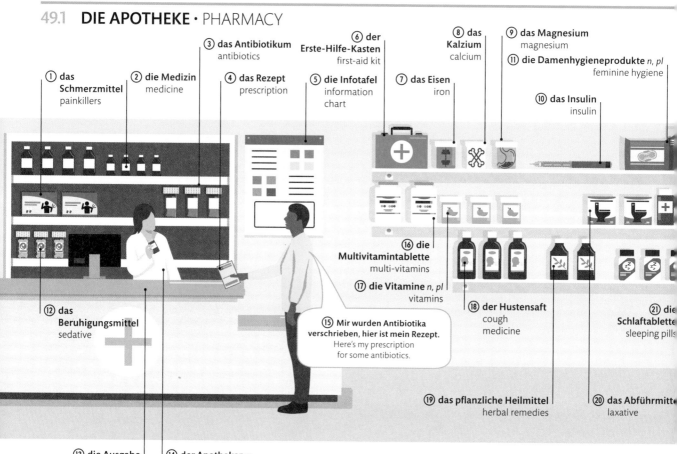

① das **Schmerzmittel** — painkillers

② die **Medizin** — medicine

③ das **Antibiotikum** — antibiotics

④ das **Rezept** — prescription

⑤ die **Infotafel** — information chart

⑥ der **Erste-Hilfe-Kasten** — first-aid kit

⑦ das **Eisen** — iron

⑧ das **Kalzium** — calcium

⑨ das **Magnesium** — magnesium

⑩ das **Insulin** — insulin

⑪ die **Damenhygieneprodukte** *n, pl* — feminine hygiene

⑫ das **Beruhigungsmittel** — sedative

⑬ die **Ausgabe** — dispensary

⑭ der **Apotheker** *m* die **Apothekerin** *f* — pharmacist

⑮ **Mir wurden Antibiotika verschrieben, hier ist mein Rezept.** — Here's my prescription for some antibiotics.

⑯ die **Multivitamintablette** — multi-vitamins

⑰ die **Vitamine** *n, pl* — vitamins

⑱ der **Hustensaft** — cough medicine

⑲ das **pflanzliche Heilmittel** — herbal remedies

⑳ das **Abführmittel** — laxative

㉑ die **Schlaftablette** — sleeping pills

㉒ die **Nebenwirkungen** *f, pl* — side effects

㉓ die **Medizin** — medication

㉔ die **Kapsel** — capsules

㉕ die **Tablette / die Pille** — pills / tablets

㉖ die **Dosierung** — dosage

㉗ **entzündungshemmend** — anti-inflammatory

㉘ das **nicht verschreibungspflichtige Arzneimittel** — over-the-counter drugs

㉙ das **Halsbonbon** — throat lozenge

㉚ die **Tablette gegen Reisekrankheit** — travel-sickness pills

㉛ das **Verfallsdatum** — expiry date

10/02/2028

See also
19 Krankheiten und Verletzungen • Illness and injury **20** Beim Arzt • Visiting the doctor **21** Das Krankenhaus • The hospital **46** Einkaufen • Shopping

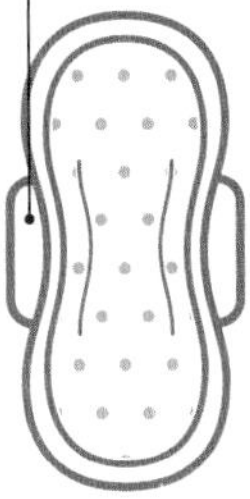

(33) **der Flügel**
wings

(32) **die Binde**
sanitary towel

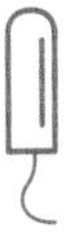

(34) **der Tampon**
tampon

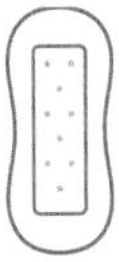

(35) **die Slipeinlage**
panty liner

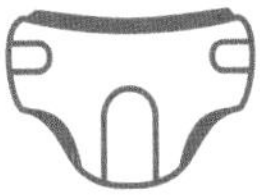

(36) **die Inkontinenzeinlage**
incontinence pads

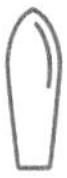

(37) **das Zäpfchen**
suppository

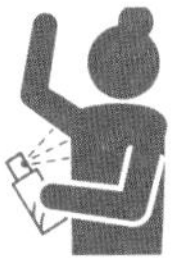

(38) **das Deodorant**
deodorant

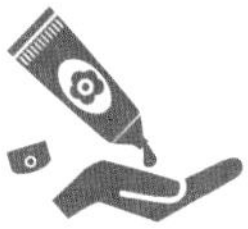

(39) **die Hautpflege**
skin care

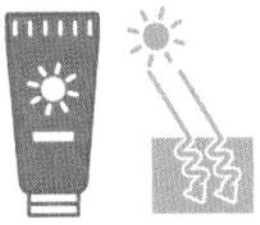

(40) **die Sonnencreme**
sun cream

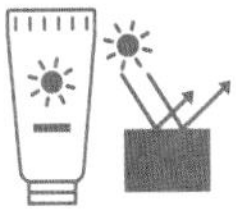

(41) **die Sonnencreme**
sunblock

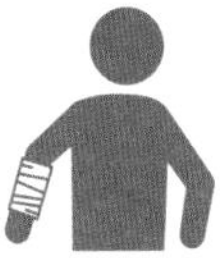

(42) **der Verband**
bandage

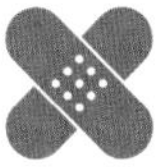

(43) **das Heftpflaster**
plaster

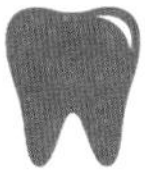

(44) **die Zahnpflege**
dental care

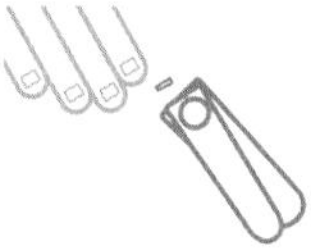

(45) **die Nagelzange**
nail clippers

(46) **das Feuchttuch**
wet wipes

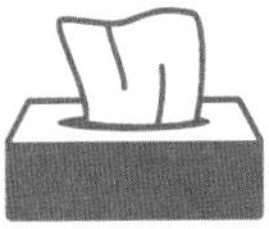

(47) **das Taschentuch**
tissue

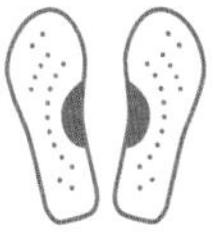

(48) **die Einlage**
insoles

(49) **die Lesebrille**
reading glasses

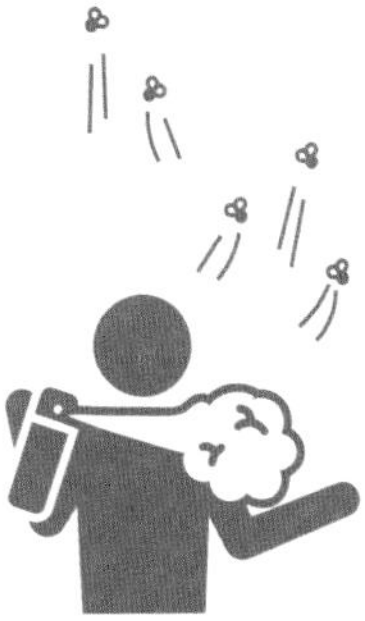

(50) **das Insektenmittel**
insect repellent

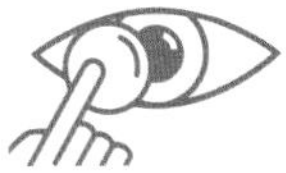

(51) **die Kontaktlinse**
contact lens

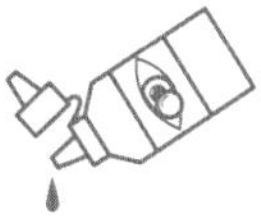

(52) **die Kontaktlinsenflüssigkeit**
lens solution

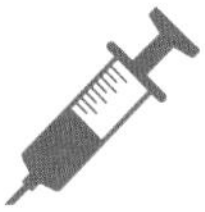

(53) **die Spritze**
syringe

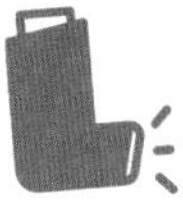

(54) **der Inhalator**
inhaler

(55) **die Tropfen** *m, pl*
drops

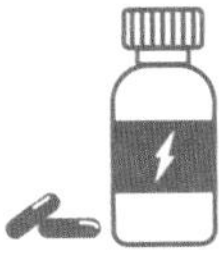

(56) **das Nahrungsergänzungsmittel**
supplement

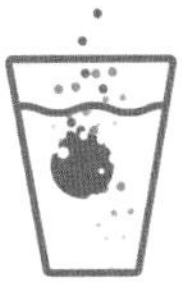

(57) **löslich**
soluble

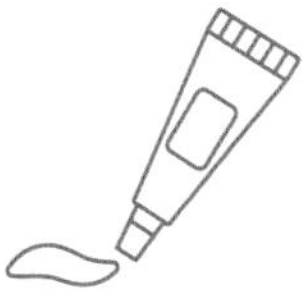

(58) **die Salbe**
ointment

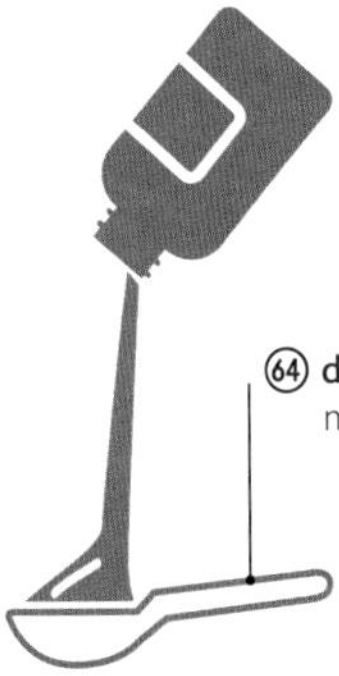

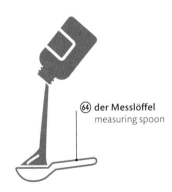

(64) **der Messlöffel**
measuring spoon

(63) **der Sirup**
syrup

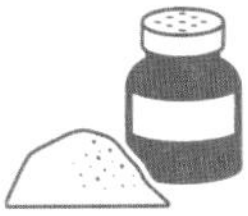

(59) **das Pulver**
powder

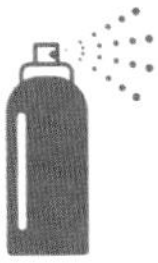

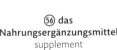

(60) **das Spray**
spray

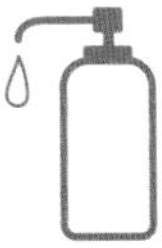

(61) **das Gel**
gel

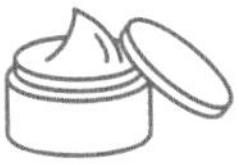

(62) **die Creme**
cream

50.1 DIE NOTAUFNAHME · ACCIDENT AND EMERGENCY

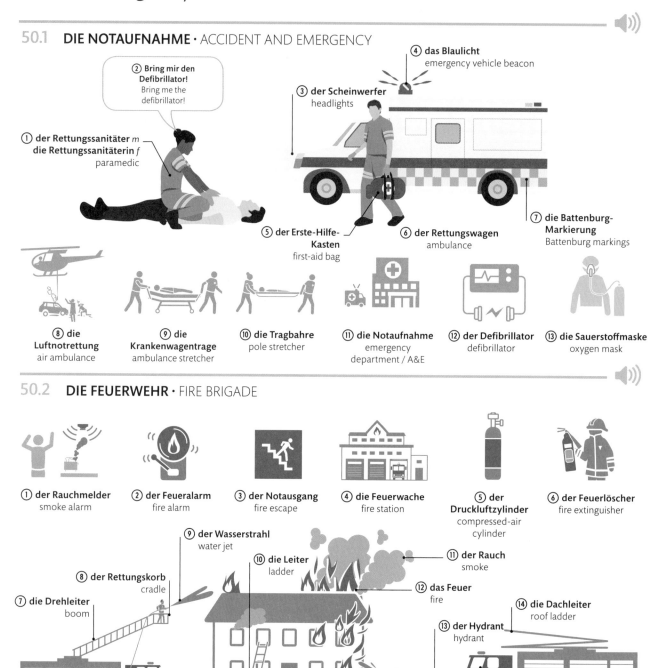

④ **das Blaulicht**
emergency vehicle beacon

② **Bring mir den Defibrillator!**
Bring me the defibrillator!

③ **der Scheinwerfer**
headlights

① **der Rettungssanitäter** *m*
die Rettungssanitäterin *f*
paramedic

⑦ **die Battenburg-Markierung**
Battenburg markings

⑤ **der Erste-Hilfe-Kasten**
first-aid bag

⑥ **der Rettungswagen**
ambulance

⑧ **die Luftnotrettung**
air ambulance

⑨ **die Krankenwagentrage**
ambulance stretcher

⑩ **die Tragbahre**
pole stretcher

⑪ **die Notaufnahme**
emergency department / A&E

⑫ **der Defibrillator**
defibrillator

⑬ **die Sauerstoffmaske**
oxygen mask

50.2 DIE FEUERWEHR · FIRE BRIGADE

① **der Rauchmelder**
smoke alarm

② **der Feueralarm**
fire alarm

③ **der Notausgang**
fire escape

④ **die Feuerwache**
fire station

⑤ **der Druckluftzylinder**
compressed-air cylinder

⑥ **der Feuerlöscher**
fire extinguisher

⑨ **der Wasserstrahl**
water jet

⑩ **die Leiter**
ladder

⑪ **der Rauch**
smoke

⑫ **das Feuer**
fire

⑧ **der Rettungskorb**
cradle

⑦ **die Drehleiter**
boom

⑭ **die Dachleiter**
roof ladder

⑬ **der Hydrant**
hydrant

⑮ **der Feuerwehrmann** *m*
die Feuerwehrfrau *f*
firefighters

⑯ **die Axt**
axe

⑰ **der Schlauch**
hose

⑱ **die Kabine**
cab

⑲ **der Feuerwehrwagen**
fire engine

See also
19 Krankheiten und Verletzungen · Illness and injury
21 Das Krankenhaus · The hospital **85** Recht · Law

50.3 DIE POLIZEI · POLICE

① **das Laserhandmessgerät**
radar speed gun

② **der Alkoholtest**
breathalyzer

③ **das Funkgerät**
walkie-talkie

④ **der Polizeihund**
police dog

⑭ **die Polizeimütze**
police hat

⑮ **die Uniform**
uniform

⑯ **das Abzeichen**
badge

⑤ **die Beschwerde**
complaint

⑥ **die Polizeiwache**
police station

⑦ **die Zelle**
police cell

⑧ **das Vernehmungszimmer**
interrogation room

⑰ **der Polizeigürtel**
duty belt

⑱ **der Schlagstock**
truncheon

⑨ **der Detektiv** *m*
die Detektivin *f*
detective

⑩ **der Kommissar** *m*
die Kommissarin *f*
inspector

⑪ **der Fingerabdruck**
fingerprint

⑫ **die Anklage**
charge

⑬ **der Polizeibeamte** *m*
die Polizeibeamtin *f*
police officer

⑳ **der motorisierte Polizeibeamte** *m*
die motorisierte Polizeibeamtin *f*
motorcycle police officer

㉑ **der Helm**
helmet

㉒ **das Megafon**
megaphone

㉓ **das Blaulicht**
lights

die Bank · BANK

㉖ **die Alarmanlage**
alarm

㉗ **der Einbruch**
break in

㉘ **der Räuber** *m, pl*
robbers

⑲ **das Polizeimotorrad**
police bike

㉔ **das Polizeiauto**
police car

㉕ **der Raub**
robbery

㉛ **das Beweisstück**
evidence

㉜ **das Funkgerät**
radio

㉞ **der Verdächtige** *m*
die Verdächtige *f*
suspect

㊱ **Sie sind verhaftet.**
You're under arrest!

㉟ **die Handschellen** *f, pl*
handcuffs

㉚ **die Ermittlung**
investigation

㉙ **der Tatort**
crime scene

㉝ **die Festnahme**
arrest

51.1 **ATOMENERGIE UND FOSSILE BRENNSTOFFE** · NUCLEAR ENERGY AND FOSSIL FUELS

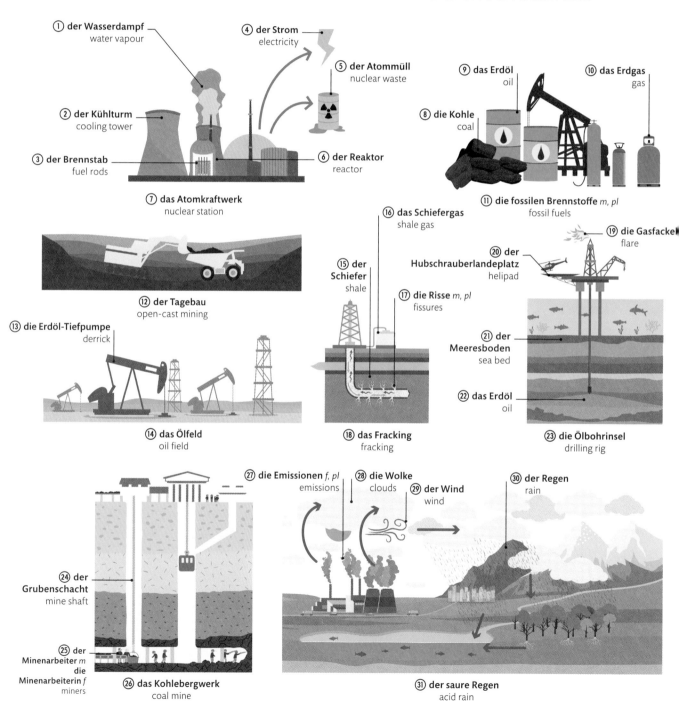

① **der Wasserdampf**
water vapour

④ **der Strom**
electricity

⑤ **der Atommüll**
nuclear waste

② **der Kühlturm**
cooling tower

③ **der Brennstab**
fuel rods

⑥ **der Reaktor**
reactor

⑦ **das Atomkraftwerk**
nuclear station

⑨ **das Erdöl**
oil

⑩ **das Erdgas**
gas

⑧ **die Kohle**
coal

⑪ **die fossilen Brennstoffe** *m, pl*
fossil fuels

⑯ **das Schiefergas**
shale gas

⑮ **der Schiefer**
shale

⑰ **die Risse** *m, pl*
fissures

⑲ **die Gasfackel**
flare

⑳ **der Hubschrauberlandeplatz**
helipad

⑫ **der Tagebau**
open-cast mining

⑬ **die Erdöl-Tiefpumpe**
derrick

㉑ **der Meeresboden**
sea bed

㉒ **das Erdöl**
oil

⑭ **das Ölfeld**
oil field

⑱ **das Fracking**
fracking

㉓ **die Ölbohrinsel**
drilling rig

㉗ **die Emissionen** *f, pl*
emissions

㉘ **die Wolke**
clouds

㉙ **der Wind**
wind

㉚ **der Regen**
rain

㉔ **der Grubenschacht**
mine shaft

㉕ **der Minenarbeiter** *m*
die Minenarbeiterin *f*
miners

㉖ **das Kohlebergwerk**
coal mine

㉛ **der saure Regen**
acid rain

See also
33 Elektrizität und Sanitärtechnik · Electrics and plumbing **42-43** In der Stadt · In town
145 Der Planet Erde · Planet Earth **155** Klima und Umwelt · Climate and the environment

51.2 ERNEUERBARE ENERGIEN · RENEWABLE ENERGY

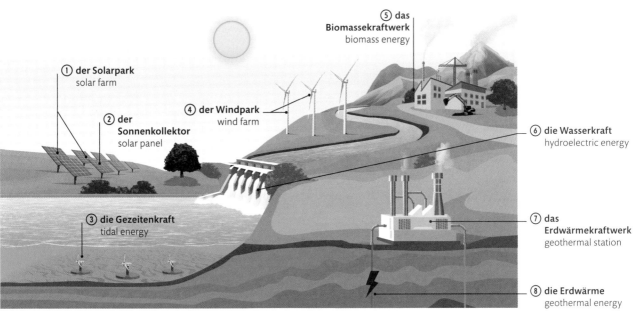

⑤ das **Biomassekraftwerk** biomass energy

① der **Solarpark** solar farm

② der **Sonnenkollektor** solar panel

④ der **Windpark** wind farm

⑥ die **Wasserkraft** hydroelectric energy

③ die **Gezeitenkraft** tidal energy

⑦ das **Erdwärmekraftwerk** geothermal station

⑧ die **Erdwärme** geothermal energy

⑨ die **grüne Energie** green energy

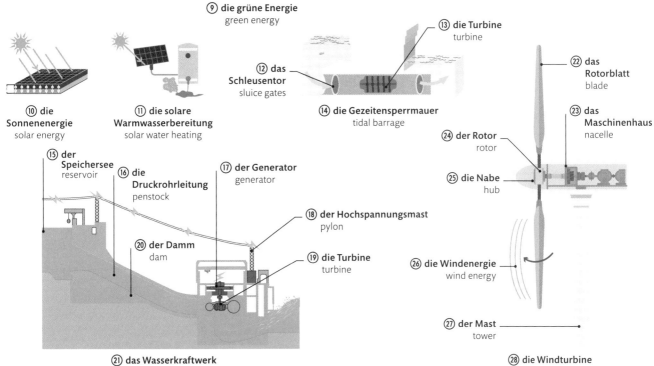

⑩ die **Sonnenenergie** solar energy

⑪ die **solare Warmwasserbereitung** solar water heating

⑫ das **Schleusentor** sluice gates

⑬ die **Turbine** turbine

⑭ die **Gezeitensperrmauer** tidal barrage

㉒ das **Rotorblatt** blade

㉓ das **Maschinenhaus** nacelle

㉔ der **Rotor** rotor

㉕ die **Nabe** hub

⑮ der **Speichersee** reservoir

⑯ die **Druckrohrleitung** penstock

⑰ der **Generator** generator

⑱ der **Hochspannungsmast** pylon

⑳ der **Damm** dam

⑲ die **Turbine** turbine

㉖ die **Windenergie** wind energy

㉗ der **Mast** tower

㉑ das **Wasserkraftwerk** hydroelectric power station

㉘ die **Windturbine** wind turbine

52.1 GETRÄNKE · DRINKS

① **der Kaffee**
coffee

② **der Tee**
tea

③ **der Kakao**
hot chocolate

④ **der Kräutertee**
herbal tea

⑤ **der Eistee**
iced tea

⑥ **die Limonade**
lemonade

⑦ **der Saft**
juice

⑧ **das Mineralwasser**
mineral water

⑨ **das Leitungswasser**
tap water

⑩ **der Smoothie**
smoothie

⑪ **die Orangeade**
orangeade

⑫ **die Cola**
cola

⑬ **der Milchshake**
milkshake

⑭ **der Energydrink**
sports drink /
energy drink

⑮ **der Rotwein**
red wine

⑯ **der Weißwein**
white wine

⑰ **der Rosé**
rosé wine

⑱ **das Bier**
beer

52.2 BEHÄLTER · CONTAINERS

① **die Flasche**
bottle

② **das Glas**
glass

③ **der Karton**
carton

④ **das Einmachglas**
jar

⑤ **die Tüte**
bag

⑥ **die Packung**
packet

⑦ **die Box**
box

⑧ **die Dose**
tin

⑨ **die Thermoskanne**
flask

⑩ **die Schüssel**
bowl

⑪ **die luftdichte Box**
airtight container

⑫ **das Einmachglas**
Mason jar

See also
27 Die Küche und das Geschirr • Kitchen and tableware **28** Küchenutensilien
Kitchenware **29** Kochen • Cooking **52-72** Lebensmittel und Nahrungsmittel • Food

52.3 ADJEKTIVE · ADJECTIVES

① süß
sweet

② herzhaft
savoury

③ sauer
sour

④ salzig
salty

⑤ bitter
bitter

⑥ scharf
spicy / hot

⑦ frisch
fresh

⑧ verdorben
off

⑨ stark
strong

⑩ gekühlt
iced / chilled

⑪ sprudelnd
carbonated / sparkling

⑫ still
non-carbonated / still

⑬ schwer
rich

⑭ saftig
juicy

⑮ knackig
crunchy

⑯ hervorragend
delicious

⑰ eklig
disgusting

⑱ lecker
tasty

④ Prost!
Cheers

52.4 VERBEN FÜR DAS TRINKEN UND ESSEN
DRINKING AND EATING VERBS

① essen
to eat

② kauen
to chew

③ probieren
to taste

⑤ zu Abend essen
to dine

⑥ knabbern
to nibble

⑦ abbeißen
to bite

⑧ schlucken
to swallow

⑨ nippen
to sip

⑩ trinken
to drink

⑪ herunterstürzen
to gulp

53 Fleisch
Meta

53.1 DER METZGER · THE BUTCHER

① Bio-
organic

② freilaufend
free-range

③ **das weiße Fleisch**
white meat

④ **das rote Fleisch**
red meat

⑤ **das magere
Fleisch**
lean meat

⑥ **das Hackfleisch**
mince

⑦ **die Salami**
salami

⑧ **die Chorizo**
chorizo

⑨ **der Schinken**
ham

⑩ **die Leber**
liver

⑪ **das Kotelett**
chop

⑫ **der
Fleischhaken**
meat hook

⑬ **der Rostbraten**
rump steak

⑭ **der Metzger** *m*
die Metzgerin *f*
butcher

⑮ **das
Kaninchen**
rabbit

⑯ **die Wurst**
sausages

⑰ **das Wild**
game

⑱ **der Bacon**
streaky bacon

⑲ **der
Rückenspeck**
back bacon

⑳ **das
Sirloin-Steak**
sirloin steak

See also
29 Kochen · Cooking **52** Trinken und essen · Drinking and eating **54** Fisch und Meeresfrüchte
Fish and seafood **69** Im Restaurant · At the restaurant **72** Das Mittagessen und das
Abendessen · Lunch and dinner **165** Bauernhoftiere · Farm animals

53.2 **FLEISCHSORTEN** · TYPES OF MEAT

① **das Lamm**
lamb

② **das Schwein**
pork

③ **das Rind**
beef

④ **das Kalb**
veal

⑤ **der Hirsch**
venison

⑥ **die Ziege**
goat

⑦ **das Kaninchen**
rabbit

⑧ **das Wildschwein**
wild boar

⑨ **das gekochte Fleisch**
cooked meat

⑩ **das rohe Fleisch**
raw meat

⑪ **das gepökelte Fleisch**
cured meat

⑫ **das geräucherte Fleisch**
smoked meat

53.3 **GEFLÜGEL** · POULTRY

④ **die Ente**
duck

⑦ **Ist das ein Huhn aus Freilandhaltung?**
Is this chicken free-range?

⑧ **Ja, es stammt von einem Bauern aus der Umgebung.**
Yes, it's locally sourced.

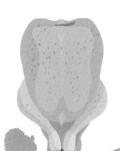  

① **der Truthahn**
turkey

② **die Gans**
goose

③ **der Fasan**
pheasant

⑤ **das Huhn**
chicken

⑥ **die Wachtel**
quail

53.4 **FLEISCHTEILE** · CUTS OF MEAT

① **der Schlegel**
leg

② **die Keule**
thigh

③ **die Brust**
breast

④ **der Flügel**
wing

⑤ **die Rippe**
rib

⑥ **das Filet**
fillet

⑦ **die Fleischstücke** *n, pl*
cuts

⑧ **die Keule**
joint

⑨ **der Schnitt**
slice

⑩ **das Herz**
heart

⑪ **die Zunge**
tongue

⑫ **die Niere**
kidney

⑬ **die Innereien** *f, pl*
offal

54 Fisch und Meeresfrüchte
Fish and seafood

54.1 FISCH · FISH

① **das Lachsfilet**
salmon fillet

② **der Schellfisch**
haddock tail

③ **der Rochenflügel**
skate wing

④ **das Kabeljaufilet**
cod fillet

⑤ **die Sardine**
sardines

⑥ **die Rotbarbe**
red mullet

⑧ **die Makrele**
mackerel

⑨ **die Scholle**
sole

⑩ **die Seebrasse**
sea bream

⑪ **der Seeteufel**
monkfish

⑫ **der Seebarsch**
sea bass

⑬ **der Katzenwels**
catfish

㉖ **der Schwertfisch**
swordfish

㉗ **der Thunfisch**
tuna

㉘ **der Fischhändler** *m*
die Fischhändlerin *f*
fishmonger

㉕ **die Forelle**
trout

㉔ **Ich hätte gerne vier Forellenfilets.**
Can I have four trout fillets, please?

㉓ **der Karpfen**
carp

㉙ **der Goldbutt**
plaice

㉚ **der Köhler**
pollock

㉛ **das Filet**
fillet

㉜ **der Fischkasten**
fish box

⑮ **die Regenbogenforelle**
rainbow trout

⑰ **der Rochen**
skate

⑲ **der Hering**
herring

㉑ **der Schlankwels**
basa

See also
29 Kochen • Cooking **52** Trinken und essen • Drinking and eating **55-56**
Gemüse Vegetables **69** Im Restaurant • At the restaurant **72** Das Mittagessen
und das Abendessen • Lunch and dinner **166** Leben im Ozean • Ocean life

54.2 MEERESFRÜCHTE · SEAFOOD

⑦ **der Weißling**
whiting

⑭ **der Heilbutt**
halibut

⑯ **der Steinbutt**
turbot

⑱ **der Aal**
eel

⑳ **der Barsch**
perch

㉒ **der Zander**
pike perch

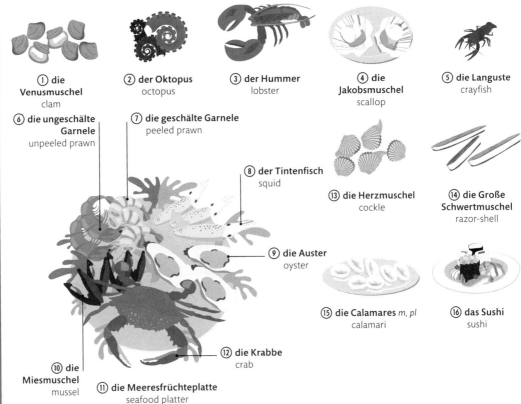

① **die Venusmuschel**
clam

② **der Oktopus**
octopus

③ **der Hummer**
lobster

④ **die Jakobsmuschel**
scallop

⑤ **die Languste**
crayfish

⑥ **die ungeschälte Garnele**
unpeeled prawn

⑦ **die geschälte Garnele**
peeled prawn

⑧ **der Tintenfisch**
squid

⑬ **die Herzmuschel**
cockle

⑭ **die Große Schwertmuschel**
razor-shell

⑨ **die Auster**
oyster

⑮ **die Calamares** *m, pl*
calamari

⑯ **das Sushi**
sushi

⑫ **die Krabbe**
crab

⑩ **die Miesmuschel**
mussel

⑪ **die Meeresfrüchteplatte**
seafood platter

54.3 ZUBEREITUNG · PREPARATION

① **die Schuppe**
scale

③ **der Schwanz**
tail

② **frisch**
fresh

④ **gefroren**
frozen

⑤ **geräuchert**
smoked

⑥ **gesalzen**
salted

⑦ **entschuppt**
descaled

⑧ **ausgenommen**
cleaned

⑨ **entgrätet**
boned

⑩ **die Lende**
loin

55.1 GEMÜSE · VEGETABLES

  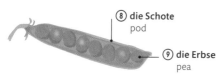 

① **die Saubohne**
broad beans

② **die Stangenbohne**
runner beans

③ **die Grüne Bohne**
green beans /
French beans

④ **die getrocknete Bohne**
dried beans

⑤ **der Sellerie**
celery

⑧ **die Schote**
pod

⑨ **die Erbse**
pea

⑦ **die Speiseerbse**
garden peas

⑩ **die Zuckererbse**
mangetout

⑪ **die Okra**
okra

⑫ **der Bambus**
bamboo

⑬ **die Bohnensprosse**
bean sprouts

⑮ **der Chicorée**
chicory

⑯ **der Fenchel**
fennel

⑰ **das Palmherz**
palm hearts

⑱ **der Jungmais**
baby sweetcorn

⑲ **der Kolben**
kernel

⑳ **der Mais**
corn / sweetcorn

㉓ **die Endivie**
endive

㉔ **der Löwenzahn**
dandelion

㉕ **der Mangold**
Swiss chard

㉖ **der Grünkohl**
kale

㉗ **der Sauerampfer**
sorrel

㉘ **der Spinat**
spinach

  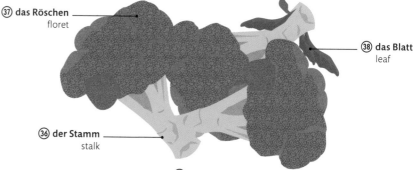

㉛ **der Pak Choi**
pak-choi

㉜ **der Kohlrabi**
kohlrabi

㉝ **der Rosenkohl**
Brussels sprouts

㉞ **der Frühkohl**
spring greens

㊲ **das Röschen**
floret

㊳ **das Blatt**
leaf

㊱ **der Stamm**
stalk

㉟ **der Brokkoli**
broccoli

See also
29 Kochen · Cooking **52** Trinken und essen · Drinking and eating **56** Gemüse (Fortsetzung) · Vegetables continued **57** Obst · Fruit **58** Obst und Nüsse · Fruit and nuts **59** Kräuter und Gewürze · Herbs and spices **69** Im Restaurant · At the restaurant **72** Das Mittagessen und das Abendessen · Lunch and dinner

⑥ **der Baumkohl**
collards

55.2   SALATGEMÜSE · SALAD VEGETABLES

① **die Kresse**
cress

② **der Rucola**
rocket

③ **der Eisbergsalat**
iceberg lettuce

④ **der Römersalat**
romaine lettuce

⑭ **der Wirsing**
savoy cabbage

⑤ **das Romanasalatherz**
little gem

⑥ **die Frühlingszwiebel**
spring onion

⑦ **die Cocktailtomate**
cherry tomatoes

⑧ **die Salatgurke**
cucumber

㉑ **der Weißkohl**
cabbage

㉒ **der Rotkohl**
red cabbage

⑨ **der Friséesalat**
frisée

⑩ **die Brunnenkresse**
watercress

⑪ **der Radicchio**
radicchio

⑫ **der Kopfsalat**
lettuce

㉙ **der Palmkohl**
cavolo nero

㉚ **die Rote-Bete-Blätter**
n, pl
beet leaves

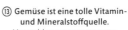

⑬ **Gemüse ist eine tolle Vitamin- und Mineralstoffquelle.**
Vegetables are a great source of vitamins and minerals.

⑭ **der Salat**
salad

⑳ **das Pestizid**
pesticides

㊴ **das Biogemüse**
organic vegetables

56.1 IM LEBENSMITTELGESCHÄFT · AT THE GREENGROCERS

① die Steckrübe
turnip

② das Radieschen
radish

③ die Pastinake
parsnip

④ der Knollensellerie
celeriac

⑤ der Maniok
cassava

⑥ die Kartoffel
potato

⑦ die Wasserkastanie
water chestnut

⑧ die Yamswurzel
yam

⑨ die Rote Bete
beetroot

⑩ die Kohlrübe
swede

⑪ der Topinambur
Jerusalem
artichoke

⑫ die Tarowurzel
taro root

⑬ der Meerrettich
horseradish

⑭ die Brotfrucht
breadfruit

⑮ die Schalotte
shallot

⑯ die Chilischote
chilli

⑰ die Eiertomate
plum tomato

⑱ die Spargelspitze
asparagus tip

**⑲ das
Artischockenherz**
artichoke heart

⑳ der Austernpilz
oyster
mushroom

㉑ der Pfifferling
chanterelle

㉒ der Shiitake
shiitake
mushroom

㉓ der Trüffel
truffle

㉔ der Enoki
enoki
mushroom

㉕ die Zucchini
marrow

㉖ der Moschuskürbis
butternut
squash

㉗ der Eichelkürbis
button acorn squash

㉘ der Kürbis
pumpkin

㉙ der Riesenkürbis
buttercup
squash

**㉚ die
Bischofsmütze**
patty pan

㉛ frisch
fresh

㉜ gefroren
frozen

㉝ konserviert
tinned

㉞ roh
raw

㉟ gekocht
cooked

㊱ scharf
hot / spicy

See also
29 Kochen • Cooking **52** Trinken und essen • Drinking and eating
57 Obst • Fruit **58** Obst und Nüsse • Fruit and nuts **69** Im Restaurant
At the restaurant **72** Das Mittagessen und das Abendessen • Lunch and dinner

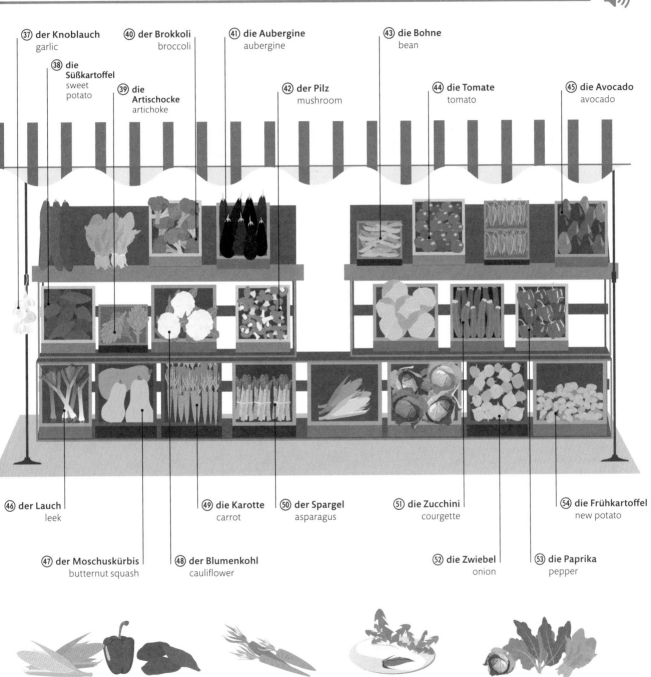

㊲ **der Knoblauch**
garlic

㊳ **die Süßkartoffel**
sweet potato

㊴ **die Artischocke**
artichoke

㊵ **der Brokkoli**
broccoli

㊶ **die Aubergine**
aubergine

㊷ **der Pilz**
mushroom

㊸ **die Bohne**
bean

㊹ **die Tomate**
tomato

㊺ **die Avocado**
avocado

㊻ **der Lauch**
leek

㊼ **der Moschuskürbis**
butternut squash

㊽ **der Blumenkohl**
cauliflower

㊾ **die Karotte**
carrot

㊿ **der Spargel**
asparagus

51 **die Zucchini**
courgette

52 **die Zwiebel**
onion

53 **die Paprika**
pepper

54 **die Frühkartoffel**
new potato

55 **süß**
sweet

56 **knackig**
crunchy

57 **bitter**
bitter

58 **grün**
leafy

123

57 Obst
Fruit

57.1 ZITRUSFRÜCHTE · CITRUS FRUIT

① **die Orange**
orange

② **die Blutorange**
blood orange

③ **die Tangelo**
ugli fruit

④ **die Pampelmuse**
pomelo

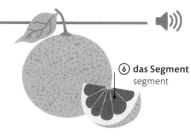
⑥ **das Segment**
segment
⑤ **die Grapefruit**
grapefruit

⑦ **die Klementine**
clementine

⑧ **die Satsuma**
satsuma

⑨ **die Kumquat**
kumquat

⑩ **die Limette**
lime

⑪ **die Zitrone**
lemon

⑫ **die Zitronenschale**
zest

57.2 OBST BESCHREIBEN · DESCRIBING FRUIT

⑤ **Diese Birnen sind reif und können geerntet werden.**
These pears are ripe and ready to pick.

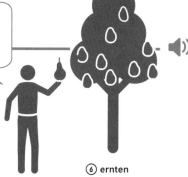

① **die Kokosnussschale**
coconut shell

② **hart**
hard

③ **weich**
soft

④ **kernlos**
seedless

⑥ **ernten**
to pick

⑦ **der Frühling**
spring
⑧ **der Sommer**
summer

⑪ **süß**
sweet

⑫ **sauer**
sour

⑬ **reif**
ripe

⑭ **verdorben**
rotten

⑨ **der Herbst**
autumn

⑩ **die Saisonfrucht**
seasonal fruit

⑮ **knackig**
crisp

⑯ **das Kerngehäuse**
core

⑰ **die Ballaststoffe** *m, pl*
fibre

⑱ **das Fruchtfleisch**
pulp

See also
29 Kochen · Cooking **52** Trinken und essen · Drinking and eating **55-56** Gemüse · Vegetables **58** Obst und Nüsse · Fruit and nuts **65-66** Im Café · At the café **69** Im Restaurant · At the restaurant **71** Das Frühstück · Breakfast **72** Das Mittagessen und das Abendessen · Lunch and dinner

57.3 BEEREN UND STEINFRÜCHTE · BERRIES AND STONE FRUIT

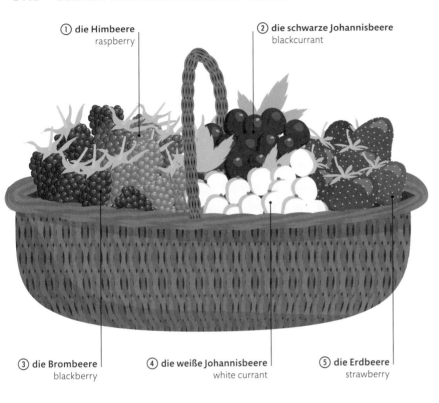

① **die Himbeere**
raspberry

② **die schwarze Johannisbeere**
blackcurrant

③ **die Brombeere**
blackberry

④ **die weiße Johannisbeere**
white currant

⑤ **die Erdbeere**
strawberry

⑥ **der Obstkorb**
basket of fruit

⑦ **die Cranberry**
cranberry

⑧ **die Blaubeere**
blueberry

⑨ **die Loganbeere**
loganberry

⑩ **die Andenkirsche**
cape gooseberry

⑪ **die Goji-Beere**
goji berry

⑫ **die Stachelbeere**
gooseberry

⑬ **die rote Johannisbeere**
redcurrant

⑭ **die Heidelbeere**
bilberry

⑮ **die Holunderbeere**
elderberry

⑯ **die Weintraube**
grapes

⑰ **die Maulbeere**
mulberry

⑱ **der Pfirsich**
peach

⑲ **die Nektarine**
nectarine

⑳ **die Aprikose**
apricot

㉑ **die Mango**
mango

㉒ **die Pflaume**
plum

㉓ **die Kirsche**
cherry

㉔ **die Dattel**
date

㉕ **die Lychee**
lychee

Obst und Nüsse
Fruit and nuts

58.1 MELONEN · MELONS

① **die Wassermelone**
watermelon

② **die Kantalupe**
cantaloupe

③ **die Honigmelone**
honeydew melon

④ **die Gelbe Kanarische**
Canary melon

⑤ **die Charentais-Melone**
charentais

⑥ **die Galiamelone**
galia

58.2 WEITERES OBST · OTHER FRUIT

③ **die Schale**
skin

④ **das Fruchtfleisch**
flesh

② **die Kerne** *m, pl*
seeds

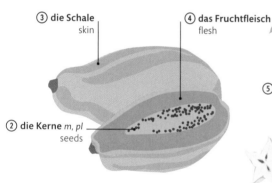

① **die Papaya**
papaya

⑤ **die Quitte**
quince

⑥ **die Passionsfrucht**
passion fruit

⑦ **die Guave**
guava

⑪ **die Ananas**
pineapple

⑧ **die Sternfrucht**
starfruit

⑨ **die Kakifrucht**
persimmon

⑩ **die Ananas-Guave**
feijoa

⑫ **die Kaktusfeige**
prickly pear

⑬ **die Baumtomate**
tamarillo

⑭ **die Jackfrucht**
jackfruit

⑮ **die Mangostinfrucht**
mangosteen

⑯ **der Granatapfel**
pomegranate

⑰ **die Banane**
banana

⑱ **die Kiwi**
kiwi fruit

⑲ **der Apfel**
apple

⑳ **der Holzapfel**
crab apples

㉑ **die Birne**
pear

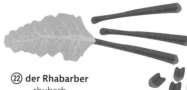

㉒ **der Rhabarber**
rhubarb

See also
29 Kochen · Cooking **52** Trinken und essen · Drinking and eating **55-56** Gemüse Vegetables
57 Obst · Fruit **65-66** Im Café · At the café **69** Im Restaurant · At the restaurant **71** Das
Frühstück · Breakfast **72** Das Mittagessen und das Abendessen · Lunch and dinner

58.3 NÜSSE UND TROCKENFRÜCHTE · NUTS AND DRIED FRUIT

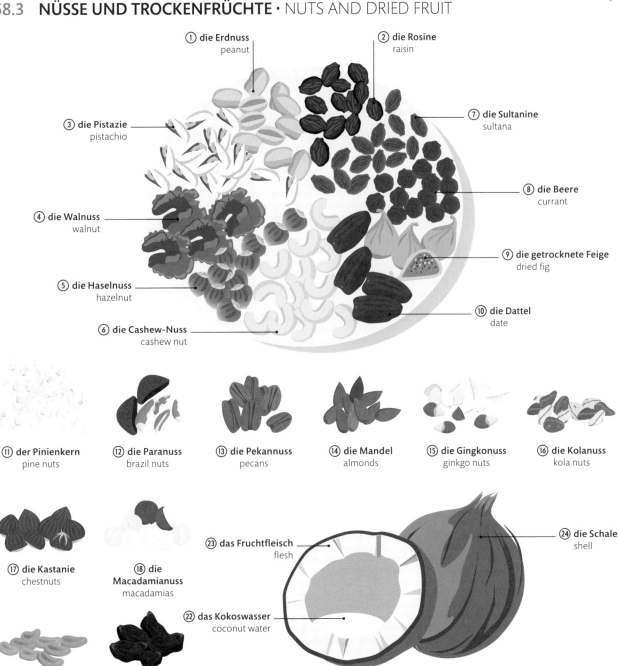

① **die Erdnuss**
peanut

② **die Rosine**
raisin

③ **die Pistazie**
pistachio

④ **die Walnuss**
walnut

⑤ **die Haselnuss**
hazelnut

⑥ **die Cashew-Nuss**
cashew nut

⑦ **die Sultanine**
sultana

⑧ **die Beere**
currant

⑨ **die getrocknete Feige**
dried fig

⑩ **die Dattel**
date

⑪ **der Pinienkern**
pine nuts

⑫ **die Paranuss**
brazil nuts

⑬ **die Pekannuss**
pecans

⑭ **die Mandel**
almonds

⑮ **die Gingkonuss**
ginkgo nuts

⑯ **die Kolanuss**
kola nuts

⑰ **die Kastanie**
chestnuts

⑱ **die Macadamianuss**
macadamias

⑲ **die getrocknete Aprikose**
dried apricots

⑳ **die Dörrpflaume**
prunes

㉑ **die Kokosnuss**
coconut

㉒ **das Kokoswasser**
coconut water

㉓ **das Fruchtfleisch**
flesh

㉔ **die Schale**
shell

59.1 GEWÜRZE · SPICES

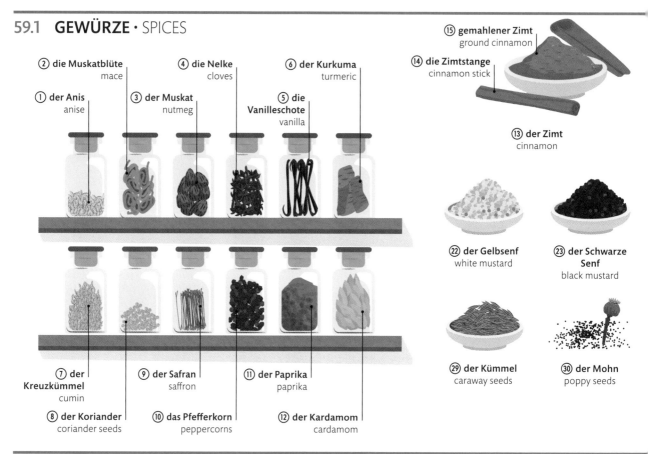

⑮ **gemahlener Zimt**
ground cinnamon

⑭ **die Zimtstange**
cinnamon stick

⑬ **der Zimt**
cinnamon

② **die Muskatblüte**
mace

④ **die Nelke**
cloves

⑥ **der Kurkuma**
turmeric

① **der Anis**
anise

③ **der Muskat**
nutmeg

⑤ **die Vanilleschote**
vanilla

⑦ **der Kreuzkümmel**
cumin

⑧ **der Koriander**
coriander seeds

⑨ **der Safran**
saffron

⑩ **das Pfefferkorn**
peppercorns

⑪ **der Paprika**
paprika

⑫ **der Kardamom**
cardamom

㉒ **der Gelbsenf**
white mustard

㉓ **der Schwarze Senf**
black mustard

㉙ **der Kümmel**
caraway seeds

㉚ **der Mohn**
poppy seeds

59.2 KRÄUTER · HERBS

① **der Fenchel**
fennel

② **der Lorbeer**
bay leaf

③ **die Petersilie**
parsley

④ **der Schnittlauch**
chives

⑤ **die Minze**
mint

⑥ **der Koriander**
coriander

⑬ **der Thymian**
thyme

⑭ **der Salbei**
sage

⑮ **der Estragon**
tarragon

⑯ **der Majoran**
marjoram

⑰ **das Basilikum**
basil

⑱ **der Oregano**
oregano

See also
29 Kochen · Cooking **52** Trinken und essen · Drinking and eating **53** Fleisch
Meat **55-56** Gemüse · Vegetables **60** In der Vorratskammer · In the pantry

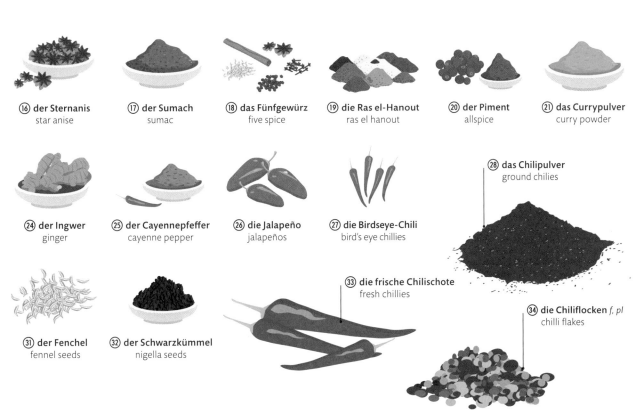

16 **der Sternanis**
star anise

17 **der Sumach**
sumac

18 **das Fünfgewürz**
five spice

19 **die Ras el-Hanout**
ras el hanout

20 **der Piment**
allspice

21 **das Currypulver**
curry powder

24 **der Ingwer**
ginger

25 **der Cayennepfeffer**
cayenne pepper

26 **die Jalapeño**
jalapeños

27 **die Birdseye-Chili**
bird's eye chillies

28 **das Chilipulver**
ground chilies

33 **die frische Chilischote**
fresh chillies

34 **die Chiliflocken** *f, pl*
chilli flakes

31 **der Fenchel**
fennel seeds

32 **der Schwarzkümmel**
nigella seeds

7 **der Ysop**
hyssop

8 **der Dill**
dill

9 **der Rosmarin**
rosemary

10 **der Kerbel**
chervil

11 **das Maggikraut**
lovage

12 **der Sauerampfer**
sorrel

19 **das Zitronengras**
lemongrass

20 **die Zitronenmelisse**
lemon balm

21 **das Gurkenkraut**
borage

22 **der Bockshornklee**
fenugreek leaves

23 **das Kräutersträußchen**
bouquet garni

60.1 ÖLE · BOTTLED OILS

① **das Öl**
oil

② **das Palmöl**
palm oil

③ **das Sonnenblumenöl**
sunflower oil

④ **das Rapsöl**
canola / rapeseed oil

⑤ **das Maisöl**
corn oil

⑫ **der Korken**
cork

⑪ **die Chilischote**
chilli

⑥ **das Sojaöl**
soybean oil

⑦ **das Erdnussöl**
groundnut oil

⑧ **das Haselnussöl**
hazelnut oil

⑨ **das Kokosnussöl**
coconut oil

⑩ **das aromatisierte Öl**
flavoured oil

⑱ **natives Olivenöl extra**
extra virgin

⑬ **das Sesamöl**
sesame seed oil

⑭ **das Mandelöl**
almond oil

⑮ **das Walnussöl**
walnut oil

⑯ **das Traubenkernöl**
grapeseed oil

⑰ **das Olivenöl**
olive oil

60.2 SÜSSER AUFSTRICH · SWEET SPREADS

④ **das Glas**
jar

⑦ **die Honigwabe**
honeycomb

⑧ **der Honiglöffel**
honey dipper

① **das Zitronenmus**
lemon curd

② **die Himbeermarmelade**
raspberry jam

③ **die Erdbeermarmelade**
strawberry jam

⑤ **der kristallisierte Honig**
set honey

⑥ **der Honig**
honey

⑭ **das Einmachglas**
preserved fruit

⑨ **die Zitrusmarmelade**
marmalade

⑩ **der Ahornsirup**
maple syrup

⑪ **die Erdnussbutter**
peanut butter

⑫ **der Schokoaufstrich**
chocolate spread

⑬ **das eingemachte Obst**
preserving jar

See also
27 Die Küche und das Geschirr • Kitchen and tableware **29** Kochen • Cooking
52 Trinken und essen • Drinking and eating **53** Fleisch • Meat **55-56** Gemüse
Vegetables **65-66** Im Café • At the café **69** Im Restaurant • At the restaurant

60.3 WÜRZSAUCEN · SAUCES AND CONDIMENTS

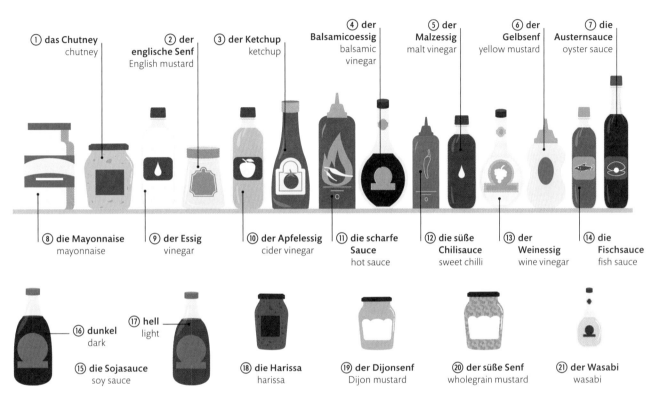

① **das Chutney**
chutney

② **der englische Senf**
English mustard

③ **der Ketchup**
ketchup

④ **der Balsamicoessig**
balsamic vinegar

⑤ **der Malzessig**
malt vinegar

⑥ **der Gelbsenf**
yellow mustard

⑦ **die Austernsauce**
oyster sauce

⑧ **die Mayonnaise**
mayonnaise

⑨ **der Essig**
vinegar

⑩ **der Apfelessig**
cider vinegar

⑪ **die scharfe Sauce**
hot sauce

⑫ **die süße Chilisauce**
sweet chilli

⑬ **der Weinessig**
wine vinegar

⑭ **die Fischsauce**
fish sauce

⑯ **dunkel**
dark

⑰ **hell**
light

⑮ **die Sojasauce**
soy sauce

⑱ **die Harissa**
harissa

⑲ **der Dijonsenf**
Dijon mustard

⑳ **der süße Senf**
wholegrain mustard

㉑ **der Wasabi**
wasabi

60.4 SAUERKONSERVEN · PICKLES

① **der Dill**
dill

③ **das Senfkorn**
mustard seeds

② **die Essiggurke**
gherkin

④ **das Sauerkraut**
sauerkraut

⑤ **das Kimchi**
kimchi

⑥ **das Limetten-Pickle**
lime pickle

⑦ **die eingelegte Zwiebel**
pickled onions

⑧ **die eingelegte Rote Bete**
beetroot

⑨ **die Mischung aus eingelegtem Gemüse**
sandwich pickle

⑩ **die Piccalilli-Sauce**
piccalilli

⑪ **das Cornichon**
cornichons

61.1 DER KÄSE · CHEESE

① der Hartkäse
hard cheese

② der Schnittkäse
semi-hard cheese

③ der halbfeste Käse
semi-soft cheese

④ der Schmelzkäse
soft cheese

⑤ der Schafskäse
sheep's milk cheese

⑥ der Ziegenkäse
goat's cheese

⑦ der Blauschimmelkäse
blue cheese

⑧ die Rinde
rind

⑨ der geriebene Käse
grated cheese

⑩ der frische Käse
fresh cheese

⑪ der Hüttenkäse
cottage cheese

⑫ der Frischkäse
cream cheese

61.2 EIER · EGGS

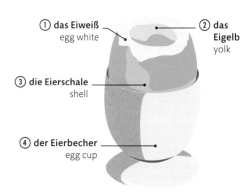
① das Eiweiß
egg white

② das Eigelb
yolk

③ die Eierschale
shell

④ der Eierbecher
egg cup

⑤ das gekochte Ei
boiled egg

⑥ das Spiegelei
fried egg

⑦ das Rührei
scrambled eggs

⑧ das pochierte Ei
poached egg

⑨ das Omelett
omelette

⑩ das Gänseei
goose egg

⑪ das Entenei
duck egg

⑫ das Hühnerei
hen's egg

⑬ das Wachtelei
quail egg

61.3 MILCH · MILK

① pasteurisiert
pasteurized

② die Rohmilch
unpasteurized

③ laktosefrei
lactose free

④ homogenisiert
homogenized

⑤ fettfrei
fat free

⑥ das Milchpulver
powdered milk

See also
29 Kochen · Cooking **52** Trinken und essen · Drinking and eating **65-66** Im Café
At · the café **69** Im Restaurant · At the restaurant **71** Das Frühstück · Breakfast

61.4 **MILCHPRODUKTE** · MILK PRODUCTS

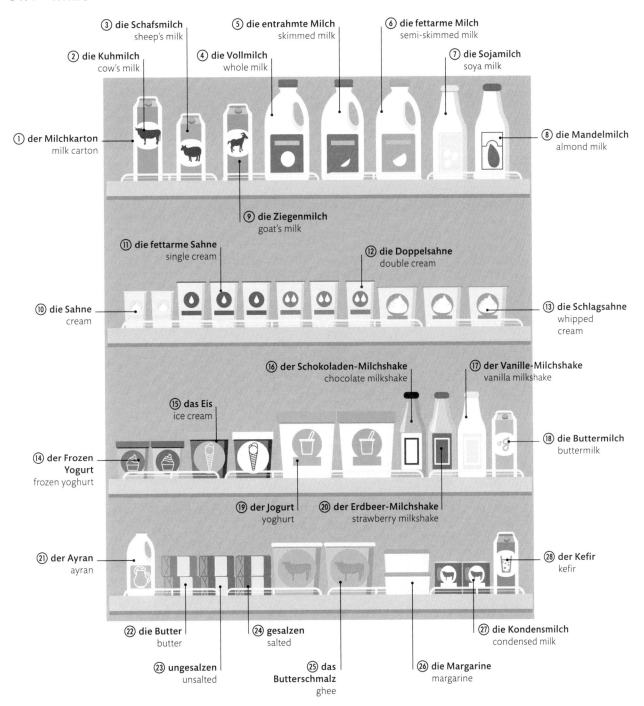

③ **die Schafsmilch** sheep's milk
② **die Kuhmilch** cow's milk
④ **die Vollmilch** whole milk
⑤ **die entrahmte Milch** skimmed milk
⑥ **die fettarme Milch** semi-skimmed milk
⑦ **die Sojamilch** soya milk
① **der Milchkarton** milk carton
⑧ **die Mandelmilch** almond milk
⑨ **die Ziegenmilch** goat's milk
⑪ **die fettarme Sahne** single cream
⑫ **die Doppelsahne** double cream
⑩ **die Sahne** cream
⑬ **die Schlagsahne** whipped cream
⑯ **der Schokoladen-Milchshake** chocolate milkshake
⑰ **der Vanille-Milchshake** vanilla milkshake
⑮ **das Eis** ice cream
⑱ **die Buttermilch** buttermilk
⑭ **der Frozen Yogurt** frozen yoghurt
⑲ **der Jogurt** yoghurt
⑳ **der Erdbeer-Milchshake** strawberry milkshake
㉑ **der Ayran** ayran
㉘ **der Kefir** kefir
㉒ **die Butter** butter
㉔ **gesalzen** salted
㉗ **die Kondensmilch** condensed milk
㉓ **ungesalzen** unsalted
㉕ **das Butterschmalz** ghee
㉖ **die Margarine** margarine

Die Bäckerei
The bakery

62.1 BROT UND MEHL · BREADS AND FLOURS

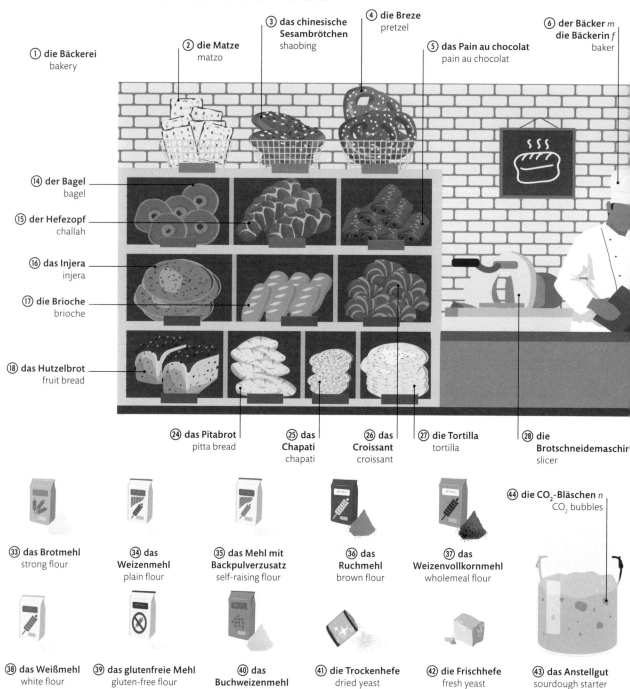

① die Bäckerei
bakery

② die Matze
matzo

③ das chinesische Sesambrötchen
shaobing

④ die Breze
pretzel

⑤ das Pain au chocolat
pain au chocolat

⑥ der Bäcker *m*
die Bäckerin *f*
baker

⑭ der Bagel
bagel

⑮ der Hefezopf
challah

⑯ das Injera
injera

⑰ die Brioche
brioche

⑱ das Hutzelbrot
fruit bread

㉔ das Pitabrot
pitta bread

㉕ das Chapati
chapati

㉖ das Croissant
croissant

㉗ die Tortilla
tortilla

㉘ die Brotschneidemaschir
slicer

㉝ das Brotmehl
strong flour

㉞ das Weizenmehl
plain flour

㉟ das Mehl mit Backpulverzusatz
self-raising flour

㊱ das Ruchmehl
brown flour

㊲ das Weizenvollkornmehl
wholemeal flour

㊸ die CO_2-Bläschen *n*
CO_2 bubbles

㊳ das Weißmehl
white flour

㊴ das glutenfreie Mehl
gluten-free flour

㊵ das Buchweizenmehl
buckwheat flour

㊶ die Trockenhefe
dried yeast

㊷ die Frischhefe
fresh yeast

㊸ das Anstellgut
sourdough starter

See also
29 Kochen · Cooking **52** Trinken und essen · Drinking and eating
63 Die Bäckerei (Fortsetzung) · The bakery continued **65-66** Im Café · At
the café **69** Im Restaurant · At the restaurant **71** Das Frühstück · Breakfast

⑦ **das aufgeschnittene Brot**
sliced bread

⑨ **das Weißbrot**
white bread

⑪ **das Roggenbrot**
rye bread

⑧ **das Knäckebrot**
crispbread

⑩ **die Kruste**
crust

⑫ **das Graubrot**
brown bread

⑬ **der Laib**
loaf

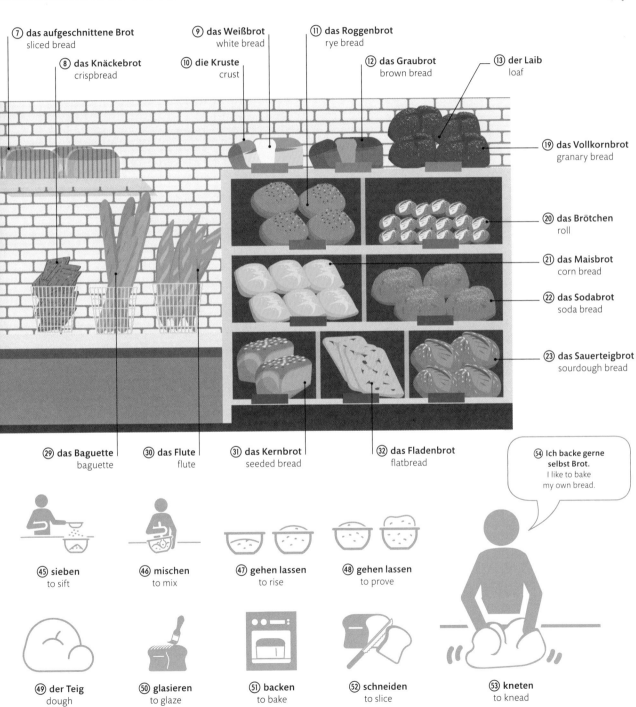

⑲ **das Vollkornbrot**
granary bread

⑳ **das Brötchen**
roll

㉑ **das Maisbrot**
corn bread

㉒ **das Sodabrot**
soda bread

㉓ **das Sauerteigbrot**
sourdough bread

㉙ **das Baguette**
baguette

㉚ **das Flute**
flute

㉛ **das Kernbrot**
seeded bread

㉜ **das Fladenbrot**
flatbread

㊹ **Ich backe gerne selbst Brot.**
I like to bake
my own bread.

㊺ **sieben**
to sift

㊻ **mischen**
to mix

㊼ **gehen lassen**
to rise

㊽ **gehen lassen**
to prove

㊾ **der Teig**
dough

㊿ **glasieren**
to glaze

51 **backen**
to bake

52 **schneiden**
to slice

53 **kneten**
to knead

63 Die Bäckerei (Fortsetzung)
The bakery continued

63.1 KUCHEN UND NACHSPEISEN · CAKES AND DESSERTS

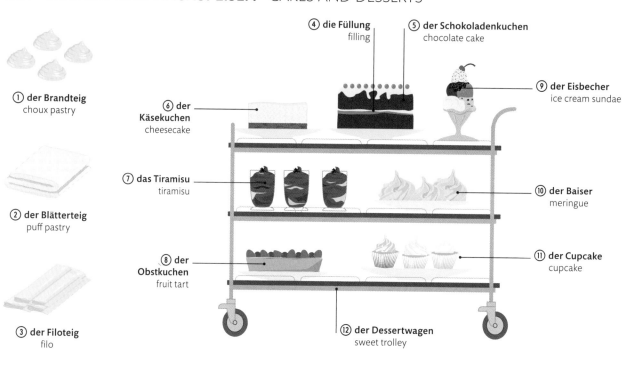

① **der Brandteig**
choux pastry

② **der Blätterteig**
puff pastry

③ **der Filoteig**
filo

④ **die Füllung**
filling

⑤ **der Schokoladenkuchen**
chocolate cake

⑥ **der Käsekuchen**
cheesecake

⑦ **das Tiramisu**
tiramisu

⑧ **der Obstkuchen**
fruit tart

⑨ **der Eisbecher**
ice cream sundae

⑩ **der Baiser**
meringue

⑪ **der Cupcake**
cupcake

⑫ **der Dessertwagen**
sweet trolley

⑬ **die Konditorcreme**
crème pâtissière

⑭ **das Mochi**
mochi

⑮ **der Donut**
doughnut

⑯ **der Berliner**
jam doughnut

⑰ **der Schokodonut**
chocolate doughnut

⑱ **der Muffin**
muffin

⑲ **die Baklava**
baklava

⑳ **die Pavlova**
pavlova

㉑ **der Schichtkuchen**
layer cake

㉒ **der Rührkuchen**
sponge cake

㉓ **das Früchtebrot**
fruitcake

㉔ **die Torte**
gateau

㉕ **die Cremeschnitte**
custard slice

㉖ **der Vanillepudding**
custard

㉗ **das Eclair**
éclair

㉘ **das Iced Bun**
iced bun

㉙ **das Plundergebäck**
pastry

㉚ **der Milchreis**
rice pudding

See also
29 Kochen • Cooking **52** Trinken und essen • Drinking and eating **67** Süßigkeiten • Sweets **71** Das Frühstück • Breakfast

63.2 KEKSE · COOKIES AND BISCUITS

① **der Schokoladen-Cookie**
chocolate chip cookie

② **der Florentiner**
Florentine

③ **das Mürbegebäck**
shortbread

④ **die Makrone**
macaron

⑤ **der Lebkuchenmann**
gingerbread man

⑥ **der Glückskeks**
fortune cookies

63.3 KUCHEN ZU FEIERLICHEN ANLÄSSEN · CELEBRATION CAKES

① **Möchtest du gerne ein Stück Kuchen?**
Would you like a piece of cake?

② **Ja, der sieht fantastisch aus!**
Yes, it looks absolutely delicious.

⑥ **der Tortenaufsatz**
cake topper

③ **der oberste Stock**
top tier

⑦ **das Marzipan**
marzipan

④ **die Dekoration**
decoration

⑤ **die Glasur**
icing

⑧ **das Band**
ribbon

⑨ **die Hochzeitstorte**
wedding cake

⑩ **glasieren**
to glaze

⑪ **backen**
to bake

⑫ **dekorieren**
to decorate

⑮ **auspusten**
to blow out

⑭ **die Geburtstagskerzen f, pl**
birthday candles

⑬ **der Geburtstagskuchen**
birthday cake

64.1 DAS FEINKOSTGESCHÄFT · DELICATESSEN

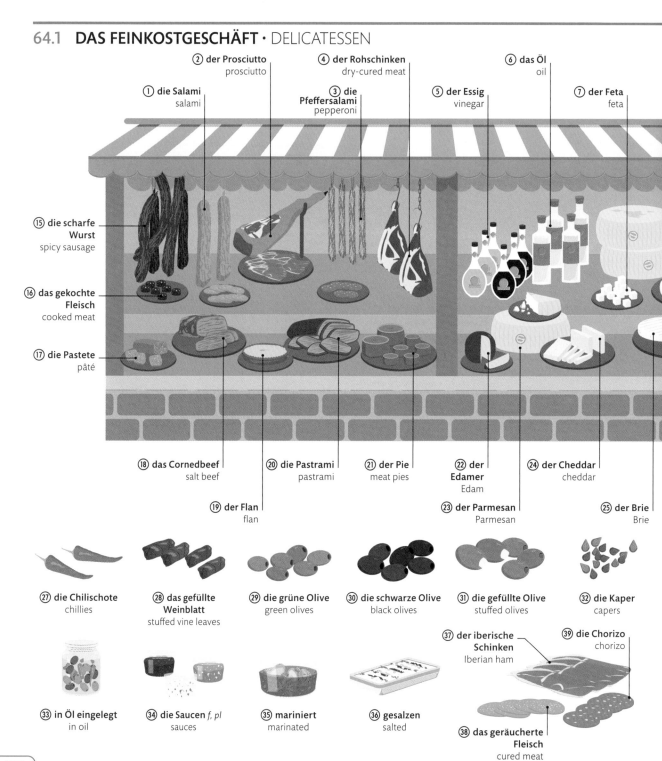

① die Salami
salami

② der Prosciutto
prosciutto

③ die Pfeffersalami
pepperoni

④ der Rohschinken
dry-cured meat

⑤ der Essig
vinegar

⑥ das Öl
oil

⑦ der Feta
feta

⑮ die scharfe Wurst
spicy sausage

⑯ das gekochte Fleisch
cooked meat

⑰ die Pastete
pâté

⑱ das Cornedbeef
salt beef

⑲ der Flan
flan

⑳ die Pastrami
pastrami

㉑ der Pie
meat pies

㉒ der Edamer
Edam

㉓ der Parmesan
Parmesan

㉔ der Cheddar
cheddar

㉕ der Brie
Brie

㉗ die Chilischote
chillies

㉘ das gefüllte Weinblatt
stuffed vine leaves

㉙ die grüne Olive
green olives

㉚ die schwarze Olive
black olives

㉛ die gefüllte Olive
stuffed olives

㉜ die Kaper
capers

㉝ in Öl eingelegt
in oil

㉞ die Saucen f, pl
sauces

㉟ mariniert
marinated

㊱ gesalzen
salted

㊲ der iberische Schinken
Iberian ham

㊳ das geräucherte Fleisch
cured meat

㊴ die Chorizo
chorizo

See also
29 Kochen • Cooking **52** Trinken und essen • Drinking and eating **53** Fleisch • Meat **60** In der Vorratskammer • In the pantry **61** Milchprodukte • Dairy produce **65-66** Im Café • At the café **69** Im Restaurant At the restaurant **71** Das Frühstück • Breakfast **72** Die Mittagessen und das Abendessen • Lunch and dinner

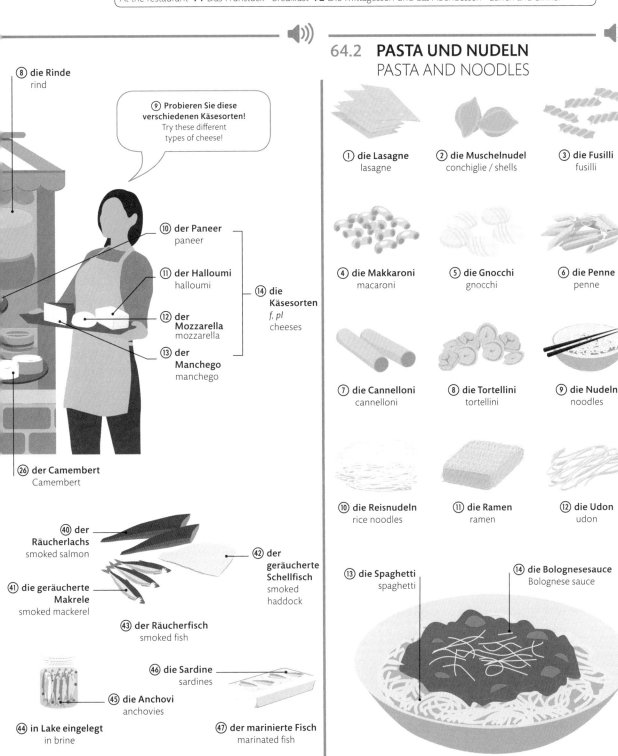

⑧ **die Rinde**
rind

⑨ **Probieren Sie diese verschiedenen Käsesorten!**
Try these different types of cheese!

⑩ **der Paneer**
paneer

⑪ **der Halloumi**
halloumi

⑫ **der Mozzarella**
mozzarella

⑬ **der Manchego**
manchego

⑭ **die Käsesorten**
f, pl
cheeses

㉖ **der Camembert**
Camembert

㊵ **der Räucherlachs**
smoked salmon

㊶ **die geräucherte Makrele**
smoked mackerel

㊷ **der geräucherte Schellfisch**
smoked haddock

㊸ **der Räucherfisch**
smoked fish

㊻ **die Sardine**
sardines

㊺ **die Anchovi**
anchovies

㊹ **in Lake eingelegt**
in brine

㊼ **der marinierte Fisch**
marinated fish

64.2 PASTA UND NUDELN
PASTA AND NOODLES

① **die Lasagne**
lasagne

② **die Muschelnudel**
conchiglie / shells

③ **die Fusilli**
fusilli

④ **die Makkaroni**
macaroni

⑤ **die Gnocchi**
gnocchi

⑥ **die Penne**
penne

⑦ **die Cannelloni**
cannelloni

⑧ **die Tortellini**
tortellini

⑨ **die Nudeln**
noodles

⑩ **die Reisnudeln**
rice noodles

⑪ **die Ramen**
ramen

⑫ **die Udon**
udon

⑬ **die Spaghetti**
spaghetti

⑭ **die Bolognesesauce**
Bolognese sauce

65.1 DAS CAFÉ · CAFÉ

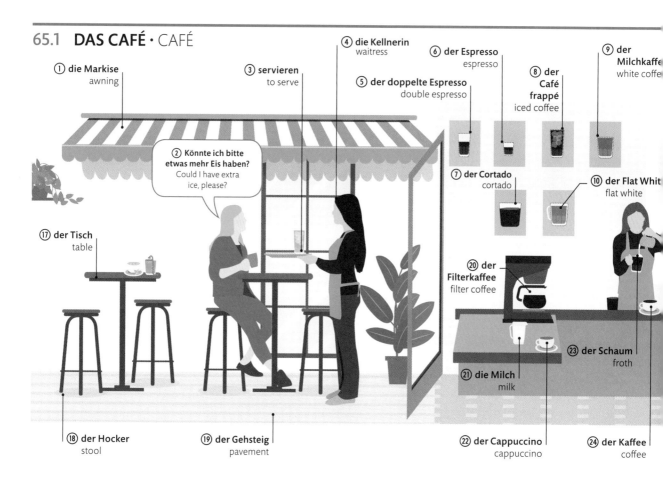

① die Markise
awning

② Könnte ich bitte etwas mehr Eis haben?
Could I have extra ice, please?

③ servieren
to serve

④ die Kellnerin
waitress

⑤ der doppelte Espresso
double espresso

⑥ der Espresso
espresso

⑦ der Cortado
cortado

⑧ der Café frappé
iced coffee

⑨ der Milchkaffe
white coffe

⑩ der Flat Whit
flat white

⑰ der Tisch
table

⑳ der Filterkaffee
filter coffee

㉓ der Schaum
froth

㉑ die Milch
milk

⑱ der Hocker
stool

⑲ der Gehsteig
pavement

㉒ der Cappuccino
cappuccino

㉔ der Kaffee
coffee

65.2 SÄFTE UND MILCHSHAKES · JUICES AND MILKSHAKES

① der Mixer
blender

② das Kokoswasser
coconut water

③ der Orangensaft mit Fruchtfleisch
orange juice with pulp

④ der Orangensaft ohne Fruchtfleisch
smooth orange juice

⑤ der Apfelsaft
apple juice

⑥ der Ananassaft
pineapple juice

⑦ der Tomatensaft
tomato juice

⑧ der Mangosaft
mango juice

⑨ der Cranberrysaft
cranberry juice

⑩ der Erdbeer-Smoothie
strawberry smoothie

⑪ der Schokoladen-Milchshake
chocolate milkshake

⑫ der Erdbeer-Milchshake
strawberry milkshake

See also
27 Die Küche und das Geschirr · Kitchen and tableware **52** Trinken und essen · Drinking and eating **66** Im Café (Fortsetzung) · At the café continued **70** Fastfood · Fast food **72** Das Mittagessen und das Abendessen · Lunch and dinner

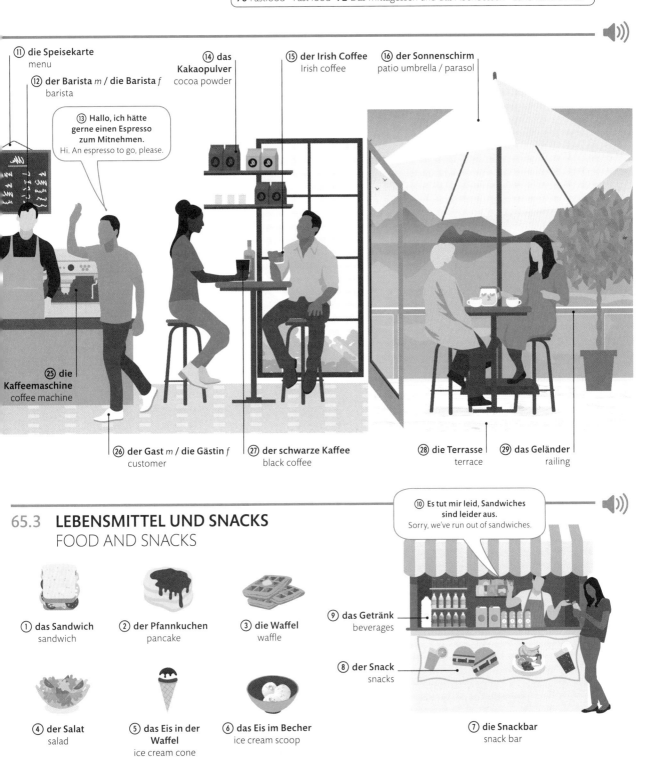

⑪ **die Speisekarte**
menu

⑫ **der Barista** *m* / **die Barista** *f*
barista

⑬ **Hallo, ich hätte gerne einen Espresso zum Mitnehmen.**
Hi. An espresso to go, please.

⑭ **das Kakaopulver**
cocoa powder

⑮ **der Irish Coffee**
Irish coffee

⑯ **der Sonnenschirm**
patio umbrella / parasol

㉕ **die Kaffeemaschine**
coffee machine

㉖ **der Gast** *m* / **die Gästin** *f*
customer

㉗ **der schwarze Kaffee**
black coffee

㉘ **die Terrasse**
terrace

㉙ **das Geländer**
railing

65.3 LEBENSMITTEL UND SNACKS
FOOD AND SNACKS

⑩ **Es tut mir leid, Sandwiches sind leider aus.**
Sorry, we've run out of sandwiches.

① **das Sandwich**
sandwich

② **der Pfannkuchen**
pancake

③ **die Waffel**
waffle

④ **der Salat**
salad

⑤ **das Eis in der Waffel**
ice cream cone

⑥ **das Eis im Becher**
ice cream scoop

⑨ **das Getränk**
beverages

⑧ **der Snack**
snacks

⑦ **die Snackbar**
snack bar

66 Im Café (Fortsetzung)
At the café continued

See also
27 Die Küche und das Geschirr • Kitchen and tableware **52** Trinken und essen • Drinking and eating **72** Das Mittagessen und das Abendessen • Lunch and dinner

66.1 TEE · TEA

① der Kräutertee
herbal tea

② der weiße Tee
white tea

③ der Eistee
iced tea

④ der Pfefferminztee
mint tea

⑥ das Teeei
tea infuser

⑤ der Tee mit Zitrone
tea with lemon

⑦ der schwarze Tee
black tea

⑧ der grüne Tee
green tea

⑨ der Kamillentee
camomile tea

⑩ das Teesieb
tea strainer

⑪ die Teekanne
teapot

⑫ der Tee mit Milch
tea with milk

See also
48 Der Supermarkt • The supermarket
62-63 Die Bäckerei • The bakery

67.1 IM SÜSSIGKEITENLADEN · SWEET SHOP

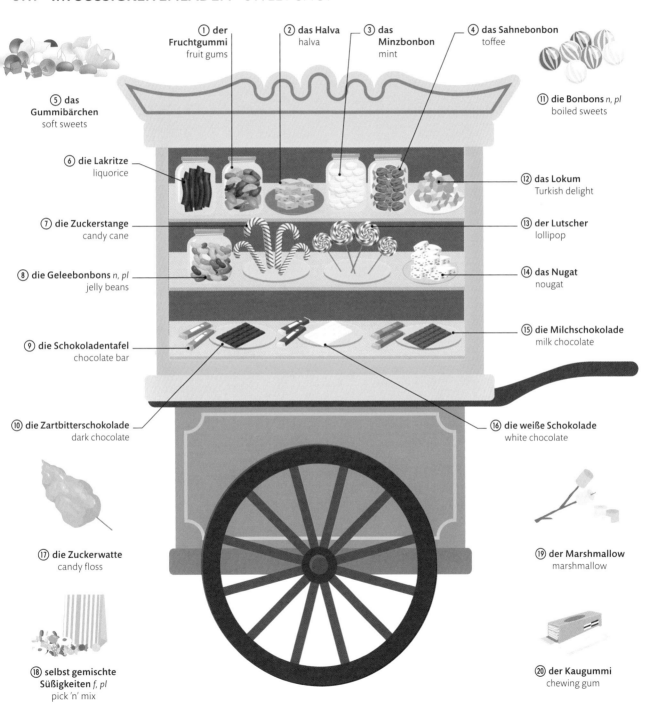

① der Fruchtgummi
fruit gums

② das Halva
halva

③ das Minzbonbon
mint

④ das Sahnebonbon
toffee

⑪ die Bonbons *n, pl*
boiled sweets

⑤ das Gummibärchen
soft sweets

⑥ die Lakritze
liquorice

⑫ das Lokum
Turkish delight

⑦ die Zuckerstange
candy cane

⑬ der Lutscher
lollipop

⑧ die Geleebonbons *n, pl*
jelly beans

⑭ das Nugat
nougat

⑨ die Schokoladentafel
chocolate bar

⑮ die Milchschokolade
milk chocolate

⑩ die Zartbitterschokolade
dark chocolate

⑯ die weiße Schokolade
white chocolate

⑰ die Zuckerwatte
candy floss

⑲ der Marshmallow
marshmallow

⑱ selbst gemischte Süßigkeiten *f, pl*
pick 'n' mix

⑳ der Kaugummi
chewing gum

68.1 DIE BAR · BAR

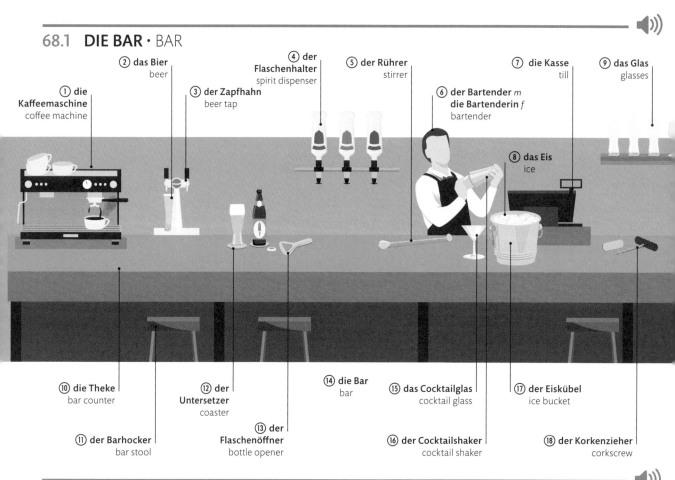

① die **Kaffeemaschine**
coffee machine

② das **Bier**
beer

③ der **Zapfhahn**
beer tap

④ der **Flaschenhalter**
spirit dispenser

⑤ der **Rührer**
stirrer

⑥ der **Bartender** *m*
die **Bartenderin** *f*
bartender

⑦ die **Kasse**
till

⑧ das **Eis**
ice

⑨ das **Glas**
glasses

⑩ die **Theke**
bar counter

⑪ der **Barhocker**
bar stool

⑫ der **Untersetzer**
coaster

⑬ der **Flaschenöffner**
bottle opener

⑭ die **Bar**
bar

⑮ das **Cocktailglas**
cocktail glass

⑯ der **Cocktailshaker**
cocktail shaker

⑰ der **Eiskübel**
ice bucket

⑱ der **Korkenzieher**
corkscrew

68.2 BIER UND WEIN · BEER AND WINE

① das **Lagerbier**
lager

② das **Pilsner**
Pilsner

③ das **Weizenbier**
wheat beer

④ das **India Pale Ale**
Indian pale ale (IPA)

⑤ das **Ale**
ale

⑥ das **Starkbier**
stout

⑦ das **alkoholfreie Bier**
alcohol-free beer

⑧ der **Rotwein**
red wine

⑨ der **Weißwein**
white wine

⑩ der **Rosé**
rosé

⑪ der **Sekt**
sparkling wine

⑫ der **Champagner**
Champagne

See also
52 Trinken und essen • Drinking and eating **69** Im Restaurant • At the restaurant **72** Das Mittagessen und das Abendessen • Lunch and dinner

68.3 GETRÄNKE · DRINKS

① das **Mineralwasser**
mineral water

② der Cidre
cider

③ der Rum
rum

④ Rum und Cola *m*
rum and cola

⑤ der Wodka
vodka

⑥ der Wodka **Orange**
vodka and orange

⑦ der Gin Tonic
gin and tonic

② der Martini
Martini

⑨ der Cocktail
cocktail

⑩ der alkoholfreie **Cocktail**
mocktail

⑪ der Sherry
sherry

⑫ der Portwein
port

⑬ der Whisky
whisky

⑭ der Whisky mit **Wasser**
Scotch and water

⑮ der Branntwein
brandy

⑯ der Likör
liqueur

⑰ mit Eis
with ice

⑱ ohne Eis
without ice

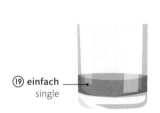

⑲ einfach
single

⑳ doppelt
double

㉑ ein Shot
shot

㉒ das Maß
measure

㉓ Eis und Zitrone *n / f*
ice and lemon

㉔ die Zange
tongs

68.4 BARSNACKS · BAR SNACKS

① die Chips *m, pl*
crisps

② die Nüsse *f, pl*
nuts

③ die Mandeln *f, pl*
almonds

④ die Cashew-Nuss *f, pl*
cashew nuts

⑤ die Erdnüsse *f, pl*
peanuts

⑥ die Oliven *f, pl*
olives

69.1 DAS RESTAURANT · RESTAURANT

② **die Weinkarte**
wine list

③ **der Bartender** *m*
die Bartenderin *f*
bartender

④ **der Gast** *m*
die Gästin *f*
customers

① **Was steht heute auf der Tageskarte?**
What are today's specials?

⑫ **die Restaurantleitung**
restaurant manager

⑭ **Ein Tisch für zwei, bitte.**
May we have a table for two, please?

⑪ **die Kellnerin**
waitress

⑬ **das Gedeck**
table setting

⑱ **das Menü**
set menu

⑲ **der Brunch**
brunch

⑳ **die Mittagskarte**
lunch menu

㉑ **das À-la-Carte-Menü**
à la carte menu

㉒ **die Tageskarte**
specials

㉓ **das Kindermenü**
child's meal

㉔ **das Buffet**
buffet

㉕ **das Dreigängemenü**
three-course meal

㉖ **die Suppe**
soup

㉗ **die Vorspeise**
starter

㉘ **die Hauptspeise**
main course

㉙ **die Beilage**
side / side order

㉚ **die Käseplatte**
cheese platter

㉛ **das Dessert**
dessert / pudding

㉜ **das Getränk**
beverage

㉝ **der Kaffee**
coffee

㉞ **der Digestif**
digestif

See also
27 Die Küche und das Geschirr · Kitchen and tableware **52** Trinken und essen
Drinking and eating **53** Fleisch · Meat **54** Fisch und Meeresfrüchte · Fish and seafood
55-56 Gemüse · Vegetables **72** Das Mittagessen und das Abendessen · Lunch and dinner

⑤ **der Preis**
price

⑥ **das Tablett**
tray

⑦ **Ich wünsche guten Appetit!**
Enjoy your meal!

⑧ **die Küche**
kitchen

⑨ **der Koch** *m*
die Köchin *f*
chef

⑩ **der Assistenzkoch** *m*
die Assistenzköchin *f*
commis chef

⑮ **die Abendkarte**
evening menu

⑯ **der Kellner**
waiter

⑰ **der Dessertwagen**
sweet trolley

㉟ **der Sommelier** *m*
die Sommelière *f*
sommelier

㊱ **essen gehen**
to eat out

㊲ **einen Tisch reservieren**
to make a reservation

㊳ **absagen**
to cancel

㊴ **bestellen**
to order

㊵ **die Rechnung**
bill

㊶ **getrennt zahlen**
to pay separately

㊷ **die Rechnung aufteilen**
to split the bill

㊸ **der Bedienungszuschlag**
service charge

㊹ **Bedienung enthalten**
service included

㊺ **Bedienung nicht enthalten**
service not included

㊻ **das Trinkgeld**
tip

㊼ **der Beleg**
receipt

㊽ **das Bistro**
bistro

70 Fastfood
Fast food

70.1 IM FASTFOOD-RESTAURANT
IN A FAST-FOOD RESTAURANT

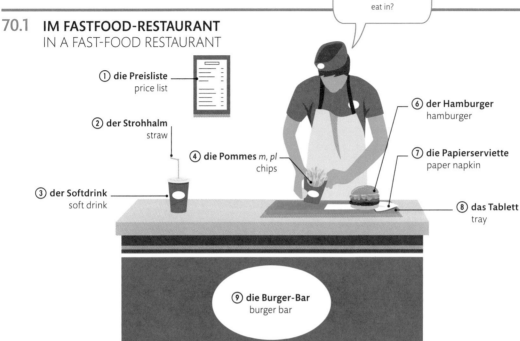

⑤ **Essen Sie hier?**
Is this to eat in?

① **die Preisliste**
price list

② **der Strohhalm**
straw

④ **die Pommes** *m, pl*
chips

③ **der Softdrink**
soft drink

⑥ **der Hamburger**
hamburger

⑦ **die Papierserviette**
paper napkin

⑧ **das Tablett**
tray

⑨ **die Burger-Bar**
burger bar

⑩ **hier essen**
to eat in

⑪ **mitnehmen**
take-away

⑫ **die Lieferung nach Hause**
home delivery

⑭ **die Karte**
menu

⑮ **der Milchshake**
milkshake

⑯ **das Dosengetränk**
canned drink

⑰ **die Limo**
fizzy drink

⑦ **Ihre Bestellung ist unterwegs.**
Your order is on its way.

⑬ **der Straßenverkauf**
street stall

⑱ **das Menü**
meal deal

⑲ **der wiederverwendbare Becher**
reusable cup

⑳ **die Sauce**
sauce

㉑ **der Foodtruck**
food van

㉒ **die Waffel**
waffle

㉓ **das Eis**
ice cream

㉔ **der Muffin**
muffin

㉕ **der Donut**
doughnut

㉖ **der Essenslieferant** *m*
die Essenslieferantin *f*
food delivery driver

See also
52 Trinken und essen • Drinking and eating **60** In der Vorratskammer In the pantry **65** Im Café • At the café **67** Süßigkeiten • Sweets

㉘ **der vegetarische Burger**
veggie burger

㉙ **der Cheeseburger**
cheeseburger

㉚ **der Hähnchenburger**
chicken burger

㉛ **der Burger**
burger

㉜ **die Chicken Nuggets** *n, pl*
chicken nuggets

㉝ **das frittierte Hähnchen**
fried chicken

㉞ **der Kartoffelpuffer**
hash browns

㉟ **Fish and Chips** *pl*
fish and chips

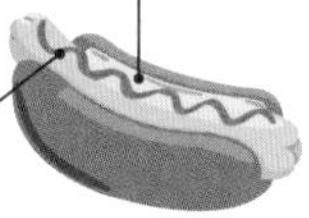

㊱ **der Hotdog**
hot dog

㊲ **der Ketchup**
ketchup

㊳ **der Senf**
mustard

㊴ **der Spieß**
kebab

㊵ **die Rippe**
ribs

㊶ **die Nudeln** *f, pl*
noodles

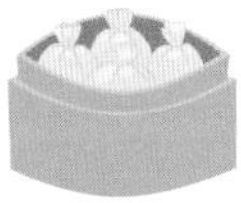

㊷ **die Klöße** *m, pl*
dumplings

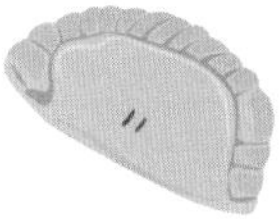

㊸ **die Empanada**
empanada

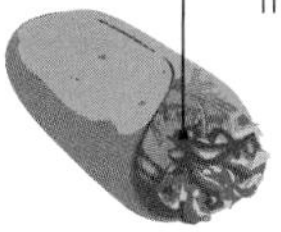

㊹ **der Wrap**
wrap

㊺ **die Füllung**
filling

㊻ **die Crêpe**
crêpe

㊼ **der Taco**
taco

㊽ **die Falafel**
falafel

㊾ **die Nachos** *m, pl*
nachos

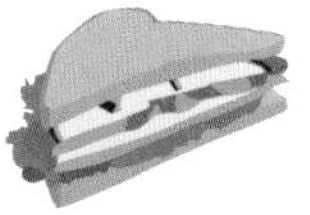

㊿ **das Sandwich**
sandwich

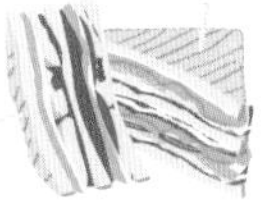

(51) **das Club-Sandwich**
club sandwich

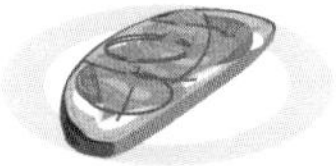

(52) **das belegte Brot**
open sandwich

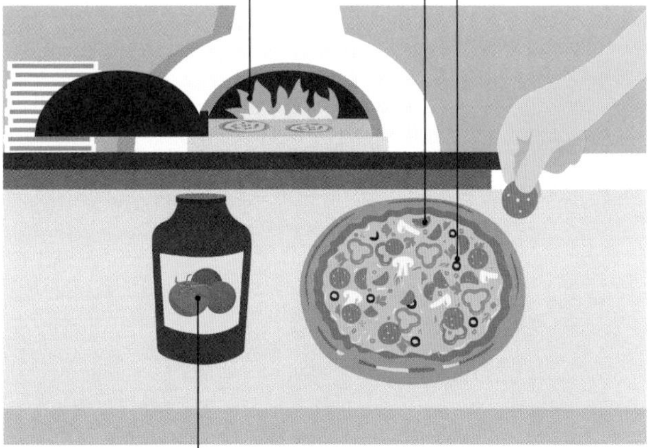

(53) **der Pizzaofen**
pizza oven

(54) **die Pizza**
pizza

(55) **der Belag**
topping

(56) **die Tomatensauce**
tomato sauce

(57) **die Pizzeria**
pizzeria

71 Das Frühstück
Breakfast

71.1 DAS FRÜHSTÜCKSBUFFET · BREAKFAST BUFFET

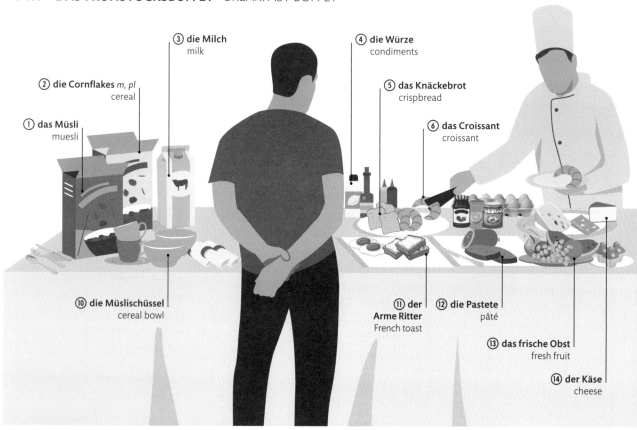

② **die Cornflakes** *m, pl*
cereal

③ **die Milch**
milk

④ **die Würze**
condiments

⑤ **das Knäckebrot**
crispbread

⑥ **das Croissant**
croissant

① **das Müsli**
muesli

⑩ **die Müslischüssel**
cereal bowl

⑪ **der Arme Ritter**
French toast

⑫ **die Pastete**
pâté

⑬ **das frische Obst**
fresh fruit

⑭ **der Käse**
cheese

⑰ **der Schinken**
ham

⑱ **das getoastete Sandwich**
toasted sandwich

⑲ **das Omelett**
omelette

⑳ **der Avocadotoast**
avocado toast

㉑ **der Bagel**
bagel

㉒ **die Zimtschnecke**
cinnamon rolls

㉕ **die Marmelade**
jam

㉖ **die Zitrusmarmelade**
marmalade

㉗ **der Honig**
honey

㉘ **der Tee**
tea

㉙ **der Kaffee**
coffee

㉚ **der Fruchtsaft**
fruit juice

See also
29 Kochen • Cooking **52** Trinken und essen • Drinking and eating **53** Fleisch • Meat
57 Obst • Fruit **58** Obst und Nüsse • Fruit and nuts **61** Milchprodukte • Dairy produce
64 Im Feinkostladen • The delicatessen **65-66** Im Café • At the café

71.2 DAS WARME FRÜHSTÜCK · COOKED BREAKFAST

⑨ **der Brotkorb**
bread basket

⑦ **der Aufschnitt**
cold meats

⑧ **das Brioche**
brioche

⑯ **das Brot**
bread

⑮ **die Butter**
butter

㉓ **die Waffel**
waffles

㉔ **die Sahne**
cream

㉛ **die Trockenfrüchte** *f, pl*
dried fruit

㉜ **der Fruchtjoghurt**
fruit yoghurt

① **das Würstchen**
sausage

② **die Frikadellen** *f, pl*
sausage patties

③ **der Bacon**
bacon

④ **der Bückling**
kippers

⑤ **der Räucherlachs**
smoked salmon

⑥ **die geräucherte Makrele**
smoked mackerel

⑦ **die Blutwurst**
black pudding /
blood sausage

⑧ **die Niere**
kidneys

⑨ **das Rührei**
scrambled eggs

⑩ **das pochierte Ei**
poached egg

⑪ **das gekochte Ei**
boiled egg

⑫ **das Eiweiß**
egg white

⑬ **das Eigelb**
yolk

⑭ **das Spiegelei**
fried egg

⑮ **der Toast**
toast

⑯ **die gebratenen Pilze**
m, pl
fried mushrooms

⑰ **der Kartoffelpuffer**
hash browns

⑱ **die gegrillte Tomate**
grilled tomato

⑲ **die Dosentomaten**
f, pl
tinned tomato

⑳ **die Baked Beans** *f, pl*
baked beans

㉑ **das Frühstücksbrötchen**
breakfast roll

㉒ **der Frühstücksburrito**
breakfast burrito

㉓ **das Kartoffelplätzchen**
potato cakes

㉔ **der Pfannkuchen**
pancakes

㉕ **der Haferbrei**
porridge

72.1 MAHLZEITEN UND GERICHTE · MEALS AND DISHES

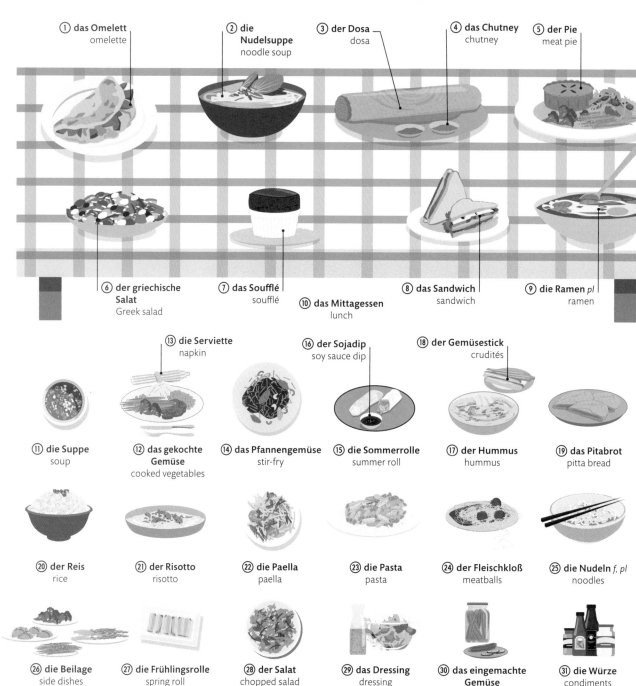

① das Omelett
omelette

② die Nudelsuppe
noodle soup

③ der Dosa
dosa

④ das Chutney
chutney

⑤ der Pie
meat pie

⑥ der griechische Salat
Greek salad

⑦ das Soufflé
soufflé

⑩ das Mittagessen
lunch

⑧ das Sandwich
sandwich

⑨ die Ramen pl
ramen

⑬ die Serviette
napkin

⑯ der Sojadip
soy sauce dip

⑱ der Gemüsestick
crudités

⑪ die Suppe
soup

⑫ das gekochte Gemüse
cooked vegetables

⑭ das Pfannengemüse
stir-fry

⑮ die Sommerrolle
summer roll

⑰ der Hummus
hummus

⑲ das Pitabrot
pitta bread

⑳ der Reis
rice

㉑ der Risotto
risotto

㉒ die Paella
paella

㉓ die Pasta
pasta

㉔ der Fleischkloß
meatballs

㉕ die Nudeln f, pl
noodles

㉖ die Beilage
side dishes

㉗ die Frühlingsrolle
spring roll

㉘ der Salat
chopped salad

㉙ das Dressing
dressing

㉚ das eingemachte Gemüse
pickles

㉛ die Würze
condiments

See also
27 Die Küche und das Geschirr • Kitchen and tableware **29** Kochen • Cooking
52 Trinken und Essen • Drinking and eating **53** Fleisch • Meat **55-56** Gemüse
Vegetables **65-66** Im Café • At the café **69** Im Restaurant • At the restaurant

㉜ **der Gartensalat**
mixed salad

㉝ **der Spieß**
kebab

㉞ **die Brühe**
broth

㉟ **die Teigtasche**
dumplings

㊱ **das chinesische Fondue**
Chinese hotpot

㊲ **das Backhähnchen**
roast chicken

㊳ **das Curry**
curry

㊴ **die Lasagne**
lasagna

㊷ **das Abendessen**
dinner

㊵ **die Spaghetti** pl
spaghetti

㊶ **der Eintopf**
stew

72.2 ZUBEREITUNG · FOOD PREPARATION

① **gefüllt**
stuffed

② **gegrillt**
grilled

③ **mariniert**
marinated

④ **in Sauce**
in sauce

⑤ **pochiert**
poached

⑥ **gekocht**
boiled

⑦ **gebacken**
baked

⑧ **in der Pfanne gebraten**
stir-fried

⑨ **gebraten**
fried

⑩ **frittiert**
deep-fried

⑪ **geräuchert**
smoked

⑫ **gedünstet**
steamed

⑬ **gestampft**
mashed

⑭ **mit Dressing versehen**
dressed

⑮ **gepökelt**
cured

⑯ **eingelegt**
pickled

⑰ **koscher**
kosher

⑱ **halal**
halal

73 In der Schule
At school

73.1 SCHULE UND LERNEN · SCHOOL AND STUDY

① **die Schule**
school

② **das Klassenzimmer**
classroom

③ **die Klasse**
class

④ **der Lehrer** *m*
die Lehrerin *f*
teacher

⑤ **das Whiteboard**
whiteboard

⑥ **der Schüler** *m*
die Schülerin *f*
pupil

⑦ **der Schreibtisch**
desk

⑧ **die Schüler** *pl*
school students

⑨ **die Schultasche**
school bag

⑩ **das Schulbuch**
literature

⑪ **Mathematik** *f*
maths

⑫ **Geografie** *f*
geography

⑬ **Geschichte** *f*
history

⑭ **Naturwissenschaften** *f, pl*
science

⑮ **Chemie** *f*
chemistry

⑯ **Physik** *f*
physics

⑰ **Biologie** *f*
biology

⑱ **Englisch** *n*
English

⑲ **Fremdsprachen** *f, pl*
languages

⑳ **Handwerk** *n*
design and
technology

㉑ **Informatik** *f*
information technology

㉒ **Kunst** *f*
art

㉓ **Musik** *f*
music

㉔ **Schauspiel** *n*
drama

㉕ **Sport** *m*
physical education

㉖ **der Rektor** *m*
die Rektorin *f*
head teacher / principal

㉗ **die
Hausaufgaben** *f, pl*
homework

㉘ **die Unterrichtsstunde**
lesson

㉙ **die Prüfung**
exam

㉚ **der Aufsatz**
essay

㉛ **die Note**
grade

㉜ **das Lexikon**
encyclopedia

㉝ **das Wörterbuch**
dictionary

㉞ **der Atlas**
atlas

㉟ **der Test**
test

See also
74 Mathematik · Mathematics **75** Physik · Physics **76** Chemie · Chemistry
77 Biologie · Biology **79** Geschichte · History **80** An der Universität · At
college **83** Computer und Technologie · Computers and technology

73.2 SCHULVERBEN · SCHOOL VERBS

① **lesen**
to read

② **schreiben**
to write

③ **fragen**
to question

④ **eine Prüfung
machen**
to take an exam

⑤ **lernen**
to learn

⑥ **zeichnen**
to draw

⑦ **antworten**
to answer

⑧ **buchstabieren**
to spell

⑨ **wiederholen**
to revise

⑩ **eine Prüfung
wiederholen**
to resit

⑪ **sich Notizen
machen**
to take notes

⑫ **etwas
besprechen**
to discuss

⑬ **nicht bestehen**
to fail

⑮ **Ich habe meine
Prüfung bestanden!**
I've passed my test.

⑭ **bestehen**
to pass

73.3 MATERIALIEN · EQUIPMENT

① **der Bleistift**
pencil

② **der Spitzer**
pencil sharpener

③ **der Stift**
pen

④ **die Feder**
nib

⑤ **der Radiergummi**
rubber

⑥ **der Buntstift**
coloured pencils

⑦ **die Federmappe**
pencil case

⑧ **das Lineal**
ruler

⑨ **das
Zeichendreieck**
set square

⑩ **der
Winkelmesser**
protractor

⑪ **der
Taschenrechner**
calculator

⑫ **der Zirkel**
compass

⑬ **das Schulbuch**
textbook

⑭ **das Heft**
notebook /
exercise book

⑮ **der Projektor**
digital projector

⑯ **der Textmarker**
highlighter

⑰ **die Büroklammer**
paper clip

⑱ **der Hefter**
stapler

74.1 FORMEN · SHAPES

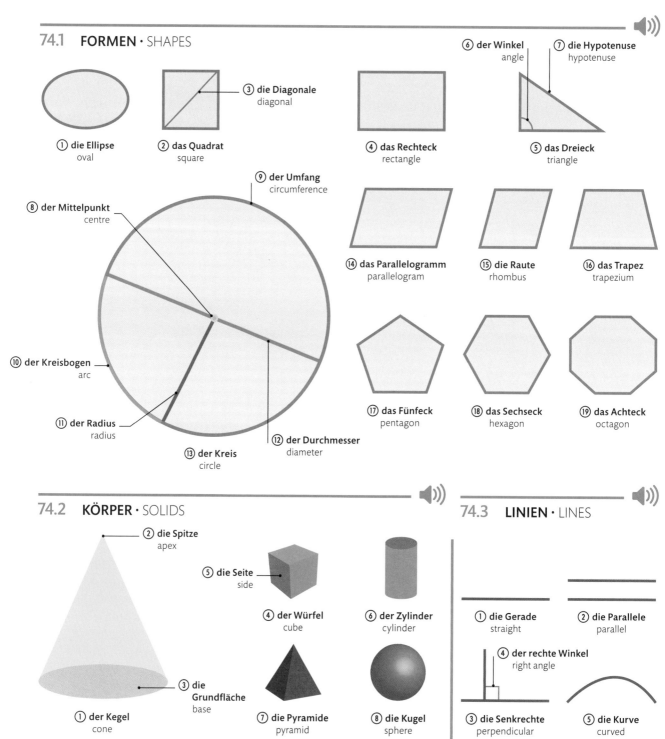

① die Ellipse
oval

② das Quadrat
square

③ die Diagonale
diagonal

④ das Rechteck
rectangle

⑤ das Dreieck
triangle

⑥ der Winkel
angle

⑦ die Hypotenuse
hypotenuse

⑧ der Mittelpunkt
centre

⑨ der Umfang
circumference

⑩ der Kreisbogen
arc

⑪ der Radius
radius

⑫ der Durchmesser
diameter

⑬ der Kreis
circle

⑭ das Parallelogramm
parallelogram

⑮ die Raute
rhombus

⑯ das Trapez
trapezium

⑰ das Fünfeck
pentagon

⑱ das Sechseck
hexagon

⑲ das Achteck
octagon

74.2 KÖRPER · SOLIDS

② die Spitze
apex

⑤ die Seite
side

④ der Würfel
cube

⑥ der Zylinder
cylinder

③ die Grundfläche
base

① der Kegel
cone

⑦ die Pyramide
pyramid

⑧ die Kugel
sphere

74.3 LINIEN · LINES

① die Gerade
straight

② die Parallele
parallel

④ der rechte Winkel
right angle

③ die Senkrechte
perpendicular

⑤ die Kurve
curved

See also
73 In der Schule · At school **94** Geld und Finanzen · Money and finance
173 Zahlen · Numbers **174** Gewichte und Maße · Weights and measures

74.4 **MESSUNGEN** · MEASUREMENTS

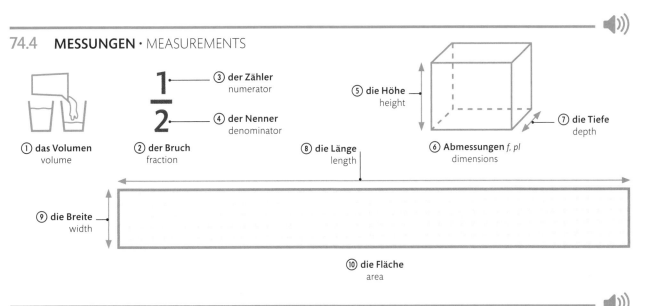

① **das Volumen**
volume

② **der Bruch**
fraction

③ **der Zähler**
numerator

④ **der Nenner**
denominator

⑤ **die Höhe**
height

⑥ **Abmessungen** *f, pl*
dimensions

⑦ **die Tiefe**
depth

⑧ **die Länge**
length

⑨ **die Breite**
width

⑩ **die Fläche**
area

74.5 **BERECHNUNGEN** · OPERATIONS

① **das Pluszeichen**
plus sign

② **das Minuszeichen**
minus sign

③ **das Multiplikationszeichen**
multiplication sign

④ **das Divisionszeichen**
division sign

⑤ **das Gleichheitszeichen**
equals

⑥ **zählen**
to count

⑦ **addieren**
to add

⑧ **subtrahieren**
to subtract

⑨ **multiplizieren**
to multiply

⑩ **dividieren**
to divide

⑪ **die Gleichung**
equation

⑫ **der Prozentsatz**
percentage

74.6 **MATHEMATISCHES WERKZEUG**
MATHEMATICAL EQUIPMENT

⑥ **Mit dem Taschenrechner ist das Addieren so viel einfacher!**
Addition is so much easier using a calculator.

① **das Zeichendreieck**
set square

② **der Winkelmesser**
protractor

③ **das Lineal**
ruler

④ **der Zirkel**
compass

⑤ **der Taschenrechner**
calculator

75.1 **PHYSIK** · PHYSICS

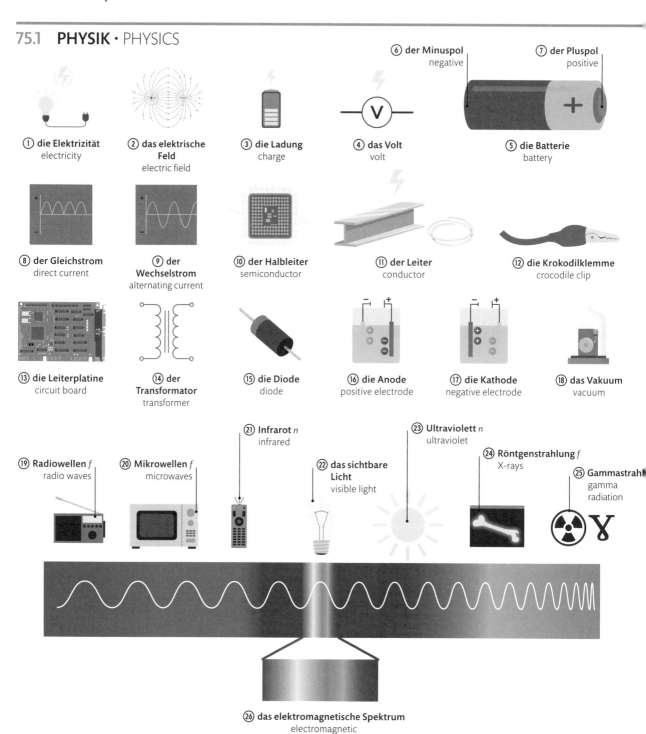

① **die Elektrizität**
electricity

② **das elektrische Feld**
electric field

③ **die Ladung**
charge

④ **das Volt**
volt

⑤ **die Batterie**
battery

⑥ **der Minuspol**
negative

⑦ **der Pluspol**
positive

⑧ **der Gleichstrom**
direct current

⑨ **der Wechselstrom**
alternating current

⑩ **der Halbleiter**
semiconductor

⑪ **der Leiter**
conductor

⑫ **die Krokodilklemme**
crocodile clip

⑬ **die Leiterplatine**
circuit board

⑭ **der Transformator**
transformer

⑮ **die Diode**
diode

⑯ **die Anode**
positive electrode

⑰ **die Kathode**
negative electrode

⑱ **das Vakuum**
vacuum

⑲ **Radiowellen** _f_
radio waves

⑳ **Mikrowellen** _f_
microwaves

㉑ **Infrarot** _n_
infrared

㉒ **das sichtbare Licht**
visible light

㉓ **Ultraviolett** _n_
ultraviolet

㉔ **Röntgenstrahlung** _f_
X-rays

㉕ **Gammastrahl**
gamma radiation

㉖ **das elektromagnetische Spektrum**
electromagnetic spectrum

See also
73 In der Schule · At school **74** Mathematik · Mathematics **76** Chemie · Chemistry
77 Biologie · Biology **78** Das Periodensystem · The periodic table

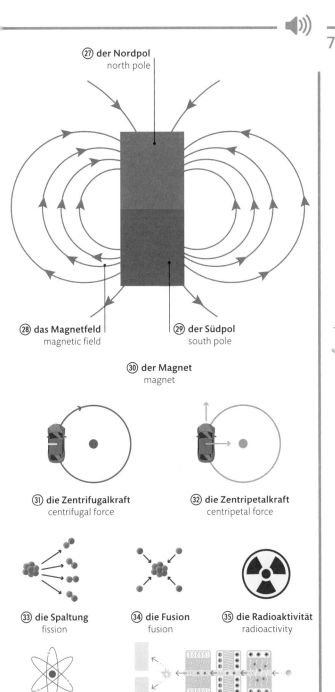

㉗ **der Nordpol**
north pole

㉘ **das Magnetfeld**
magnetic field

㉙ **der Südpol**
south pole

㉚ **der Magnet**
magnet

㉛ **die Zentrifugalkraft**
centrifugal force

㉜ **die Zentripetalkraft**
centripetal force

㉝ **die Spaltung**
fission

㉞ **die Fusion**
fusion

㉟ **die Radioaktivität**
radioactivity

㊱ **das Teilchen**
particle

㊲ **der Teilchenbeschleuniger**
particle accelerator

75.2 **OPTIK** · OPTICS

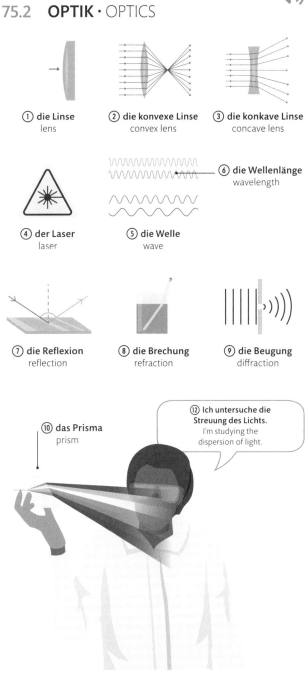

① **die Linse**
lens

② **die konvexe Linse**
convex lens

③ **die konkave Linse**
concave lens

⑥ **die Wellenlänge**
wavelength

④ **der Laser**
laser

⑤ **die Welle**
wave

⑦ **die Reflexion**
reflection

⑧ **die Brechung**
refraction

⑨ **die Beugung**
diffraction

⑩ **das Prisma**
prism

⑫ **Ich untersuche die Streuung des Lichts.**
I'm studying the dispersion of light.

⑪ **die Streuung**
dispersion

76 Chemie
Chemistry

76.1 IM LABOR · IN THE LABORATORY

⑧ **Ich mache ein Experiment.**
I'm carrying out an experiment.

① **der Rundkolben**
glass bottle

② **die Klemme**
clamp

③ **das Experiment**
experiment

④ **der Trichter**
funnel

⑦ **der Chemiker** *m*
die Chemikerin *f*
chemist

⑤ **der Stopfen**
stopper

⑥ **das Reagenzglas**
test tube

⑩ **der Tiegel**
crucible

⑫ **der Erlmeierkolben**
flask

⑬ **der Reagenzglasständer**
test tube rack

⑪ **der Bunsenbrenner**
Bunsen burner

⑨ **der Dreifuß**
tripod

⑭ **das Labor**
laboratory / lab

⑮ **die Waage**
scales

⑯ **der Zeitmesser**
timer

⑰ **das Thermometer**
thermometer

⑱ **die Zange**
tongs

⑲ **der Spatel**
spatula

⑳ **der Stößel**
pestle

㉑ **der Mörser**
mortar

㉒ **das Filterpapier**
filter paper

㉓ **die Pipette**
dropper

㉔ **die Pipette**
pipette

㉕ **der Becher**
beaker

㉖ **der Glasstab**
glass rod

㉗ **die Schutzbrille**
safety goggles

See also
73 In der Schule • At school **74** Mathematik • Mathematics **75** Physik • Physics **77** Biologie • Biology
78 Das Periodensystem • The periodic table

Wasserstoffmoleküle
2 hydrogen molecules

1 Sauerstoffmolekül
1 oxygen molecule

2 Wassermoleküle
2 water molecules

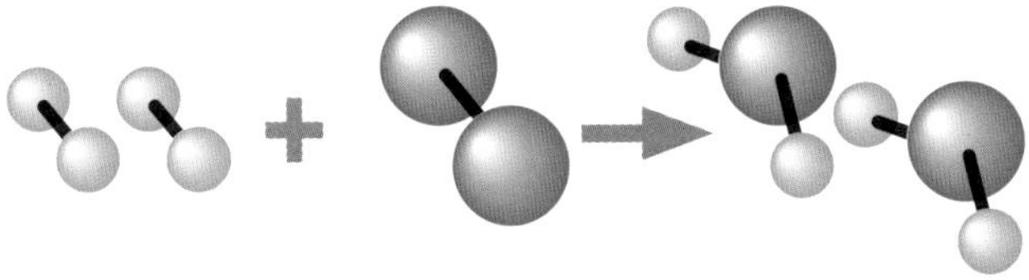

$$2H_2 + O_2 \rightarrow 2H_2O$$

㉙ **das chemische Symbol**
chemical symbol

㉚ **das tiefgestellte Zeichen**
subscript

㉘ **die Reaktionsgleichung**
chemical equation

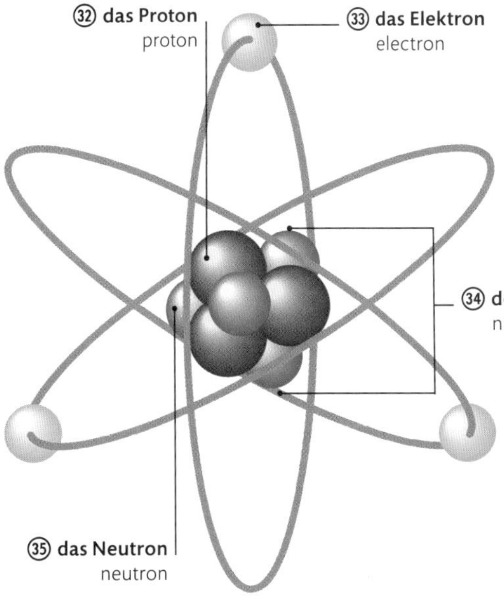

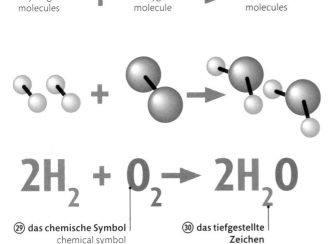

㉜ **das Proton**
proton

㉝ **das Elektron**
electron

㉞ **der Kern**
nucleus

㉟ **das Neutron**
neutron

㉛ **das Atom**
atom

$$H_2O$$

㊱ **die chemische Formel**
chemical formula

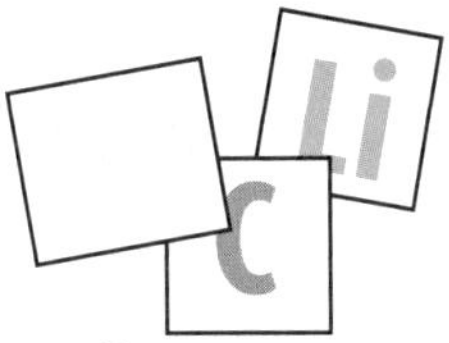
Li
C

㊲ **das Element**
elements

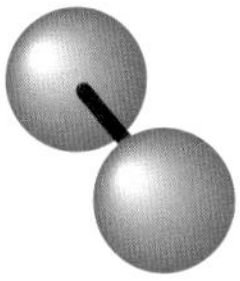

㊳ **das Molekül**
molecule

㊵ **die Sauer**
acid

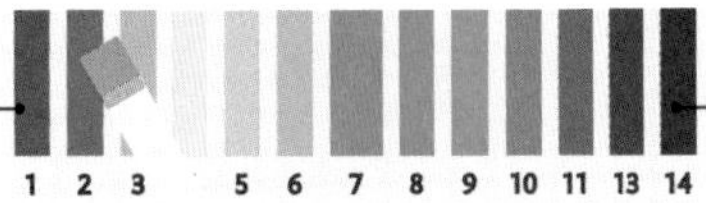
1 2 3 5 6 7 8 9 10 11 13 14

㊶ **das Basisch**
alkali

㊴ **der pH-Wert**
pH level

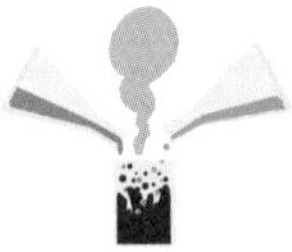

㊷ **die Reaktion**
reaction

$$Q<K$$

㊸ **die Reaktionsrichtung**
reaction direction

$$Q \rightleftharpoons K$$

㊹ **die umkehrbare Reaktion**
reversible direction

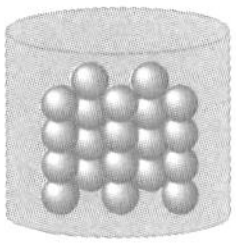

㊺ **der Feststoff**
solid

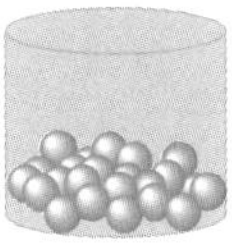

㊻ **die Flüssigkeit**
liquid

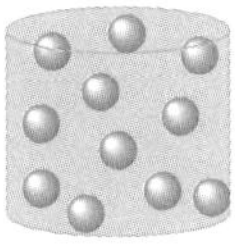

㊼ **das Gas**
gas

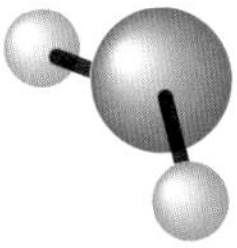

㊽ **die Verbindung**
compound

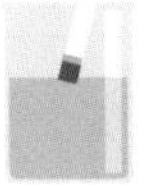

㊾ **die Base**
base

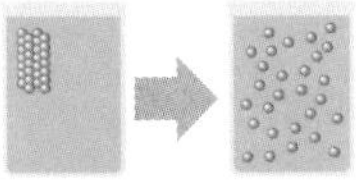

㊿ **die Diffusion**
diffusion

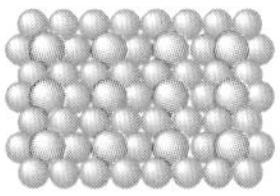

(51) **die Legierung**
alloy

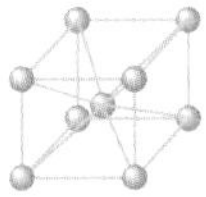

(52) **der Kristall**
crystal

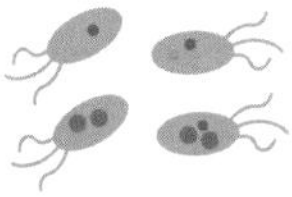

(53) **die Biochemie**
biochemistry

77.1 BIOLOGIE · BIOLOGY

① der Biologe *m*
die Biologin *f*
biologist

② die Mikrobiologie
microbiology

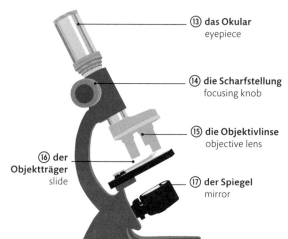

③ der Mikrobiologe *m*
die Mikrobiologin *f*
microbiologist

⑬ das Okular
eyepiece

⑭ die Scharfstellung
focusing knob

⑮ die Objektivlinse
objective lens

⑯ der Objektträger
slide

⑰ der Spiegel
mirror

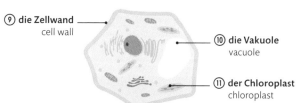

④ der Zellkern
nucleus

⑤ die Mitochondrie
mitochondria

⑥ die Zellmembran
cell membrane

⑦ das Zytoplasma
cytoplasm

⑧ die tierische Zelle
animal cell

⑱ das Mikroskop
microscope

⑨ die Zellwand
cell wall

⑩ die Vakuole
vacuole

⑪ der Chloroplast
chloroplast

⑫ die pflanzliche Zelle
plant cell

⑲ das rote Blutkörperchen
red blood cell

⑳ das weiße Blutkörperchen
white blood cell

㉑ das Chromosom
chromosome

㉒ das Ge[n]
gene

㉓ die DNS
DNA

㉔ das Virus
virus

㉕ die Bakterie
bacteria

㉗ die Pinzette
tweezers

㉖ die Petrischale
petri dish

㉘ das Skalpell
scalpel

㉙ die Spritze
syringe

㉚ die Zoologie
zoology

㉛ der Zoologe *m*
die Zoologin *f*
zoologist

㉜ das Plankton
plankton

㉝ das wirbellose Tier
invertebrate

㉞ das Wirbeltier
vertebrate

㉟ die Art
species

See also
157 Die Naturgeschichte · Natural history **158-159** Säugetiere · Mammals **160-161** Vögel · Birds
162 Insekten und Käfer · Insects and bugs **163** Amphibien und Reptilien · Amphibians and reptiles
166 Leben im Ozean · Ocean life **167-169** Pflanzen und Bäume · Plants and trees **170** Pilze · Fungi

㊱ **das Ökosystem**
ecosystem

㊲ **das Exoskelett**
exoskeleton

㊳ **das Endoskelett**
endoskeleton

㊴ **die Vermehrung**
reproduction

㊵ **der Winterschlaf**
hibernation

㊶ **die Botanik**
botany

㊷ **der Botaniker** *m*
die Botanikerin *f*
botanist

㊸ **die Pflanze**
plant

㊹ **der Pilz**
fungi

㊺ **die Fotosynthese**
photosynthesis

㊻ **der Paläontologe** *m*
die Paläontologin *f*
paleontologist

㊼ **das Fossil**
fossil

㊽ **die Evolution**
evolution

77.2 **METAMORPHOSE** · METAMORPHOSIS

① **der Schmetterling**
butterfly

② **das Ei**
egg

④ **die Puppe**
chrysalis

③ **die Raupe**
caterpillar

⑤ **der Lebenszyklus eines Schmetterlings**
life cycle of a butterfly

⑥ **der ausgewachsene Frosch**
adult frog

⑦ **der Froschlaich**
frog spawn

⑧ **die Kaulquappe**
tadpole

⑨ **der junge Frosch**
young frog

⑩ **der Lebenszyklus eines Froschs**
life cycle of a frog

Das Periodensystem
The periodic table

78.1 DAS PERIODENSYSTEM DER ELEMENTE • THE PERIODIC TABLE

- (119) **Alkalimetalle** *n, pl* alkali metals
- (120) **Erdalkalimetalle** *n, pl* alkaline earth metals
- (121) **Übergangsmetalle** *n, pl* transition metals
- (122) **Lanthanoide** *n, pl* lanthanide series
- (124) **Metalle** *n, pl* other metals
- (125) **Halbmetalle** *n, pl* semi-metals
- (126) **Nichtmetalle** *n, pl* non-metals
- (127) **Halogene** *n, pl* halogens

(1) **H** **Wasserstoff** *m* hydrogen								
(3) **Li** **Lithium** *n* lithium	(4) **Be** **Beryllium** *n* beryllium							
(11) **Na** **Natrium** *n* sodium	(12) **Mg** **Magnesium** *n* magnesium							
(19) **K** **Kalium** *n* potassium	(20) **Ca** **Kalzium** *n* calcium	(21) **Sc** **Skandium** *n* scandium	(22) **Ti** **Titan** *n* titanium	(23) **V** **Vanadium** *n* vanadium	(24) **Cr** **Chrom** *n* chromium	(25) **Mn** **Mangan** *n* manganese	(26) **Fe** **Eisen** *n* iron	(27) **Co** **Kobalt** *n* cobalt
(37) **Rb** **Rubidium** *n* rubidium	(38) **Sr** **Strontium** *n* strontium	(39) **Y** **Yttrium** *n* yttrium	(40) **Zr** **Zirkonium** *n* zirconium	(41) **Nb** **Niob** *n* niobium	(42) **Mo** **Molybdän** *n* molybdenum	(43) **Tc** **Technetium** *n* technetium	(44) **Ru** **Ruthenium** *n* ruthenium	(45) **Rh** **Rhodium** *n* rhodium
(55) **Cs** **Cäsium** *n* caesium	(56) **Ba** **Barium** *n* barium	**La-Lu**	(72) **Hf** **Hafnium** *n* hafnium	(73) **Ta** **Tantal** *n* tantalum	(74) **W** **Wolfram** *n* tungsten	(75) **Re** **Rhenium** *n* rhenium	(76) **Os** **Osmium** *n* osmium	(77) **Ir** **Iridium** *n* iridium
(87) **Fr** **Francium** *n* francium	(88) **Ra** **Radium** *n* radium	**Ac-Lr**	(104) **Rf** **Rutherfordium** *n* rutherfordium	(105) **Db** **Dubnium** *n* dubnium	(106) **Sg** **Seaborgium** *n* seaborgium	(107) **Bh** **Bohrium** *n* bohrium	(108) **Hs** **Hassium** *n* hassium	(109) **Mt** **Meitnerium** *n* meitnerium

(57) **La** **Lanthan** *n* lanthanum	(58) **Ce** **Cer** *n* cerium	(59) **Pr** **Praseodym** *n* praseodymium	(60) **Nd** **Neodym** *n* neodymium	(61) **Pm** **Promethium** *n* promethium	(62) **Sm** **Samarium** *n* samarium
(89) **Ac** **Actinium** *n* actinium	(90) **Th** **Thorium** *n* thorium	(91) **Pa** **Protactinium** *n* protactinium	(92) **U** **Uran** *n* uranium	(93) **Np** **Neptunium** *n* neptunium	(94) **Pu** **Plutonium** *n* plutonium

(130) **Elemente sind Reinstoffe.**
Elements are pure substances.

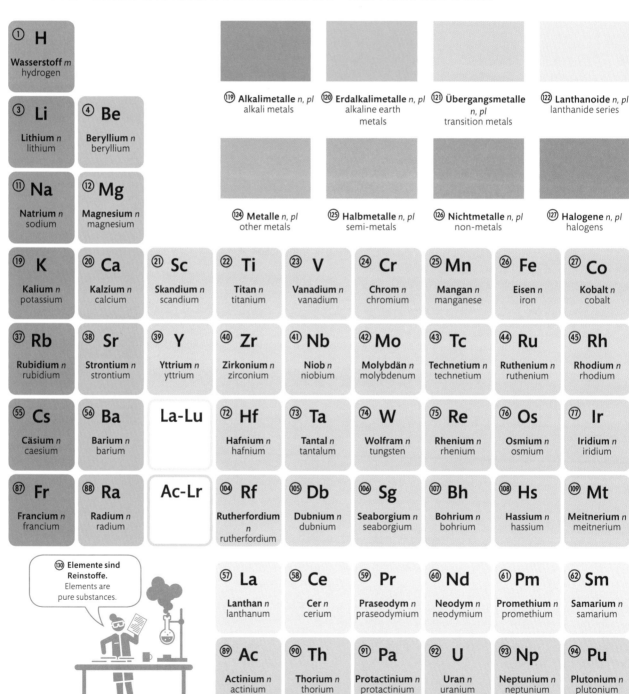

See also
73 In der Schule · At school **75** Physik · Physics **76** Chemie · Chemistry
156 Gesteine und Mineralien · Rocks and minerals

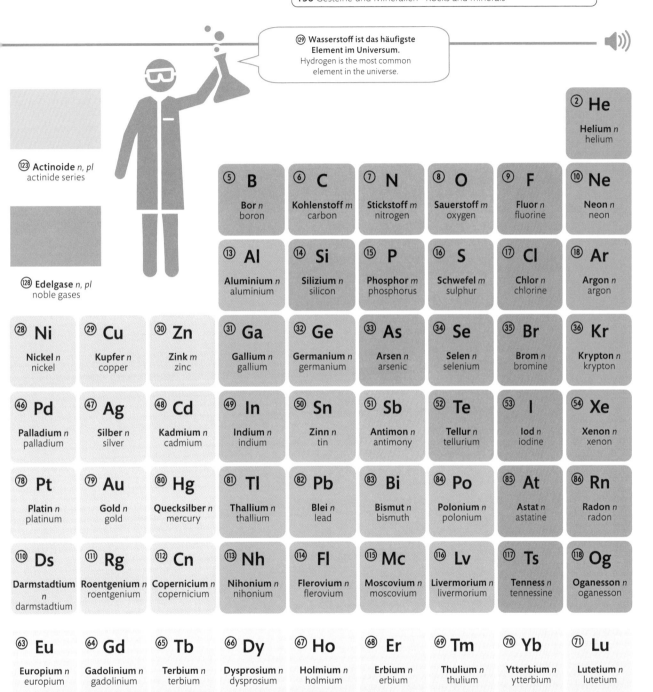

⑫⑨ **Wasserstoff ist das häufigste Element im Universum.**
Hydrogen is the most common element in the universe.

⑫③ **Actinoide** *n, pl*
actinide series

⑫⑧ **Edelgase** *n, pl*
noble gases

② **He**
Helium *n*
helium

⑤ **B**
Bor *n*
boron

⑥ **C**
Kohlenstoff *m*
carbon

⑦ **N**
Stickstoff *m*
nitrogen

⑧ **O**
Sauerstoff *m*
oxygen

⑨ **F**
Fluor *n*
fluorine

⑩ **Ne**
Neon *n*
neon

⑬ **Al**
Aluminium *n*
aluminium

⑭ **Si**
Silizium *n*
silicon

⑮ **P**
Phosphor *m*
phosphorus

⑯ **S**
Schwefel *m*
sulphur

⑰ **Cl**
Chlor *n*
chlorine

⑱ **Ar**
Argon *n*
argon

㉘ **Ni**
Nickel *n*
nickel

㉙ **Cu**
Kupfer *n*
copper

㉚ **Zn**
Zink *m*
zinc

㉛ **Ga**
Gallium *n*
gallium

㉜ **Ge**
Germanium *n*
germanium

㉝ **As**
Arsen *n*
arsenic

㉞ **Se**
Selen *n*
selenium

㉟ **Br**
Brom *n*
bromine

㊱ **Kr**
Krypton *n*
krypton

㊻ **Pd**
Palladium *n*
palladium

㊼ **Ag**
Silber *n*
silver

㊽ **Cd**
Kadmium *n*
cadmium

㊾ **In**
Indium *n*
indium

㊿ **Sn**
Zinn *n*
tin

51 **Sb**
Antimon *n*
antimony

52 **Te**
Tellur *n*
tellurium

53 **I**
Iod *n*
iodine

54 **Xe**
Xenon *n*
xenon

78 **Pt**
Platin *n*
platinum

79 **Au**
Gold *n*
gold

80 **Hg**
Quecksilber *n*
mercury

81 **Tl**
Thallium *n*
thallium

82 **Pb**
Blei *n*
lead

83 **Bi**
Bismut *n*
bismuth

84 **Po**
Polonium *n*
polonium

85 **At**
Astat *n*
astatine

86 **Rn**
Radon *n*
radon

110 **Ds**
Darmstadtium *n*
darmstadtium

111 **Rg**
Roentgenium *n*
roentgenium

112 **Cn**
Copernicium *n*
copernicium

113 **Nh**
Nihonium *n*
nihonium

114 **Fl**
Flerovium *n*
flerovium

115 **Mc**
Moscovium *n*
moscovium

116 **Lv**
Livermorium *n*
livermorium

117 **Ts**
Tenness *n*
tennessine

118 **Og**
Oganesson *n*
oganesson

63 **Eu**
Europium *n*
europium

64 **Gd**
Gadolinium *n*
gadolinium

65 **Tb**
Terbium *n*
terbium

66 **Dy**
Dysprosium *n*
dysprosium

67 **Ho**
Holmium *n*
holmium

68 **Er**
Erbium *n*
erbium

69 **Tm**
Thulium *n*
thulium

70 **Yb**
Ytterbium *n*
ytterbium

71 **Lu**
Lutetium *n*
lutetium

95 **Am**
Americium *n*
americium

96 **Cm**
Curium *n*
curium

97 **Bk**
Berkelium *n*
berkelium

98 **Cf**
Californium *n*
californium

99 **Es**
Einsteinium *n*
einsteinium

100 **Fm**
Fermium *n*
fermium

101 **Md**
Mendelevium *n*
mendelevium

102 **No**
Nobelium *n*
nobelium

103 **Lr**
Lawrencium *n*
lawrencium

79.1 KRIEG UND WAFFEN · WAR AND WEAPONS

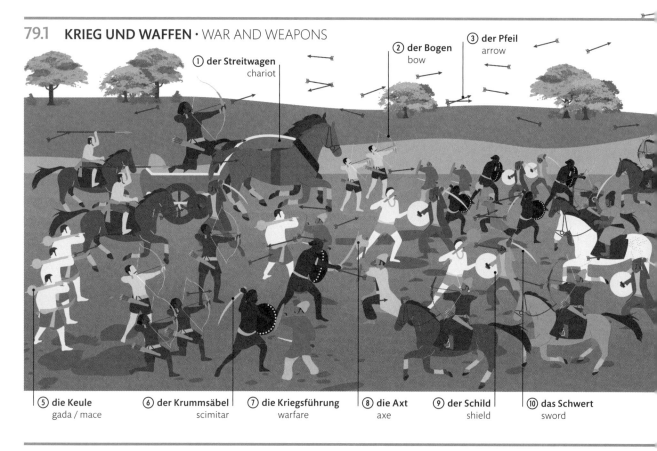

① **der Streitwagen**
chariot

② **der Bogen**
bow

③ **der Pfeil**
arrow

⑤ **die Keule**
gada / mace

⑥ **der Krummsäbel**
scimitar

⑦ **die Kriegsführung**
warfare

⑧ **die Axt**
axe

⑨ **der Schild**
shield

⑩ **das Schwert**
sword

79.2 DER MENSCH IM WANDEL DER ZEIT · PEOPLE THROUGH TIME

② **das Feuersteinwerkzeug**
flint tools

① **die Steinzeit**
the Stone Age

③ **die Bronzezeit**
the Bronze Age

④ **die Eisenzeit**
the Iron age

⑤ **der Bauer** m
die Bäuerin f
farmer

⑥ **der Händler** m
die Händlerin f
merchant

⑦ **der Handwerker** m
die Handwerkerin f
artisan

⑫ **der Kaiser**
emperor

⑬ **die Kaiserin**
empress

⑭ **der König**
king

⑮ **die Königin**
queen

⑯ **der Prinz** m
die Prinzessin f
prince / princess

⑰ **der Adel**
nobles

㉒ **die Blütezeit des Islam**
the Islamic Golden Age

㉔ **die Aufklärung**
the Enlightenment

㉕ **die industrielle Revolution**
the Industrial Revolution

㉓ **der Philosoph** m
die Philosophin f
philosopher

See also
44 Gebäude und Architektur • Buildings and architecture **73** In der Schule • At school
80 An der Universität • At college **88** Das Militär • Military

④ **der Speer**
spear

⑬ **die Schlacht**
battle

⑭ **die Kanone**
cannon

⑮ **das Katapult**
catapult

⑯ **der Rammbock**
battering ram

⑰ **der Ritter**
knight

⑱ **die Rüstung**
armour

⑲ **der Krieger** *m*
die Kriegerin *f*
warrior

⑪ **das Schlachtross**
warhorse

⑫ **der Kriegselefant**
war elephant

79.3 DIE ERFORSCHUNG DER VERGANGENHEIT
STUDYING THE PAST

① **der Historiker** *m*
die Historikerin *f*
historian

② **das Archiv**
archive

③ **die Quelle**
sources

④ **die Schriftrolle**
scroll

⑤ **das Dokument**
document

⑥ **die Archäologie**
archaeology

⑦ **der Archäologe** *m*
die Archäologin *f*
archaeologist

⑧ **die Ausgrabung**
dig / excavation

⑩ **das Torfmoor**
peat bog

⑨ **die Überreste** *m, pl*
remains

⑪ **das Fundstück**
finds

⑫ **das Grab**
tomb

⑬ **die historische Stätte**
historical site

⑧ **der Schmied** *m*
die Schmiedin *f*
blacksmith

⑨ **die Bauernschaft**
peasants

⑩ **das Königreich**
kingdom

⑪ **das Kaiserreich**
empire

⑱ **der Adelsherr** *m*
die Dame *f*
lord / lady

⑲ **der Minnesänger** *m*
die Minnesängerin *f*
minstrel

⑳ **der Narr** *m*
die Närrin *f*
jester

㉑ **der Schreiber** *m*
die Schreiberin *f*
scribe

㉖ **die technologische Revolution**
the Technological Revolution

㉗ **das Informationszeitalter**
the Information Age

㉔

80.1 DIE UNIVERSITÄT · UNIVERSITY

① **der Campus**
campus

② **der Hörsaal**
lecture theatre

③ **der Dozent** m / **die Dozentin** f
lecturer

④ **der Sportplatz**
sports field

⑤ **die Mensa**
refectory

⑥ **das Studentenwohnheim**
halls of residence

⑦ **das Stipendium**
scholarship

⑧ **die Aufnahme**
admissions

⑨ **der Bachelorstudent** m
die Bachelorstudentin f
undergraduate

⑩ **das Diplom**
diploma

⑪ **die Bachelorarbeit**
dissertation

⑫ **der Abschluss**
degree

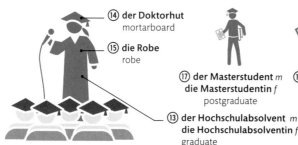

⑭ **der Doktorhut**
mortarboard

⑮ **die Robe**
robe

⑰ **der Masterstudent** m
die Masterstudentin f
postgraduate

⑱ **die Masterarbeit**
thesis

⑲ **der Masterabschluss**
master's degree

⑳ **der Doktortitel**
doctorate

⑬ **der Hochschulabsolvent** m
die Hochschulabsolventin f
graduate

⑯ **die Abschlussfeier**
graduation ceremony

80.2 FACHBEREICHE · DEPARTMENTS AND SCHOOLS

① **Geisteswissenschaften** f, pl
humanities

② **Politik** f
politics

③ **Literatur** f
literature

④ **Sprachen** f, pl
languages

⑤ **Wirtschaft** f
economics

⑥ **Philosophie** f
philosophy

⑦ **Geschichte** f
history

⑧ **Sozialwissenschaften** f, pl
social sciences

⑨ **Soziologie** f
sociology

⑩ **Jura**
law

⑪ **Medizin** f
medicine

⑫ **Krankenpflege** f
nursing

See also
73 In der Schule · At school **74** Mathematik · Mathematics **75** Physik · Physics
76 Chemie · Chemistry **77** Biologie · Biology **79** Geschichte · History
85 Recht · Law **138** Bücher und Lesen · Books and reading

80.3 IN DER BIBLIOTHEK · LIBRARY

① **der Lesesaal**
reading room

② **die Literaturliste**
reading list

③ **ausleihen**
to borrow

④ **verlängern**
to renew

⑤ **zurückgeben**
to return

⑥ **reservieren**
to reserve

⑦ **der Gang**
aisle

⑧ **das Bücherregal**
bookshelf

⑨ **der Bibliothekar** *m*
die Bibliothekarin *f*
librarian

⑩ **der Bibliotheksausweis**
library card

⑪ **die Fachzeitschrift**
periodical / journal

⑫ **das Buch**
book

⑬ **die Bibliothek**
library

⑭ **die Ausleihtheke**
loans desk

⑭ **Ich habe Fördergelder für wissenschaftliche Forschungen erhalten.**
I received a grant to do scientific research.

⑬ **Naturwissenschaften** *f, pl*
sciences

⑮ **Chemie** *f*
chemistry

⑯ **Physik** *f*
physics

⑰ **Biologie** *f*
biology

⑱ **Maschinenbau** *m*
engineering

⑲ **Zoologie** *f*
zoology

⑳ **Musikschule** *f*
music school

㉑ **Tanzschule** *f*
dance school

㉒ **Kunstakademie** *f*
art college / school

81 Auf der Arbeit
At work

81.1 BÜROARBEIT · OFFICE WORK

① **das Unternehmen**
company

② **die Niederlassung**
branch

③ **die Anstellung**
employment

④ **verdienen**
to earn

⑤ **unbefristet**
permanent

⑥ **befristet**
temporary

⑩ **der Bürojob**
nine-to-five job

⑪ **Teilzeit arbeiten**
to work part-time

⑫ **die Schichtarbeit**
to work shifts

⑬ **der Urlaub**
annual leave

⑭ **einen Tag freinehmen**
to have a day off

⑮ **in Elternzeit gehen**
to go on maternity leave

⑲ **sich krank melden**
to call in sick

⑳ **kündigen**
to hand in your notice

㉑ **gekündigt werden**
to get fired

㉒ **entlassen werden**
to be laid off

㉓ **arbeitslos sein**
to be unemployed

㉔ **das Arbeitslosengeld**
unemployment benefit

㉝ **der Vorstandsvorsitzende** *m*
die Vorstandsvorsitzende *f*
CEO (chief executive officer)

㉞ **der Geschäftsmann**
businessman

㊴ **der Manager** *m*
die Managerin *f*
manager

㉙ **der Firmensitz**
headquarters

㉚ **der Rezeptionist** *m*
die Rezeptionistin *f*
receptionist

㊳ **der Auszubildende** *m*
die Auszubildende *f*
apprentice

㊵ **der Assistent** *m*
die Assistentin *f*
PA (personal assistant)

㊶ **die Führungsperson**
leader

㉛ **der Wartebereich**
waiting area

㉟ **der Geschäftsabschluss**
business deal

㊱ **die Geschäftsfrau**
businesswoman

㊷ **der Kunde** *m*
die Kundin *f*
clients

㉘ **der Empfang**
office reception

㉜ **das Vorstandszimmer**
CEO's office

㊲ **die Besprechung**
meeting

See also
82 Im Büro • In the office **89-90** Berufe • Jobs **91** Branchen und Abteilungen • Industries and departments **92** Bewerbungen • Applying for a job **93** Nützliche Fähigkeiten für den Arbeitsplatz • Workplace skills **95** Besprechen and präsentieren • Meeting and presenting

⑦ **die Gleitzeit**
flexitime

⑧ **im Homeoffice arbeiten**
to work from home

⑨ **Vollzeit arbeiten**
to work full-time

⑯ **befördert werden**
to be promoted

⑰ **kündigen**
to resign

⑱ **in Rente gehen**
to retire

㉕ **die Geschäftsreise**
business trip

㉖ **der Termin**
appointment

㉗ **das Geschäftsessen**
business lunch

81.2 ENTLOHNUNG • PAY

① **der Stundensatz**
hourly rate

② **die Überstunde**
overtime

③ **das Gehalt**
salary

④ **der Lohn**
wages

⑤ **die Lohnabrechnung**
pay slip

⑥ **die Prämie**
bonus

⑦ **Zusatzleistungen**
benefits

⑧ **die Gehaltserhöhung**
raise

⑨ **die Gehaltskürzung**
pay cut

㊹ **der Interviewer** *m*
die Interviewerin *f*
interviewer

㊺ **der Bewerber** *m*
die Bewerberin *f*
applicant

㊽ **der Mitarbeiter** *m*
die Mitarbeiterin *f*
worker

㊾ **der Kollege** *m*
die Kollegin *f*
co-worker / colleague

(50) **der Arbeitnehmer** *m*
die Arbeitnehmerin *f*
employee

(51) **die Führungskraft**
supervisor

(52) **der Praktikant** *m*
die Praktikantin *f*
intern

㊻ **der Arbeitgeber** *m* / **die Arbeitgeberin** *f*
employer

㊸ **das Vorstellungsgespräch**
interview

㊼ **das Personal**
staff

(53) **die Büroleitung**
office manager

82.1 DAS BÜRO · OFFICE

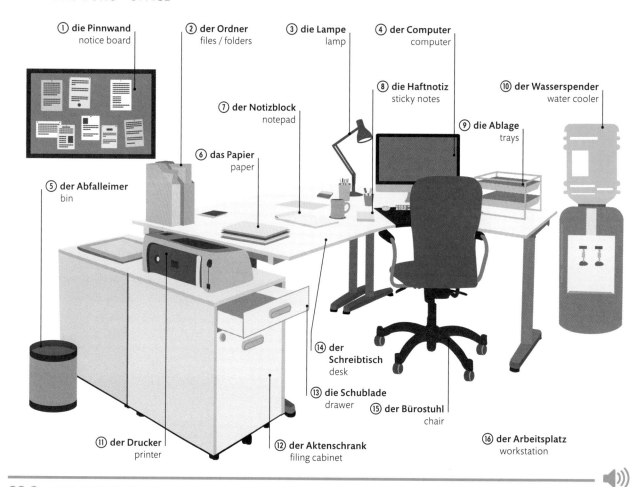

① **die Pinnwand** notice board
② **der Ordner** files / folders
③ **die Lampe** lamp
④ **der Computer** computer
⑦ **der Notizblock** notepad
⑧ **die Haftnotiz** sticky notes
⑩ **der Wasserspender** water cooler
⑨ **die Ablage** trays
⑥ **das Papier** paper
⑤ **der Abfalleimer** bin
⑭ **der Schreibtisch** desk
⑬ **die Schublade** drawer
⑮ **der Bürostuhl** chair
⑯ **der Arbeitsplatz** workstation
⑪ **der Drucker** printer
⑫ **der Aktenschrank** filing cabinet

82.2 DIE AUSSTATTUNG DES BESPRECHUNGSZIMMERS · MEETING-ROOM EQUIPMENT

① **die Präsentation** presentation
② **das Angebot** proposal
③ **der Bericht** report
⑥ **das Flip** flip char
④ **der Beamer** digital projector
⑤ **die Besprechung** meeting
⑦ **der Stän** easel

See also
81 Auf der Arbeit · At work **83** Computer und Technologie · Computers and technology **91** Branchen und Abteilungen · Industries and departments **92** Bewerbungen · Applying for a job **93** Nützliche Fähigkeiten für den Arbeitsplatz · Workplace skills **95** Besprechen and präsentieren · Meeting and presenting

82.3 BÜROMATERIAL UND BÜROZUBEHÖR · OFFICE EQUIPMENT

① **der Kopierer**
photocopier

② **der Scanner**
scanner

③ **das Telefon**
telephone / phone

④ **der Laptop**
laptop

⑤ **der Beamer**
projector

⑥ **das Headset**
headset

⑦ **der Schredder**
shredder

⑧ **das Handy**
mobile phone

⑨ **die Fußbank**
footrest

⑩ **der Kniestuhl**
kneeling chair

⑪ **die bewegliche Wand**
movable panel

⑫ **das Büromaterial**
stationery

⑬ **der Brief**
letter

⑭ **der Umschlag**
envelope

⑮ **der Kalender**
calendar

⑯ **der Planer**
diary

⑰ **das Klemmbrett**
clipboard

⑱ **der Locher**
hole punch

⑲ **das Gummiband**
rubber bands

⑳ **die Vielzweckklemme**
binder clip

㉑ **die Schere**
scissors

㉒ **der Spitzer**
pencil sharpener

㉓ **der Hefter**
stapler

㉔ **die Heftklammern**
f, pl
staples

㉕ **die Korrekturflüssigkeit**
correction fluid

㉖ **das Protokoll**
minutes

㉗ **das Ringbuch**
ring binder

㉘ **der Textmarker**
highlighter

㉙ **der Kleber**
glue

㉚ **der Tesafilm**
tape

㉛ **die Reißzwecke**
drawing pin

㉜ **der Bleistift**
pencil

㉝ **der Kugelschreiber**
pen

㉞ **die Büroklammer**
paper clips

㉟ **der Radiergummi**
rubber

㊱ **das Lineal**
ruler

83 Computer und Technologie
Computers and technology

🔊

83.1 GERÄTE UND TECHNOLOGIE · GADGETS AND TECHNOLOGY

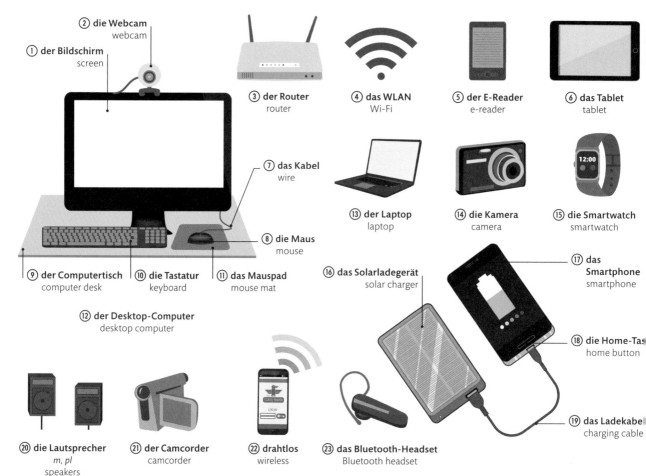

② die Webcam
webcam

① der Bildschirm
screen

③ der Router
router

④ das WLAN
Wi-Fi

⑤ der E-Reader
e-reader

⑥ das Tablet
tablet

⑦ das Kabel
wire

⑬ der Laptop
laptop

⑭ die Kamera
camera

⑮ die Smartwatch
smartwatch

⑧ die Maus
mouse

⑨ der Computertisch
computer desk

⑩ die Tastatur
keyboard

⑪ das Mauspad
mouse mat

⑯ das Solarladegerät
solar charger

⑰ das Smartphone
smartphone

⑱ die Home-Tas
home button

⑫ der Desktop-Computer
desktop computer

⑲ das Ladekabe
charging cable

⑳ die Lautsprecher
m, pl
speakers

㉑ der Camcorder
camcorder

㉒ drahtlos
wireless

㉓ das Bluetooth-Headset
Bluetooth headset

㉔ die Batterie / der Akku
battery

㉕ der USB-Stick
USB drive

㉖ das Diktiergerät
voice recorder

㉗ das Passwort
password

㉘ die Speicherkarte
memory card

㉙ die Festplatte
hard drive

㉚ der Stecker
plug

㉛ das Stromkabel
power lead

㉜ der Stromkreis
circuit

㉝ die Fernbedienung
remote control

㉞ die künstliche Intelligenz
artificial intelligence

See also
73 In der Schule • At school **80** An der Universität • At college
81 Auf der Arbeit • At work **82** Im Büro • In the office **95** Besprechen
and präsentieren • Meeting and presenting **140** Spiele • Games

83.2 ONLINE-KOMMUNIKATION · ONLINE COMMUNICATION

① **einschalten**
to turn on

② **ausschalten**
to turn off

③ **sich anmelden**
to log in

④ **sich abmelden**
to log out

⑤ **herunterladen**
to download

⑥ **hochladen**
to upload

⑦ **sichern**
to back up

⑧ **klicken**
to click

⑨ **einstecken**
to plug in

⑩ **löschen**
to delete

⑪ **ausdrucken**
to print

⑫ **der Kontakt**
contact

⑬ **die E-Mail**
email

⑭ **antworten**
to reply

⑮ **allen antworten**
to reply to all

⑯ **senden**
to send

⑰ **weiterleiten**
to forward

⑱ **der Entwurf**
draft

⑲ **der Posteingang**
inbox

⑳ **der Postausgang**
outbox

㉑ **der Betreff**
subject

㉒ **der Spam**
junk mail / spam

㉓ **der Papierkorb**
trash

㉔ **der Anhang**
attachment

㉕ **der Chat**
chat

㉖ **der Videochat**
video chat

㉗ **die Unterschrift**
signature

㉘ **das Hashtag**
hashtag

㉙ **das At-Zeichen**
at sign / at symbol

㉚ **Sie müssen Ihr Mikrofon
einschalten, Liz.**
You need to turn on your
microphone, Liz.

㉛ **die
Videokonferenz**
video
conference

84.1 DAS FERNSEHSTUDIO · TELEVISION STUDIO

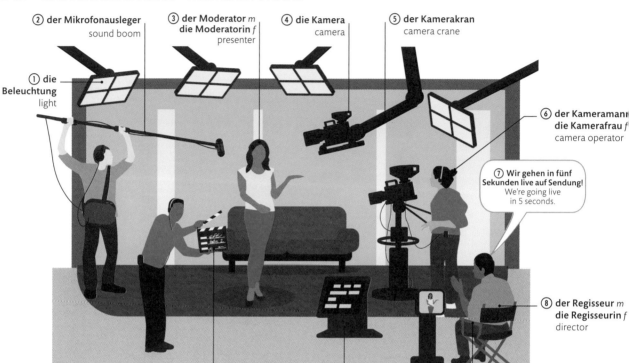

① **die Beleuchtung** light

② **der Mikrofonausleger** sound boom

③ **der Moderator** *m* **die Moderatorin** *f* presenter

④ **die Kamera** camera

⑤ **der Kamerakran** camera crane

⑥ **der Kameramann** *m* **die Kamerafrau** *f* camera operator

⑦ **Wir gehen in fünf Sekunden live auf Sendung!** We're going live in 5 seconds.

⑧ **der Regisseur** *m* **die Regisseurin** *f* director

⑨ **die Klappe** clapper board

⑩ **das Fernsehstudio** television studio

⑪ **der Teleprompter** teleprompter / autocue

⑫ **der Regiestuhl** director's chair

84.2 RADIO · RADIO

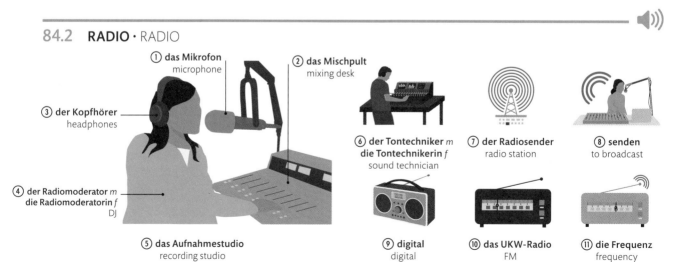

① **das Mikrofon** microphone

② **das Mischpult** mixing desk

③ **der Kopfhörer** headphones

④ **der Radiomoderator** *m* **die Radiomoderatorin** *f* DJ

⑤ **das Aufnahmestudio** recording studio

⑥ **der Tontechniker** *m* **die Tontechnikerin** *f* sound technician

⑦ **der Radiosender** radio station

⑧ **senden** to broadcast

⑨ **digital** digital

⑩ **das UKW-Radio** FM

⑪ **die Frequenz** frequency

See also
83 Computer und Technologie • Computers and technology **128-129** Musik • Music
136 Unterhaltung zu Hause • Home entertainment **137** Fernsehen • Television

84.3 SOZIALE UND ONLINE-MEDIEN
SOCIAL AND ONLINE MEDIA

 ① folgen
to follow

② liken
to like

③ viral werden
to go viral

④ trenden
to trend

⑨ Mein Blog hat über
500 Follower.
My blog has over
500 followers.

⑤ der Avatar
avatar

⑥ der Videoblog
vlog

⑦ der Vlogger *m*
die Vloggerin *f*
vlogger

⑧ der Blog
blog

⑩ der Blogger *m* / die Bloggerin *f*
blogger

⑪ teilen
to share

⑫ blockieren
to block

⑬ posten
to post

⑭ jemandem eine
Direktnachricht
schreiben
to DM someone

⑮ der Influencer *m*
die Influencerin *f*
influencer

⑯ der Follower *m*
die Followerin *f*
follower

⑰ der Podcast
podcast

⑱ das Emoji
emoji

⑲ das Hashtag
hashtag

⑳ der Thread
thread

㉑ der Feed
newsfeed

㉒ das Statusupdate
status update

㉓ das CMS (Content-Management-System)
CMS (content management system)

㉔ die Plattform
platform

㉕ das Cookie
cookie

㉖ das Pop-up
pop-up

㉗ die
Nachrichtenseite
news website

㉘ die
Zeitschriftenseite
magazine website

㉙ die Community-
Seite
community website

㉚ das Trolling
trolling

85.1 DAS RECHTSSYSTEM · THE LEGAL SYSTEM

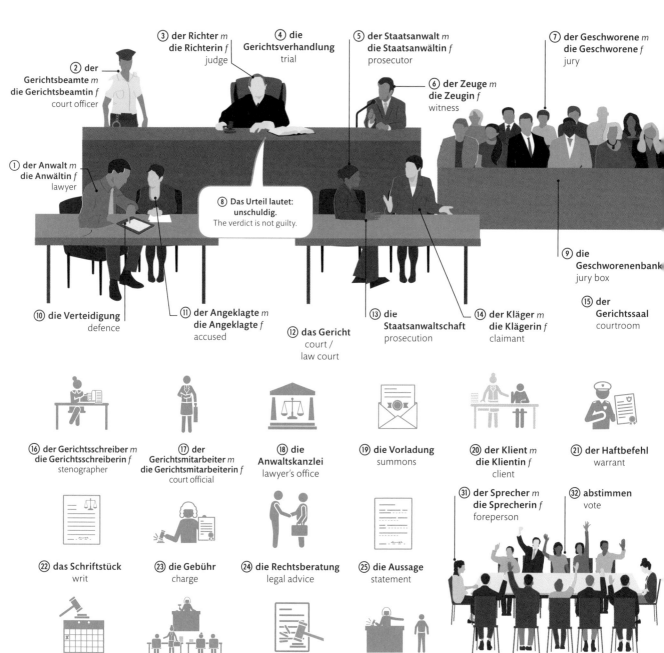

③ der Richter m
die Richterin f
judge

④ die Gerichtsverhandlung
trial

⑤ der Staatsanwalt m
die Staatsanwältin f
prosecutor

⑦ der Geschworene m
die Geschworene f
jury

② der Gerichtsbeamte m
die Gerichtsbeamtin f
court officer

⑥ der Zeuge m
die Zeugin f
witness

① der Anwalt m
die Anwältin f
lawyer

⑧ Das Urteil lautet: unschuldig.
The verdict is not guilty.

⑨ die Geschworenenbank
jury box

⑩ die Verteidigung
defence

⑪ der Angeklagte m
die Angeklagte f
accused

⑫ das Gericht
court /
law court

⑬ die Staatsanwaltschaft
prosecution

⑭ der Kläger m
die Klägerin f
claimant

⑮ der Gerichtssaal
courtroom

⑯ der Gerichtsschreiber m
die Gerichtsschreiberin f
stenographer

⑰ der Gerichtsmitarbeiter m
die Gerichtsmitarbeiterin f
court official

⑱ die Anwaltskanzlei
lawyer's office

⑲ die Vorladung
summons

⑳ der Klient m
die Klientin f
client

㉑ der Haftbefehl
warrant

㉒ das Schriftstück
writ

㉓ die Gebühr
charge

㉔ die Rechtsberatung
legal advice

㉕ die Aussage
statement

㉛ der Sprecher m
die Sprecherin f
foreperson

㉜ abstimmen
vote

㉖ der Gerichtstermin
court date

㉗ der Fall
court case

㉘ das Urteil
verdict

㉙ verurteilen
to sentence

㉚ die Geschworenenberatung
jury deliberation

See also
50 Die Rettungsdienste • Emergency services
91 Branchen und Abteilungen • Industries and departments

㉝ **das Phantombild**
photofit

㉞ **die Beweise** *m, pl*
evidence

㉟ **der Verdächtige** *m*
die Verdächtige *f*
suspect

㊱ **das Vorstrafenregister**
criminal record

㊲ **der Straftäter** *m*
die Straftäterin *f*
criminal

㊳ **der Beschuldigte** *m*
die Beschuldigte *f*
accused

㊴ **plädieren**
to plead

㊵ **unschuldig**
innocent

㊶ **schuldig**
guilty

㊷ **in Berufung gehen**
to appeal

㊸ **der Strafgefangene** *m*
die Strafgefangene *f*
prisoners

㊹ **der Gefängniswärter** *m*
die Gefängniswärterin *f*
prison guards

㊺ **das Gefängnis**
prison

㊻ **die Zelle**
cell

㊼ **die Kaution**
bail

㊽ **die Bewährung**
parole

㊾ **die Strafe**
fine

㊿ **freigesprochen werden**
to be acquitted

85.2 VERBRECHEN · CRIME

① **der Überfall / der Einbruch**
robbery / burglary

② **der Raubüberfall**
mugging

③ **der Autodiebstahl**
car theft

④ **der Krawall**
hooliganism

⑤ **der Vandalismus**
vandalism

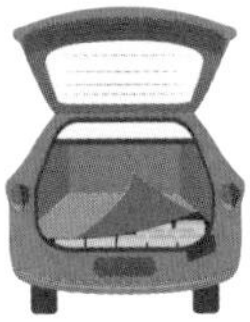
⑥ **das Schmuggeln**
smuggling

⑦ **der Betrug**
fraud

⑧ **das Hacken**
hacking

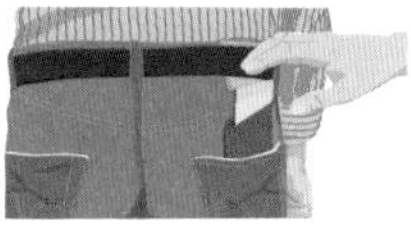
⑨ **der Taschendiebstahl**
pickpocketing

⑩ **die Bestechung**
bribery

⑪ **die Geschwindigkeitsübertretung**
speeding

⑫ **der Drogenhandel**
drug dealing

⑬ **das Graffiti**
graffiti

⑭ **der Ladendiebstahl**
shoplifting

86 Landwirtschaft
Farming

86.1 AUF DEM BAUERNHOF · ON THE FARM

③ der Traktor
tractor

⑤ das Silo
silo

⑦ der Mähdrescher
combine harvester

⑨ der Stall
stable

① die Hecke
hedge

② die Scheune
barn

④ das Ackerland
farmland

⑥ die
Vogelscheuche
scarecrow

⑧ der Bauernhof
farmhouse

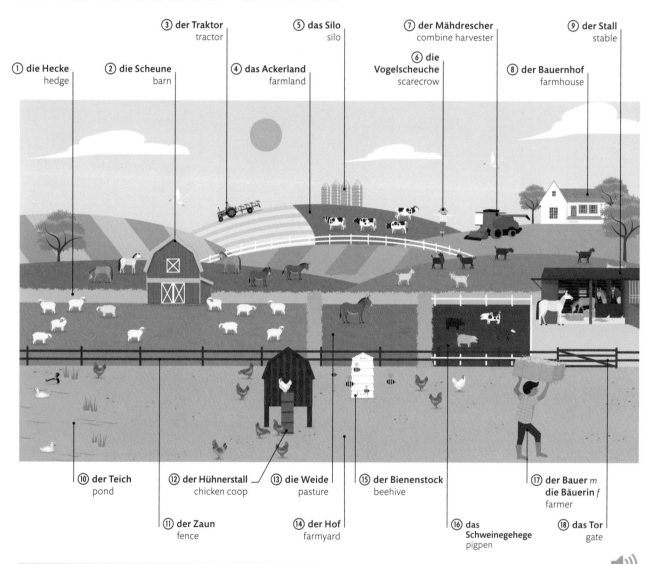

⑩ der Teich
pond

⑫ der Hühnerstall
chicken coop

⑬ die Weide
pasture

⑮ der Bienenstock
beehive

⑰ der Bauer *m*
die Bäuerin *f*
farmer

⑪ der Zaun
fence

⑭ der Hof
farmyard

⑯ das
Schweinegehege
pigpen

⑱ das Tor
gate

86.2 LANDWIRTSCHAFTLICHE VERBEN · FARMING VERBS

① **pflügen**
to plough

② **säen**
to sow

③ **melken**
to milk

④ **füttern**
to feed

⑤ **anpflanzen**
to plant

⑥ **ernten**
to harvest

See also
53 Fleisch · Meat **55-56** Gemüse · Vegetables **57** Obst · Fruit **58** Obst und Nüsse
Fruit and nuts **61** Milchprodukte · Dairy produce **165** Bauernhoftiere · Farm animals

86.3 LANDWIRTSCHAFTLICHE BEGRIFFE · FARMING TERMS

① der Ackerbaubetrieb
arable farm

② der Milchbetrieb
dairy farm

③ die Schafzucht
sheep farm

④ die Hühnerzucht
poultry farm

⑤ die Schweinezucht
pig farm

⑥ die Fischzucht
fish farm

⑦ die Herde
herd

⑧ die Obstplantage
fruit farm

⑨ der Weinberg
vineyard

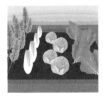
⑩ der Gemüsegarten
vegetable garden / vegetable plot

⑪ der Unkrautvernichter
herbicide

⑫ das Pestizid
pesticide

86.4 FELDFRÜCHTE · CROPS

① der Weizen
wheat

② der Mais
maize

③ die Gerste
barley

④ der Raps
rapeseed

⑤ die Sonnenblume
sunflowers

⑥ das Heu
hay

⑦ die Alfalfa
alfalfa

⑧ der Tabak
tobacco

⑨ der Reis
rice

⑩ der Tee
tea

⑪ der Kaffee
coffee

⑫ das Zuckerrohr
sugar cane

⑬ der Flachs
flax

⑭ die Baumwolle
cotton

⑮ die Kartoffel
potatoes

⑯ die Yamswurzel
yams

⑰ die Hirse
millet

⑱ die Kochbanane
plantains

87.1 DIE BAUSTELLE · BUILDING SITE

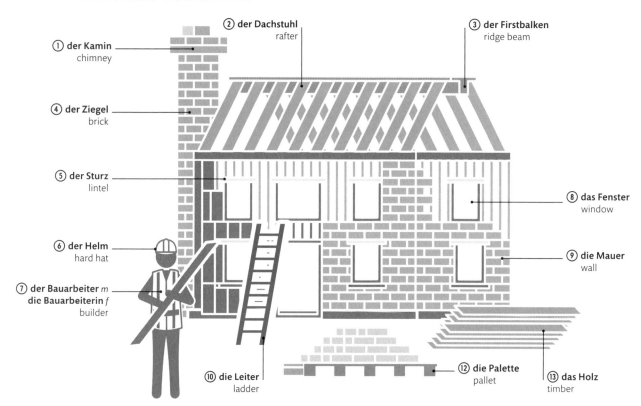

① **der Kamin**
chimney

② **der Dachstuhl**
rafter

③ **der Firstbalken**
ridge beam

④ **der Ziegel**
brick

⑤ **der Sturz**
lintel

⑧ **das Fenster**
window

⑥ **der Helm**
hard hat

⑨ **die Mauer**
wall

⑦ **der Bauarbeiter** *m*
die Bauarbeiterin *f*
builder

⑩ **die Leiter**
ladder

⑫ **die Palette**
pallet

⑬ **das Holz**
timber

⑪ **die Baustelle**
building site

⑭ **der Aushang mit**
Sicherheitshinweisen
safety notice board

⑮ **der Ohrschutz**
ear protectors / ear muffs

⑯ **die Warnweste**
high-visibility vest

⑰ **die**
Schutzhandschuhe *m, pl*
safety gloves

⑱ **die Schutzbrille**
safety glasses

⑲ **der**
Werkzeuggürtel
tool belt

⑳ **der Träger**
girder

㉑ **das Rohr**
pipe

㉒ **der Zement / der Mörtel**
cement / mortar

㉓ **der Formstein**
breeze block

㉔ **die Schindel**
roof tiles

㉕ **bauen**
to build

See also
25 Ein Ort zum Leben • A place to live **32** Haus und Heim • House and home
33 Elektrizität und Sanitärtechnik • Electrics and plumbing **35** Heimwerken • Home
improvements **36** Werkzeuge • Tools **37** Wohnraumverschönerung • Decorating

87.2 **MASCHINEN** · MACHINERY

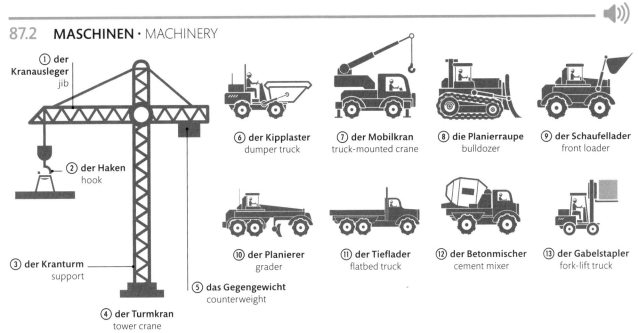

① **der Kranausleger** jib

② **der Haken** hook

③ **der Kranturm** support

④ **der Turmkran** tower crane

⑤ **das Gegengewicht** counterweight

⑥ **der Kipplaster** dumper truck

⑦ **der Mobilkran** truck-mounted crane

⑧ **die Planierraupe** bulldozer

⑨ **der Schaufellader** front loader

⑩ **der Planierer** grader

⑪ **der Tieflader** flatbed truck

⑫ **der Betonmischer** cement mixer

⑬ **der Gabelstapler** fork-lift truck

87.3 **WERKZEUGE UND STRASSENBAUARBEITEN**
TOOLS AND ROADWORKS

① **die Kelle** trowel

② **die Wasserwaage** spirit level

③ **der Griff** handle

④ **die Schaufel** shovel

⑤ **die Spitzhacke** pickaxe

⑥ **der Vorschlaghammer** sledgehammer

⑦ **der Bagger** excavator / digger

⑧ **Auf der Baustelle muss ein Helm getragen werden.** You must wear a hard hat while you're on the site.

⑨ **die Dampfwalze** roller

⑩ **der Leitkegel** cone

⑪ **die Belagsarbeiten** f, pl resurfacing

⑫ **der Presslufthammer** pneumatic drill

⑬ **Straßenbauarbeiten** f, pl roadworks

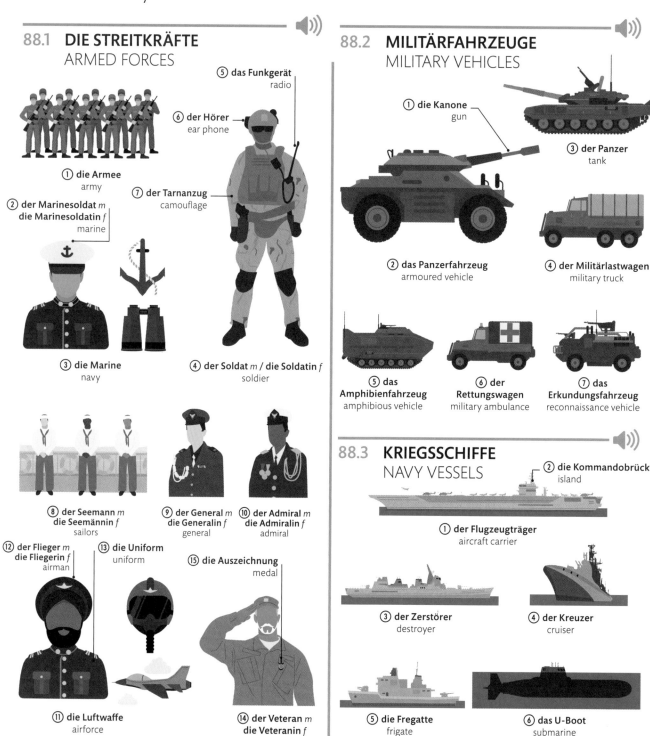

88.1 DIE STREITKRÄFTE
ARMED FORCES

① die Armee
army

② der Marinesoldat *m*
die Marinesoldatin *f*
marine

③ die Marine
navy

⑤ das Funkgerät
radio

⑥ der Hörer
ear phone

⑦ der Tarnanzug
camouflage

④ der Soldat *m* / die Soldatin *f*
soldier

⑧ der Seemann *m*
die Seemännin *f*
sailors

⑨ der General *m*
die Generalin *f*
general

⑩ der Admiral *m*
die Admiralin *f*
admiral

⑫ der Flieger *m*
die Fliegerin *f*
airman

⑬ die Uniform
uniform

⑮ die Auszeichnung
medal

⑪ die Luftwaffe
airforce

⑭ der Veteran *m*
die Veteranin *f*
veteran

88.2 MILITÄRFAHRZEUGE
MILITARY VEHICLES

① die Kanone
gun

③ der Panzer
tank

② das Panzerfahrzeug
armoured vehicle

④ der Militärlastwagen
military truck

⑤ das Amphibienfahrzeug
amphibious vehicle

⑥ der Rettungswagen
military ambulance

⑦ das Erkundungsfahrzeug
reconnaissance vehicle

88.3 KRIEGSSCHIFFE
NAVY VESSELS

② die Kommandobrück
island

① der Flugzeugträger
aircraft carrier

③ der Zerstörer
destroyer

④ der Kreuzer
cruiser

⑤ die Fregatte
frigate

⑥ das U-Boot
submarine

See also
79 Geschichte · History **148** Karten und Richtungsangaben
Maps and directions **149-151** Länder · Countries

88.4 **KAMPFFLUGZEUGE** · COMBAT AIRCRAFT

① **das militärische Transportflugzeug**
military transport aircraft

② **das Bombenflugzeug**
bomber

③ **der Kampfhubschrauber**
attack helicopter

④ **das Kampfflugzeug**
fighter

⑤ **der Aufklärer**
reconnaissance aircraft

⑥ **der Lastenhubschrauber**
transport helicopter

88.5 **KRIEG UND WAFFEN** · WAR AND WEAPONS

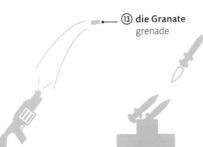

① **die Schlacht**
battle

② **die Front**
front

③ **das Geschützfeuer**
gunfire

④ **der Verwundete** *m*
die Verwundete *f*
casualty

⑤ **das Feldlazarett**
field hospital

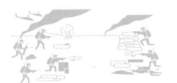

⑥ **die Kantine**
mess

⑦ **die Feuerwaffe**
guns

⑧ **das Maschinengewehr**
machine gun

⑨ **die Pistole**
pistol

⑩ **die Schrotflinte**
shotgun

⑪ **das Gewehr**
rifle

⑬ **die Granate**
grenade

⑫ **der Granatwerfer**
grenade launcher

⑭ **die Boden-Luft-Rakete**
surface-to-air missile

⑮ **die ballistische Rakete**
ballistic missile

⑯ **das tragbare Luftabwehrsystem**
shoulder-launched missile

⑰ **der Marschflugkörper**
cruise missile

⑱ **die bewaffnete Drohne**
armed drone

89.1 BERUFSBEZEICHNUNGEN · OCCUPATIONS

⑩ **Dieses Rohr leckt.**
This pipe has sprung a leak.

① der Schauspieler *m*
die Schauspielerin *f*
actor

② der Soziologe *m*
die Soziologin *f*
sociologist

③ der Friseur *m*
die Friseurin *f*
barber

④ der Lektor *m*
die Lektorin *f*
editor

⑤ der Bartender *m*
die Bartenderin *f*
bartender

⑥ der Fischer *m*
die Fischerin *f*
fisherman

⑦ der Physiotherapeut *m*
die Physiotherapeutin *f*
physical therapist / physiotherapist

⑧ der Optiker *m*
die Optikerin *f*
optician

⑨ der Klempner *m* / die Klempnerin *f*
plumber

⑪ der Schreiner *m*
die Schreinerin *f*
carpenter

⑫ der Schiffskapitän *m*
die Schiffskapitänin *f*
ship's captain

⑬ der Dozent *m*
die Dozentin *f*
lecturer

⑭ der Komiker *m*
die Komikerin *f*
comedian

⑮ der Tänzer *m*
die Tänzerin *f*
dancer

⑯ der Clown *m*
die Clownin *f*
clown

⑰ die Reinigungskraft
cleaner

⑱ der Arzt *m*
die Ärztin *f*
doctor

⑲ der Fahrlehrer *m*
die Fahrlehrerin *f*
driving instructor

⑳ der Maler *m*
die Malerin *f*
painter

㉑ der Elektriker *m*
die Elektrikerin *f*
electrician

㉒ der Designer *m*
die Designerin *f*
designer

㉓ der Barista *m*
die Barista *f*
barista

㉔ der Feuerwehrmann *m*
die Feuerwehrfrau *f*
firefighter

㉕ der App-Entwickler *m*
die App-Entwicklerin *f*
app developer

㉖ der Spion *m*
die Spionin *f*
spy

㉗ der Florist *m*
die Floristin *f*
florist

㉘ der Grundstückspfleger *m*
die Grundstückspflegerin *f*
ground maintenance

㉙ der Gärtner *m*
die Gärtnerin *f*
gardener

㉚ der Gemüsehändler *m*
die Gemüsehändlerin *f*
greengrocer

㉛ der Bergarbeiter *m*
die Bergarbeiterin *f*
miner

㉜ der IT-Manager *m*
die IT-Managerin *f*
IT manager

㉝ der Juwelier *m*
die Juwelierin *f*
jeweller

㉞ der Zahnarzt *m*
die Zahnärztin *f*
dentist

See also

81 Auf der Arbeit · At work **82** Im Büro · In the office **90** Berufe (Fortsetzung) · Jobs continued **91** Branchen und Abteilungen · Industries and departments **92** Bewerbungen · Applying for a job **93** Nützliche Fähigkeiten für den Arbeitsplatz · Workplace skills **95** Besprechen and präsentieren · Meeting and presenting

35 die **Haushaltshilfe**
maid / housekeeper

36 der **Friseur / Stylist** m
die **Friseurin / Stylistin** f
hairdresser / stylist

37 der **Mechaniker** m
die **Mechanikerin** f
mechanic

38 der **Dolmetscher** m
die **Dolmetscherin** f
interpreter

39 der **Kurator** m
die **Kuratorin** f
museum curator

40 der **Privatdetektiv** m
die **Privatdetektivin** f
private investigator

41 der **Bauleiter** m
die **Bauleiterin** f
site manager

42 der **Kieferorthopäde** m
die **Kieferorthopädin** f
orthodontist

43 der **Nachrichtensprecher** m
die **Nachrichtensprecherin** f
newsreader

44 der **Apotheker** m
die **Apothekerin** f
pharmacist

45 der **Metzger** m
die **Metzgerin** f
butcher

46 der **Fotograf** m
die **Fotografin** f
photographer

47 der **Polizeibeamte** m
die **Polizeibeamtin** f
police officer

48 der **Krankenpfleger** m
die **Krankenschwester** f
nurse

49 der **Seemann** m
die **Seefrau** f
sailor

50 der **Verkäufer** m
die **Verkäuferin** f
sales assistant

51 die **Kellnerin**
waitress

52 der **Kellner**
waiter

53 der **Bildhauer** m
die **Bildhauerin** f
sculptor

54 der **Wachmann** m
die **Wachfrau** f
security guard

55 der **Schneider** m
die **Schneiderin** f
tailor

56 der **Skilehrer** m
die **Skilehrerin** f
ski instructor

57 der **Soldat** m
die **Soldatin** f
soldier

58 der **Bauer** m
die **Bäuerin** f
farmer

59 der **Sportler** m
die **Sportlerin** f
sportsperson

60 der **Fischhändler** m
die **Fischhändlerin** f
fishmonger

61 der **Sänger** m
die **Sängerin** f
singer

62 der **Makler** m
die **Maklerin** f
estate agent

63 der **Marktforscher** m
die **Marktforscherin** f
market researcher

65 Ihr Hund hat nun alle nötigen Impfungen.
Your dog is up to date with its vaccinations.

64 der **Tierarzt** m / die **Tierärztin** f
vet

90.1 BERUFSBEZEICHNUNGEN · OCCUPATIONS

① **der Security-Mitarbeiter** m
die Security-Mitarbeiterin f
security guard

② **der Fensterputzer** m
die Fensterputzerin f
window cleaner

③ **der Künstler** m
die Künstlerin f
artist

④ **der Leibwächter** m
die Leibwächterin f
bodyguard

⑤ **der Psychologe** m
die Psychologin f
psychologist

⑥ **der Geschäftsmann** m
businessman

⑦ **die Geschäftsfrau**
businesswoman

⑧ **der Steuerberater** m
die Steuerberaterin f
accountant

⑨ **der Koch** m
die Köchin f
chef

⑩ **der Bauarbeiter** m
die Bauarbeiterin f
builder

⑪ **der Radiomoderator** m
die Radiomoderatorin f
radio DJ

⑫ **der Techniker** m
die Technikerin f
engineer

⑬ **der Modedesigner** m
die Modedesignerin f
fashion designer

⑭ **der Rockstar** m / f
rock star

⑮ **der Fluglehrer** m
die Fluglehrerin f
flight instructor

⑯ **der Hausmeister** m
die Hausmeisterin f
janitor

⑰ **der Touristenführer** m
die Touristenführerin f
tour guide

⑱ **der Postbote** m
die Postbotin f
postman / postwoman

⑲ **der Assistent** m
die Assistentin f
personal assistant (PA)

⑳ **der Bibliothekar** m
die Bibliothekarin f
librarian

㉑ **der Schlosser** m
die Schlosserin f
locksmith

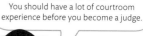

㉙ **Man sollte viel Erfahrung im Gericht sammeln, bevor man Richter wird.**
You should have a lot of courtroom experience before you become a judge.

㉒ **der Rettungssanitäter** m
die Rettungssanitäterin f
paramedic

㉓ **der Musiklehrer** m
die Musiklehrerin f
teacher

㉔ **der Erzieher** m
die Erzieherin f
childcare provider

㉕ **der Küchenmonteur** m
die Küchenmonteurin f
kitchen installer / fitter

㉖ **der Taxifahrer** m
die Taxifahrerin f
taxi driver

㉗ **der Tierpfleger** m
die Tierpflegerin f
zookeeper

㉘ **der Richter** m / **die Richterin** f
judge

See also
81 Auf der Arbeit · At work **82** Im Büro · In the office **91** Branchen und Abteilungen
Industries and departments **92** Bewerbungen · Applying for a job **93** Nützliche Fähigkeiten für
den Arbeitsplatz · Workplace skills **95** Besprechen und präsentieren · Meeting and presenting

㉜ **Meine Schicht hat heute um 8 Uhr begonnen.**
My shift started at 8 o'clock this morning.

㉚ **der Anästhesiologe** m / **die Anästhesiologin** f
anaesthetist

㉛ **der Chirurg** m / **die Chirurgin** f
surgeon

㉝ **der Chauffeur** m
die Chauffeurin f
driver

㉞ **der Sekretär** m
die Sekretärin f
secretary

㉟ **der Rezeptionist** m
die Rezeptionistin f
receptionist

㊱ **der Flugbegleiter** m
die Flugbegleiterin f
flight attendant

㊲ **der Wissenschaftler** m
die Wissenschaftlerin f
scientist

㊳ **der Busfahrer** m
die Busfahrerin f
bus driver

㊴ **der Musiker** m
die Musikerin f
musician

㊵ **der Landvermesser** m
die Landvermesserin f
surveyor

㊶ **der Anwalt** m
die Anwältin f
lawyer

㊷ **der Lehrer** m
die Lehrerin f
teacher

㊸ **der Journalist** m
die Journalistin f
journalist

㊹ **der Zugführer** m
die Zugführerin f
train driver

㊺ **der Reiseberater** m
die Reiseberaterin f
travel agent

㊻ **der Lastwagenfahrer** m
die Lastwagenfahrerin f
lorry driver

㊼ **der Architekt** m
die Architektin f
architect

㊽ **der Schriftsteller** m
die Schriftstellerin f
writer

㊾ **der Yogalehrer** m
die Yogalehrerin f
yoga teacher

㊿ **der Pilot** m
die Pilotin f
pilot

91.1 BRANCHEN · INDUSTRIES

① die Werbung
advertising

② personenbezogene Dienstleistungen *f, pl*
personal services

③ die Landwirtschaft
agriculture / farming

④ das Militär
military

⑤ die Immobilienwirtschaft
property

⑥ die Automobilindustrie
automotiveindustry

⑩ das Bankwesen
banking

⑪ die Luft- und Raumfahrt
aerospace

⑫ die Ölbranche
petroleum engineering

⑬ die Chemie
chemical industry

⑭ die Kunst
arts

⑮ die Lehre
education

⑲ die Gaming-Industrie
gaming

⑳ die Energieversorgung
energy

㉑ die Wissenschaft
research

㉒ die Mode
fashion

㉓ die Recyclingwirtschaft
recycling

㉔ die Unterhaltung
entertainment

㉘ die Logistik
shipping

㉙ der Online-Handel
online retail

㉚ der Journalismus
journalism

㉛ die Textilindustrie
textiles

㉜ die Medienbranche
media

㉝ das Gastgewerbe
hospitality

㊲ der Lieferdienst
online delivery

㊳ die Wasserwirtschaft
water

㊴ die darstellenden Künste *f, pl*
performing arts

㊵ die Biotechnologie
biotechnology

㊷ Unsere Aktien sind dramatisch abgestürzt.
Our stocks have fallen dramatically.

㊶ das Finanzwesen
finance

See also
81 Auf der Arbeit · At work **82** Im Büro · In the office **89-90** Berufe · Jobs **92** Bewerbungen Applying for a job **93** Nützliche Fähigkeiten für den Arbeitsplatz · Workplace skills

⑧ **Hier sehen Sie eines unserer berühmtesten Gebäude.**
This is one of our most famous buildings.

91.2 ABTEILUNGEN · DEPARTMENTS

⑦ **die Tourismusbranche**
tourism

⑨ **die Veterinärversorgung**
pet services

① **die Buchhaltung**
accounts / finance

② **die Fertigung**
production

③ **die Rechtsabteilung**
legal

⑯ **das Catering / e Lebensmittelindustrie**
catering / food

⑰ **die Pharmaindustrie**
pharmaceuticals

⑱ **das Bauwesen**
construction

④ **das Marketing**
marketing

⑤ **die IT**
information technology (IT)

⑥ **die Büroverwaltung und Anlagenverwaltung**
facilities / office services

㉕ **die Fischerei**
fishing

㉖ **die Elektronikbranche**
electronics

㉗ **der Einzelhandel**
retail

⑦ **der Vertrieb**
sales

⑧ **die Verwaltung**
administration

⑨ **Public Relations**
public relations (PR)

㉞ **das Gesundheitswesen**
healthcare

㉟ **die Produktionsindustrie**
manufacturing

㊱ **der Bergbau**
mining

⑩ **der Einkauf**
purchasing

⑬ **Diese Ideen für das neue Projekt gefallen mir.**
I love these ideas for the new project.

⑪ **die Personalabteilung**
human resources (HR)

㊸ **das Transportwesen**
transport

⑫ **Forschung und Entwicklung (F&E)**
research and development (R&D)

191

92.1 BEWERBUNGEN · JOB APPLICATIONS

① die Stellenanzeige
job ads

② das Bewerbungsformular
application form

③ das Anschreiben
cover letter

④ das Portfolio
portfolio

⑤ der Lebenslauf
CV

⑦ ein Formular ausfüllen
to fill out a form

⑥ die Personalvermittlung
recruitment agency

⑧ Nach welcher Art Job sehen Sie sich derzeit um?
What kind of work are you looking for?

92.2 SICH BEWERBEN · APPLYING FOR A JOB

② die Stellenausschreibung
vacancies

④ Was macht Sie zur perfekten Kandidatin für diese Stelle?
What makes you the perfect candidate for this job?

⑤ Ich bin sehr fleißig und arbeite gerne im Team.
I'm hardworking and I'm a team player.

① sich um eine Stelle bewerben
to apply for a job

③ ein Bewerbungsgespräch haben
to have an interview

See also
81 Auf der Arbeit • At work **89-90** Berufe • Jobs **91** Branchen und Abteilungen
Industries and departments **93** Nützliche Fähigkeiten für den Arbeitsplatz
Workplace skills **95** Besprechen and präsentieren • Meeting and presenting

92.3 TEAMARBEIT · TEAMWORK

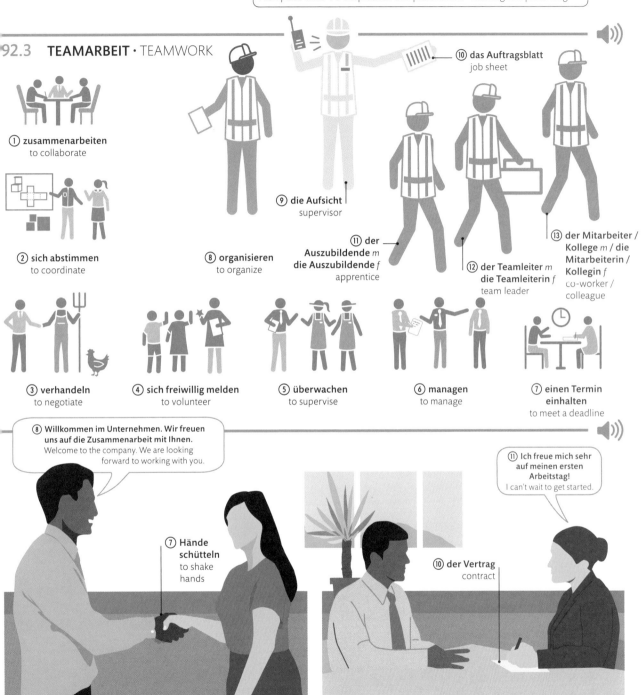

① **zusammenarbeiten**
to collaborate

② **sich abstimmen**
to coordinate

⑧ **organisieren**
to organize

⑨ **die Aufsicht**
supervisor

⑩ **das Auftragsblatt**
job sheet

⑪ **der Auszubildende** *m*
die Auszubildende *f*
apprentice

⑫ **der Teamleiter** *m*
die Teamleiterin *f*
team leader

⑬ **der Mitarbeiter /
Kollege** *m* **/ die
Mitarbeiterin /
Kollegin** *f*
co-worker /
colleague

③ **verhandeln**
to negotiate

④ **sich freiwillig melden**
to volunteer

⑤ **überwachen**
to supervise

⑥ **managen**
to manage

⑦ **einen Termin
einhalten**
to meet a deadline

⑧ Willkommen im Unternehmen. Wir freuen
uns auf die Zusammenarbeit mit Ihnen.
Welcome to the company. We are looking
forward to working with you.

⑪ Ich freue mich sehr
auf meinen ersten
Arbeitstag!
I can't wait to get started.

⑦ **Hände
schütteln**
to shake
hands

⑩ **der Vertrag**
contract

⑥ **eine Stelle bekommen**
to get the job

⑨ **einen Vertrag unterschreiben**
to sign a contract

93.1 WICHTIGE EIGENSCHAFTEN FÜR DEN BERUF · PROFESSIONAL ATTRIBUTES

① **gut organisiert**
organized

② **geduldig**
patient

③ **kreativ**
creative

④ **ehrlich**
honest

⑤ **praktisch veranlagt**
practical

⑥ **professionell**
professional

⑦ **anpassungsfähig**
adaptable

⑧ **ehrgeizig**
ambitious

⑨ **ruhig**
calm

⑩ **selbstbewusst**
confident

⑪ **pünktlich**
punctual

⑫ **zuverlässig**
reliable

⑬ **kundenorientiert**
customer-focused

⑭ **unabhängig**
independent

⑮ **effizient**
efficient

⑯ **ein Teamplayer** *m* / **eine Teamplayerin** *f*
team player

⑰ **verantwortungsbewusst**
responsible

⑱ **innovativ**
innovative

⑲ **motiviert**
motivated

⑳ **entschlossen**
determined

㉑ **energiegeladen**
energetic

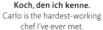

㉓ **Carlo ist der fleißigste Koch, den ich kenne.**
Carlo is the hardest-working chef I've ever met.

㉔ **Freude am Wettkampf haben**
competitive

㉕ **durchsetzungsfähig**
assertive

㉖ **einfallsreich**
imaginative

㉗ **neugierig**
curious

㉒ **fleißig**
hard-working

㉘ **originell**
original

㉙ **genau**
accurate

㉚ **ein guter Zuhörer** *m*
eine gute Zuhörerin *f*
good listener

㉛ **flexibel**
flexible

See also
10 Eigenschaften · Personality traits **11** Fähigkeiten und Handlungen
Abilities and actions **81** Auf der Arbeit · At work **82** Im Büro · In the office

93.2 BERUFLICHE FÄHIGKEITEN · PROFESSIONAL EXPERTISE

① die Organisation
organization

② die Softwarekenntnis
computer literacy

③ das Computing
computing

④ die
Problemlösungskompetenz
problem-solving

⑤ die Analyse
analytics

⑥ die
Entscheidungsfindung
decision-making

⑦ die Teamarbeit
teamwork

⑧ eine schnelle
Auffassungsgabe haben
being a fast learner

⑨ detailorientiert
arbeiten
paying attention
to detail

⑩ der Kundenservice
customer service

⑪ die
Führungskompetenz
leadership

⑫ die Forschung
research

⑬ die Fremdsprachenkenntnisse
f, pl
fluent in languages

⑭ die
Technologiekenntnisse
f, pl
technology literate

⑮ das Halten von
Vorträgen
public speaking

⑯ die Verhandlung
negotiating

⑰ die schriftliche
Kommunikation
written communication

⑱ die Initiative
initiative

⑲ der freundliche
Umgang am Telefon
telephone manner

⑳ gut unter Druck
arbeiten können
working well
under pressure

㉑ die
Rechenkenntnis
numeracy

㉒ der
Führerscheinbesitz
ability to drive

㉜ Sie müssen dringend an Ihrem
Zeitmanagement arbeiten,
der Bericht ist überfällig!
You must improve your time
management! This report is late.

㉓ hochqualifiziert
well-qualified

㉔ das
Selbstmanagement
self management

㉕ die
Serviceorientiertheit
service focused

㉖ die
Einflussnahme
influencer

㉗ die geschäftliche
Einstellung
businesslike attitude

㉘ die
zwischenmenschliche
Kompetenz
interpersonal skills

㉙ das
Projektmanagement
project management

㉚ die Verwaltung
administration

㉛ das Zeitmanagement
time management

94.1 DAS GELD · MONEY

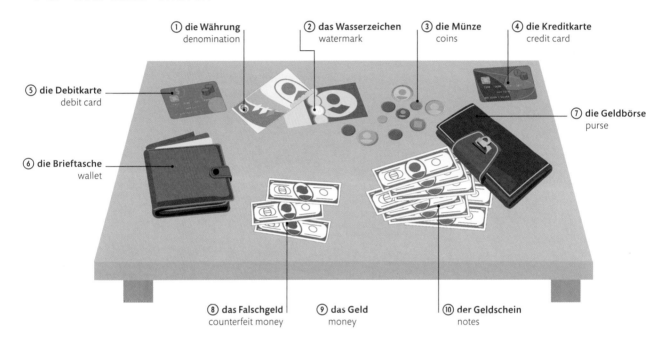

① die Währung
denomination

② das Wasserzeichen
watermark

③ die Münze
coins

④ die Kreditkarte
credit card

⑤ die Debitkarte
debit card

⑦ die Geldbörse
purse

⑥ die Brieftasche
wallet

⑧ das Falschgeld
counterfeit money

⑨ das Geld
money

⑩ der Geldschein
notes

⑪ die digitale
Brieftasche
digital wallet

⑫ die digitale
Währung
digital currency

⑬ die Bank
bank

⑭ das Online-
Banking
online banking

⑮ das Mobile
Banking
mobile banking

⑯ das Telefon-
Banking
telephone banking

⑰ der Beleg
receipt

⑱ die Währung
currency

⑲ die Rechnung
invoice

㉔ Nehmen Sie
auch Bargeld?
Do you accept
cash here?

⑳ der Scheck
cheque

㉑ die Kasse
till

㉒ mit der Karte
zahlen
to pay by card

㉓ bar zahlen
to pay with cash

See also
45 Bank und post · The bank and post office
91 Branchen und Abteilungen · Industries and departments

94.2 **FINANZEN** · FINANCE

① **der Aktienbroker** *m*
die Aktienbrokerin *f*
stockbroker

② **die Börse**
stock exchange

③ **die Anteile** *m, pl*
shares

④ **der Aktienpreis**
share price

⑤ **die Dividenden** *f, pl*
dividends

⑥ **die Provision**
commission

⑦ **das Kapital**
equity

⑧ **die Investition**
investment

⑨ **das Portfolio**
portfolio

⑩ **die Aktien** *f, pl*
stocks

⑪ **der Wechselkurs**
exchange rate

⑫ **das Einkommen**
income

⑬ **das Budget**
budget

⑭ **Schulden machen**
to get into debt

⑮ **einen Gewinn
machen**
to make a profit

⑯ **einen Verlust
machen**
to make a loss

⑰ **die Kosten
decken**
to break even

⑱ **pleite gehen**
to go out of business

㉔ **Ich kann Sie dazu beraten,
wie Sie Ihr Geld anlegen sollten.**
I can advise you where to
invest your money.

⑲ **der Dispo**
overdraft

⑳ **die Ausgabe**
expenditure / outlay

㉑ **die Rezession**
economic downturn

㉒ **der Buchhalter** *m*
die Buchhalterin *f*
accountant

㉓ **der Finanzberater** *m*
die Finanzberaterin *f*
financial advisor

95.1 BESPRECHEN · MEETING

② **Was steht heute auf der Tagesordnung, Maria?**
What's on the agenda today, Maria?

③ **Wir wollten über die Präsentationen kommende Woche sprechen.**
We're discussing the presentations for next week.

① **an einer Besprechung teilnehmen**
to attend a meeting

④ **eine Telefonkonferenz abhalten**
to have a conference call

⑤ **Protokoll führen**
to take minutes

⑥ **Fragen beantworten**
to take questions

⑦ **abwesend sein**
to be absent

⑧ **stören**
to interrupt

⑨ **sich einigen**
to reach a consensus

⑩ **einstimmig**
unanimous vote

⑪ **der Aktionspunkt**
action points

⑫ **per Handzeichen** n
show of hands

⑬ **sonstige Anliegen** n, pl
any other business

⑭ **das Aufsichtsratszimmer**
boardroom

⑮ **der Aufsichtsrat**
board of directors

⑯ **sich einigen**
to reach an agreement

⑰ **die Jahreshauptversammlung**
annual general meeting (AGM)

⑱ **eine Besprechung beenden**
to wrap up the meeting

⑲ **das Whiteboard**
whiteboard

⑳ **das Notizbuch**
notebook

㉑ **die Tagesordnung**
agenda

See also
81 Auf der Arbeit · At work **82** Im Büro · In the office
83 Computer und Technologie · Computers and technology **84** Medien · Media

95.2 **PRÄSENTIEREN** · PRESENTING

① **anfangen**
to commence

② **zusammenfassen**
to sum up

③ **keine Zeit mehr haben**
to run out of time

④ **die Folie**
slide

⑤ **die Roadmap**
roadmap

⑥ **eine Präsentation halten**
to give a presentation

⑦ **der Beamer**
projector

⑧ **der Timer**
timer

⑨ **das HDMI-Kabel**
HDMI cable

⑩ **der tragbare Lautsprecher**
portable speakers

⑪ **das Handout**
handouts

⑫ **die Notizen** f, pl
notes

⑬ **der Smartpen**
smartpen

⑭ **das Mikrofon**
microphone

⑮ **die Kopfhörer**
headphones

⑯ **das Flipchart**
flip chart

⑰ **den Bildschirm teilen**
to share your screen

⑱ **die Fernbedienung**
presenter remote

⑲ **die Konferenz**
conference

⑳ **der Gastredner** m / **die Gastrednerin** f
guest speaker

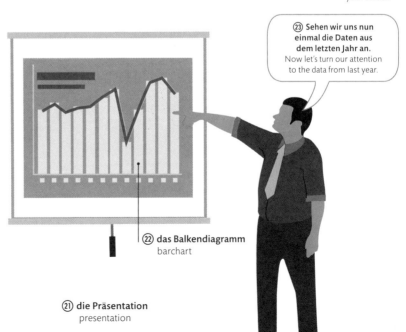

㉓ **Sehen wir uns nun einmal die Daten aus dem letzten Jahr an.**
Now let's turn our attention to the data from last year.

㉒ **das Balkendiagramm**
barchart

㉑ **die Präsentation**
presentation

96.1 AUF DER STRASSE · ON THE ROAD

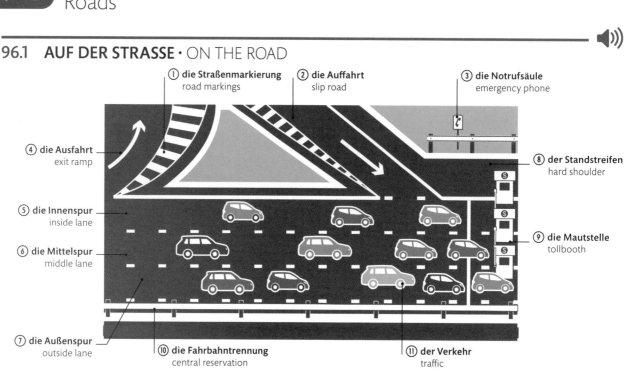

① **die Straßenmarkierung**
road markings

② **die Auffahrt**
slip road

③ **die Notrufsäule**
emergency phone

④ **die Ausfahrt**
exit ramp

⑧ **der Standstreifen**
hard shoulder

⑤ **die Innenspur**
inside lane

⑨ **die Mautstelle**
tollbooth

⑥ **die Mittelspur**
middle lane

⑦ **die Außenspur**
outside lane

⑩ **die Fahrbahntrennung**
central reservation

⑪ **der Verkehr**
traffic

⑫ **die Autobahn**
motorway

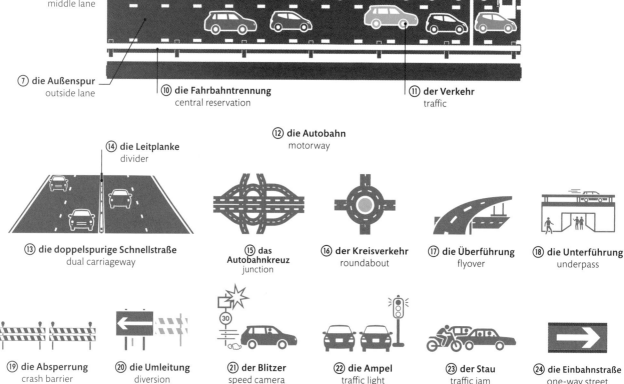

⑭ **die Leitplanke**
divider

⑬ **die doppelspurige Schnellstraße**
dual carriageway

⑮ **das Autobahnkreuz**
junction

⑯ **der Kreisverkehr**
roundabout

⑰ **die Überführung**
flyover

⑱ **die Unterführung**
underpass

⑲ **die Absperrung**
crash barrier

⑳ **die Umleitung**
diversion

㉑ **der Blitzer**
speed camera

㉒ **die Ampel**
traffic light

㉓ **der Stau**
traffic jam

㉔ **die Einbahnstraße**
one-way street

㉕ **der Fußgängerüberweg**
pedestrian crossing

㉖ **die Straßenbauarbeiten** *f, pl*
roadworks

㉗ **der Behindertenparkplatz**
disabled parking

㉘ **der Parkplatzwächter** *m*
die Parkplatzwächterin *f*
parking attendant

㉙ **die Parkuhr**
parking meter

See also
42-43 In der Stadt • In town **97-98** Autos • Cars **99** Autos und Busse • Cars and buses **100** Motorräder • Motorcycles **101** Radfahren • Cycling **123** Motorsport Motorsports **148** Karten und Richtungsangaben • Maps and directions

96.2 VERKEHRSSCHILDER · ROAD SIGNS

① **Einfahrt verboten**
no entry

② **Geschwindigkeitsbegrenzung** f
speed limit

③ **Gefahrenstelle** f
hazard

④ **rechts abbiegen verboten**
no right turn

⑤ **umdrehen verboten**
no U-turn

⑥ **Rechtskurve** f
right bend

⑦ **Vorfahrt gewähren**
give way

⑧ **Vorfahrt** f
priority traffic

⑨ **überholen verboten**
no overtaking

⑩ **Achtung, Schulkinder**
school zone

⑪ **unebene Fahrbahn**
bumps

⑫ **Wildwechsel** m
deer crossing

⑬ **hier entlang**
direction to follow

⑭ **Baustelle** f
roadworks ahead

⑮ **Ampel** f
traffic light ahead

⑯ **keine Einfahrt für Fahrräder**
closed to bicycles

⑰ **kein Zutritt für Fußgänger**
closed to pedestrians

96.3 VERKEHRSVERBEN · VERBS FOR DRIVING

⑤ **der Verkehrspolizist** m / **die Verkehrspolizistin** f
traffic warden

① **fahren**
to drive

② **rückwärts fahren**
to reverse

③ **anhalten**
to stop

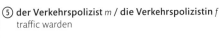

④ **abschleppen**
to tow away

⑥ **links abbiegen**
to turn left

⑦ **rechts abbiegen**
to turn right

⑧ **geradeaus fahren**
to go straight ahead /
to go straight on

⑨ **die erste Abzweigung links nehmen**
to take the first left

⑩ **die zweite Abzweigung rechts nehmen**
to take the second right

97.1 DAS AUTO VON AUSSEN · CAR EXTERIOR

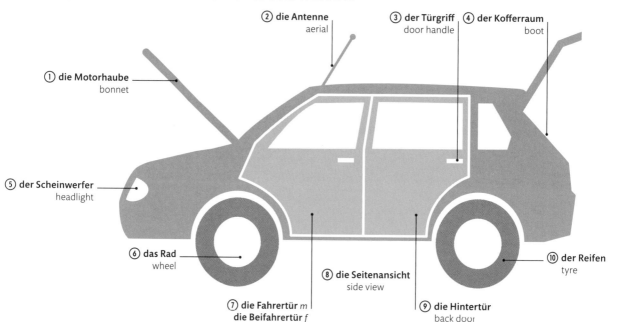

② die Antenne
aerial

③ der Türgriff
door handle

④ der Kofferraum
boot

① die Motorhaube
bonnet

⑤ der Scheinwerfer
headlight

⑥ das Rad
wheel

⑩ der Reifen
tyre

⑧ die Seitenansicht
side view

⑦ die Fahrertür *m*
die Beifahrertür *f*
front door

⑨ die Hintertür
back door

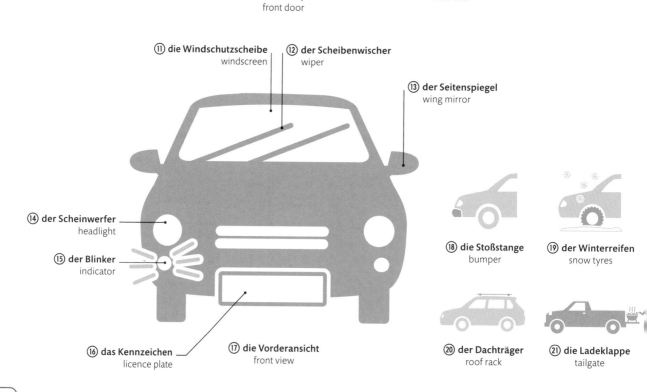

⑪ die Windschutzscheibe
windscreen

⑫ der Scheibenwischer
wiper

⑬ der Seitenspiegel
wing mirror

⑭ der Scheinwerfer
headlight

⑮ der Blinker
indicator

⑯ das Kennzeichen
licence plate

⑰ die Vorderansicht
front view

⑱ die Stoßstange
bumper

⑲ der Winterreifen
snow tyres

⑳ der Dachträger
roof rack

㉑ die Ladeklappe
tailgate

See also
42-43 In der Stadt · In town **96** Straßen · Roads **98** Autos (Fortsetzung) · Cars continued
99 Autos und Busse · Cars and buses **100** Motorräder · Motorcycles **123** Motorsport · Motorsports

97.2 **AUTOTYPEN** · TYPES OF CARS

① das Elektroauto
electric car

② der Hybrid
hybrid

③ der Plug-in-Hybrid
plug-in hybrid

④ das Steilheck
hatchback

⑤ die Limousine
saloon

⑥ der Kombi
estate

⑦ das Allradfahrzeug
four-wheel drive

⑧ der Minivan
people carrier

⑨ die Stretch-Limousine
limousine

⑪ der Spoiler
spoiler

⑩ der Sportwagen
sports car

⑮ der Überrollbügel
roller bar

⑱ der Heckflügel
rear wing

⑫ das Cabrio
convertible

⑬ der Oldtimer
vintage

⑭ der Strandbuggy
beach buggy

⑰ der Vorderkotflügel
front wing

⑯ der Rennwagen
racing car

97.3 **DIE TANKSTELLE** · PETROL STATION

① die Zapfsäule
petrol pump

② die Überdachung
forecourt

③ die Ladestelle
electric charge point

④ der Scheibenreiniger
screen wash

⑤ das Gefrierschutzmittel
antifreeze

⑥ das Benzin
petrol

⑦ bleifrei
unleaded

⑧ bleihaltig
leaded

⑨ der Diesel
diesel

⑩ das Öl
oil

⑪ die Autowaschanlage
car wash

Autos (Fortsetzung)
Cars continued

98.1 PANNENHILFE · BREAKDOWN ASSISTANCE

② **der Mechatroniker** *m*
die Mechatronikerin *f*
mechanic

④ **der Ersatzreifen**
spare tyre

③ **der Abschleppwagen**
tow truck

⑤ **der Platten**
flat tyre

① **die Autowerkstatt**
garage

98.2 DIE MECHANIK · MECHANICS

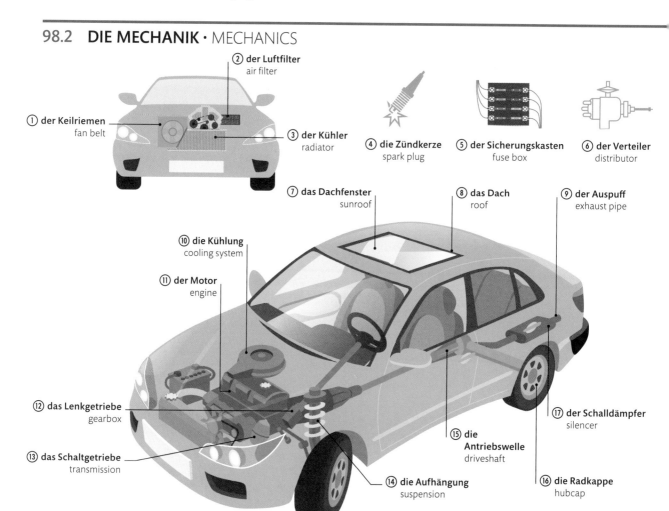

② **der Luftfilter**
air filter

① **der Keilriemen**
fan belt

③ **der Kühler**
radiator

④ **die Zündkerze**
spark plug

⑤ **der Sicherungskasten**
fuse box

⑥ **der Verteiler**
distributor

⑦ **das Dachfenster**
sunroof

⑧ **das Dach**
roof

⑨ **der Auspuff**
exhaust pipe

⑩ **die Kühlung**
cooling system

⑪ **der Motor**
engine

⑫ **das Lenkgetriebe**
gearbox

⑬ **das Schaltgetriebe**
transmission

⑭ **die Aufhängung**
suspension

⑮ **die Antriebswelle**
driveshaft

⑰ **der Schalldämpfer**
silencer

⑯ **die Radkappe**
hubcap

See also
42-43 In der Stadt · In town **96** Straßen · Roads **99** Autos und Busse · Cars and buses
100 Motorräder · Motorcycles **123** Motorsport · Motorsports

⑯ der Schraubschlüssel
wrench

⑰ die Radmutter
wheel nuts

⑱ der Wagenheber
jack

98.3 AUTOVERBEN · VERBS FOR DRIVING

① tanken
to fill up

② den Ölstand prüfen
to check the oil

③ den Reifendruck prüfen
to check the tyres

④ das Auto warten
to service the car

⑤ parken
to park

⑥ losfahren
to set off

⑦ blinken
to indicate

⑧ bremsen
to brake

⑨ abbremsen
to slow down

⑱ der Scheibenwischwasserbehälter
screen wash reservoir

⑲ die Motorhaube
bonnet

⑳ der Bremsflüssigkeitsbehälter
brake fluid reservoir

㉑ der Ölmessstab
dipstick

⑩ beschleunigen
to speed up

⑪ jemanden mitnehmen
to pick someone up

⑫ jemanden absetzen
to drop someone off

㉒ das Rohr
pipe

㉓ der Kühlmittelbehälter
coolant reservoir

⑬ einen Autounfall haben
to have a car accident

㉔ die Batterie
battery

㉕ die Karosserie
bodywork

㉖ der Zylinderkopf
cylinder head

⑭ liegenbleiben
to break down

⑮ überholen
to overtake

99.1 DER AUTOINNENRAUM · CAR INTERIOR

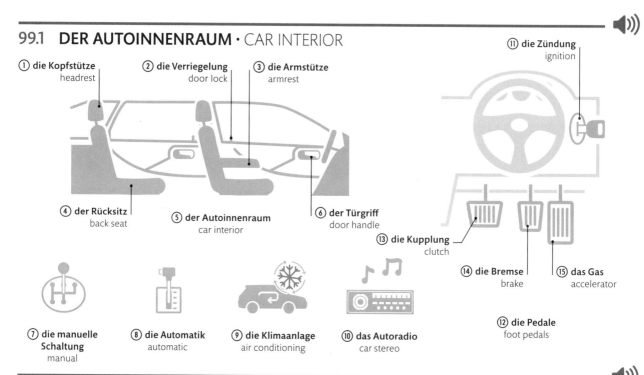

① die Kopfstütze
headrest

② die Verriegelung
door lock

③ die Armstütze
armrest

⑪ die Zündung
ignition

④ der Rücksitz
back seat

⑤ der Autoinnenraum
car interior

⑥ der Türgriff
door handle

⑬ die Kupplung
clutch

⑭ die Bremse
brake

⑮ das Gas
accelerator

⑦ die manuelle Schaltung
manual

⑧ die Automatik
automatic

⑨ die Klimaanlage
air conditioning

⑩ das Autoradio
car stereo

⑫ die Pedale
foot pedals

99.2 DAS ARMATURENBRETT UND BEDIENELEMENTE · DASHBOARD AND CONTROLS

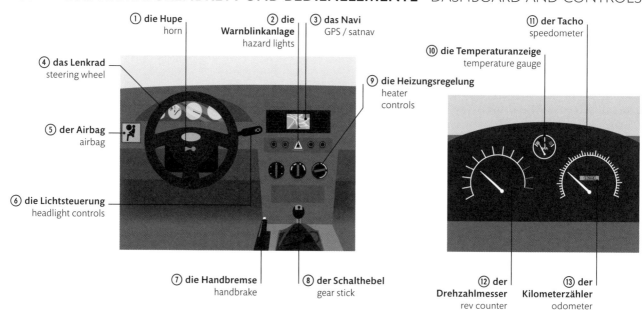

① die Hupe
horn

② die Warnblinkanlage
hazard lights

③ das Navi
GPS / satnav

⑪ der Tacho
speedometer

④ das Lenkrad
steering wheel

⑩ die Temperaturanzeige
temperature gauge

⑨ die Heizungsregelung
heater controls

⑤ der Airbag
airbag

⑥ die Lichtsteuerung
headlight controls

⑦ die Handbremse
handbrake

⑧ der Schalthebel
gear stick

⑫ der Drehzahlmesser
rev counter

⑬ der Kilometerzähler
odometer

See also
42-43 In der Stadt · In town **96** Straßen · Roads **97-98** Autos · Cars
100 Motorräder · Motorcycles **123** Motorsport · Motorsports

99.3 **DER BUS** · BUS

① **das Bushäuschen** bus shelter

② **der Busbahnhof** bus station

③ **die Fahrkarte** bus ticket

④ **der Fahrpreis** fare

⑤ **die Glocke** bell

⑥ **die Stopptaste** stop button

⑦ **der Fahrersitz** driver's seat

⑧ **der Handlauf** handrail

⑨ **das Fenster** window

⑩ **die Tür** door

⑪ **das Hinterrad** rear wheel

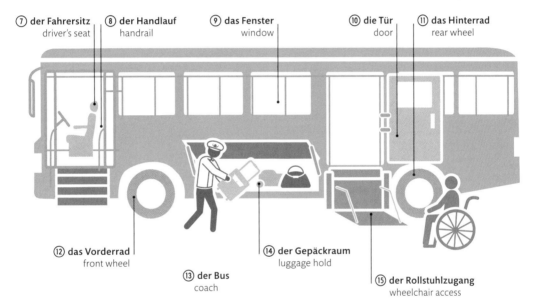

⑫ **das Vorderrad** front wheel

⑬ **der Bus** coach

⑭ **der Gepäckraum** luggage hold

⑮ **der Rollstuhlzugang** wheelchair access

99.4 **BUSTYPEN** · TYPES OF BUSES

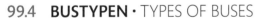

② **das obere Stockwerk** upper deck

③ **das untere Stockwerk** lower deck

④ **der Fahrer** *m* **die Fahrerin** *f* driver

① **der Doppeldeckerbus** double-decker bus

⑥ **das Sightseeing** sightseeing

⑤ **der Touristenbus** tourist bus

⑦ **die Linie** route number

⑧ **der Schulbus** school bus

⑨ **der Minibus** minibus

⑩ **der Gelenkbus** articulated bus

⑪ **der Shuttlebus** shuttle bus

⑫ **der Oberleitungsbus** trolley bus

⑬ **die Straßenbahn** tram

100.1   DAS MOTORRAD · MOTORBIKE

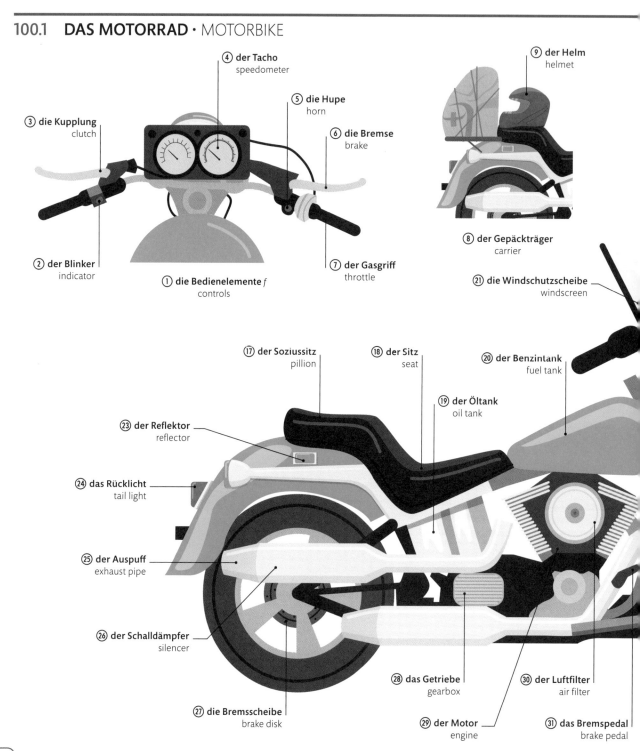

④ der Tacho
speedometer

⑤ die Hupe
horn

③ die Kupplung
clutch

⑥ die Bremse
brake

⑨ der Helm
helmet

② der Blinker
indicator

⑦ der Gasgriff
throttle

① die Bedienelemente *f*
controls

⑧ der Gepäckträger
carrier

㉑ die Windschutzscheibe
windscreen

⑰ der Soziussitz
pillion

⑱ der Sitz
seat

⑳ der Benzintank
fuel tank

⑲ der Öltank
oil tank

㉓ der Reflektor
reflector

㉔ das Rücklicht
tail light

㉕ der Auspuff
exhaust pipe

㉖ der Schalldämpfer
silencer

㉘ das Getriebe
gearbox

㉚ der Luftfilter
air filter

㉗ die Bremsscheibe
brake disk

㉙ der Motor
engine

㉛ das Bremspedal
brake pedal

⑪ das Visier
visor

⑫ das Reflektorband
reflector strap

⑬ der Handschuh
glove

⑭ die Lederkombi
leathers

⑮ der Knieschoner
knee pad

⑯ der Stiefel
boot

⑩ die Motorradkleidung
clothing

㉒ der Scheinwerfer
headlight

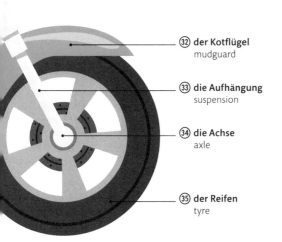

㉜ der Kotflügel
mudguard

㉝ die Aufhängung
suspension

㉞ die Achse
axle

㉟ der Reifen
tyre

See also
42-43 In der Stadt · In town **96** Straßen · Roads
97-98 Autos · Cars **123** Motorsport · Motorsports

100.2 **MOTORRADTYPEN** · TYPES OF MOTORCYCLES

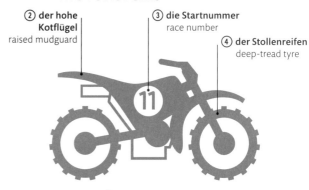

② der hohe
Kotflügel
raised mudguard

③ die Startnummer
race number

④ der Stollenreifen
deep-tread tyre

① das Geländemotorrad
off road motorcycle

⑤ das
Rennmotorrad
racing bike

⑥ das
Tourenmotorrad
tourer

⑦ das Quad
all-terrain vehicle /
quad bike

⑧ der Beiwagen
side car

⑨ das elektrische
Motorrad
electric motorcycle

⑩ der Elektroroller
electric scooter

⑪ das Dreirad
three-wheeler

⑫ der Motorroller
motor scooter

⑬ der Fahrer *m*
die Fahrerin *f*
rider

⑭ auf dem
Beifahrersitz
mitfahren
to ride pillion

⑮ aufsteigen
to get on / mount

⑯ absteigen
to get off / dismount

209

101.1 DAS FAHRRAD · BICYCLE

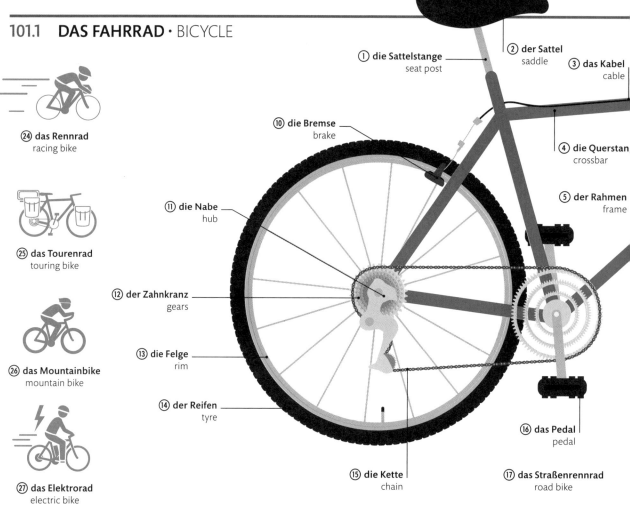

① die Sattelstange
seat post

② der Sattel
saddle

③ das Kabel
cable

④ die Querstan
crossbar

⑤ der Rahmen
frame

⑩ die Bremse
brake

⑪ die Nabe
hub

⑫ der Zahnkranz
gears

⑬ die Felge
rim

⑭ der Reifen
tyre

⑮ die Kette
chain

⑯ das Pedal
pedal

⑰ das Straßenrennrad
road bike

㉔ das Rennrad
racing bike

㉕ das Tourenrad
touring bike

㉖ das Mountainbike
mountain bike

㉗ das Elektrorad
electric bike

㉘ das Tandem
tandem

㉙ der Korb
basket

㉚ der Kindersitz
child seat

㉛ der Radständer
kickstand

㉜ die Bremsbacke
brake pad

㉝ das Stützrad
stabilizers

㉞ das Einrad
unicycle

㉟ der Pedalhaken
toe clip

㊱ der Fußriemen
toe strap

㊲ die Lampe
lamp

㊳ das Rücklicht
rear light

㊴ der Schlauch
inner tube

See also
42-43 In der Stadt • In town **96** Straßen • Roads **100** Motorräder Motorcycles **133** Aktivitäten im Freien • Outdoor activities

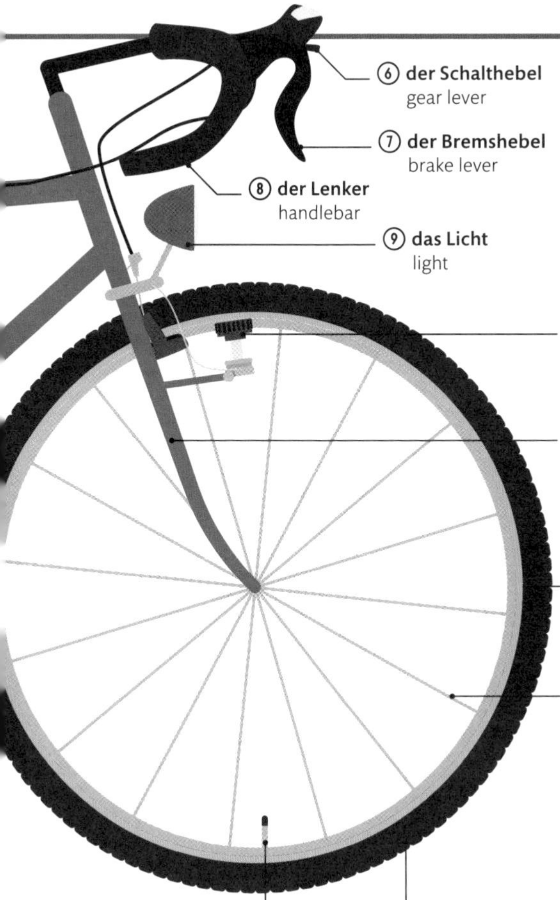

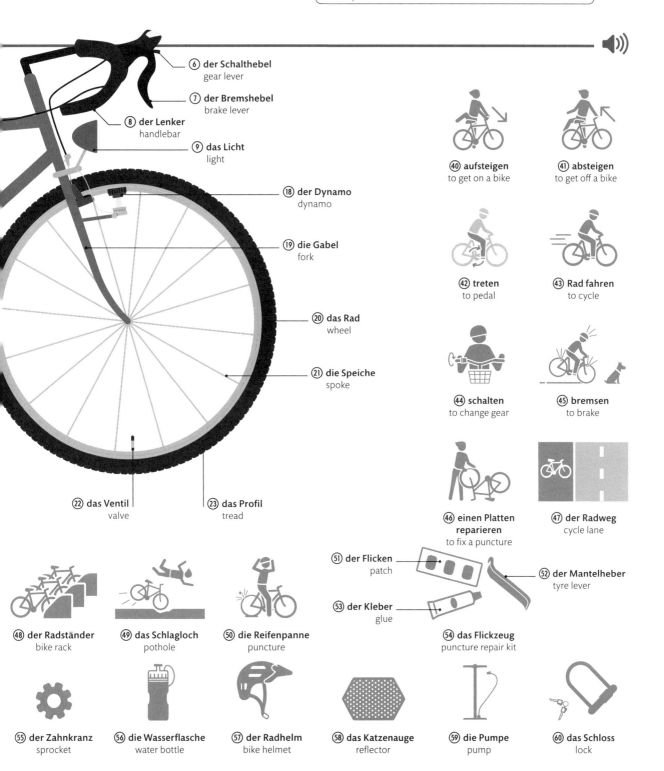

⑥ **der Schalthebel**
gear lever

⑦ **der Bremshebel**
brake lever

⑧ **der Lenker**
handlebar

⑨ **das Licht**
light

⑱ **der Dynamo**
dynamo

⑲ **die Gabel**
fork

⑳ **das Rad**
wheel

㉑ **die Speiche**
spoke

㉒ **das Ventil**
valve

㉓ **das Profil**
tread

㊵ **aufsteigen**
to get on a bike

㊶ **absteigen**
to get off a bike

㊷ **treten**
to pedal

㊸ **Rad fahren**
to cycle

㊹ **schalten**
to change gear

㊺ **bremsen**
to brake

㊻ **einen Platten reparieren**
to fix a puncture

㊼ **der Radweg**
cycle lane

㊽ **der Radständer**
bike rack

㊾ **das Schlagloch**
pothole

㊿ **die Reifenpanne**
puncture

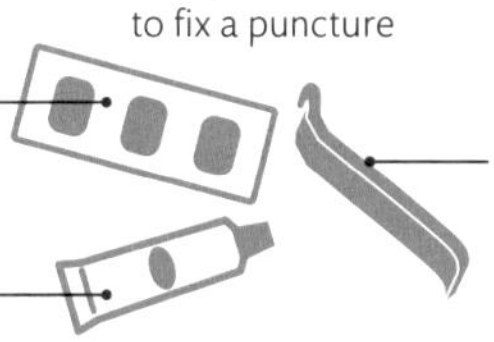

(51) **der Flicken**
patch

(52) **der Mantelheber**
tyre lever

(53) **der Kleber**
glue

(54) **das Flickzeug**
puncture repair kit

(55) **der Zahnkranz**
sprocket

(56) **die Wasserflasche**
water bottle

(57) **der Radhelm**
bike helmet

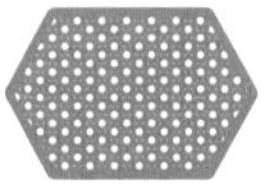

(58) **das Katzenauge**
reflector

(59) **die Pumpe**
pump

(60) **das Schloss**
lock

102 Züge
Trains

102.1 DER BAHNHOF · TRAIN STATION

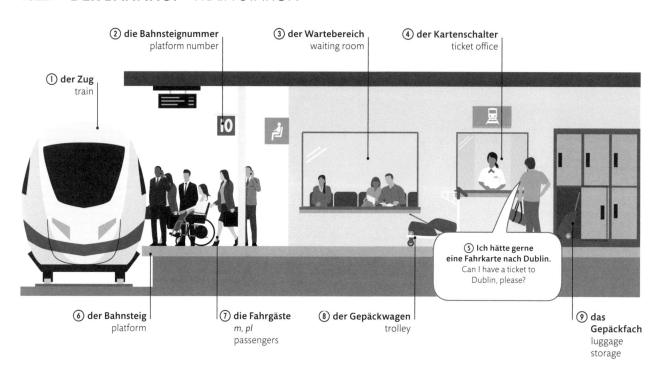

② **die Bahnsteignummer**
platform number

③ **der Wartebereich**
waiting room

④ **der Kartenschalter**
ticket office

① **der Zug**
train

⑤ **Ich hätte gerne eine Fahrkarte nach Dublin.**
Can I have a ticket to Dublin, please?

⑥ **der Bahnsteig**
platform

⑦ **die Fahrgäste**
m, pl
passengers

⑧ **der Gepäckwagen**
trolley

⑨ **das Gepäckfach**
luggage storage

⑩ **das Fundbüro**
lost property office

⑪ **die Fahrkarte**
ticket

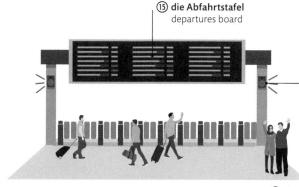

⑮ **die Abfahrtstafel**
departures board

⑯ **die Lautsprechanlage**
public address system

⑫ **der Fahrpreis**
fare

⑬ **die Sperre**
ticket barrier

⑭ **der Querbahnsteig**
concourse

㉒ **der Pendler** *m*
die Pendlerin *f*
commuters

⑰ **das Zugnetz**
rail network

⑱ **der Netzplan**
underground map

⑲ **der Intercity**
intercity train

⑳ **die Verspätung**
delay

㉑ **der Berufsverkehr**
rush hour

㉓ **einen Zug nehmen**
to catch a train

See also
42-43 In der Stadt · In town **131** Reise und Unterkunft · Travel and accommodation

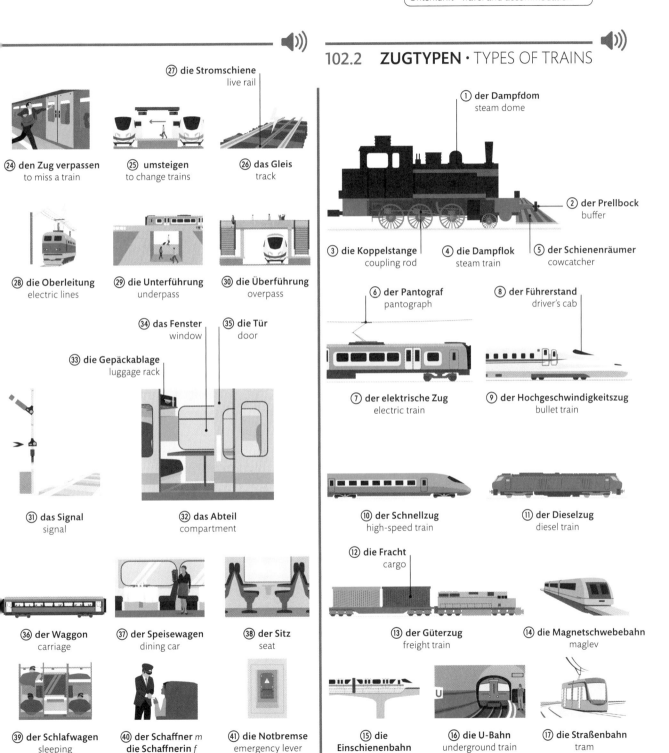

㉗ **die Stromschiene**
live rail

102.2 ZUGTYPEN · TYPES OF TRAINS

㉔ **den Zug verpassen**
to miss a train

㉕ **umsteigen**
to change trains

㉖ **das Gleis**
track

① **der Dampfdom**
steam dome

② **der Prellbock**
buffer

㉘ **die Oberleitung**
electric lines

㉙ **die Unterführung**
underpass

㉚ **die Überführung**
overpass

③ **die Koppelstange**
coupling rod

④ **die Dampflok**
steam train

⑤ **der Schienenräumer**
cowcatcher

㉞ **das Fenster**
window

㉟ **die Tür**
door

⑥ **der Pantograf**
pantograph

⑧ **der Führerstand**
driver's cab

㉝ **die Gepäckablage**
luggage rack

⑦ **der elektrische Zug**
electric train

⑨ **der Hochgeschwindigkeitszug**
bullet train

㉛ **das Signal**
signal

㉜ **das Abteil**
compartment

⑩ **der Schnellzug**
high-speed train

⑪ **der Dieselzug**
diesel train

⑫ **die Fracht**
cargo

㊱ **der Waggon**
carriage

㊲ **der Speisewagen**
dining car

㊳ **der Sitz**
seat

⑬ **der Güterzug**
freight train

⑭ **die Magnetschwebebahn**
maglev

㊴ **der Schlafwagen**
sleeping compartment

㊵ **der Schaffner** *m*
die Schaffnerin *f*
ticket inspector

㊶ **die Notbremse**
emergency lever

⑮ **die Einschienenbahn**
monorail

⑯ **die U-Bahn**
underground train

⑰ **die Straßenbahn**
tram

103.1 DAS PASSAGIERFLUGZEUG · PASSENGER AEROPLANE

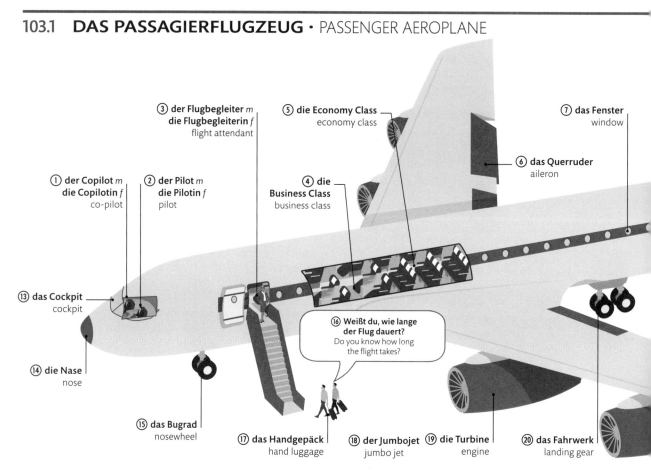

③ der Flugbegleiter *m*
die Flugbegleiterin *f*
flight attendant

⑤ die Economy Class
economy class

⑦ das Fenster
window

① der Copilot *m*
die Copilotin *f*
co-pilot

② der Pilot *m*
die Pilotin *f*
pilot

④ die
Business Class
business class

⑥ das Querruder
aileron

⑬ das Cockpit
cockpit

⑯ Weißt du, wie lange
der Flug dauert?
Do you know how long
the flight takes?

⑭ die Nase
nose

⑮ das Bugrad
nosewheel

⑰ das Handgepäck
hand luggage

⑱ der Jumbojet
jumbo jet

⑲ die Turbine
engine

⑳ das Fahrwerk
landing gear

103.3 LUFTFAHRZEUGE · TYPES OF AIRCRAFT

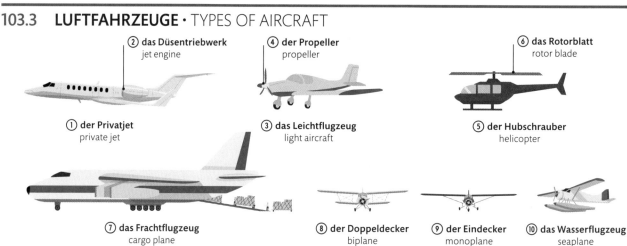

② das Düsentriebwerk
jet engine

④ der Propeller
propeller

⑥ das Rotorblatt
rotor blade

① der Privatjet
private jet

③ das Leichtflugzeug
light aircraft

⑤ der Hubschrauber
helicopter

⑦ das Frachtflugzeug
cargo plane

⑧ der Doppeldecker
biplane

⑨ der Eindecker
monoplane

⑩ das Wasserflugzeug
seaplane

See also
42-43 In der Stadt · In town **104** Am Flughafen · At the airport
131 Reise und Unterkunft · Travel and accommodation

⑧ die **kflosse**
fin

⑨ **das Seitenruder**
rudder

⑩ **das Heck**
tail

⑫ **der Notausgang**
emergency exit

⑪ **das Höhenleitwerk**
tailplane

㉑ **die Tragfläche**
wing

103.2 DIE KABINE · CABIN

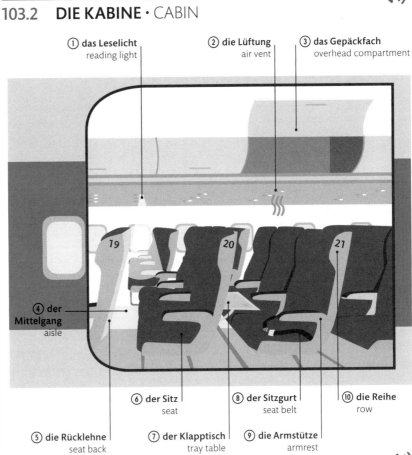

① **das Leselicht**
reading light

② **die Lüftung**
air vent

③ **das Gepäckfach**
overhead compartment

④ **der Mittelgang**
aisle

⑥ **der Sitz**
seat

⑧ **der Sitzgurt**
seat belt

⑩ **die Reihe**
row

⑤ **die Rücklehne**
seat back

⑦ **der Klapptisch**
tray table

⑨ **die Armstütze**
armrest

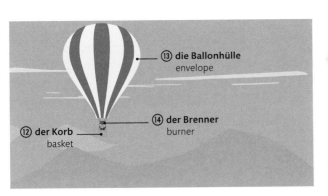

⑬ **die Ballonhülle**
envelope

⑭ **der Brenner**
burner

⑫ **der Korb**
basket

⑪ **der Heißluftballon**
hot-air balloon

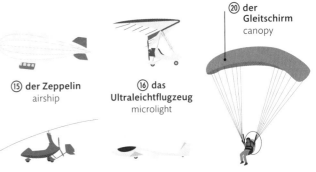

⑳ **der Gleitschirm**
canopy

⑮ **der Zeppelin**
airship

⑯ **das Ultraleichtflugzeug**
microlight

⑰ **der Tragschrauber**
gyrocopter

⑱ **das Gleitflugzeug**
glider

⑲ **der Motorschirm**
paramotor

104.1 AM TERMINAL · AT THE TERMINAL

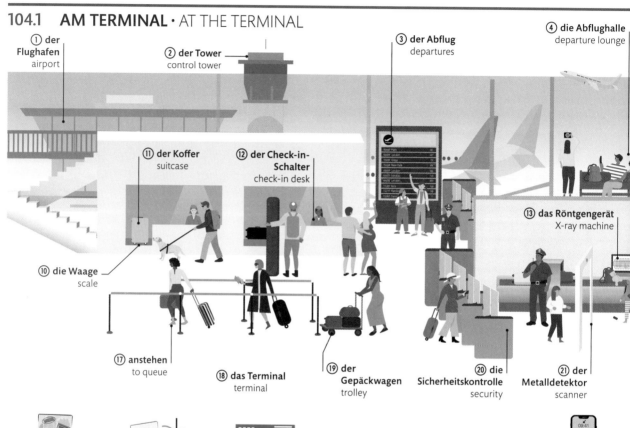

① der Flughafen
airport

② der Tower
control tower

③ der Abflug
departures

④ die Abflughalle
departure lounge

⑪ der Koffer
suitcase

⑫ der Check-in-Schalter
check-in desk

⑬ das Röntgengerät
X-ray machine

⑩ die Waage
scale

⑰ anstehen
to queue

⑱ das Terminal
terminal

⑲ der Gepäckwagen
trolley

⑳ die Sicherheitskontrolle
security

㉑ der Metalldetektor
scanner

㉘ der Pass
passport

㉙ der biometrische Pass
biometric passport

㉚ das Visum
visa

㉛ das Ticket
ticket

㉜ die Bordkarte
boarding pass

㉝ der Online-Check-in
online check-in

㊵ der Urlaub
holiday

㊶ der Inlandsflug
domestic flight

㊷ der internationale Flug
international flight

㊸ ins Ausland gehen
to go abroad

㊹ der Direktflug
direct flight

㊺ der Anschlussflug
connection

㉛ das Übergepäck
excess baggage

㊺ die Passkontrolle
passport control

㊾ die Wechselstube
currency exchange

㊾ das zollfreie Geschäft
duty-free shop

㊾ das Fundbüro
lost and found

㊾ Verspätung haben
to be delayed

See also
103 Luftfahrzeuge • Aircraft **131** Reise und Unterkunft
Travel and accommodation **149-151** Länder • Countries

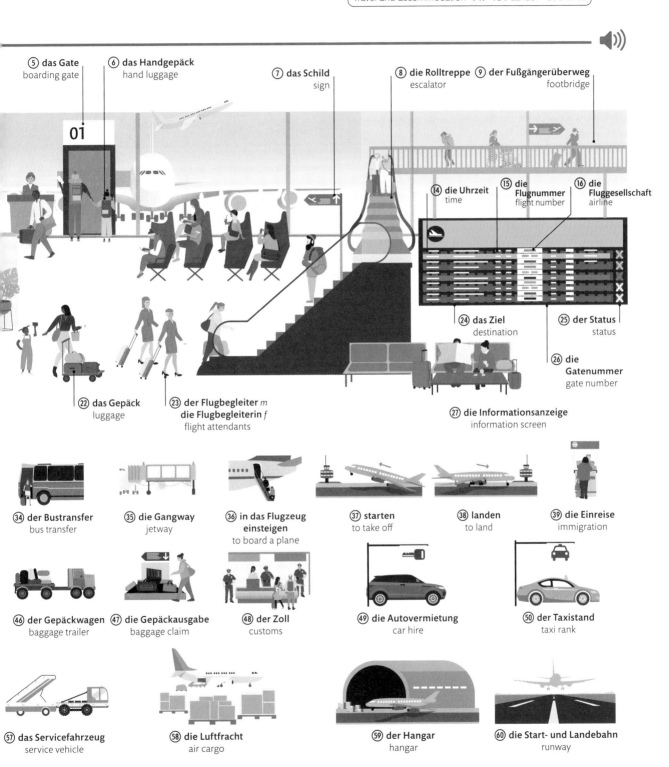

⑤ **das Gate**
boarding gate

⑥ **das Handgepäck**
hand luggage

⑦ **das Schild**
sign

⑧ **die Rolltreppe**
escalator

⑨ **der Fußgängerüberweg**
footbridge

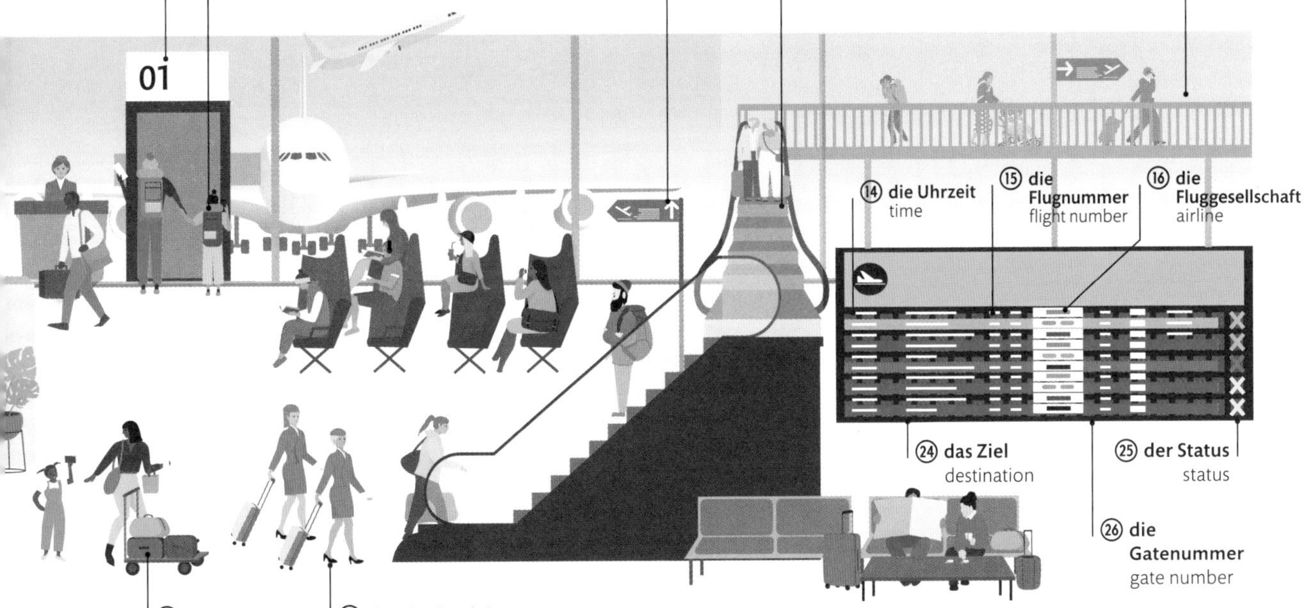

⑭ **die Uhrzeit**
time

⑮ **die Flugnummer**
flight number

⑯ **die Fluggesellschaft**
airline

㉔ **das Ziel**
destination

㉕ **der Status**
status

㉖ **die Gatenummer**
gate number

㉒ **das Gepäck**
luggage

㉓ **der Flugbegleiter** *m*
die Flugbegleiterin *f*
flight attendants

㉗ **die Informationsanzeige**
information screen

㉞ **der Bustransfer**
bus transfer

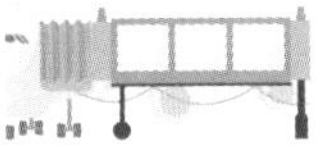

㉟ **die Gangway**
jetway

㊱ **in das Flugzeug einsteigen**
to board a plane

㊲ **starten**
to take off

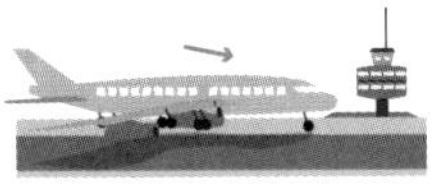

㊳ **landen**
to land

㊴ **die Einreise**
immigration

㊻ **der Gepäckwagen**
baggage trailer

㊼ **die Gepäckausgabe**
baggage claim

㊽ **der Zoll**
customs

㊾ **die Autovermietung**
car hire

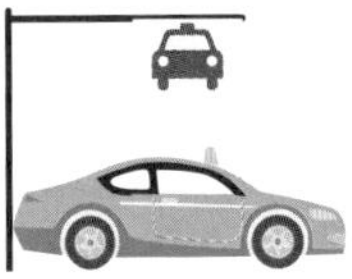

㊿ **der Taxistand**
taxi rank

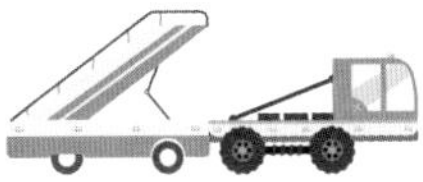

(57) **das Servicefahrzeug**
service vehicle

(58) **die Luftfracht**
air cargo

(59) **der Hangar**
hangar

(60) **die Start- und Landebahn**
runway

105.1 DAS SCHIFF · SHIP

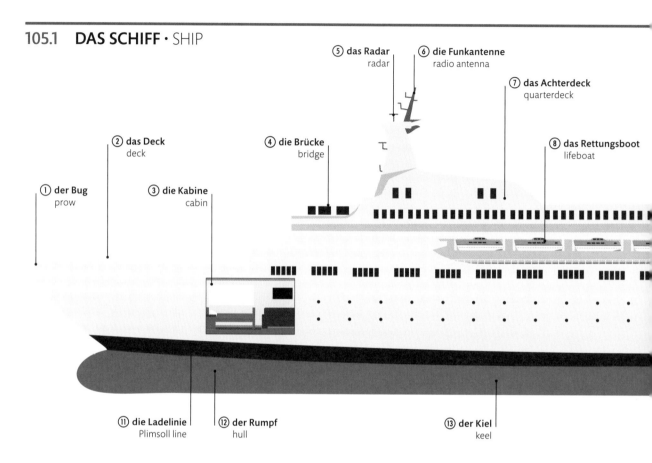

⑤ **das Radar**
radar

⑥ **die Funkantenne**
radio antenna

⑦ **das Achterdeck**
quarterdeck

② **das Deck**
deck

④ **die Brücke**
bridge

⑧ **das Rettungsboot**
lifeboat

① **der Bug**
prow

③ **die Kabine**
cabin

⑪ **die Ladelinie**
Plimsoll line

⑫ **der Rumpf**
hull

⑬ **der Kiel**
keel

105.2 WEITERE BOOTE UND SCHIFFE · OTHER BOATS AND SHIPS

⑤ **der Außenborder**
outboard motor

⑧ **der Mast**
mast

① **das Kanu**
canoe

② **das Kajak**
kayak

③ **das Ruderboot**
rowing boat

④ **das Schlauchboot**
inflatable dinghy

⑥ **der Katamaran**
catamaran

⑦ **das Segelboot**
sailing boat

⑮ **das Schnellboot**
speedboat

⑯ **die Jacht**
yacht

⑰ **das Tragflügelboot**
hydrofoil

⑱ **das Luftkissenboot**
hovercraft

⑲ **der Schlepper**
tugboat

⑳ **der Trawler**
trawler

See also
106 Der Hafen · The port **119** Segeln und Wassersport · Sailing and
watersports **131** Reise und Unterkunft · Travel and accommodation

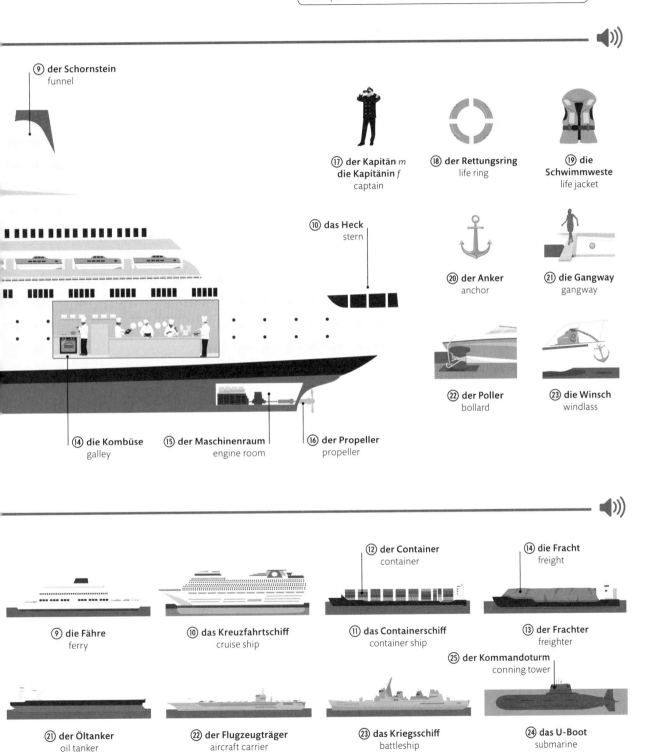

⑨ **der Schornstein**
funnel

⑰ **der Kapitän** *m*
die Kapitänin *f*
captain

⑱ **der Rettungsring**
life ring

⑲ **die
Schwimmweste**
life jacket

⑩ **das Heck**
stern

⑳ **der Anker**
anchor

㉑ **die Gangway**
gangway

㉒ **der Poller**
bollard

㉓ **die Winsch**
windlass

⑭ **die Kombüse**
galley

⑮ **der Maschinenraum**
engine room

⑯ **der Propeller**
propeller

⑫ **der Container**
container

⑭ **die Fracht**
freight

⑨ **die Fähre**
ferry

⑩ **das Kreuzfahrtschiff**
cruise ship

⑪ **das Containerschiff**
container ship

⑬ **der Frachter**
freighter

㉕ **der Kommandoturm**
conning tower

㉑ **der Öltanker**
oil tanker

㉒ **der Flugzeugträger**
aircraft carrier

㉓ **das Kriegsschiff**
battleship

㉔ **das U-Boot**
submarine

106.1 AM DOCK · AT THE DOCKS

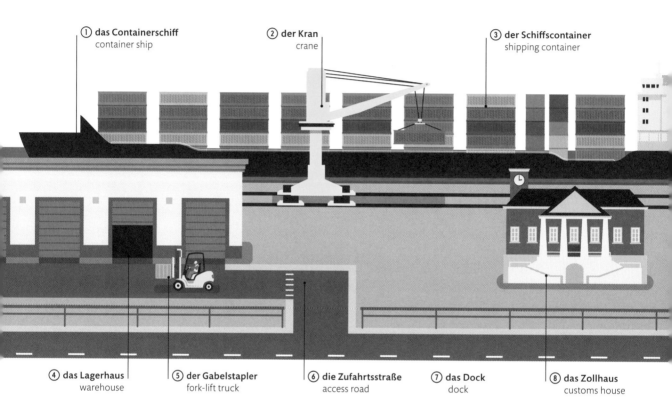

① **das Containerschiff**
container ship

② **der Kran**
crane

③ **der Schiffscontainer**
shipping container

④ **das Lagerhaus**
warehouse

⑤ **der Gabelstapler**
fork-lift truck

⑥ **die Zufahrtsstraße**
access road

⑦ **das Dock**
dock

⑧ **das Zollhaus**
customs house

⑱ **die Fähre**
ferry

⑳ **der Passagier** *m*
die Passagierin *f*
passengers

⑰ **der Fährhafen**
ferry terminal

⑲ **der Passagierhafen**
passenger port

㉑ **der Fischereihafen**
fishing port

㉒ **der Fahrkartenschalter**
ticket office

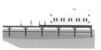

㉗ **der Liegeplatz**
mooring

㉘ **der Hafen**
harbour

㉙ **die Marina**
marina

㉚ **der Pier**
pier

㉛ **der Steg**
jetty

㉜ **das Werftgelände**
shipyard

See also
96 Straßen • Roads **102** Züge • Trains
105 Seefahrzeuge • Sea vessels

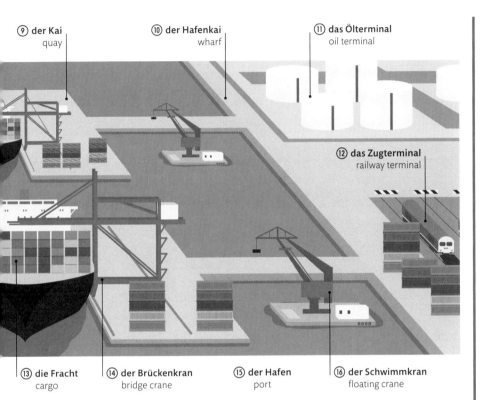

⑨ **der Kai**
quay

⑩ **der Hafenkai**
wharf

⑪ **das Ölterminal**
oil terminal

⑫ **das Zugterminal**
railway terminal

⑬ **die Fracht**
cargo

⑭ **der Brückenkran**
bridge crane

⑮ **der Hafen**
port

⑯ **der Schwimmkran**
floating crane

㉓ **das Trockendock**
dry dock

㉔ **die Boje**
buoy

㉕ **der Leuchtturm**
lighthouse

㉖ **die Laterne**
lamp

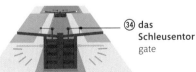

㉝ **die Schleuse**
lock

㉞ **das Schleusentor**
gate

㉟ **die Küstenwache**
coastguard

㊱ **der Hafenmeister** *m*
die Hafenmeisterin *f*
harbour master

106.2 VERBEN
VERBS

① **an Bord gehen**
to board

② **anlegen**
to moor

③ **von Bord gehen**
to disembark

④ **den Anker werfen**
to drop anchor

⑤ **anlanden**
to dock

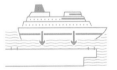

⑥ **die Segel setzen**
to set sail

107.1 AMERICAN FOOTBALL · AMERICAN FOOTBALL

① der Left Cornerback *m* / die Left Cornerback *f*
left cornerback

② der Outside Linebacker *m* die Outside Linebacker *f*
outside linebacker

③ der Left Defensive End *m* / die Left Defensive End *f*
left defensive end

④ der Left Safety *m* die Left Safety *f*
left safety

⑤ der Left Defensive Tackle *m* / die Left Defensive Tackle *f*
left defensive tackle

⑥ der Middle Linebacker *m* / die Middle Linebacker *f*
middle linebacker

⑦ der Right Defensive Tackle *m* / die Right Defensive Tackle *f*
right defensive tackle

⑧ der Right Safety *m* die Right Safety *f*
right safety

⑨ der Right Defensive End *m* die Right Defensive End *f*
right defensive end

⑩ der Outside Linebacker *m* / die Outside Linebacker *f*
outside linebacker

⑪ der Right Cornerback *m* / die Right Cornerback *f*
right cornerback

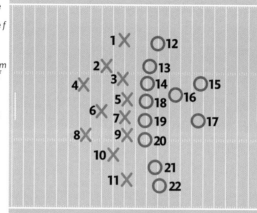

⑫ der Wide Receiver *m* / die Wide Receiver *f*
wide receiver

⑬ der Right Tackle *m* die Right Tackle *f*
right tackle

⑭ der Right Guard *m* die Right Guard *f*
right guard

⑮ der Running Back / Halfback *m* / die Running Back / Halfback *f*
running back / halfback

⑯ der Fullback *m* die Fullback *f*
fullback

⑰ der Quarterba die Quarterba
quarterback

⑱ der Center *m* die Center *f*
centre

⑲ der Left Guarc die Left Guard
left guard

⑳ der Left Tackle die Left Tackle
left tackle

㉑ ㉒ der Wide Receiver *m* / d Wide Receiver
wide receiver

㉔ die Verteidigung
defence

㉓ die Aufstellung im American Football
American football positions

㉕ der Angriff
offence

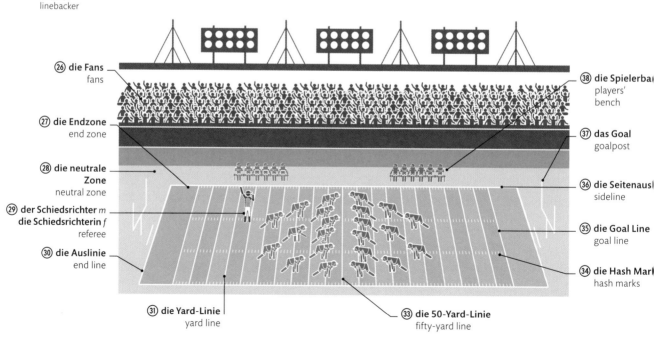

㉖ die Fans
fans

㉗ die Endzone
end zone

㉘ die neutrale Zone
neutral zone

㉙ der Schiedsrichter *m* die Schiedsrichterin *f*
referee

㉚ die Auslinie
end line

㉛ die Yard-Linie
yard line

㉜ das Spielfeld
field / pitch

㉝ die 50-Yard-Linie
fifty-yard line

㉞ die Hash Mar
hash marks

㉟ die Goal Line
goal line

㊱ die Seitenaus
sideline

㊲ das Goal
goalpost

㊳ die Spielerba
players' bench

See also
108 Rugby • Rugby **109** Fußball • Football
110 Hockey und Lacrosse • Hockey and lacrosse

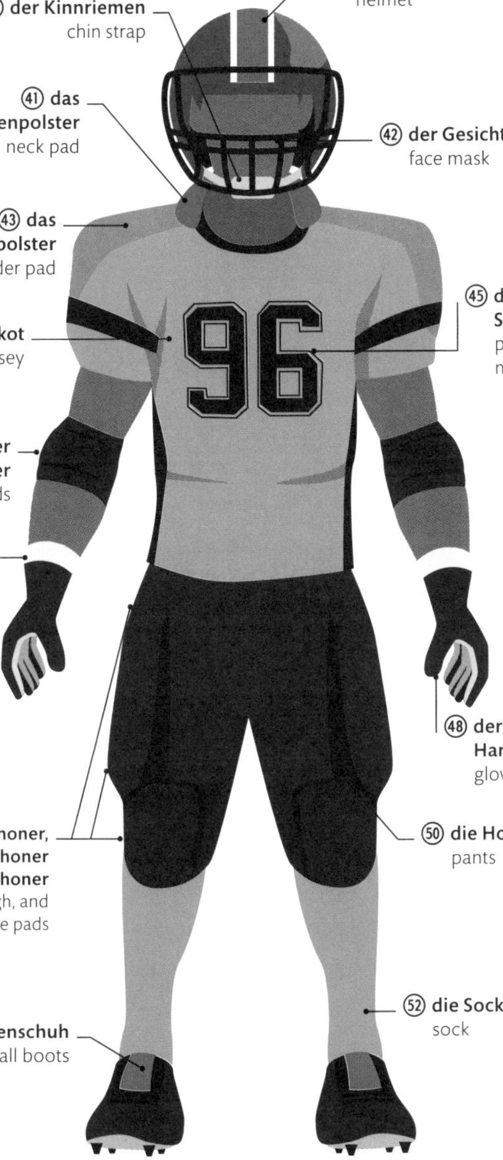

(39) **der Kinnriemen**
chin strap

(40) **der Helm**
helmet

(41) **das Nackenpolster**
neck pad

(42) **der Gesichtsschutz**
face mask

(43) **das Schulterpolster**
shoulder pad

(44) **das Trikot**
team jersey

(45) **die Spielernummer**
player's number

(46) **der ogenschoner**
elbow pads

(47) **das weißband**
wrist band

(48) **der Handschuh**
gloves

) **der Hüftschoner, rschenkelschoner und Knieschoner**
hip, thigh, and knee pads

(50) **die Hose**
pants

(51) **der Stollenschuh**
football boots

(52) **die Socke**
sock

(53) **der Footballspieler** *m* / **die Footballspielerin** *f*
football player

(54) **der Mundschutz**
mouth guard

(55) **der Brustschutz**
chest protector

(56) **die Mannschaft**
team

(57) **angreifen**
to tackle

(58) **passen**
to pass

(59) **fangen**
to catch

(60) **die Auszeit**
time out

(61) **Yards gewinnen**
to gain yards

(62) **fumbeln**
to fumble

(63) **werfen**
to throw

(64) **schießen**
to kick

(65) **der Touchdown**
touchdown

(66) **verfolgen**
to chase

(67) **der Cheerleader** *m*
die Cheerleaderin *f*
cheerleader

(70) **die Naht**
lace

(69) **das Leder**
leather

(68) **der Football**
football

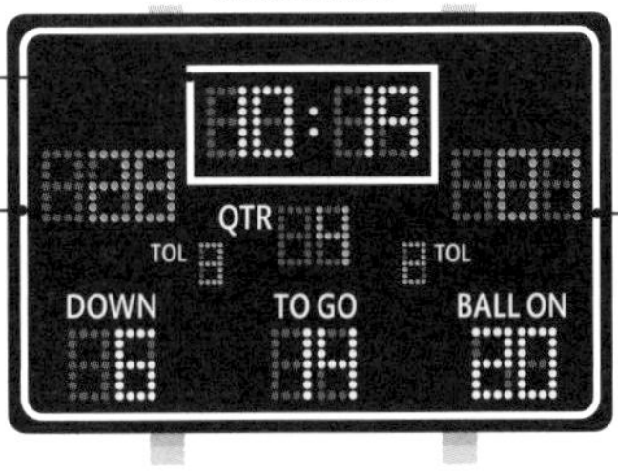

(71) **die Zeit**
time

(72) **die Heimmannschaft**
home

(73) **die Gastmannschaft**
visitor

(74) **die Anzeigetafel**
scoreboard

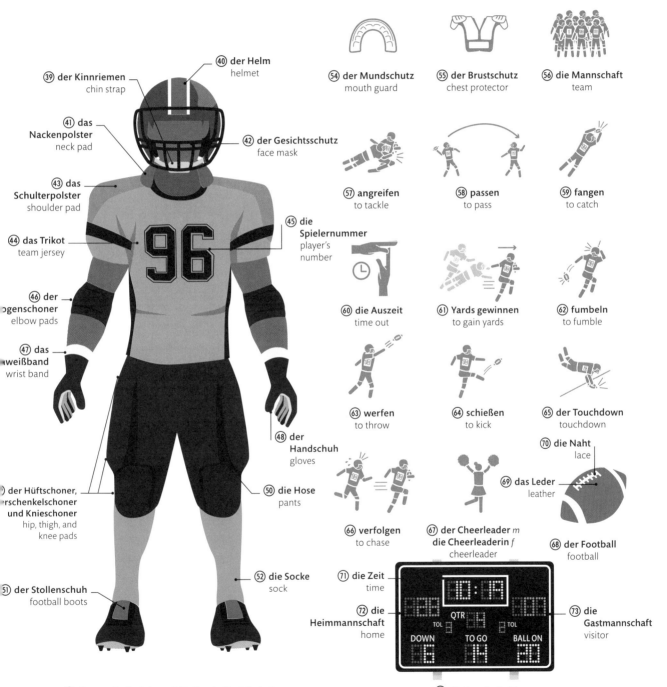

108.1 RUGBY · RUGBY

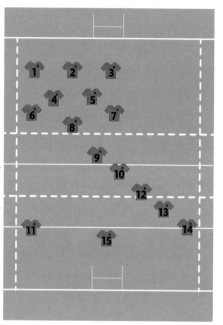

① der linke Pfeiler *m*
die linke Pfeilerin *f*
loosehead prop

② der Hakler *m*
die Haklerin *f*
hooker

③ der rechte Pfeiler *m*
die rechte Pfeilerin *f*
tighthead prop

④ der Zweite-Reihe-Stürmer *m*
die Zweite-Reihe-Stürmerin *f*
second row

⑤ der Zweite-Reihe-Stürmer *m*
die Zweite-Reihe-Stürmerin *f*
second row

⑥ der linke Flügelstürmer *m*
die linke Flügelstürmerin *f*
blindside flanker

⑦ der rechte Flügelstürmer *m*
die rechte Flügelstürmerin *f*
openside flanker

⑧ die Nummer Acht
number eight

⑯ die Aufstellung im Rugby
rugby positions

⑨ der Gedrängehalb *m*
die Gedrängehalb *f*
scrum-half

⑩ der Verbindungshalb *m*
die Verbindungshalb *f*
fly-half

⑪ der linke Außendreiviertel *m*
die linke Außendreiviertel *f*
left-wing

⑫ der erste Innendreiviertel *m*
die erste Innendreiviertel *f*
inside centre

⑬ der zweite Innendreiviertel *m*
die zweite Innendreiviertel *f*
outside centre

⑭ der rechte Außendreiviertel *m*
die rechte Außendreiviertel *f*
right wing

⑮ der Schlussmann *m*
die Schlussfrau *f*
full back

㊱ das Rollstuhl-Rugby
wheelchair rugby

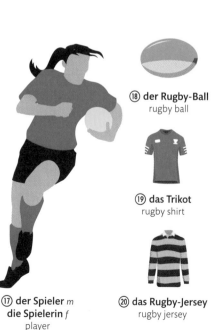

⑱ der Rugby-Ball
rugby ball

⑲ das Trikot
rugby shirt

⑳ das Rugby-Jersey
rugby jersey

⑰ der Spieler *m*
die Spielerin *f*
player

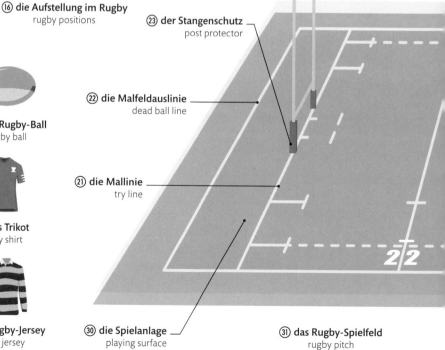

㉔ die Malstange
goal posts

㉓ der Stangenschutz
post protector

㉒ die Malfeldauslinie
dead ball line

㉑ die Mallinie
try line

㉚ die Spielanlage
playing surface

㉛ das Rugby-Spielfeld
rugby pitch

See also
107 American Football · American football **109** Fußball · Football **110** Hockey und Lacrosse · Hockey and lacrosse **112** Basketball und Volleyball · Basketball and volleyball

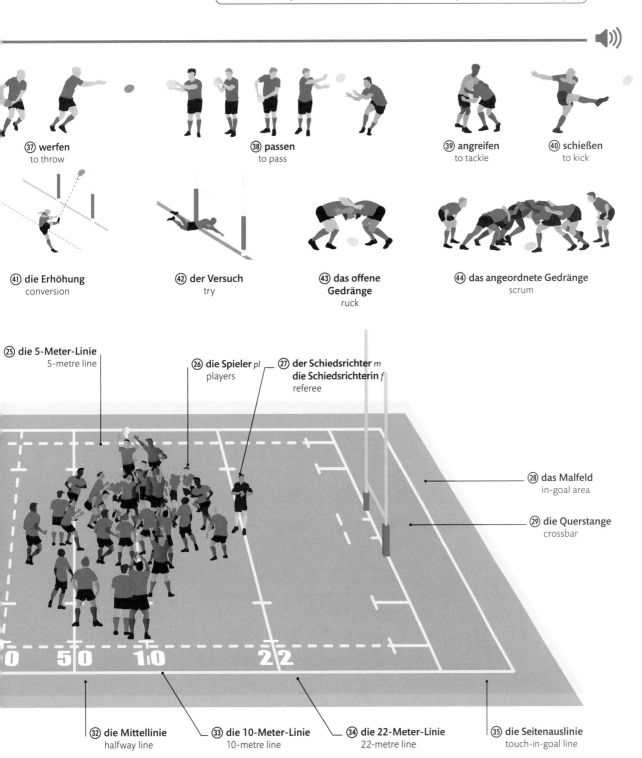

㊲ **werfen**
to throw

㊳ **passen**
to pass

㊴ **angreifen**
to tackle

㊵ **schießen**
to kick

㊶ **die Erhöhung**
conversion

㊷ **der Versuch**
try

㊸ **das offene Gedränge**
ruck

㊹ **das angeordnete Gedränge**
scrum

㉕ **die 5-Meter-Linie**
5-metre line

㉖ **die Spieler** *pl*
players

㉗ **der Schiedsrichter** *m*
die Schiedsrichterin *f*
referee

㉘ **das Malfeld**
in-goal area

㉙ **die Querstange**
crossbar

㉜ **die Mittellinie**
halfway line

㉝ **die 10-Meter-Linie**
10-metre line

㉞ **die 22-Meter-Linie**
22-metre line

㉟ **die Seitenauslinie**
touch-in-goal line

109.1 DAS FUSSBALLSPIEL · FOOTBALL GAME

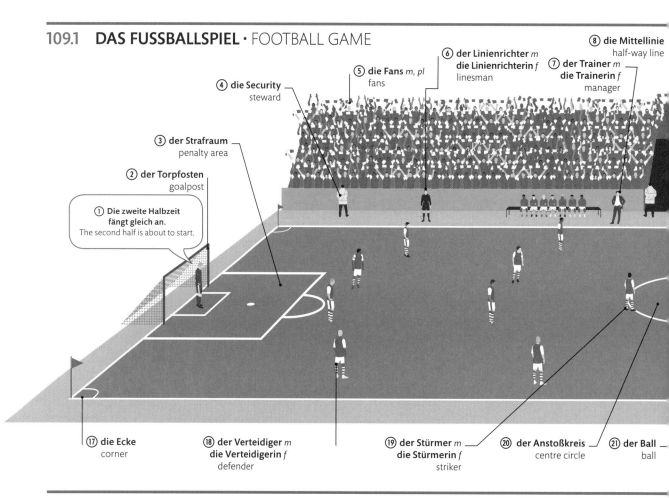

⑧ **die Mittellinie** half-way line

⑥ **der Linienrichter** *m* **die Linienrichterin** *f* linesman

⑦ **der Trainer** *m* **die Trainerin** *f* manager

⑤ **die Fans** *m, pl* fans

④ **die Security** steward

③ **der Strafraum** penalty area

② **der Torpfosten** goalpost

① **Die zweite Halbzeit fängt gleich an.** The second half is about to start.

⑰ **die Ecke** corner

⑱ **der Verteidiger** *m* **die Verteidigerin** *f* defender

⑲ **der Stürmer** *m* **die Stürmerin** *f* striker

⑳ **der Anstoßkreis** centre circle

㉑ **der Ball** ball

109.2 ZEITEN UND REGELN · TIMING AND RULES

① **der Anstoß** kickoff

② **die Halbzeit** half time

③ **das Spielzeitende** full time

④ **der Einwurf** throw-in

⑤ **der Abpfiff** final whistle

⑥ **die Nachspielzeit** injury time

⑨ **der Eckstoß** corner kick

⑩ **die gelbe Karte** yellow card

⑪ **die rote Karte** red card

⑫ **einen Platzverweis erhalten** to be sent off

⑬ **unentschieden spielen** to draw

⑭ **verlieren** to lose

See also
107 American Football · American football **108** Rugby · Rugby **110** Hockey und
Lacrosse · Hockey and lacrosse **112** Basketball und Volleyball · Basketball and volleyball

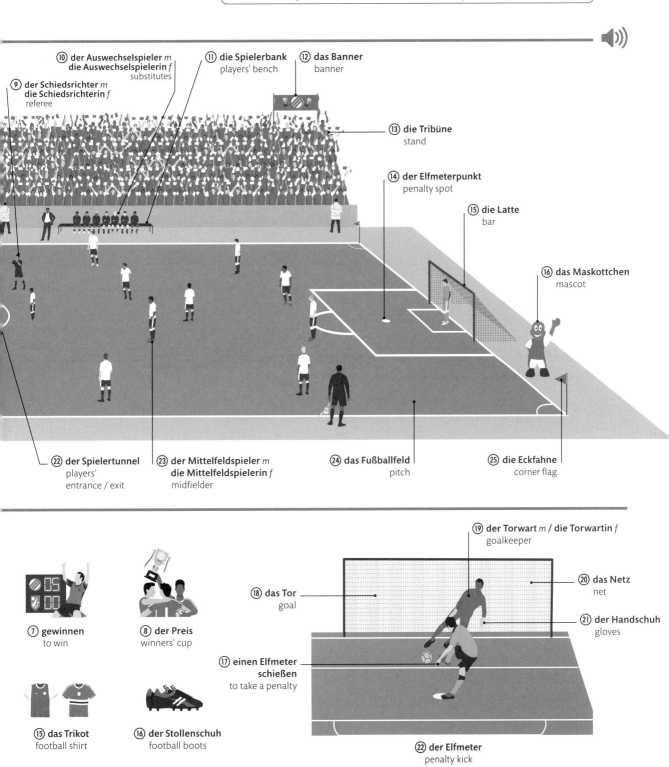

⑩ **der Auswechselspieler** *m*
die Auswechselspielerin *f*
substitutes

⑪ **die Spielerbank**
players' bench

⑫ **das Banner**
banner

⑨ **der Schiedsrichter** *m*
die Schiedsrichterin *f*
referee

⑬ **die Tribüne**
stand

⑭ **der Elfmeterpunkt**
penalty spot

⑮ **die Latte**
bar

⑯ **das Maskottchen**
mascot

㉒ **der Spielertunnel**
players'
entrance / exit

㉓ **der Mittelfeldspieler** *m*
die Mittelfeldspielerin *f*
midfielder

㉔ **das Fußballfeld**
pitch

㉕ **die Eckfahne**
corner flag

⑲ **der Torwart** *m* / **die Torwartin** *f*
goalkeeper

⑱ **das Tor**
goal

⑳ **das Netz**
net

㉑ **der Handschuh**
gloves

⑰ **einen Elfmeter
schießen**
to take a penalty

⑦ **gewinnen**
to win

⑧ **der Preis**
winners' cup

⑮ **das Trikot**
football shirt

⑯ **der Stollenschuh**
football boots

㉒ **der Elfmeter**
penalty kick

227

110.1 EISHOCKEY · ICE HOCKEY

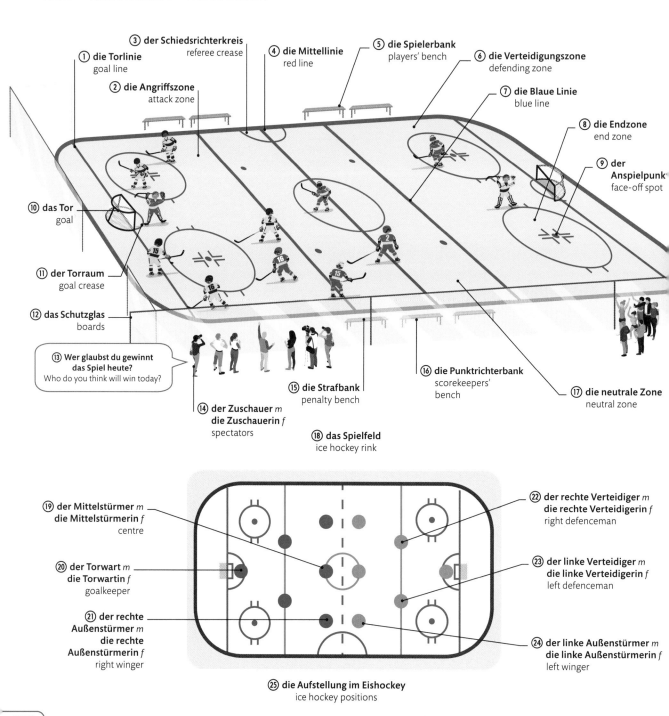

① die Torlinie
goal line

② die Angriffszone
attack zone

③ der Schiedsrichterkreis
referee crease

④ die Mittellinie
red line

⑤ die Spielerbank
players' bench

⑥ die Verteidigungszone
defending zone

⑦ die Blaue Linie
blue line

⑧ die Endzone
end zone

⑨ der Anspielpunkt
face-off spot

⑩ das Tor
goal

⑪ der Torraum
goal crease

⑫ das Schutzglas
boards

⑬ Wer glaubst du gewinnt das Spiel heute?
Who do you think will win today?

⑭ der Zuschauer m
die Zuschauerin f
spectators

⑮ die Strafbank
penalty bench

⑯ die Punktrichterbank
scorekeepers' bench

⑰ die neutrale Zone
neutral zone

⑱ das Spielfeld
ice hockey rink

⑲ der Mittelstürmer m
die Mittelstürmerin f
centre

⑳ der Torwart m
die Torwartin f
goalkeeper

㉑ der rechte Außenstürmer m
die rechte Außenstürmerin f
right winger

㉒ der rechte Verteidiger m
die rechte Verteidigerin f
right defenceman

㉓ der linke Verteidiger m
die linke Verteidigerin f
left defenceman

㉔ der linke Außenstürmer m
die linke Außenstürmerin f
left winger

㉕ die Aufstellung im Eishockey
ice hockey positions

See also
107 American Football · American football **111** Kricket · Cricket **112** Basketball und Volleyball · Basketball and volleyball **113** Baseball · Baseball **114** Tennis · Tennis

㉖ **eislaufen**
to skate

㉗ **das Schulterpolster**
shoulder pad

㉘ **der Helm**
helmet

㉙ **die Schutzpolsterung**
protective padding

㉚ **der Handschuh**
glove

㉜ **der Schläger**
stick

㉛ **der Schlittschuh**
ice skate

㉝ **der Puck**
puck

㉞ **der Eishockeyspieler** *m*
die Eishockeyspielerin *f*
ice hockey player

㉟ **der Stockhandschuh**
blocking glove

㊱ **die Goalie-Maske**
face mask

㊲ **der Fanghandschuh**
catching glove

㊳ **der Beinschoner**
leg guard

㊴ **der Torwart** *m*
die Torwartin *f*
goalkeeper

㊴ **der Goalie-Schläger**
goalie stick

110.2 HOCKEY · FIELD HOCKEY

① **schlagen**
to hit

② **der Schienbeinschoner**
shin guard

③ **der Hockeyschläger**
hockey stick

⑤ **der Ball**
ball

④ **der Hockeyspieler** *m*
die Hockeyspielerin *f*
field hockey player

110.3 LACROSSE · LACROSSE

① **das Netz**
head pocket

② **der Schläger**
crosse

③ **der Armschutz**
arm protection

④ **der Griff**
handle

⑤ **der Lacrossespieler** *m*
die Lacrossespielerin *f*
lacrosse player

⑥ **passen**
to pass

⑦ **aufnehmen**
to scoop

⑧ **der Face-Off**
face-off

111.1 DAS KRICKETSPIELFELD UND DIE KRICKETAUFSTELLUNG
CRICKET PITCH AND POSITIONS

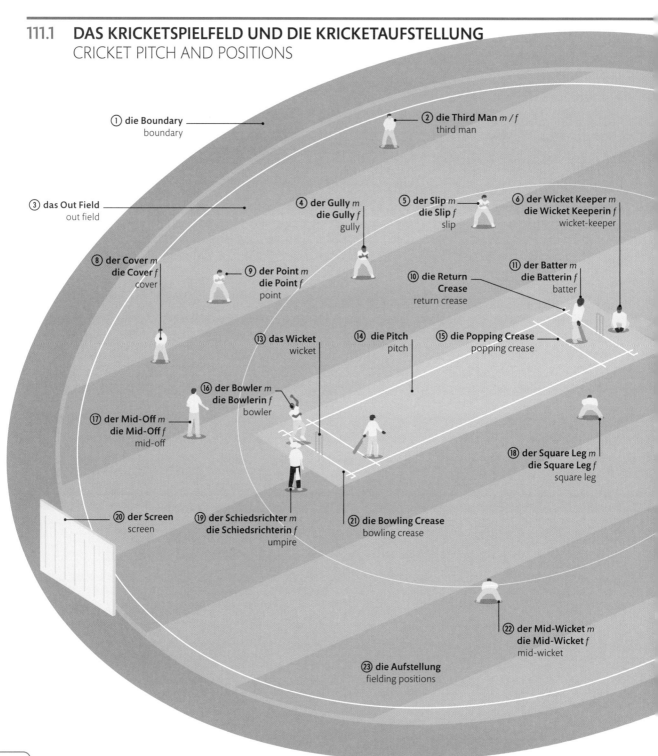

① **die Boundary**
boundary

② **die Third Man** *m / f*
third man

③ **das Out Field**
out field

④ **der Gully** *m*
die Gully *f*
gully

⑤ **der Slip** *m*
die Slip *f*
slip

⑥ **der Wicket Keeper** *m*
die Wicket Keeperin *f*
wicket-keeper

⑧ **der Cover** *m*
die Cover *f*
cover

⑨ **der Point** *m*
die Point *f*
point

⑩ **die Return Crease**
return crease

⑪ **der Batter** *m*
die Batterin *f*
batter

⑬ **das Wicket**
wicket

⑭ **die Pitch**
pitch

⑮ **die Popping Crease**
popping crease

⑯ **der Bowler** *m*
die Bowlerin *f*
bowler

⑰ **der Mid-Off** *m*
die Mid-Off *f*
mid-off

⑱ **der Square Leg** *m*
die Square Leg *f*
square leg

⑳ **der Screen**
screen

⑲ **der Schiedsrichter** *m*
die Schiedsrichterin *f*
umpire

㉑ **die Bowling Crease**
bowling crease

㉒ **der Mid-Wicket** *m*
die Mid-Wicket *f*
mid-wicket

㉓ **die Aufstellung**
fielding positions

See also
109 Fußball · Football **110** Hockey und Lacrosse · Hockey and lacrosse **113** Baseball · Baseball **115** Golf · Golf

111.2 KRICKETAUSRÜSTUNG · CRICKET EQUIPMENT

① **der Kricketschuh**
cricket shoes

② **die Stollen** m, pl
studs

③ **der Kricketball**
cricket ball

④ **die Naht**
seam

⑤ **der Stab**
stumps

⑥ **der Querstab**
bail

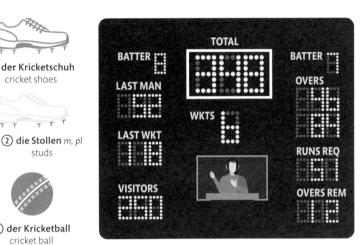

⑦ **die Anzeigetafel**
scoreboard

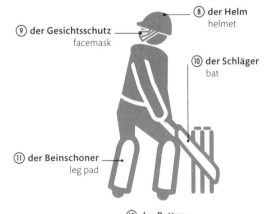

⑧ **der Helm**
helmet

⑨ **der Gesichtsschutz**
facemask

⑩ **der Schläger**
bat

⑪ **der Beinschoner**
leg pad

⑫ **der Batter** m
die Batterin f
batter / batsman

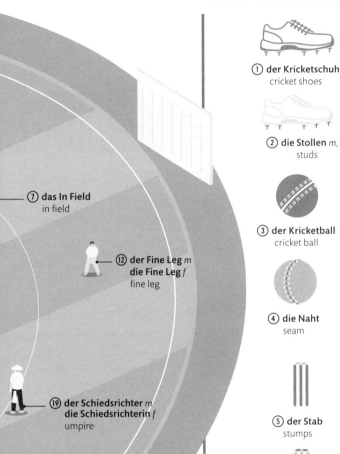

⑦ **das In Field**
in field

⑫ **der Fine Leg** m
die Fine Leg f
fine leg

⑲ **der Schiedsrichter** m
die Schiedsrichterin f
umpire

111.3 KRICKETVERBEN · CRICKET VERBS

① **laufen**
to run

② **werfen**
to bowl

③ **schlagen**
to bat

④ **fangen**
to field

⑤ **ins Aus schlagen**
to strike out

⑥ **ausschalten**
to stump

112.1 **BASKETBALL** · BASKETBALL

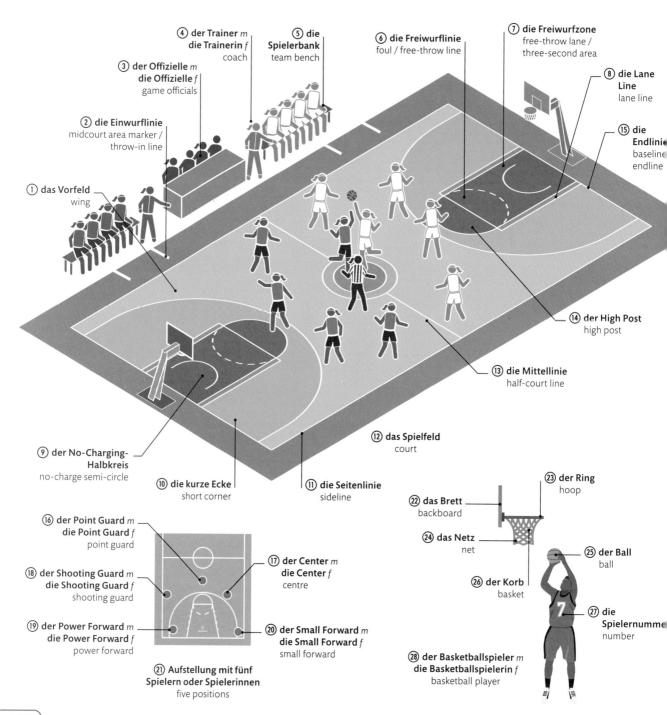

④ **der Trainer** m
die Trainerin f
coach

⑤ **die Spielerbank**
team bench

③ **der Offizielle** m
die Offizielle f
game officials

⑥ **die Freiwurflinie**
foul / free-throw line

⑦ **die Freiwurfzone**
free-throw lane /
three-second area

⑧ **die Lane Line**
lane line

② **die Einwurflinie**
midcourt area marker /
throw-in line

① **das Vorfeld**
wing

⑮ **die Endlinie**
baseline
endline

⑭ **der High Post**
high post

⑬ **die Mittellinie**
half-court line

⑫ **das Spielfeld**
court

⑨ **der No-Charging-Halbkreis**
no-charge semi-circle

⑩ **die kurze Ecke**
short corner

⑪ **die Seitenlinie**
sideline

⑯ **der Point Guard** m
die Point Guard f
point guard

⑰ **der Center** m
die Center f
centre

⑱ **der Shooting Guard** m
die Shooting Guard f
shooting guard

⑲ **der Power Forward** m
die Power Forward f
power forward

⑳ **der Small Forward** m
die Small Forward f
small forward

㉑ **Aufstellung mit fünf Spielern oder Spielerinnen**
five positions

㉒ **das Brett**
backboard

㉓ **der Ring**
hoop

㉔ **das Netz**
net

㉕ **der Ball**
ball

㉖ **der Korb**
basket

㉗ **die Spielernummer**
number

㉘ **der Basketballspieler** m
die Basketballspielerin f
basketball player

See also
107 American Football · American football **108** Rugby · Rugby **109** Fußball · Football
124 Im Fitnessstudio · At the gym **125** Weitere Sportarten · Other sports

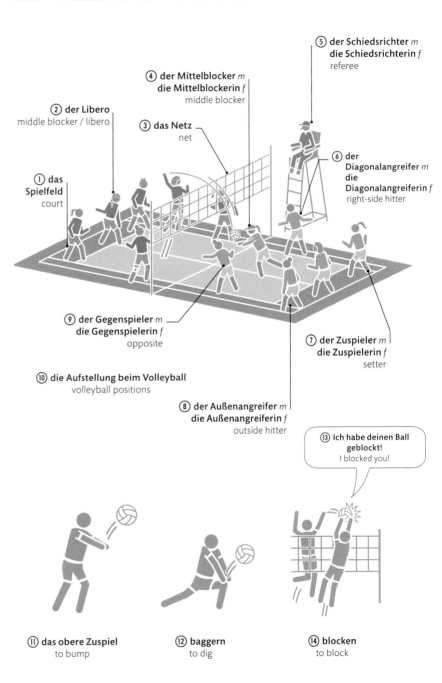

㉙ **passen**
pass

㉚ **im Aus**
out of bounds

㉛ **der Einwurf**
throw-in

㉜ **der Rebound**
rebound

㉝ **der Airball**
airball

㉞ **der Schiedsrichterball**
jump ball

㉟ **das Foul**
foul

㊱ **decken**
to mark

㊲ **dribbeln**
to bounce

㊳ **dunken**
to dunk

㊴ **werfen**
to shoot

㊵ **abwehren**
to block

112.2 **VOLLEYBALL** · VOLLEYBALL

⑤ **der Schiedsrichter** *m*
die Schiedsrichterin *f*
referee

④ **der Mittelblocker** *m*
die Mittelblockerin *f*
middle blocker

② **der Libero**
middle blocker / libero

③ **das Netz**
net

① **das Spielfeld**
court

⑥ **der Diagonalangreifer** *m*
die Diagonalangreiferin *f*
right-side hitter

⑨ **der Gegenspieler** *m*
die Gegenspielerin *f*
opposite

⑩ **die Aufstellung beim Volleyball**
volleyball positions

⑧ **der Außenangreifer** *m*
die Außenangreiferin *f*
outside hitter

⑦ **der Zuspieler** *m*
die Zuspielerin *f*
setter

⑬ Ich habe deinen Ball geblockt!
I blocked you!

⑪ **das obere Zuspiel**
to bump

⑫ **baggern**
to dig

⑭ **blocken**
to block

113.1 DAS BASEBALLSPIEL · BASEBALL GAME

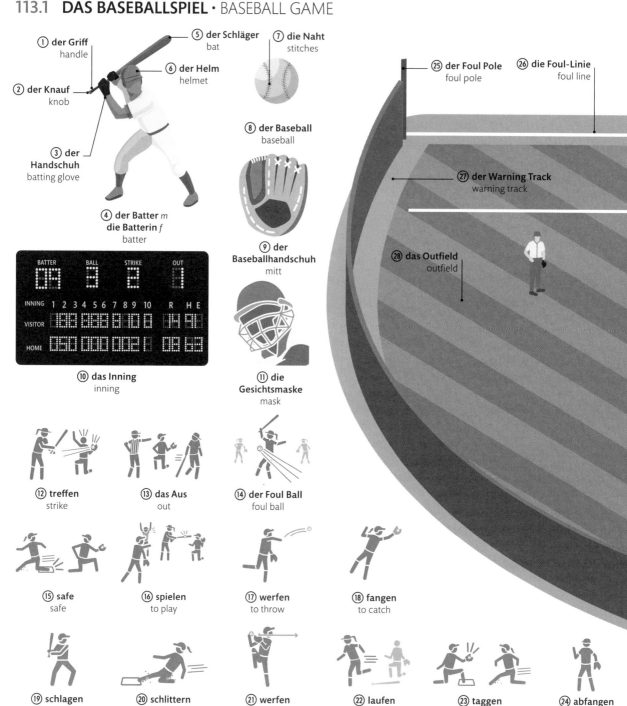

① **der Griff**
handle

② **der Knauf**
knob

③ **der Handschuh**
batting glove

④ **der Batter** *m*
die Batterin *f*
batter

⑤ **der Schläger**
bat

⑥ **der Helm**
helmet

⑦ **die Naht**
stitches

⑧ **der Baseball**
baseball

⑨ **der Baseballhandschuh**
mitt

⑩ **das Inning**
inning

⑪ **die Gesichtsmaske**
mask

⑫ **treffen**
strike

⑬ **das Aus**
out

⑭ **der Foul Ball**
foul ball

⑮ **safe**
safe

⑯ **spielen**
to play

⑰ **werfen**
to throw

⑱ **fangen**
to catch

⑲ **schlagen**
to bat

⑳ **schlittern**
to slide

㉑ **werfen**
to pitch

㉒ **laufen**
to run

㉓ **taggen**
to tag

㉔ **abfangen**
to field

㉕ **der Foul Pole**
foul pole

㉖ **die Foul-Linie**
foul line

㉗ **der Warning Track**
warning track

㉘ **das Outfield**
outfield

BATTER BALL STRIKE OUT

INNING 1 2 3 4 5 6 7 8 9 10 R H E
VISITOR
HOME

See also
107 American Football · American football **110** Hockey und Lacrosse · Hockey and lacrosse
111 Kricket · Cricket **112** Basektball und Volleyball · Basketball and volleyball

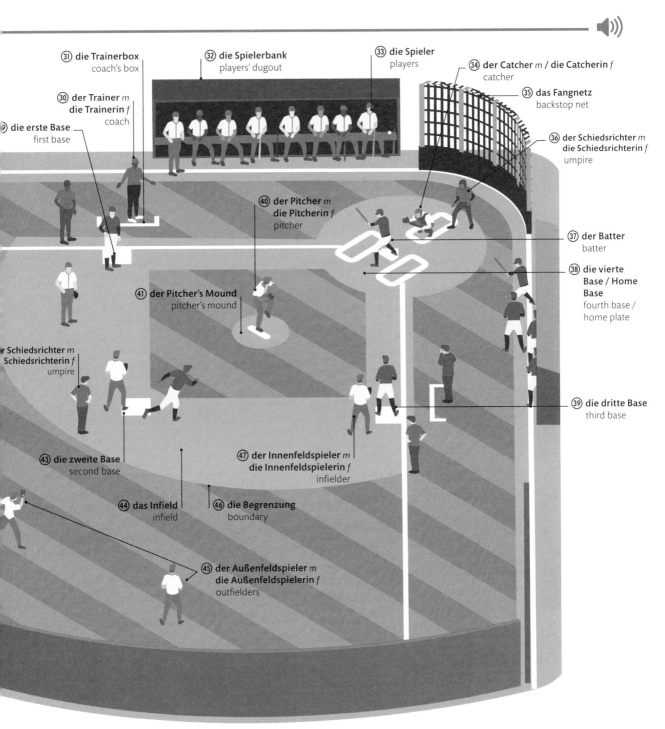

③① **die Trainerbox**
coach's box

③② **die Spielerbank**
players' dugout

③③ **die Spieler**
players

③④ **der Catcher** *m* / **die Catcherin** *f*
catcher

③⑤ **das Fangnetz**
backstop net

③⓪ **der Trainer** *m*
die Trainerin *f*
coach

die erste Base
first base

③⑥ **der Schiedsrichter** *m*
die Schiedsrichterin *f*
umpire

④⓪ **der Pitcher** *m*
die Pitcherin *f*
pitcher

③⑦ **der Batter**
batter

③⑧ **die vierte
Base / Home
Base**
fourth base /
home plate

④① **der Pitcher's Mound**
pitcher's mound

Schiedsrichter *m*
Schiedsrichterin *f*
umpire

③⑨ **die dritte Base**
third base

④③ **die zweite Base**
second base

④⑦ **der Innenfeldspieler** *m*
die Innenfeldspielerin *f*
infielder

④④ **das Infield**
infield

④⑥ **die Begrenzung**
boundary

④⑤ **der Außenfeldspieler** *m*
die Außenfeldspielerin *f*
outfielders

④⑧ **das Baseballfeld**
baseball field

114.1 DAS TENNISMATCH · TENNIS MATCH

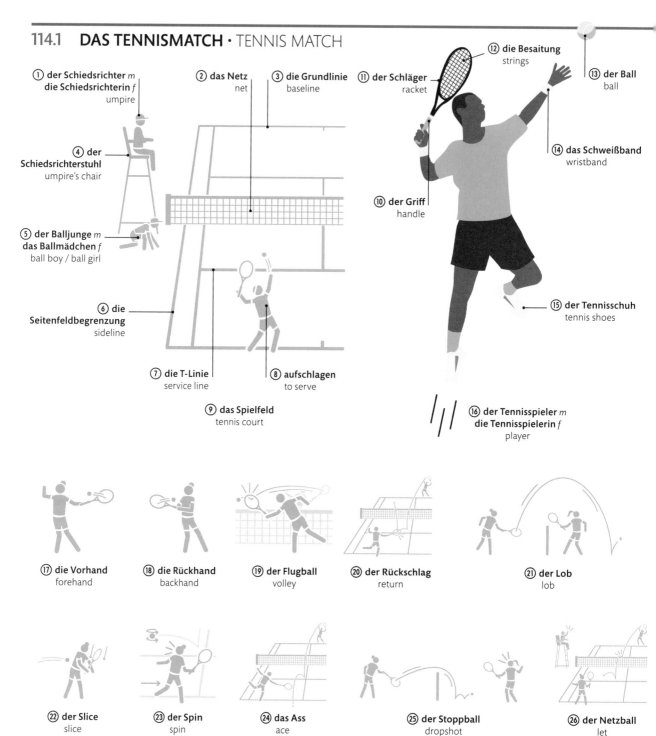

① der Schiedsrichter *m*
die Schiedsrichterin *f*
umpire

② das Netz
net

③ die Grundlinie
baseline

⑪ der Schläger
racket

⑫ die Besaitung
strings

⑬ der Ball
ball

④ der Schiedsrichterstuhl
umpire's chair

⑤ der Balljunge *m*
das Ballmädchen *f*
ball boy / ball girl

⑥ die Seitenfeldbegrenzung
sideline

⑦ die T-Linie
service line

⑧ aufschlagen
to serve

⑨ das Spielfeld
tennis court

⑩ der Griff
handle

⑭ das Schweißband
wristband

⑮ der Tennisschuh
tennis shoes

⑯ der Tennisspieler *m*
die Tennisspielerin *f*
player

⑰ die Vorhand
forehand

⑱ die Rückhand
backhand

⑲ der Flugball
volley

⑳ der Rückschlag
return

㉑ der Lob
lob

㉒ der Slice
slice

㉓ der Spin
spin

㉔ das Ass
ace

㉕ der Stoppball
dropshot

㉖ der Netzball
let

See also
111 Kricket · Cricket **113** Baseball · Baseball
115 Golf · Golf **116** Leichtathletik · Athletics

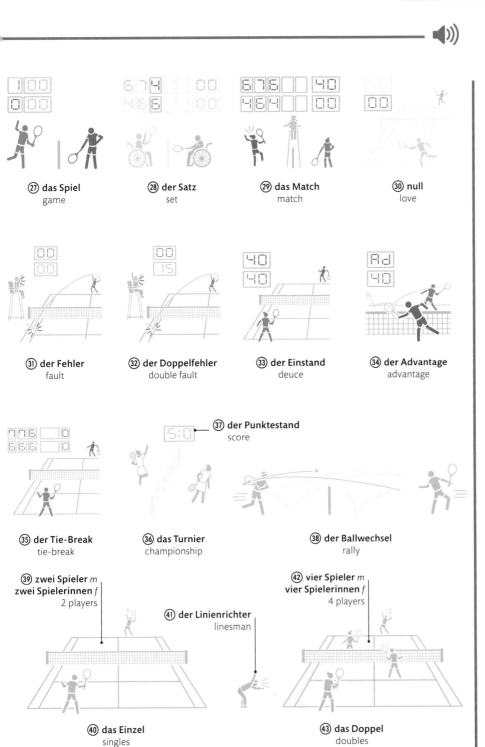

㉗ **das Spiel**
game

㉘ **der Satz**
set

㉙ **das Match**
match

㉚ **null**
love

㉛ **der Fehler**
fault

㉜ **der Doppelfehler**
double fault

㉝ **der Einstand**
deuce

㉞ **der Advantage**
advantage

㉟ **der Tie-Break**
tie-break

㊱ **das Turnier**
championship

㊲ **der Punktestand**
score

㊳ **der Ballwechsel**
rally

㊴ **zwei Spieler** *m*
zwei Spielerinnen *f*
2 players

㊶ **der Linienrichter**
linesman

㊷ **vier Spieler** *m*
vier Spielerinnen *f*
4 players

㊵ **das Einzel**
singles

㊸ **das Doppel**
doubles

114.2 BALLSPORTARTEN MIT SCHLÄGER
RACKET GAMES

① **das Squash**
squash

② **der Racquetball**
racquetball

③ **das Tischtennis / Pingpong**
ping pong / table tennis

④ **der Schläger**
bat

⑤ **das Badminton**
badminton

⑥ **der Federball**
shuttlecock

115.1 AUF DEM GOLFPLATZ · ON THE GOLF COURSE

① **das Loch**
hole

② **die Fahne**
flag

③ **das Grün**
green

⑩ **der Schwung**
swing

④ **der Bunker**
bunker

⑪ **der Stand**
stance

⑤ **das Wasserhindernis**
water hazard

⑥ **die Fairway**
fairway

⑫ **der Golfspieler** *m*
die Golfspielerin *f*
golfer

⑦ **das Rough**
rough

⑧ **der Golfplatz**
golf course

⑨ **der Abschlagplatz**
teeing ground

⑬ **das Clubhaus**
clubhouse

⑭ **der Golfwagen**
buggy

⑮ **der Caddie**
caddy

⑯ **das Par**
par

⑰ **über Par**
over par

⑱ **unter Par**
under par

⑲ **das Handicap**
handicap

⑳ **die Ziellinie**
line of play

㉑ **der Probeschwung**
practice swing

㉒ **der Rückschwung**
backswing

㉓ **das Hole-in-One**
hole in one

㉔ **das Turnier**
tournament

㉕ **der Zuschauer** *m*
die Zuschauerin *f*
spectators

See also
111 Kricket · Cricket **113** Baseball
Baseball **114** Tennis · Tennis

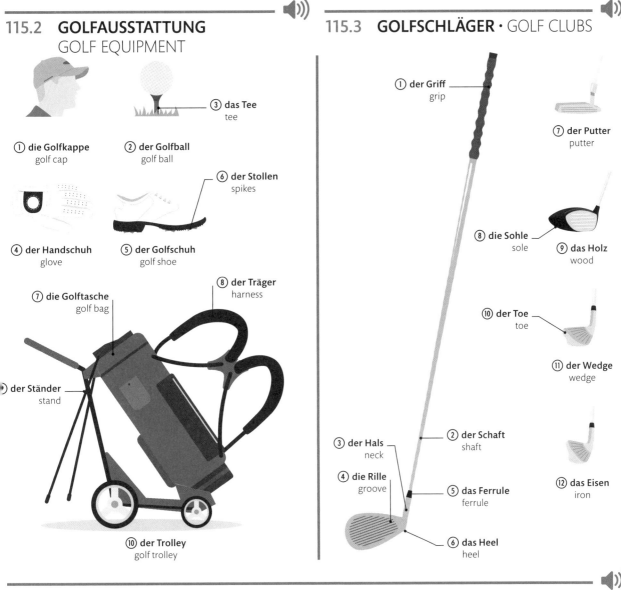

115.2 GOLFAUSSTATTUNG
GOLF EQUIPMENT

③ **das Tee**
tee

① **die Golfkappe**
golf cap

② **der Golfball**
golf ball

⑥ **der Stollen**
spikes

④ **der Handschuh**
glove

⑤ **der Golfschuh**
golf shoe

⑦ **die Golftasche**
golf bag

⑧ **der Träger**
harness

⑨ **der Ständer**
stand

⑩ **der Trolley**
golf trolley

115.3 GOLFSCHLÄGER · GOLF CLUBS

① **der Griff**
grip

⑦ **der Putter**
putter

⑧ **die Sohle**
sole

⑨ **das Holz**
wood

⑩ **der Toe**
toe

⑪ **der Wedge**
wedge

② **der Schaft**
shaft

③ **der Hals**
neck

④ **die Rille**
groove

⑤ **das Ferrule**
ferrule

⑫ **das Eisen**
iron

⑥ **das Heel**
heel

115.4 GOLFVERBEN · GOLF VERBS

① **abschlagen**
to tee off

② **driven**
to drive

③ **schwingen**
to swing

④ **putten**
to putt

⑤ **chippen**
to chip

⑥ **gewinnen**
to win

116.1 DIE LAUFBAHN · ATHLETICS TRACK

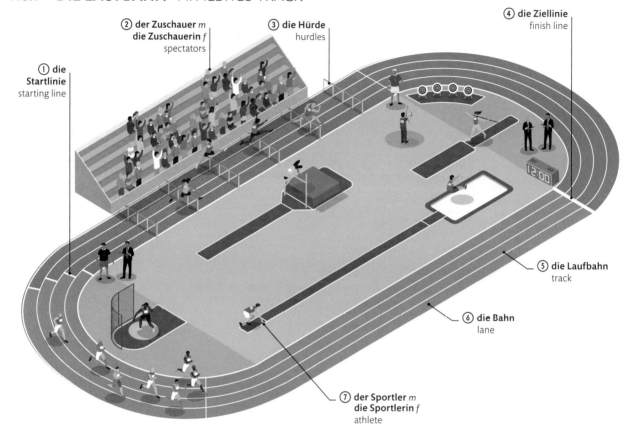

① **die Startlinie**
starting line

② **der Zuschauer** m
die Zuschauerin f
spectators

③ **die Hürde**
hurdles

④ **die Ziellinie**
finish line

⑤ **die Laufbahn**
track

⑥ **die Bahn**
lane

⑦ **der Sportler** m
die Sportlerin f
athlete

116.2 WETTLÄUFE · RACING EVENTS

① **der Wettlauf**
race

② **der Startblock**
starting block

③ **der Sprinter** m
die Sprinterin f
sprinter

④ **der Wettlauf für Sehbehinderte**
T11 (visual impairment) race

⑤ **das Rollstuhlrennen**
wheelchair race

⑥ **die Staffel**
relay race

⑦ **der Staffelstab**
baton

⑧ **der Marathon**
marathon

⑨ **das Fotofinish**
photo finish

See also
117 Kampfsportarten · Combat sports **118** Schwimmen · Swimming **119** Segeln
und Wassersport · Sailing and watersports **120** Reiten · Horse riding **122** Wintersport
Winter sports **124** Im Fitnessstudio · At the gym **125** Weitere Sportarten · Other sports

116.3 DISZIPLINEN · FIELD EVENTS

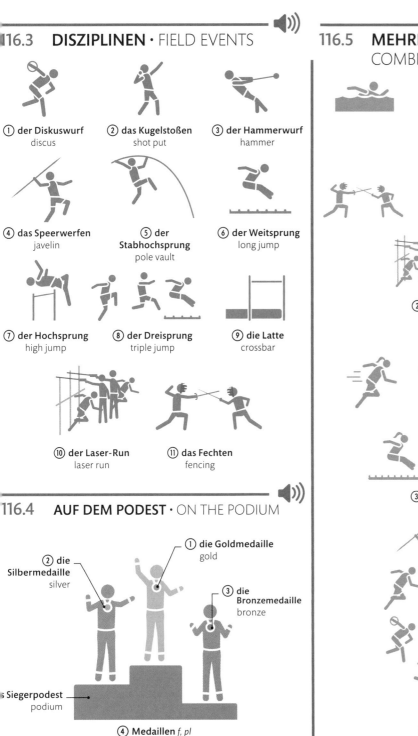

① der Diskuswurf
discus

② das Kugelstoßen
shot put

③ der Hammerwurf
hammer

④ das Speerwerfen
javelin

⑤ der Stabhochsprung
pole vault

⑥ der Weitsprung
long jump

⑦ der Hochsprung
high jump

⑧ der Dreisprung
triple jump

⑨ die Latte
crossbar

⑩ der Laser-Run
laser run

⑪ das Fechten
fencing

116.4 AUF DEM PODEST · ON THE PODIUM

① die Goldmedaille
gold

② die Silbermedaille
silver

③ die Bronzemedaille
bronze

s Siegerpodest
podium

④ Medaillen f, pl
medals

116.5 MEHRKÄMPFE
COMBINED EVENTS

① der Triathlon
triathlon

② der moderne Fünfkampf
modern pentathlon

③ der Damen-Siebenkampf
women's heptathlon

④ der Herren-Zehnkampf
men's decathlon

117.1 DER KAMPFSPORT · MARTIAL ARTS

① der Leistenschutz
groin protector

② der Handschuh
glove

③ der Gurt
belt

④ der Kopfschutz
head guard

⑤ der Brustschutz
chest protection

⑥ Taekwondo n
taekwondo

⑦ der Schwarzgurt
black belt

⑧ die Karatematte
karate mat

⑨ der Gegner m
die Gegnerin f
opponent

⑩ die Sicherheitszone
safety area

⑪ Karate n
karate

⑫ die Gefahrenzon
danger area

⑬ Judo n
judo

⑭ Aikido n
aikido

⑮ der Hakama
hakama

⑯ Kung-Fu n
kung fu

⑰ Jiu-Jitsu n
jujitsu

⑱ Capoeira f
capoeira

⑲ Kickboxen n
kickboxing

⑳ Tai-Chi n
tai chi

㉑ Wrestling n
wrestling

㉒ Sumoringen n
sumo wrestling

㉓ die Maske
mask

㉔ das Schw
sword

㉕ Kendo n
kendo

117.2 HANDLUNGEN · ACTIONS

① fallen
to fall

② festhalten
to hold

③ werfen
to throw

④ niederhalten
to pin

⑤ der Front-Kick
front kick

⑥ der Sprungtritt
flying kick

See also
116 Leichtathletik · Athletics **124** Im Fitnessstudio At the gym **125** Weitere Sportarten · Other sports

117.3 **BOXEN** · BOXING

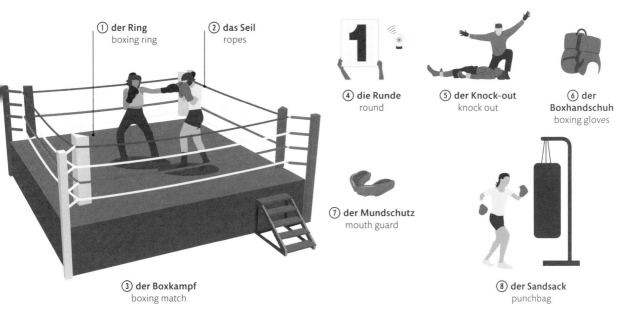

① **der Ring**
boxing ring

② **das Seil**
ropes

④ **die Runde**
round

⑤ **der Knock-out**
knock out

⑥ **der Boxhandschuh**
boxing gloves

⑦ **der Mundschutz**
mouth guard

③ **der Boxkampf**
boxing match

⑧ **der Sandsack**
punchbag

117.4 **FECHTEN** · FENCING

③ **das Heft**
hilt

⑤ **die Klinge**
blade

④ **das Florett**
foil

⑥ **der Degen**
épée

⑦ **der Säbel**
sabre

① **einen Ausfallschritt machen**
to lunge

② **parieren**
to parry

⑦ **schlagen**
to punch

⑧ **treffen**
to strike

⑨ **blocken**
to block

⑩ **springen**
to jump

⑪ **zerschlagen**
to chop

118.1 SCHWIMMEN · SWIMMING

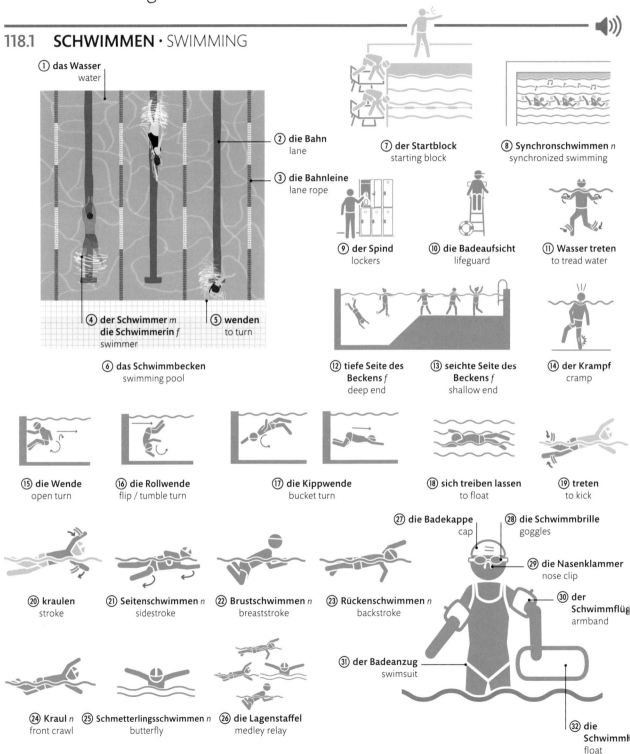

① **das Wasser**
water

② **die Bahn**
lane

③ **die Bahnleine**
lane rope

④ **der Schwimmer** m
die Schwimmerin f
swimmer

⑤ **wenden**
to turn

⑥ **das Schwimmbecken**
swimming pool

⑦ **der Startblock**
starting block

⑧ **Synchronschwimmen** n
synchronized swimming

⑨ **der Spind**
lockers

⑩ **die Badeaufsicht**
lifeguard

⑪ **Wasser treten**
to tread water

⑫ **tiefe Seite des Beckens** f
deep end

⑬ **seichte Seite des Beckens** f
shallow end

⑭ **der Krampf**
cramp

⑮ **die Wende**
open turn

⑯ **die Rollwende**
flip / tumble turn

⑰ **die Kippwende**
bucket turn

⑱ **sich treiben lassen**
to float

⑲ **treten**
to kick

⑳ **kraulen**
stroke

㉑ **Seitenschwimmen** n
sidestroke

㉒ **Brustschwimmen** n
breaststroke

㉓ **Rückenschwimmen** n
backstroke

㉔ **Kraul** n
front crawl

㉕ **Schmetterlingsschwimmen** n
butterfly

㉖ **die Lagenstaffel**
medley relay

㉗ **die Badekappe**
cap

㉘ **die Schwimmbrille**
goggles

㉙ **die Nasenklammer**
nose clip

㉚ **der Schwimmflüg**
armband

㉛ **der Badeanzug**
swimsuit

㉜ **die Schwimml**
float

See also
119 Segeln und Wassersport • Sailing and watersports
134 Am Strand • On the beach **166** Leben im Ozean • Ocean life

118.2 **TURMSPRINGEN** DIVING

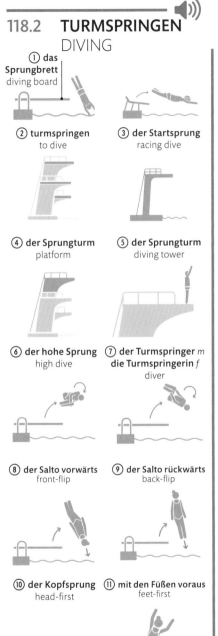

① **das Sprungbrett**
diving board

② **turmspringen**
to dive

③ **der Startsprung**
racing dive

④ **der Sprungturm**
platform

⑤ **der Sprungturm**
diving tower

⑥ **der hohe Sprung**
high dive

⑦ **der Turmspringer** *m*
die Turmspringerin *f*
diver

⑧ **der Salto vorwärts**
front-flip

⑨ **der Salto rückwärts**
back-flip

⑩ **der Kopfsprung**
head-first

⑪ **mit den Füßen voraus**
feet-first

⑫ **das Sprungbrett**
springboard

118.3 **TAUCHEN** · UNDERWATER DIVING

① **der Schnorchel**
snorkel

② **der Rifffisch**
coral
reef fish

③ **das Schnorcheln**
snorkelling

④ **der Taucheranzug**
wet suit

⑤ **der Tauchgurt**
weight belt

⑥ **die Sauerstoffflasche**
air cylinder

⑦ **die Flosse**
fins / flippers

⑧ **das Gerätetauchen**
scuba diving

⑨ **die Taucherbrille**
mask

⑩ **der Regler**
regulator

⑪ **die Unterwasserkamera**
underwater camera

⑫ **der Tiefenmesser**
depth gauge

⑬ **das Korallenriff**
coral reef

⑭ **das Tiefseetauchen**
deep diving

119.1 SEGELN · SAILING

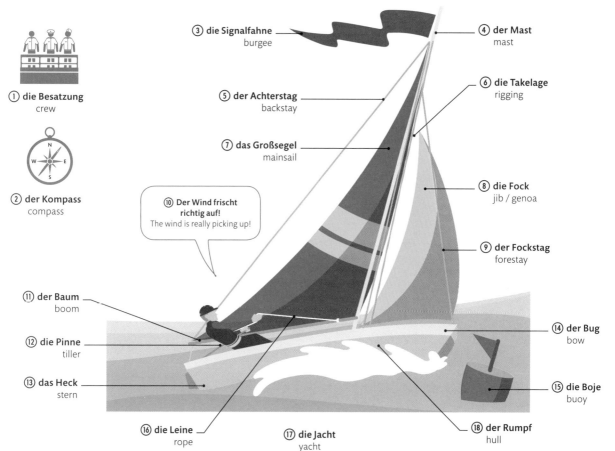

③ die Signalfahne
burgee

④ der Mast
mast

⑤ der Achterstag
backstay

⑥ die Takelage
rigging

⑦ das Großsegel
mainsail

⑧ die Fock
jib / genoa

⑩ Der Wind frischt richtig auf!
The wind is really picking up!

⑨ der Fockstag
forestay

① die Besatzung
crew

② der Kompass
compass

⑪ der Baum
boom

⑫ die Pinne
tiller

⑬ das Heck
stern

⑭ der Bug
bow

⑮ die Boje
buoy

⑯ die Leine
rope

⑰ die Jacht
yacht

⑱ der Rumpf
hull

⑲ der Anker
anchor

⑳ die Schot
sheet

㉑ die Klampe
cleat

㉒ das Seitendeck
sidedeck

㉓ das Steuerrad
boat's wheel

㉔ das Steuer
helm

㉕ das Kielschwert
centreboard

㉖ das Ruder
rudder

㉗ der Kiel
keel

㉘ die Leuchtfackel
flare

㉙ der Rettungsring
life ring

㉚ die Schwimmweste
life jacket

㉛ das Rettungsboot
life raft

See also
105 Seefahrzeuge • Sea vessels **106** Der Hafen • The port **118** Schwimmen • Swimming
121 Fischen • Fishing **134** Am Strand • On the beach

119.2 WASSERSPORT · WATERSPORTS

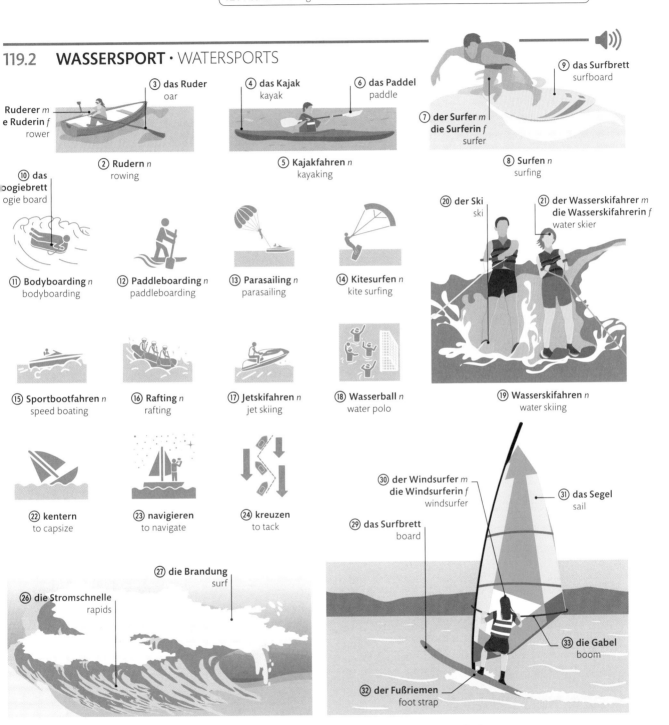

③ **das Ruder**
oar

④ **das Kajak**
kayak

⑥ **das Paddel**
paddle

⑨ **das Surfbrett**
surfboard

Ruderer *m*
e Ruderin *f*
rower

⑦ **der Surfer** *m*
die Surferin *f*
surfer

② **Rudern** *n*
rowing

⑤ **Kajakfahren** *n*
kayaking

⑧ **Surfen** *n*
surfing

⑩ **das**
ogiebrett
ogie board

⑳ **der Ski**
ski

㉑ **der Wasserskifahrer** *m*
die Wasserskifahrerin *f*
water skier

⑪ **Bodyboarding** *n*
bodyboarding

⑫ **Paddleboarding** *n*
paddleboarding

⑬ **Parasailing** *n*
parasailing

⑭ **Kitesurfen** *n*
kite surfing

⑮ **Sportbootfahren** *n*
speed boating

⑯ **Rafting** *n*
rafting

⑰ **Jetskifahren** *n*
jet skiing

⑱ **Wasserball** *n*
water polo

⑲ **Wasserskifahren** *n*
water skiing

㉒ **kentern**
to capsize

㉓ **navigieren**
to navigate

㉔ **kreuzen**
to tack

㉚ **der Windsurfer** *m*
die Windsurferin *f*
windsurfer

㉛ **das Segel**
sail

㉙ **das Surfbrett**
board

㉗ **die Brandung**
surf

㉖ **die Stromschnelle**
rapids

㉝ **die Gabel**
boom

㉜ **der Fußriemen**
foot strap

㉘ **Windsurfen** *n*
windsurfing

㉕ **die Welle**
wave

120.1 REITEN · HORSE RIDING

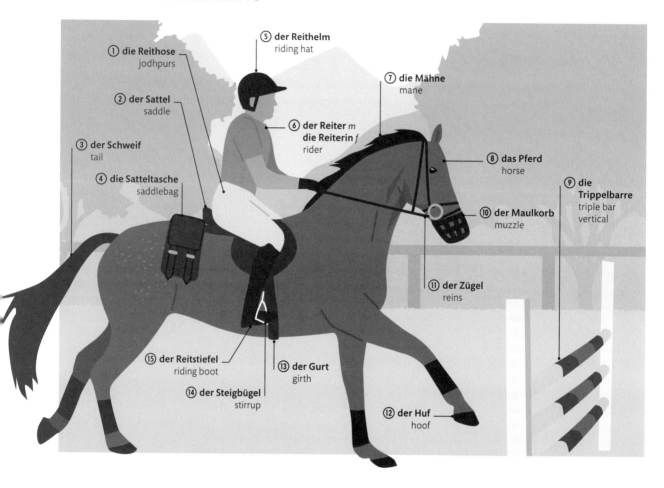

① die Reithose
jodhpurs

② der Sattel
saddle

③ der Schweif
tail

④ die Satteltasche
saddlebag

⑤ der Reithelm
riding hat

⑥ der Reiter *m*
die Reiterin *f*
rider

⑦ die Mähne
mane

⑧ das Pferd
horse

⑨ die Trippelbarre
triple bar
vertical

⑩ der Maulkorb
muzzle

⑪ der Zügel
reins

⑮ der Reitstiefel
riding boot

⑬ der Gurt
girth

⑭ der Steigbügel
stirrup

⑫ der Huf
hoof

⑯ das Hufeisen
horseshoe

⑰ das Halfter
halter

⑱ der Nasenriemen
noseband

⑲ das Gebiss
bit

⑳ der Stirnriemen
browband

㉑ das Zaumzeug
bridle

㉒ der Vorderzwiesel
pommel

㉓ der Sitz
seat

㉔ die Gerte
riding crop

㉕ der Jockey
jockey

㉖ das Rennpferd
racehorse

㉗ das Hindernis
verticals

See also
116 Leichtathletik · Athletics **125** Weitere Sportarten · Other sports
133 Aktivitäten im Freien · Outdoor activities

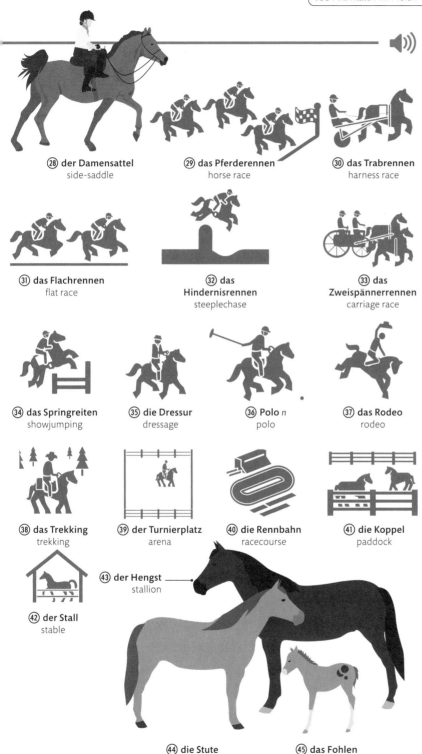

㉘ **der Damensattel**
side-saddle

㉙ **das Pferderennen**
horse race

㉚ **das Trabrennen**
harness race

㉛ **das Flachrennen**
flat race

㉜ **das Hindernisrennen**
steeplechase

㉝ **das Zweispännerrennen**
carriage race

㉞ **das Springreiten**
showjumping

㉟ **die Dressur**
dressage

㊱ **Polo** *n*
polo

㊲ **das Rodeo**
rodeo

㊳ **das Trekking**
trekking

㊳ **der Turnierplatz**
arena

㊵ **die Rennbahn**
racecourse

㊶ **die Koppel**
paddock

㊸ **der Hengst**
stallion

㊷ **der Stall**
stable

㊹ **die Stute**
mare

㊺ **das Fohlen**
foal

120.2 VERBEN · VERBS

① **striegeln**
to groom

② **im Schritt reiten**
to walk

③ **traben**
to trot

④ **im leichten Galopp reiten**
to canter

⑤ **galoppieren**
to gallop

⑥ **springen**
to jump

⑦ **züchten**
to breed

⑧ **ausmisten**
to muck out

249

121.1 ANGLER · ANGLER

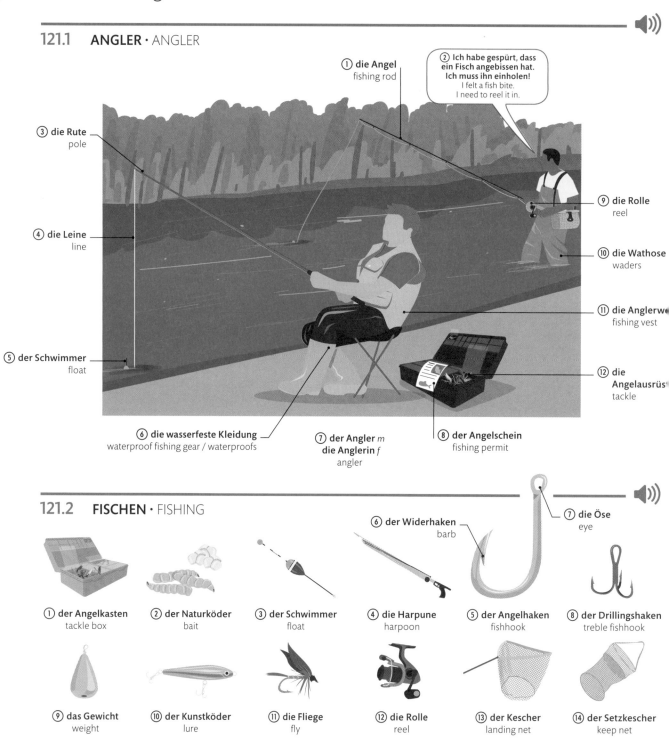

① die Angel
fishing rod

② Ich habe gespürt, dass ein Fisch angebissen hat. Ich muss ihn einholen!
I felt a fish bite. I need to reel it in.

③ die Rute
pole

④ die Leine
line

⑤ der Schwimmer
float

⑥ die wasserfeste Kleidung
waterproof fishing gear / waterproofs

⑦ der Angler m
die Anglerin f
angler

⑧ der Angelschein
fishing permit

⑨ die Rolle
reel

⑩ die Wathose
waders

⑪ die Anglerwe
fishing vest

⑫ die Angelausrüs
tackle

121.2 FISCHEN · FISHING

⑥ der Widerhaken
barb

⑦ die Öse
eye

① der Angelkasten
tackle box

② der Naturköder
bait

③ der Schwimmer
float

④ die Harpune
harpoon

⑤ der Angelhaken
fishhook

⑧ der Drillingshaken
treble fishhook

⑨ das Gewicht
weight

⑩ der Kunstköder
lure

⑪ die Fliege
fly

⑫ die Rolle
reel

⑬ der Kescher
landing net

⑭ der Setzkescher
keep net

See also
54 Fisch und Meeresfrüchte · Fish and seafood **119** Segeln und Wassersport
Sailing and watersports **166** Leben im Ozean · Ocean life

121.3 FISCHEREIDISZIPLINEN
TYPES OF FISHING

① die Fliegenfischerei
fly fishing

② die Süßwasserfischerei
freshwater fishing

③ die Seefischerei
marine fishing

④ die Tiefseefischerei
deep sea fishing

⑤ die Sportfischerei
sport fishing

⑥ die Unterwasserfischerei
spearfishing

⑦ die Eisfischerei
ice fishing

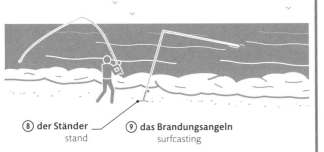

⑧ der Ständer
stand

⑨ das Brandungsangeln
surfcasting

121.4 FISCHEREIVERBEN · FISHING VERBS

① ködern
to bait

② auswerfen
to cast

③ anbeißen
to bite

④ fangen
to catch

⑤ einholen
to reel in

⑥ mit dem Netz fangen
to net

⑦ freilassen
to release

121.5 KNOTEN · KNOTS

① der Clinchknoten
clinch knot

② der Blutknoten
blood knot

③ der Arborknoten
arbor knot

④ der Snell-Knoten
snell knot

⑤ der Turle-Knoten
turle knot

⑥ der Palomar-Knoten
palomar knot

122.1 SKIFAHREN · SKIING

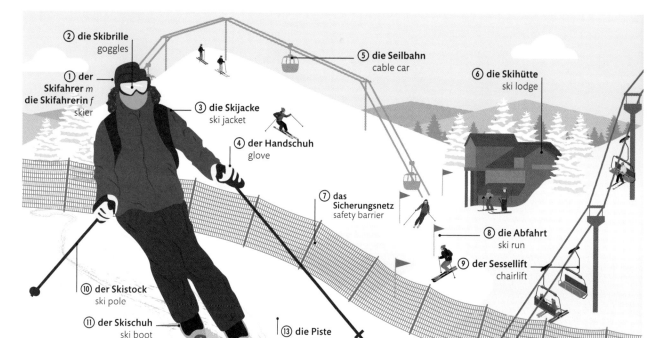

② **die Skibrille**
goggles

① **der Skifahrer** *m*
die Skifahrerin *f*
skier

③ **die Skijacke**
ski jacket

④ **der Handschuh**
glove

⑤ **die Seilbahn**
cable car

⑥ **die Skihütte**
ski lodge

⑦ **das Sicherungsnetz**
safety barrier

⑧ **die Abfahrt**
ski run

⑨ **der Sessellift**
chairlift

⑩ **der Skistock**
ski pole

⑪ **der Skischuh**
ski boot

⑫ **der Ski**
ski

⑬ **die Piste**
ski slope

⑭ **die Spitze**
tip

⑮ **das Skigebiet**
ski resort

⑯ **Ski fahren**
to ski

⑰ **die Abfahrt**
downhill skiing

⑱ **der Slalom**
slalom

⑲ **der Riesenslalom**
giant slalom

⑳ **der Skilanglauf**
cross-country skiing

㉑ **abseits der Piste**
off-piste

㉒ **der Biathlon**
biathlon

㉓ **die Lawine**
avalanche

㉔ **die Aufsprungbahn**
landing hill

㉕ **das Tor**
gate

㉖ **der Skisprung**
ski jump

㉗ **die Sprungschanze**
jumping ramp

See also
116 Leichtathletik · Athletics **124** Im Fitnessstudio · At the gym
125 Weitere Sportarten · Other sports

122.2 WEITERE WINTERSPORTARTEN · OTHER WINTER SPORTS

① **Wintersport** *m*
winter sports

② **der Schlittschuh**
skate

③ **Eislaufen** *n*
ice-skating

④ **Eisschnelllauf** *m*
speed skating

⑤ **Eiskunstlauf** *m*
figure skating

⑥ **Snowboardfahren** *n*
snowboarding

⑫ **der Bob**
sleigh

⑪ **der Anschieber** *m*
die Anschieberin *f*
runners

⑦ **Rodeln** *n*
luge

⑧ **Skeleton** *m*
skeleton

⑨ **Schlittenfahren** *n*
sledging

⑩ **Bobfahren** *n*
bobsleigh

⑲ **der Curlingbesen**
curling brush

⑱ **der Curlingstein**
curling stone

⑬ **Eisklettern** *n*
ice climbing

⑭ **das Schneemobil**
snowmobile

⑮ **Para-Eishockey** *n*
para ice hockey

⑯ **Rollstuhlcurling** *n*
wheelchair curling

⑰ **Curling** *n*
curling

⑳ **der Hundeschlittenführer** *m*
die Hundeschlittenführerin *f*
musher

㉑ **das Geschirr**
harness

㉒ **der Hundeschlitten**
dogsled

㉓ **der Hund**
dog

㉕ **die Olympischen Winterspiele** *pl*
Winter Olympics

㉔ **das Schlittenhunderennen**
dog sledding

123.1 DER RENNWAGEN · RACING CAR

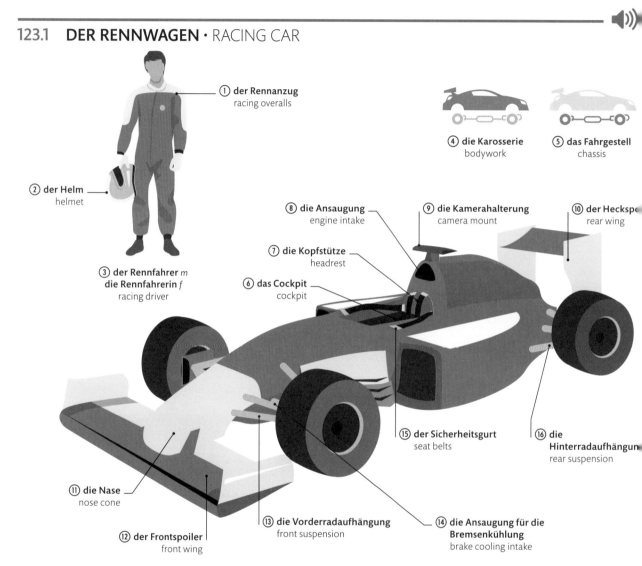

① der Rennanzug
racing overalls

④ die Karosserie
bodywork

⑤ das Fahrgestell
chassis

② der Helm
helmet

③ der Rennfahrer *m*
die Rennfahrerin *f*
racing driver

⑧ die Ansaugung
engine intake

⑨ die Kamerahalterung
camera mount

⑩ der Heckspo[iler]
rear wing

⑦ die Kopfstütze
headrest

⑥ das Cockpit
cockpit

⑮ der Sicherheitsgurt
seat belts

⑯ die
Hinterradaufhängun[g]
rear suspension

⑪ die Nase
nose cone

⑬ die Vorderradaufhängung
front suspension

⑭ die Ansaugung für die
Bremsenkühlung
brake cooling intake

⑫ der Frontspoiler
front wing

123.2 MOTORSPORTDISZIPLINEN · TYPES OF MOTORSPORTS

① das Autorennen
motor racing

② die Rallye
rally driving

③ das Dragracing
drag racing

See also
96 Straßen · Roads **97-98** Autos · Cars **99** Autos und Busse
Cars and buses **100** Motorräder · Motorcycles

123.3 **DIE RENNSTRECKE** · RACE TRACK

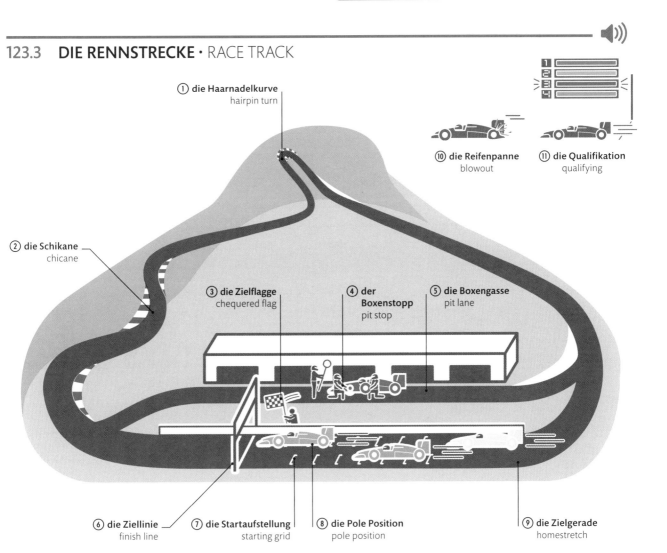

① **die Haarnadelkurve**
hairpin turn

② **die Schikane**
chicane

③ **die Zielflagge**
chequered flag

④ **der Boxenstopp**
pit stop

⑤ **die Boxengasse**
pit lane

⑥ **die Ziellinie**
finish line

⑦ **die Startaufstellung**
starting grid

⑧ **die Pole Position**
pole position

⑨ **die Zielgerade**
homestretch

⑩ **die Reifenpanne**
blowout

⑪ **die Qualifikation**
qualifying

④ **das Motorradrennen**
motorbike racing

⑤ **das Speedwayrennen**
speedway

⑥ **das Motocrossrennen**
motocross

⑦ **das Monstertruckrennen**
monster truck

⑧ **das Go-Kart-Rennen**
go-cart

124.1 SPORT TREIBEN · WORKING OUT

② Ich mache dreimal die Woche Sport.
I exercise three times a week.

① Wie oft treibst du Sport?
How often do you work out?

③ der Cross-Trainer
cross-trainer

⑤ das Rudergerät
rowing machine

④ Sport treiben
working out

⑥ der Heimtrainer
exercise bike

⑫ die Fitnessgeräte n, pl
gym machines

⑬ die Umkleide
changing room

⑭ der Spind
lockers

⑮ der Trainingskurs
exercise class

⑯ Pilates n
Pilates

⑰ die Dehnung
stretch

⑲ die Übung
exercises

⑱ das Zirkeltraining
circuit training

⑳ Aerobic n
aerobics

㉑ der Hampelmann
star jumps

㉒ das Armkreisen
arm circles

㉓ der Seitensprung
side shuffles

㉔ das Laufen
running

㉕ der Ausfallschritt
lunge

㉖ der Bizepscurl
bicep curl

㉗ die Kniebeuge
squat

㉘ der Situp
sit-up

㉙ Boxgymnastik f
boxercise

㉚ Seilspringen n
to skip

㉛ die Muskeln anspannen
to flex

㉜ auf der Stelle laufen
to jog on the spot

㉝ trainieren
to train

㉞ einen Klimmzug machen
to pull up

㉟ strecken
to extend

㊱ sich aufwärmen
to warm up

㊲ sich abkühlen
to cool down

See also
116 Leichtathletik • Athletics **117** Kampfsportarten • Combat sports **118** Schwimmen • Swimming
122 Wintersport • Winter sports **125** Weitere Sportarten • Other sports

⑦ **Gewichtheben** *n*
weight training
⑧ **die Hantel**
free weights
⑨ **die Sportmatte**
exercise mat
⑩ **der Liegestütz**
push ups / press ups
⑪ **das Laufband**
treadmill

㊳ **die Mitgliedschaft**
membership

㊴ **das Fitnessgerät**
gym equipment

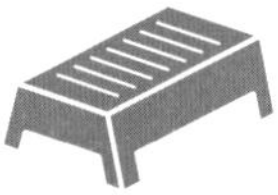
㊵ **der Aerobic-Stepper**
aerobics step

㊶ **die Hantel**
dumbbell

㊷ **der Handgriff**
hand grips

㊸ **die Hantelstange**
weight bar

㊹ **die Stange**
bar

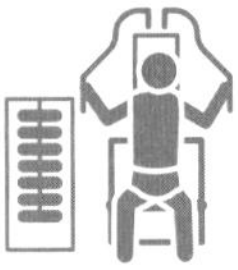
㊺ **das Brustdrücken**
chest press

㊻ **das Springseil**
skipping rope

㊼ **der Gymnastikball**
exercise ball

㊽ **die Drehstange**
twist bar

㊾ **die Gewichtsmanschette**
ankle weights / wrist weights

㊿ **die Beinpresse**
leg press

(51) **der Brustexpander**
chest expander

(52) **das Ab Wheel**
wheel roller

(53) **das Laufband**
running machine

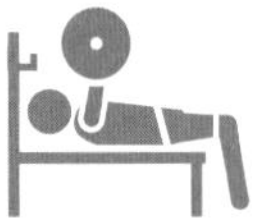
(54) **die Bank**
bench

(55) **der Puls**
heart rate

(56) **die Sauna**
sauna

(57) **der Whirlpool**
hot tub

(58) **der Personal Trainer** *m*
die Personal Trainerin *f*
personal trainer

125.1 TURNEN · GYMNASTICS

① **die Bodenmatte** floor mat

② **der Reifen** hoop

③ **das Band** ribbon

④ **der Barren** horizontal bar

⑤ **der Sprungtisch** vault

⑪ **das Sprungbrett** springboard

⑥ **der Stufenbarren** uneven bars

⑦ **der Schwebebalken** beam

⑧ **das Pferd** pommel horse

⑨ **die Ringe** *m, pl* rings

⑩ **der Parallelbarren** parallel bars

125.2 WEITERE SPORTARTEN · OTHER SPORTS

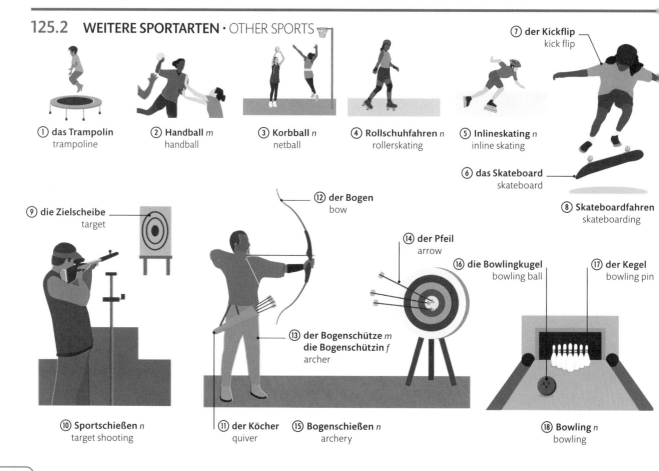

① **das Trampolin** trampoline

② **Handball** *m* handball

③ **Korbball** *n* netball

④ **Rollschuhfahren** *n* rollerskating

⑤ **Inlineskating** *n* inline skating

⑥ **das Skateboard** skateboard

⑦ **der Kickflip** kick flip

⑧ **Skateboardfahren** skateboarding

⑨ **die Zielscheibe** target

⑫ **der Bogen** bow

⑭ **der Pfeil** arrow

⑯ **die Bowlingkugel** bowling ball

⑰ **der Kegel** bowling pin

⑬ **der Bogenschütze** *m* **die Bogenschützin** *f* archer

⑩ **Sportschießen** *n* target shooting

⑪ **der Köcher** quiver

⑮ **Bogenschießen** *n* archery

⑱ **Bowling** *n* bowling

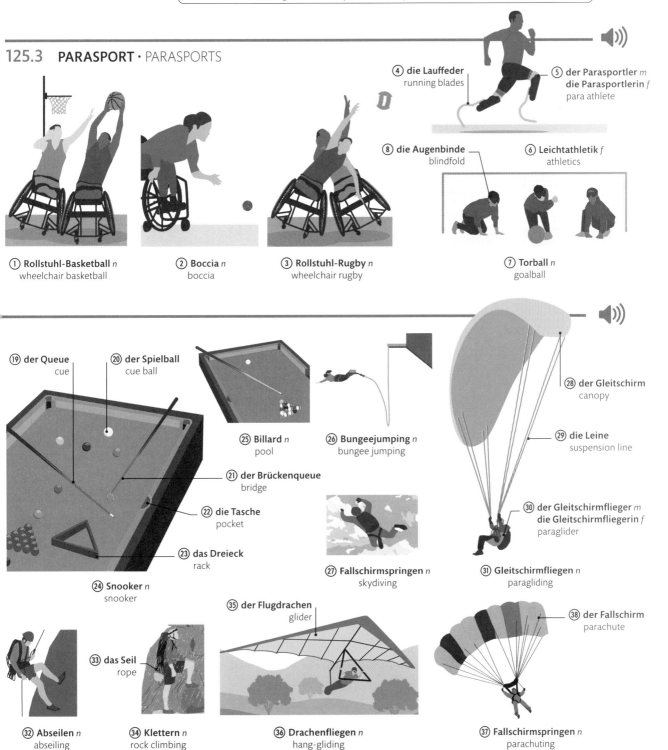

See also
116 Leichtathletik · Athletics **117** Kampfsportarten · Combat sports **118** Schwimmen · Swimming
120 Reiten · Horse riding **122** Wintersport · Winter sports **124** Im Fitnessstudio · At the gym

125.3 PARASPORT · PARASPORTS

④ **die Lauffeder**
running blades

⑤ **der Parasportler** *m*
die Parasportlerin *f*
para athlete

⑧ **die Augenbinde**
blindfold

⑥ **Leichtathletik** *f*
athletics

① **Rollstuhl-Basketball** *n*
wheelchair basketball

② **Boccia** *n*
boccia

③ **Rollstuhl-Rugby** *n*
wheelchair rugby

⑦ **Torball** *n*
goalball

⑲ **der Queue**
cue

⑳ **der Spielball**
cue ball

㉘ **der Gleitschirm**
canopy

㉙ **die Leine**
suspension line

㉕ **Billard** *n*
pool

㉖ **Bungeejumping** *n*
bungee jumping

㉑ **der Brückenqueue**
bridge

㉒ **die Tasche**
pocket

㉓ **das Dreieck**
rack

㉚ **der Gleitschirmflieger** *m*
die Gleitschirmfliegerin *f*
paraglider

㉗ **Fallschirmspringen** *n*
skydiving

㉛ **Gleitschirmfliegen** *n*
paragliding

㉔ **Snooker** *n*
snooker

㉟ **der Flugdrachen**
glider

㊳ **der Fallschirm**
parachute

㉝ **das Seil**
rope

㉜ **Abseilen** *n*
abseiling

㉞ **Klettern** *n*
rock climbing

㊱ **Drachenfliegen** *n*
hang-gliding

㊲ **Fallschirmspringen** *n*
parachuting

126.1 DAS THEATER · THEATRE

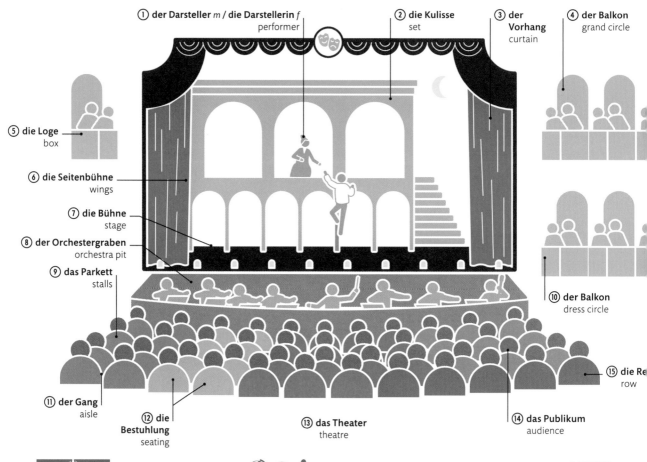

① der Darsteller *m* / die Darstellerin *f*
performer

② die Kulisse
set

③ der Vorhang
curtain

④ der Balkon
grand circle

⑤ die Loge
box

⑥ die Seitenbühne
wings

⑦ die Bühne
stage

⑧ der Orchestergraben
orchestra pit

⑨ das Parkett
stalls

⑩ der Balkon
dress circle

⑪ der Gang
aisle

⑫ die Bestuhlung
seating

⑬ das Theater
theatre

⑭ das Publikum
audience

⑮ die Re...
row

⑯ das Theaterstück
play

⑰ das Kostüm
costumes

⑱ die Requisite
props

⑲ das Bühnenbild
sets

⑳ der Hintergrund
backdrop

㉑ das Textbuch
script

㉒ der Produzent *m*
die Produzentin *f*
producer

㉓ der Regisseur *m*
die Regisseurin *f*
director

㉔ der Schauspieler *m*
die Schauspielerin *f*
actor

㉕ die Besetzung
cast

㉖ die Premiere
opening night

㉗ die Pause
interval

See also
127 Filme · Films **128-129** Musik · Music **139** Fantasy und Mythologie · Fantasy and myth

126.2 **BALLETT** · BALLET

① **der Arm**
arm

② **das Knie**
knee

③ **der Zehenraum**
toe box

④ **eine Pirouette machen / sich drehen**
to pirouette / to turn

⑤ **einen Plié machen / die Beine beugen**
to plié / to bend

⑥ **der Balletttänzer**
male ballet dancer

⑦ **die Ballerina**
ballerina

⑧ **das Tütü**
tutu

⑨ **das Balletttrikot**
ballet leotard

⑩ **der Ballettschuh**
ballet shoes

⑪ **die Aufführung**
performance

⑫ **die Zugabe**
encore

⑬ **der Beifall**
applause

㉘ **das Programm**
programme

der Platzanweiser *m*
die Platzanweiserin *f*
usher

㉚ **die Tragödie**
tragedy

㉛ **die Komödie**
comedy

㉜ **das Musical**
musical

㉝ **der Stehbeifall**
standing ovation

126.3 **DIE OPER** · OPERA

① **der Bass**
bass

② **der Bariton**
baritone

③ **der Tenor**
tenor

④ **das Opernhaus**
opera house

⑤ **der Alt**
alto

⑥ **der Mezzosopran**
mezzo-soprano

⑦ **der Sopran**
soprano

⑧ **die Primadonna**
prima donna

⑨ **das Libretto**
libretto

261

127.1 IM KINO · AT THE CINEMA

① **das Drama**
drama

② **das Musical**
musical

③ **der Science-Fiction-Film**
science fiction

④ **der Thriller**
thriller

⑤ **die Komödie**
comedy

⑥ **der Actionfilm**
action movie

⑦ **der Horrorfilm**
horror

⑧ **der Animationsfilm**
animation

⑨ **die romantische Komödie**
romantic comedy

⑩ **der Krimi**
crime drama

⑪ **der Western**
western

⑫ **das Historiendrama**
historical drama

⑬ **der Fantasyfilm**
fantasy

⑭ **der Kampfsportfilm**
martial arts

⑮ **der Spezialeffekt**
special effects

⑯ **die Kasse**
box office

⑰ **das Multiplexkino**
multiplex

⑱ **das Popcorn**
popcorn

⑲ **der Filmstar**
film star

⑳ **die Leinwand**
screen

㉑ **das Publikum**
audience

㉒ **das Kino**
cinema

㉓ **die Hauptfigur**
main character

㉔ **der Held** m
die Heldin f
hero

㉕ **der Bösewicht**
villain

See also
126 Auf der Bühne · On stage **136** Unterhaltung zu Hause · Home entertainment **137** Fernsehen · Television

127.2 **DAS FILMSTUDIO** · FILM STUDIO

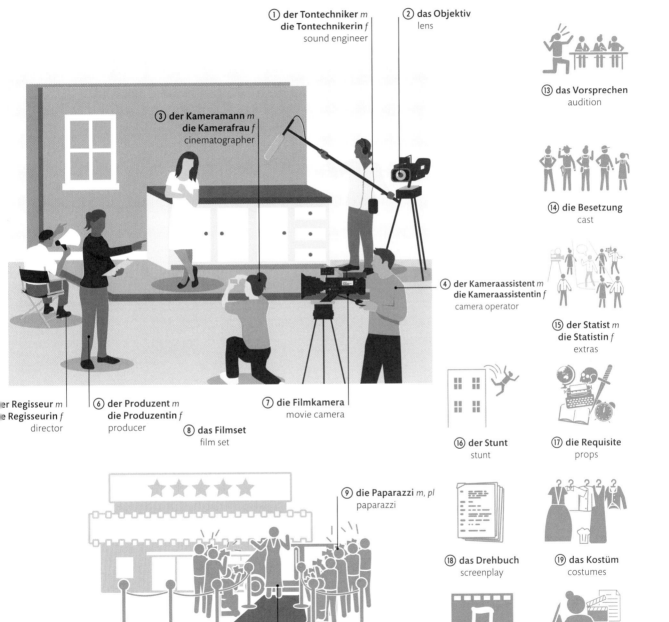

① **der Tontechniker** m
die Tontechnikerin f
sound engineer

② **das Objektiv**
lens

③ **der Kameramann** m
die Kamerafrau f
cinematographer

④ **der Kameraassistent** m
die Kameraassistentin f
camera operator

er Regisseur m
e Regisseurin f
director

⑥ **der Produzent** m
die Produzentin f
producer

⑦ **die Filmkamera**
movie camera

⑧ **das Filmset**
film set

⑨ **die Paparazzi** m, pl
paparazzi

⑩ **der rote Teppich**
red carpet

⑪ **der Star**
celebrity

⑫ **die Premiere**
premiere

⑬ **das Vorsprechen**
audition

⑭ **die Besetzung**
cast

⑮ **der Statist** m
die Statistin f
extras

⑯ **der Stunt**
stunt

⑰ **die Requisite**
props

⑱ **das Drehbuch**
screenplay

⑲ **das Kostüm**
costumes

⑳ **der Soundtrack**
soundtrack

㉑ **der Drehbuchautor** m
die Drehbuchautorin f
screenwriter

128.1 ORCHESTERINSTRUMENTE · ORCHESTRAL INSTRUMENTS

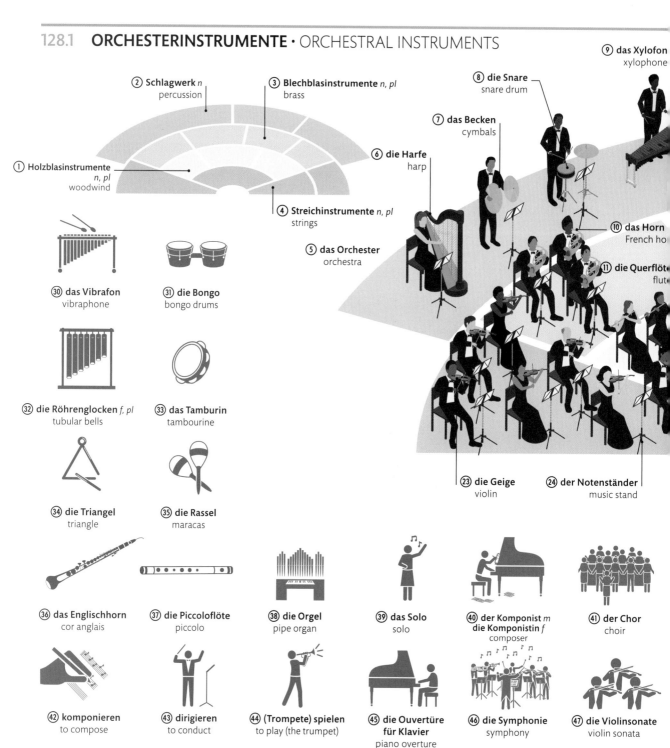

⑨ das Xylofon
xylophone

② Schlagwerk *n*
percussion

③ Blechblasinstrumente *n, pl*
brass

⑧ die Snare
snare drum

⑦ das Becken
cymbals

⑥ die Harfe
harp

① Holzblasinstrumente
n, pl
woodwind

④ Streichinstrumente *n, pl*
strings

⑤ das Orchester
orchestra

⑩ das Horn
French ho

⑪ die Querflöt
flut

㉚ das Vibrafon
vibraphone

㉛ die Bongo
bongo drums

㉜ die Röhrenglocken *f, pl*
tubular bells

㉝ das Tamburin
tambourine

㉓ die Geige
violin

㉔ der Notenständer
music stand

㉞ die Triangel
triangle

㉟ die Rassel
maracas

㊱ das Englischhorn
cor anglais

㊲ die Piccoloflöte
piccolo

㊳ die Orgel
pipe organ

㊴ das Solo
solo

㊵ der Komponist *m*
die Komponistin *f*
composer

㊶ der Chor
choir

㊷ komponieren
to compose

㊸ dirigieren
to conduct

㊹ (Trompete) spielen
to play (the trumpet)

㊺ die Ouvertüre
für Klavier
piano overture

㊻ die Symphonie
symphony

㊼ die Violinsonate
violin sonata

See also
126 Auf der Bühne · On stage **127** Filme · Films **129** Musik (Fortsetzung)
Music continued **136** Unterhaltung zu Hause · Home entertainment

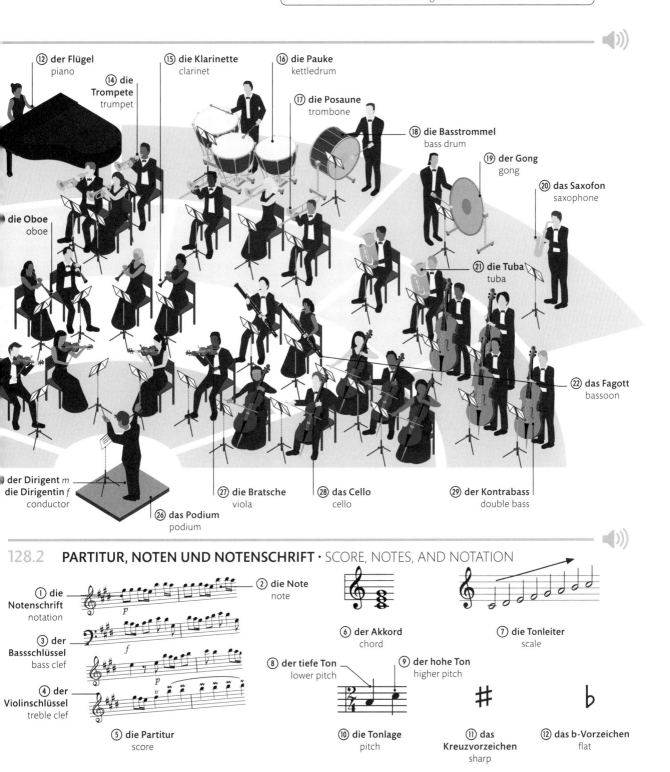

⑫ **der Flügel**
piano

⑭ **die Trompete**
trumpet

⑮ **die Klarinette**
clarinet

⑯ **die Pauke**
kettledrum

⑰ **die Posaune**
trombone

⑱ **die Basstrommel**
bass drum

⑲ **der Gong**
gong

⑳ **das Saxofon**
saxophone

die Oboe
oboe

㉑ **die Tuba**
tuba

㉒ **das Fagott**
bassoon

der Dirigent *m*
die Dirigentin *f*
conductor

㉗ **die Bratsche**
viola

㉘ **das Cello**
cello

㉙ **der Kontrabass**
double bass

㉖ **das Podium**
podium

128.2 PARTITUR, NOTEN UND NOTENSCHRIFT · SCORE, NOTES, AND NOTATION

① **die Notenschrift**
notation

② **die Note**
note

③ **der Bassschlüssel**
bass clef

④ **der Violinschlüssel**
treble clef

⑤ **die Partitur**
score

⑥ **der Akkord**
chord

⑦ **die Tonleiter**
scale

⑧ **der tiefe Ton**
lower pitch

⑨ **der hohe Ton**
higher pitch

⑩ **die Tonlage**
pitch

⑪ **das Kreuzvorzeichen**
sharp

⑫ **das b-Vorzeichen**
flat

265

129.1 POPMUSIK · POPULAR MUSIC

① die Traverse
rig

② der Schlagzeuger *m*
die Schlagzeugerin *f*
drummer

③ der Akustikgitarrist *m*
die Akustikgitarristin *f*
acoustic guitarist

④ der Frontsänger *m*
die Frontsängerin *f*
lead singer

⑤ der E-Gitarrist *m* / die E-Gitarristin *f*
electric guitarist

⑥ die Bühnenbeleuchtung
stage lights

⑦ der Bassist *m*
die Bassistin *f*
bass guitarist

⑧ der Lautsprecher
speaker

⑨ die Fans *m, pl*
fans

⑩ das Popkonzert
pop concert

⑪ der Verstärker
amplifier

⑫ der Plattenspieler
turntable

⑬ das Mischpult
DJ console

⑭ die Schallplatte
vinyl records

⑮ der Begleitsänger *m*
die Begleitsängerin *f*
backing singers

⑯ das Lied
song

⑰ die Melodie
melody

⑱ der Takt
beat

⑲ die Band
band

⑳ das Album
album

㉑ der Jazz
jazz

㉒ der Blues
the blues

㉓ der Punk
punk

㉔ die Folk-Musik
folk

㉕ der Pop
pop

㉖ der K-Pop
K-pop

㉗ der Heavy Metal
heavy metal

㉘ der Hiphop
hip-hop

㉙ die Countrymusik
country

㉚ der Rock
rock

㉛ der Soul
soul

㉜ die lateinamerikanische Musik
Latin

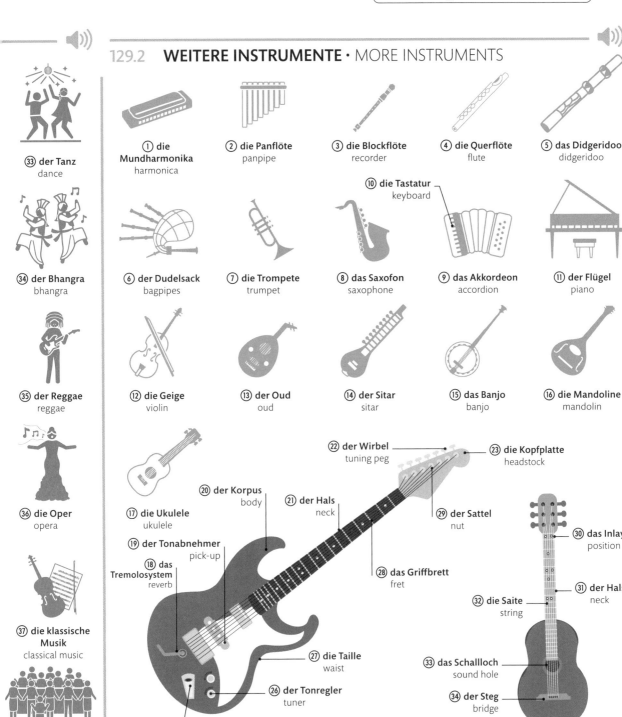

See also
126 Auf der Bühne • On stage **127** Filme • Films
136 Unterhaltung zu Hause • Home entertainment

129.2 WEITERE INSTRUMENTE · MORE INSTRUMENTS

① die Mundharmonika — harmonica
② die Panflöte — panpipe
③ die Blockflöte — recorder
④ die Querflöte — flute
⑤ das Didgeridoo — didgeridoo
⑥ der Dudelsack — bagpipes
⑦ die Trompete — trumpet
⑧ das Saxofon — saxophone
⑨ das Akkordeon — accordion
⑩ die Tastatur — keyboard
⑪ der Flügel — piano
⑫ die Geige — violin
⑬ der Oud — oud
⑭ der Sitar — sitar
⑮ das Banjo — banjo
⑯ die Mandoline — mandolin
⑰ die Ukulele — ukulele
⑱ das Tremolosystem — reverb
⑲ der Tonabnehmer — pick-up
⑳ der Korpus — body
㉑ der Hals — neck
㉒ der Wirbel — tuning peg
㉓ die Kopfplatte — headstock
㉔ die Kabelbuchse — jack connector
㉕ die E-Gitarre — electric guitar
㉖ der Tonregler — tuner
㉗ die Taille — waist
㉘ das Griffbrett — fret
㉙ der Sattel — nut
㉚ das Inlay — position markers
㉛ der Hals — neck
㉜ die Saite — string
㉝ das Schallloch — sound hole
㉞ der Steg — bridge
㉟ die Akustikgitarre — acoustic guitar

㉝ der Tanz — dance
㉞ der Bhangra — bhangra
㉟ der Reggae — reggae
㊱ die Oper — opera
㊲ die klassische Musik — classical music
㊳ der Gospel — gospel

130.1 IM MUSEUM UND IN DER KUNSTGALERIE · AT THE MUSEUM AND ART GALLERY

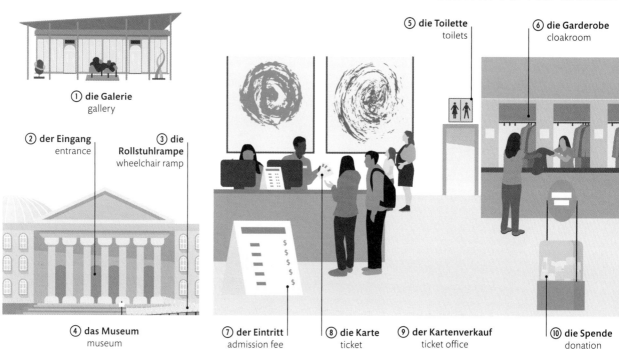

① die Galerie
gallery

② der Eingang
entrance

③ die Rollstuhlrampe
wheelchair ramp

④ das Museum
museum

⑤ die Toilette
toilets

⑥ die Garderobe
cloakroom

⑦ der Eintritt
admission fee

⑧ die Karte
ticket

⑨ der Kartenverkauf
ticket office

⑩ die Spende
donation

⑪ der Gebäudeplan
floor plan

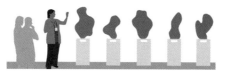

⑫ der Kurator m / die Kuratorin f
curator

⑬ die Ausstellung
exhibition

⑭ das Ausstellung
exhibit

⑰ die Installation
installation

⑮ die Dauerausstellung
permanent exhibition

⑯ die Sonderausstellung
temporary exhibition

⑱ die Sammlung
collection

⑲ die Restaurierung
conservation

⑳ der Museumsführer m
die Museumsführerin f
tour guide

㉑ der Audioguide
audio guide

㉒ fotografieren verboten
no photography

㉓ der Geschenkeladen
gift shop

See also
42-43 In der Stadt · In town **132** Sightseeing · Sightseeing
141-142 Kunst und Handwerk · Arts and crafts

㉔ **die Skulptur**
sculpture

㉕ **die Überwachungskamera**
surveillance camera

㉙ **Dieses Meisterwerk ist unbezahlbar!**
This masterpiece is priceless!

㉚ **der Rahmen**
frame

㉖ **das Schild**
label

㉗ **das Meisterwerk**
masterpiece

㉘ **der Museumswächter** *m*
die Museumswächterin *f*
security guard

㉛ **das Gemälde**
painting

㉜ **das Ölgemälde**
oil painting

㉝ **das Aquarell**
watercolour

㉞ **der Klassizismus**
Classicism

㉟ **der Impressionismus**
Impressionism

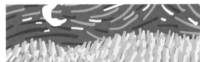

㊱ **der Postimpressionismus**
Post-Impressionism

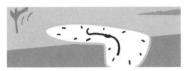

㊳ **der Surrealismus**
Surrealism

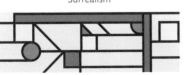

㊶ **das Art-déco**
Art Deco

㊷ **der Jugendstil**
Art Nouveau

㊲ **der Kubismus**
Cubism

㊴ **das Bauhaus**
Bauhaus

㊵ **die Pop-Art**
Pop Art

㊸ **die Konzeptkunst**
conceptual art

131.1 REISEN · TRAVEL

① **der Reiseführer**
guidebook

② **das Wörterbuch mit praktischen Redewendungen**
phrasebook

③ **der Einzelfahrschein**
one-way ticket

④ **die Hin- und Rückfahrkarte**
return ticket

⑤ **einen Urlaub buchen**
to book a holiday

⑥ **den Koffer packen**
to pack your bags

⑦ **in den Urlaub fahren**
to go on a holiday

⑧ **eine Kreuzfahrt machen**
to go on a cruise

⑨ **ins Ausland gehen**
to go abroad

⑩ **reservieren**
to make a reservation

⑪ **ein Ferienhaus mieten**
to rent a cottage

⑫ **eine Rucksacktour machen**
to go backpacking

⑬ **einchecken**
to check in

⑭ **auschecken**
to check out

⑮ **im Hotel übernachten**
to stay in a hotel

131.2 UNTERKÜNFTE · ACCOMMODATION

① **das Hotel**
hotel

② **die Wohnung**
apartment

③ **das Hostel**
hostel

⑨ **das Gasthaus**
guest house

⑩ **die Übernachtung mit Frühstück**
bed and breakfast

⑪ **die Villa**
villa

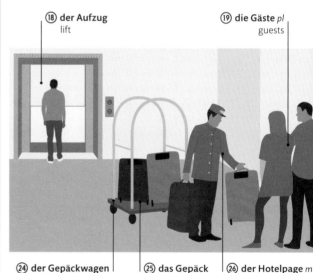

⑱ **der Aufzug**
lift

⑲ **die Gäste** *pl*
guests

㉔ **der Gepäckwagen**
trolley

㉕ **das Gepäck**
luggage

㉖ **der Hotelpage** *m*
die Pförtnerin *f*
porter

131.3 LEISTUNGEN · SERVICES

① **das Restaurant**
restaurant

② **das Fitnessstudio**
gym

③ **das Schwimmbecken**
swimming pool

See also
104 Am Flughafen • At the airport **132** Sightseeing • Sightseeing
133 Aktivitäten im Freien • Outdoor activities **134** Am Strand • On the beach

④ **die Skihütte**
chalet

⑤ **die Hütte**
cabin

⑥ **der Ökotourismus**
ecotourism

⑦ **das Einzelzimmer**
single room

⑧ **das Zweibettzimmer**
twin room

⑫ **das Doppelzimmer**
double room

⑬ **das private Badezimmer**
en suite bathroom

⑭ **der Schlafsaal**
dorm

⑮ **das Zimmer mit Ausblick**
room with a view

⑯ **Zimmer frei**
vacancies

⑰ **alle Zimmer besetzt**
no vacancies

⑳ **der Rezeptionist** *m*
die Rezeptionistin *f*
receptionist

㉑ **die Rezeption**
reception

㉒ **die Toilette**
toilets

㉓ **der Notausgang**
emergency exit

㉗ **der Tresen**
counter

㉘ **die Lobby**
hotel lobby

⑤ **das Frühstückstablett**
breakfast tray

④ **der Zimmerservice**
room service

⑥ **der Wäscheservice**
laundry service

⑦ **die Zimmerreinigung**
maid service

⑧ **die Minibar**
minibar

⑨ **der Tresor**
safe

132.1 DIE TOURISTENATTRAKTION · TOURIST ATTRACTION

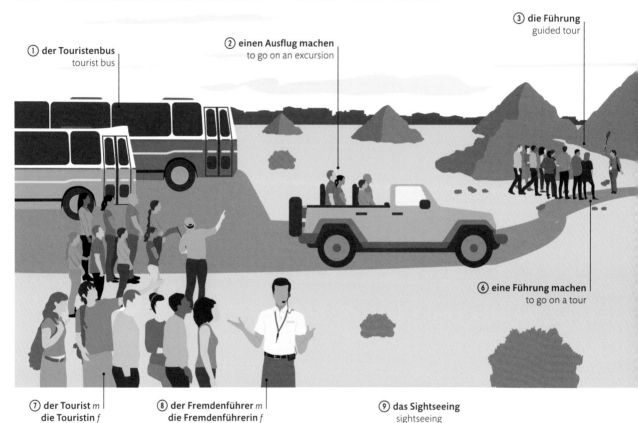

③ **die Führung**
guided tour

② **einen Ausflug machen**
to go on an excursion

① **der Touristenbus**
tourist bus

⑥ **eine Führung machen**
to go on a tour

⑦ **der Tourist** *m*
die Touristin *f*
tourist

⑧ **der Fremdenführer** *m*
die Fremdenführerin *f*
tour guide

⑨ **das Sightseeing**
sightseeing

132.2 SEHENSWÜRDIGKEITEN · ATTRACTIONS

① **die Kunstgalerie**
art gallery

② **das Museum**
museum

③ **das Denkmal**
monument

④ **das Schloss**
palace

⑧ **die Landschaft**
landscape

⑨ **malerisch**
scenic

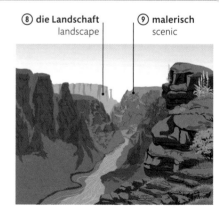

⑤ **das historische Gebäude**
historic building

⑥ **der botanische Garten**
botanical gardens

⑦ **der Nationalpark**
national park

See also
99 Autos und Busse • Cars and buses **130** Museen und Kunstgalerien • Museums and galleries
131 Reise und Unterkunft • Travel and accommodation **149-151** Länder • Countries

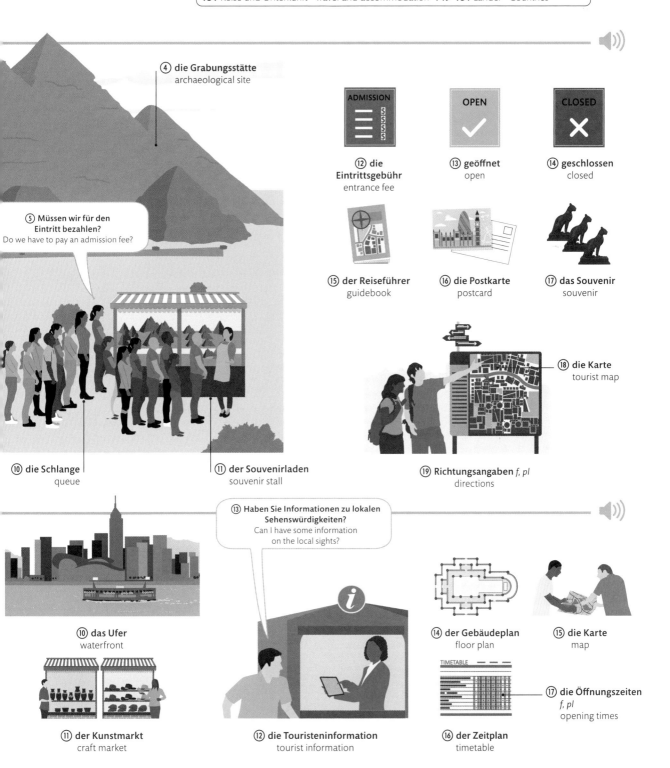

④ **die Grabungsstätte**
archaeological site

⑫ **die Eintrittsgebühr**
entrance fee

⑬ **geöffnet**
open

⑭ **geschlossen**
closed

⑤ **Müssen wir für den Eintritt bezahlen?**
Do we have to pay an admission fee?

⑮ **der Reiseführer**
guidebook

⑯ **die Postkarte**
postcard

⑰ **das Souvenir**
souvenir

⑱ **die Karte**
tourist map

⑩ **die Schlange**
queue

⑪ **der Souvenirladen**
souvenir stall

⑲ **Richtungsangaben** *f, pl*
directions

⑬ **Haben Sie Informationen zu lokalen Sehenswürdigkeiten?**
Can I have some information on the local sights?

⑩ **das Ufer**
waterfront

⑭ **der Gebäudeplan**
floor plan

⑮ **die Karte**
map

⑪ **der Kunstmarkt**
craft market

⑫ **die Touristeninformation**
tourist information

⑯ **der Zeitplan**
timetable

⑰ **die Öffnungszeiten**
f, pl
opening times

133.1 AKTIVITÄTEN AN DER FRISCHEN LUFT · OPEN-AIR ACTIVITIES

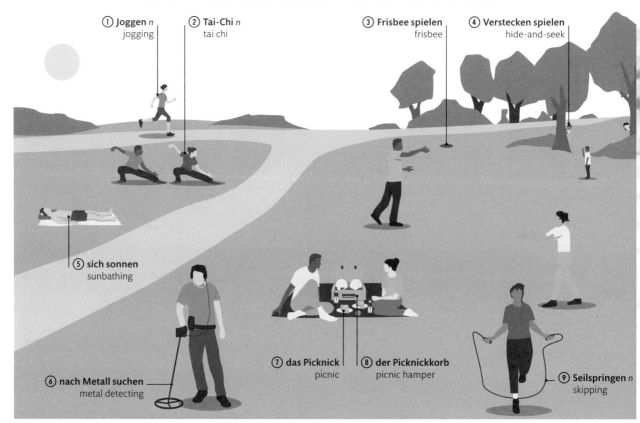

① **Joggen** n
jogging

② **Tai-Chi** n
tai chi

③ **Frisbee spielen**
frisbee

④ **Verstecken spielen**
hide-and-seek

⑤ **sich sonnen**
sunbathing

⑥ **nach Metall suchen**
metal detecting

⑦ **das Picknick**
picnic

⑧ **der Picknickkorb**
picnic hamper

⑨ **Seilspringen** n
skipping

⑩ **der Park**
park

㉓ **das Baumhaus**
tree house

㉔ **die Schaukel**
swing

㉒ **auf Bäume klettern**
tree climbing

㉕ **Gärtnern** n
gardening

㉖ **Krocket** n
croquet

㉗ **Vögel beobachten**
bird-watching

㉘ **Paintball spielen**
paintballing

㉛ **das Planschbecken**
paddling pool

㉜ **Skateboardfahren** n
skateboarding

㉝ **Rollerfahren** n
scootering

㉞ **Rollschuhfahren** n
rollerblading

㉟ **Radfahren** n
cycling

㊱ **Parcours** m
parkour

See also
11 Fähigkeiten und Handlungen • Abilities and actions **134** Am Strand • On the beach
135 Camping • Camping **148** Karten und Richtungsangaben • Maps and directions

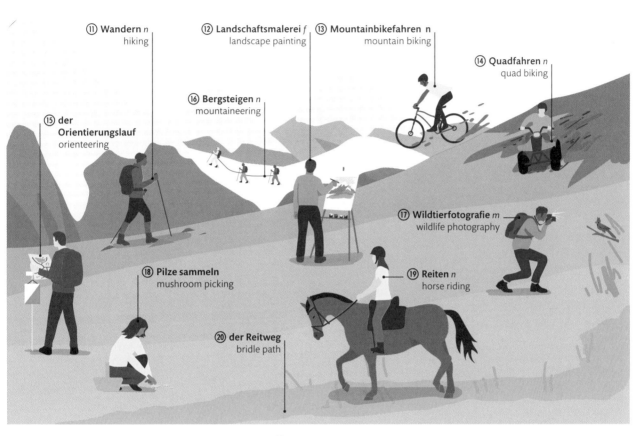

⑪ **Wandern** *n*
hiking

⑫ **Landschaftsmalerei** *f*
landscape painting

⑬ **Mountainbikefahren** *n*
mountain biking

⑭ **Quadfahren** *n*
quad biking

⑯ **Bergsteigen** *n*
mountaineering

⑮ **der Orientierungslauf**
orienteering

⑰ **Wildtierfotografie** *m*
wildlife photography

⑱ **Pilze sammeln**
mushroom picking

⑲ **Reiten** *n*
horse riding

⑳ **der Reitweg**
bridle path

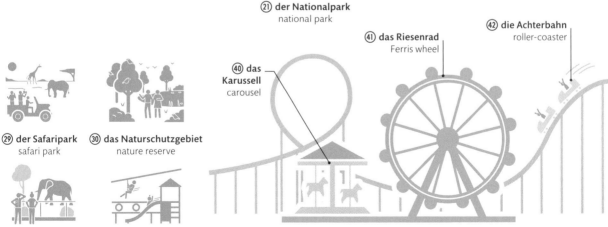

㉑ **der Nationalpark**
national park

㊶ **das Riesenrad**
Ferris wheel

㊷ **die Achterbahn**
roller-coaster

㊵ **das Karussell**
carousel

㉙ **der Safaripark**
safari park

㉚ **das Naturschutzgebiet**
nature reserve

㊲ **der Tierpark**
zoo

㊳ **der Abenteuerspielplatz**
adventure playground

㊴ **der Erlebnispark**
theme park

134.1 DER STRAND · THE BEACH

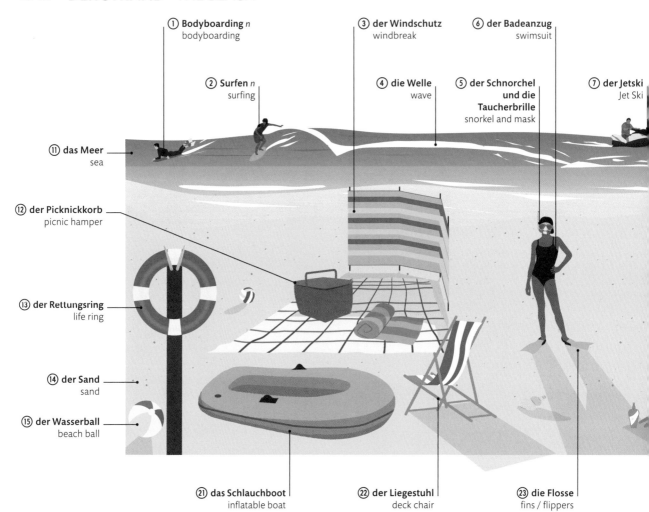

① **Bodyboarding** n
bodyboarding

② **Surfen** n
surfing

③ **der Windschutz**
windbreak

④ **die Welle**
wave

⑥ **der Badeanzug**
swimsuit

⑤ **der Schnorchel
und die
Taucherbrille**
snorkel and mask

⑦ **der Jetski**
Jet Ski

⑪ **das Meer**
sea

⑫ **der Picknickkorb**
picnic hamper

⑬ **der Rettungsring**
life ring

⑭ **der Sand**
sand

⑮ **der Wasserball**
beach ball

㉑ **das Schlauchboot**
inflatable boat

㉒ **der Liegestuhl**
deck chair

㉓ **die Flosse**
fins / flippers

㉕ **das Segel**
sail

㉖ **die Jacht**
yacht

㉗ **der Bohlenweg**
boardwalk

㉘ **die Strandpromenade**
promenade

㉙ **das Strandhäuschen**
beach hut

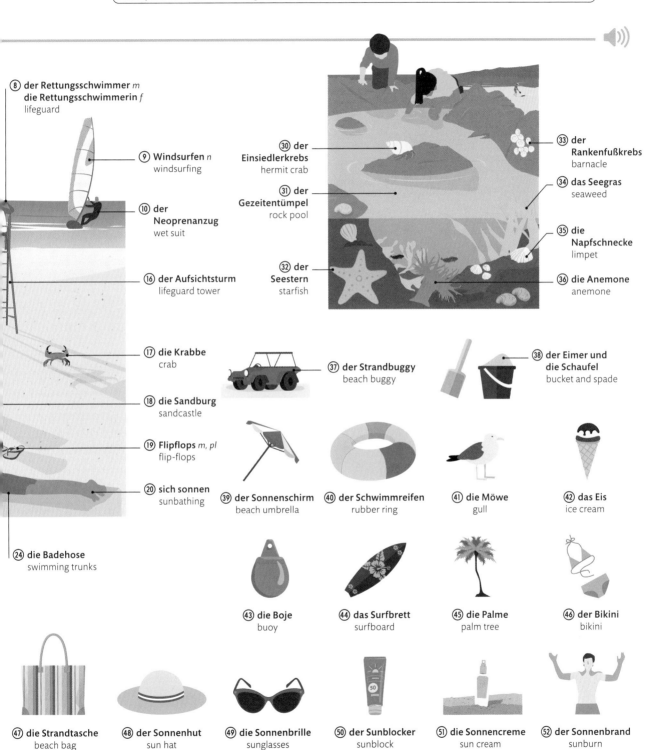

See also
105 Seefahrzeuge • Sea vessels **118** Schwimmen • Swimming **119** Segeln und Wassersport • Sailing and watersports **121** Fischen • Fishing **133** Aktivitäten im Freien • Outdoor activities **166** Leben im Ozean • Ocean life

⑧ **der Rettungsschwimmer** *m*
die Rettungsschwimmerin *f*
lifeguard

⑨ **Windsurfen** *n*
windsurfing

⑩ **der Neoprenanzug**
wet suit

⑯ **der Aufsichtsturm**
lifeguard tower

⑰ **die Krabbe**
crab

⑱ **die Sandburg**
sandcastle

⑲ **Flipflops** *m, pl*
flip-flops

⑳ **sich sonnen**
sunbathing

㉔ **die Badehose**
swimming trunks

㉚ **der Einsiedlerkrebs**
hermit crab

㉛ **der Gezeitentümpel**
rock pool

㉜ **der Seestern**
starfish

㉝ **der Rankenfußkrebs**
barnacle

㉞ **das Seegras**
seaweed

㉟ **die Napfschnecke**
limpet

㊱ **die Anemone**
anemone

㊲ **der Strandbuggy**
beach buggy

㊳ **der Eimer und die Schaufel**
bucket and spade

㊴ **der Sonnenschirm**
beach umbrella

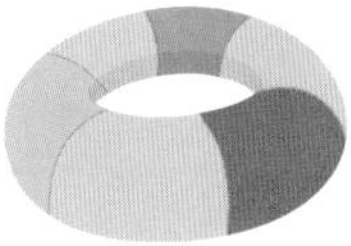

㊵ **der Schwimmreifen**
rubber ring

㊶ **die Möwe**
gull

㊷ **das Eis**
ice cream

㊸ **die Boje**
buoy

㊹ **das Surfbrett**
surfboard

㊺ **die Palme**
palm tree

㊻ **der Bikini**
bikini

㊼ **die Strandtasche**
beach bag

㊽ **der Sonnenhut**
sun hat

㊾ **die Sonnenbrille**
sunglasses

㊿ **der Sunblocker**
sunblock

(51) **die Sonnencreme**
sun cream

(52) **der Sonnenbrand**
sunburn

135.1 CAMPINGAUSRÜSTUNG UND ZUBEHÖR · CAMPING EQUIPMENT AND FACILITIES

① **campen**
to camp

② **ein Zelt aufstellen**
to pitch a tent

③ **das Zweipersonenzelt**
two-person tent

④ **der Stellplatz**
pitch

⑤ **freie Stellplätze**
pitches available

⑥ **alles besetzt**
full

⑧ **der Stromanschluss**
electric hook-up

⑨ **der Anhänger**
trailer

⑩ **das Wohnmobil**
camper van

⑪ **die Hängematte**
hammock

⑫ **das Lagerfeuer**
campfire

⑬ **Feuer machen**
to light a fire

⑮ **die Kohle**
charcoal

⑯ **der Grill**
barbecue

⑰ **der Gaskocher**
single-burner
camping stove

⑱ **der Campingkocher mit zwei Herdplatten**
double-burner camping stove

⑲ **der Faltrost**
folding grill

⑳ **die Picknickbank**
picnic bench

㉒ **das Duschhaus**
shower block

㉓ **das Toilettenhaus**
toilet block

㉔ **die Abfallsammelstelle**
waste disposal

㉕ **das Campingbüro**
site manager's office

㉖ **der Rucksack**
rucksack

㉗ **die Taschenlampe**
torch

㉙ **der Kompass**
compass

㉚ **die Thermounterwäsche**
thermals

㉛ **die Wanderschuhe** m, pl
walking boots

㉜ **die Regenjacke**
waterproofs

㉝ **das Mehrzweckmesser**
multi-purpose knife

㉞ **das Insektenschutzmittel**
insect repellent

㊱ **der Schlafsack**
sleeping bag

㊲ **die Isomatte**
sleeping mat

㊳ **das Campingbett**
camp bed

㊴ **die selbst aufblasende Matratze**
self-inflating mattress

㊵ **die Luftmatratze**
air bed /
air mattress

㊶ **die Luftpumpe**
air pump

See also
131 Reise und Unterkunft • Travel and accommodation **133** Aktivitäten im Freien • Outdoor activities **146-147** Geografie • Geography

135.2 **DER CAMPINGPLATZ** · CAMPSITE

⑦ der **Wohnwagen**
caravan

⑭ der **Anzünder**
firelighter

㉑ die **Wasserflasche**
water bottles

㉘ die **Stirnlampe**
headlamp

㉟ das **Mückennetz**
mosquito net

㊷ die **elektrische Pumpe**
electric pump

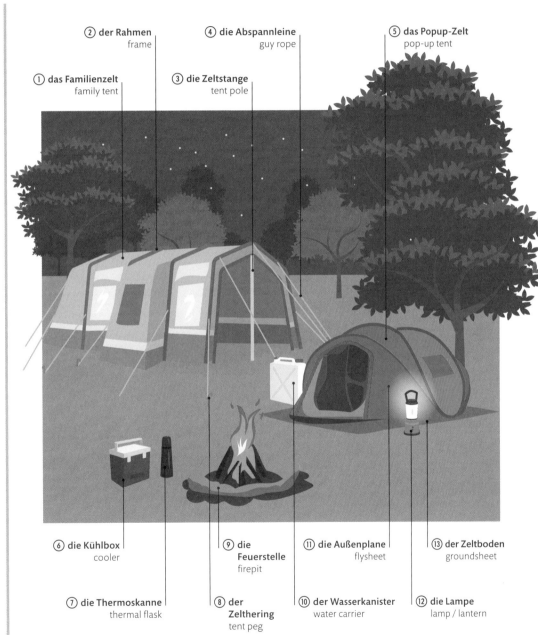

② der **Rahmen**
frame

④ die **Abspannleine**
guy rope

⑤ das **Popup-Zelt**
pop-up tent

① das **Familienzelt**
family tent

③ die **Zeltstange**
tent pole

⑥ die **Kühlbox**
cooler

⑨ die **Feuerstelle**
firepit

⑪ die **Außenplane**
flysheet

⑬ der **Zeltboden**
groundsheet

⑦ die **Thermoskanne**
thermal flask

⑧ der **Zelthering**
tent peg

⑩ der **Wasserkanister**
water carrier

⑫ die **Lampe**
lamp / lantern

279

136.1 FERNSEHER UND LAUTSPRECHER · TELEVISION AND AUDIO

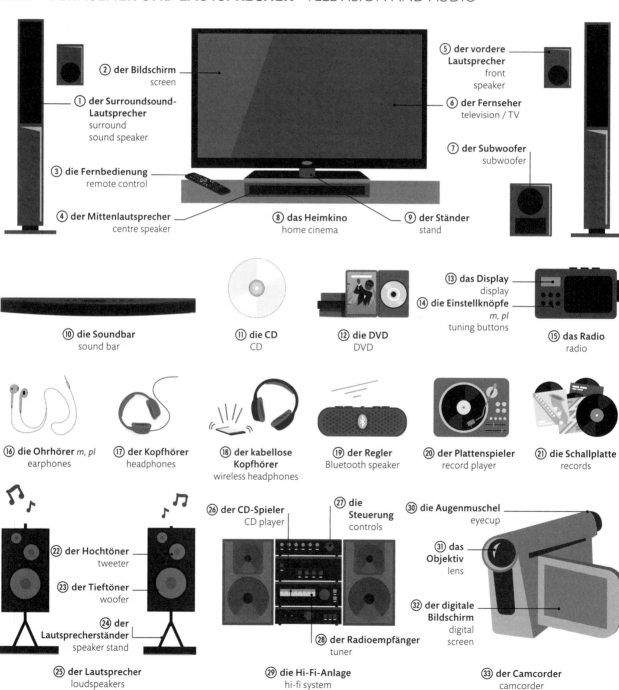

② der Bildschirm
screen

① der Surroundsound-
Lautsprecher
surround
sound speaker

③ die Fernbedienung
remote control

④ der Mittenlautsprecher
centre speaker

⑤ der vordere
Lautsprecher
front
speaker

⑥ der Fernseher
television / TV

⑦ der Subwoofer
subwoofer

⑧ das Heimkino
home cinema

⑨ der Ständer
stand

⑩ die Soundbar
sound bar

⑪ die CD
CD

⑫ die DVD
DVD

⑬ das Display
display

⑭ die Einstellknöpfe
m, pl
tuning buttons

⑮ das Radio
radio

⑯ die Ohrhörer m, pl
earphones

⑰ der Kopfhörer
headphones

⑱ der kabellose
Kopfhörer
wireless headphones

⑲ der Regler
Bluetooth speaker

⑳ der Plattenspieler
record player

㉑ die Schallplatte
records

㉒ der Hochtöner
tweeter

㉓ der Tieftöner
woofer

㉔ der
Lautsprecherständer
speaker stand

㉕ der Lautsprecher
loudspeakers

㉖ der CD-Spieler
CD player

㉗ die
Steuerung
controls

㉘ der Radioempfänger
tuner

㉙ die Hi-Fi-Anlage
hi-fi system

㉚ die Augenmuschel
eyecup

㉛ das
Objektiv
lens

㉜ der digitale
Bildschirm
digital
screen

㉝ der Camcorder
camcorder

See also
127 Filme · Films **128-129** Musik · Music
137 Fernsehen · Television **140** Spiele · Games

136.2 **VIDEOSPIELE** · VIDEO GAMES

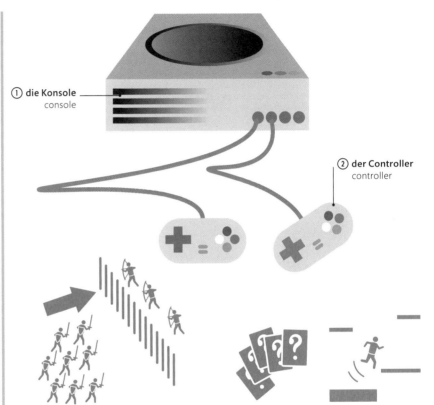

① die Konsole
console

② der Controller
controller

③ das Strategiespiel
strategy game

④ das Wissensquiz
trivia game

⑤ das Plattformspiel
platform game

⑥ das Abenteuerspiel
adventure game

⑦ das Rollenspiel
role-playing game

⑧ das Actionspiel
action game

⑨ das Spiel für mehrere Spieler
multiplayer game

⑩ das Simulationsspiel
simulation game

⑪ das Sportspiel
sports game

⑫ das Blockpuzzle
puzzle game

⑬ das Logikspiel
logic game

㉞ stereo
stereo

㉟ mono
mono

㊱ den Sender einstellen
to tune in

㊲ die Lautstärke
volume

㊳ lauter machen
to turn up

㊴ leiser machen
to turn down

㊵ die Satellitenschüssel
satellite dish

㊶ der Digitalempfänger
digital box

㊷ das Mikrofon
microphone

㊸ Karaoke *n*
karaoke

137.1 FERNSEHEN · WATCHING TELEVISION

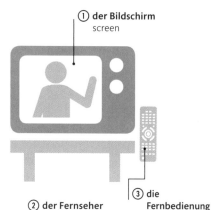

① **der Bildschirm**
screen

② **der Fernseher**
TV set

③ **die Fernbedienung**
remote control

④ **HD**
high-definition

⑤ **das Kabelfernsehen**
cable TV

⑥ **das Satellitenfernsehen**
satellite TV

⑦ **das Video-on-Demand**
video on demand

⑧ **der Kanal**
channel

⑨ **der Bezahlkanal**
pay-per-view channel

⑩ **die Folge**
episode

⑪ **die Staffel**
series

⑫ **die Sendung**
programme

⑬ **der Untertitel**
subtitles

⑭ **das Interview**
interview

⑮ **die Fernsehzeitung**
TV guide / schedule

⑯ **die Vorschau**
preview

⑰ **der Reporter** *m*
die Reporterin *f*
reporter

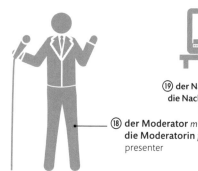

⑱ **der Moderator** *m*
die Moderatorin *f*
presenter

⑲ **der Nachrichtensprecher** *m*
die Nachrichtensprecherin *f*
newsreader

⑳ **die Werbepause**
adverts

㉑ **der Meteorologe** *m*
die Meteorologin *f*
weather forecaster

㉒ **der Stubenhocker** *m*
die Stubenhockerin *f*
couch potato

137.2 FERNSEHVERBEN · TELEVISION VERBS

① **einschalten**
to turn on

② **ausschalten**
to turn off

③ **lauter machen**
to turn up the volume

④ **leiser machen**
to turn down the volume

⑤ **umschalten**
to change the channel

⑥ **streamen**
to stream

See also
26 Das Wohnzimmer und das Esszimmer · Living room and dining room **84** Medien
Media **127** Filme · Films **136** Unterhaltung zu Hause · Home entertainment

137.3 FERNSEHSENDUNGEN UND KANÄLE · TV SHOWS AND CHANNELS

① **die Kochsendung**
cooking show

② **die Talkshow**
chat show

③ **der Sport**
sports

④ **die Dokumentation**
documentary

⑤ **die Naturdokumentation**
nature documentary

⑥ **das Historiendrama**
period drama /
costume drama

⑦ **die Sitcom**
sitcom

⑧ **die Quizshow**
quiz show

⑨ **das Tagesgeschehen** *n, pl*
current affairs

⑩ **die Nachrichten** *pl*
news

⑪ **das Wetter**
weather

⑫ **die Seifenoper**
soap opera

⑬ **die Gameshow**
game show

⑭ **die Komödie**
comedy

⑮ **der Cartoon**
cartoon

⑯ **der Krimi**
crime

⑰ **der Thriller**
thriller

⑱ **die Satire**
satire

⑲ **die Kindersendung**
children's TV

⑳ **das Frühstücksfernsehen**
breakfast TV

㉑ **die Realityshow**
reality TV

㉒ **die TV-Mediathek**
catch-up TV

㉓ **der Shoppingkanal**
shopping channel

㉔ **der Musikkanal**
music channel

⑦ **abspielen**
to play

⑧ **anhalten**
to stop

⑨ **unterbrechen**
to pause

⑩ **zurückspulen**
to rewind

⑪ **vorspulen**
to fast forward

⑫ **aufzeichnen**
to record

138.1 BÜCHER · BOOKS

① **die Illustration**
illustration

② **die Seite**
page

③ **der Text**
text

④ **der Rücken**
spine

⑤ **das Buch**
book

⑥ **der Umschlag**
cover

⑦ **der Schriftsteller** *m*
die Schriftstellerin *f*
author

⑧ **das Taschenbuch**
paperback

⑨ **das gebundene Buch**
hardback

⑬ **die Rezension**
review

⑭ **der Inhalt**
contents

⑮ **das Kapitel**
chapter

138.2 LESEN UND GENRES · READING AND GENRES

① **das Sachbuch**
non-fiction

② **das Wörterbuch**
dictionary

③ **das Lexikon**
encyclopedia

④ **das Gartenbuch**
gardening book

⑤ **die Fernsehzeitung**
TV guide

⑥ **der Ratgeber**
self-help

⑦ **die Autobiografie**
autobiography

⑧ **die Biografie**
biography

⑨ **das Kochbuch**
cookbook

⑩ **der Reiseführer**
guidebook

⑪ **das Natursachbuch**
nature writing

⑫ **das Kursbuch**
textbook / course book

⑬ **die Erzählliteratur**
fiction

⑭ **der Roman**
novel

⑮ **das Science-Fiction-Buch**
science fiction

⑯ **das Fantasy-Buch**
fantasy

⑰ **der Comic**
comic

⑱ **der Reisebericht**
travel writing

See also
127 Filme • Films **136** Unterhaltung zu Hause • Home entertainment
139 Fantasy und Mythologie • Fantasy and myth **175** Schreiben • Writing

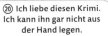

⑳ Ich liebe diesen Krimi. Ich kann ihn gar nicht aus der Hand legen.
I love this crime novel. It's a real page-turner.

㉑ Ich hasse diesen Fantasy-Roman. Die Handlung ist lächerlich.
I hate this fantasy novel. The plot is ridiculous.

⑩ der Titel
title

⑪ durchblättern
to flip through

⑫ der E-Reader
e-reader

⑯ das Literaturverzeichnis
bibliography

⑰ das Glossar
glossary

⑱ das Wortverzeichnis
index

⑲ das Lesen
reading

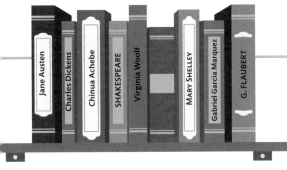

⑲ die Belletristik
literary fiction

㉑ die Figur
character

⑳ das Kinderbuch
children's book

㉒ das Malbuch
colouring book

㉓ das Märchen
fairy tale

㉔ die Romanze
romance

㉕ der Krimi
crime fiction

㉖ die Unterhaltungsliteratur
humour

㉗ der Kalender
diary

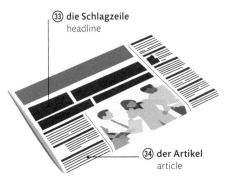

㉝ die Schlagzeile
headline

㉞ der Artikel
article

㉘ der Bestseller
bestseller

㉙ das Horoskop
horoscope

㉚ das Klatschmagazin
gossip magazine

㉛ das Rätselbuch
puzzles

㉜ die Zeitung
newspaper

139.1 MYTHEN, GESCHICHTEN UND FABELWESEN · MYTHS, STORIES, AND FANTASTIC CREATURES

② **Es war einmal, in einem weit entfernten Land...**
Once upon a time in a land far away...

⑥ **zaubern**
to cast a spell

⑤ **der Zauberstab**
wand

④ **das Zauberbuch**
spell book

① **das Märchen**
fairy tale

③ **das Einhorn**
unicorn

⑧ **der Zaubertrank**
witches' brew

⑦ **der Kessel**
cauldron

⑨ **die Kristallkugel**
crystal ball

⑩ **der Zaubertrank**
potion

⑪ **die Kerzenmagie**
candle magic

⑱ **der Stab**
staff

⑭ **der Held** *m*
die Heldin *f*
hero

⑬ **der Minotaurus**
Minotaur

⑫ **die griechische Mythologie**
Greek mythology

⑮ **das Elixier**
elixir

⑯ **das Amulett**
amulet

⑰ **der Zauberer**
wizard

⑲ **die Aufgabe**
quest

⑳ **der Schatz**
treasure

㉑ **der fliegende Teppich**
flying carpet

㉒ **der Flaschengeist**
genie

㉓ **die Wunderlampe**
lamp

See also
127 Filme • Films **137** Fernsehen • Television
138 Bücher und lesen • Books and reading

㉔ **die Seeschlange**
sea serpent

㉕ **Hugin und Munin**
Hugin and Munin

㉖ **die Disen** *pl*
the Disir

㉗ **das Monster**
monster

㉘ **der Zombie**
zombie

㉙ **der Werwolf**
werewolf

㉚ **der Vampir**
vampire

㉛ **das Gespenst**
ghost

㉜ **die Kürbisfratze**
jack-o'-lantern

㉝ **der Drache**
dragon

㉞ **der Ritter**
knight

㊱ **der Besen**
broomstick

㉟ **die Hexe**
witch

㊲ **die Fee**
fairy

㊳ **die Elfe**
pixie

㊴ **der Faun**
faun

㊵ **der Zwerg**
gnome

㊶ **der Kobold**
leprechaun

㊷ **der Gremlin**
gremlin

㊸ **der Goblin**
goblin

㊹ **der Troll**
troll

㊺ **der Oger**
ogre

㊻ **der Ork**
orc

㊼ **der Riese**
giant

㊽ **der Elf**
elf

㊾ **der Zwerg**
dwarf

㊿ **die Meerjungfrau**
mermaid

(51) **der Meermann**
merman

(52) **der Phönix**
phoenix

(53) **der Greif**
griffin

(54) **die Hydra**
hydra

(55) **der Zentaur**
centaur

(56) **die Sphinx**
sphinx

(57) **Kerberos**
Cerberus

(58) **der böse Roboter**
bad robot

(59) **der Außerirdische**
alien

140.1 SCHACH · CHESS

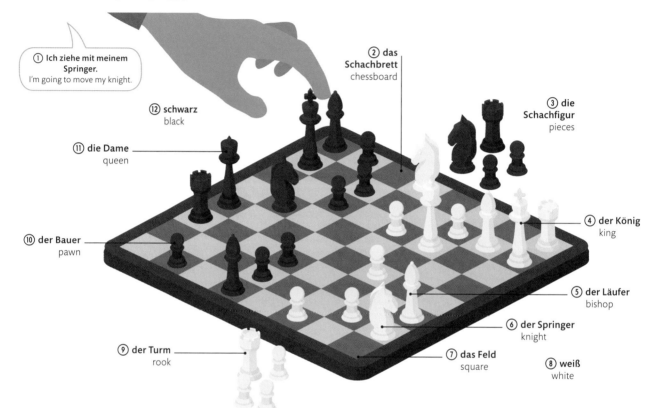

① Ich ziehe mit meinem Springer.
I'm going to move my knight.

② das Schachbrett
chessboard

③ die Schachfigur
pieces

⑫ schwarz
black

⑪ die Dame
queen

④ der König
king

⑩ der Bauer
pawn

⑤ der Läufer
bishop

⑥ der Springer
knight

⑨ der Turm
rook

⑦ das Feld
square

⑧ weiß
white

140.3 SPIELE · GAMES

① das Brettspiel
board games

② der Punkt
points

③ das Ergebnis
score

④ Tic-Tac-Toe n
noughts and crosses

⑤ der Würfel
dice

⑥ Solitär n
solitaire

⑦ die Figur
pieces

⑧ das Puzzle
jigsaw puzzle

⑨ Domino n
dominoes

⑩ der Dartpfeil
darts

⑪ die Dartscheibe
dartboard

⑫ das Bullseye
bullseye

See also
136 Unterhaltung zu Hause · Home entertainment **138** Bücher und Lesen
Books and reading **141-142** Kunst und Handwerk · Arts and crafts

140.2 **SPIELKARTEN** · PLAYING CARDS

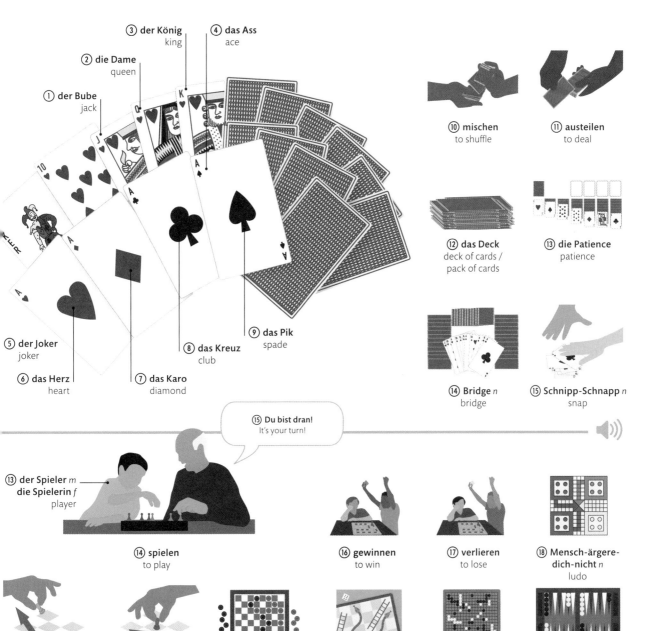

① der Bube
jack

② die Dame
queen

③ der König
king

④ das Ass
ace

⑤ der Joker
joker

⑥ das Herz
heart

⑦ das Karo
diamond

⑧ das Kreuz
club

⑨ das Pik
spade

⑩ mischen
to shuffle

⑪ austeilen
to deal

⑫ das Deck
deck of cards /
pack of cards

⑬ die Patience
patience

⑭ Bridge *n*
bridge

⑮ Schnipp-Schnapp *n*
snap

⑮ **Du bist dran!**
It's your turn!

⑬ der Spieler *m*
die Spielerin *f*
player

⑭ spielen
to play

⑯ gewinnen
to win

⑰ verlieren
to lose

⑱ Mensch-ärgere-
dich-nicht *n*
ludo

⑲ nehmen
to take

⑳ ziehen
to move

㉑ Dame *n*
draughts

㉒ Leiterspiel *n*
snakes and ladders

㉓ Go *n*
go

㉔ Backgammon *n*
backgammon

141.1 DAS MALEN · PAINTING

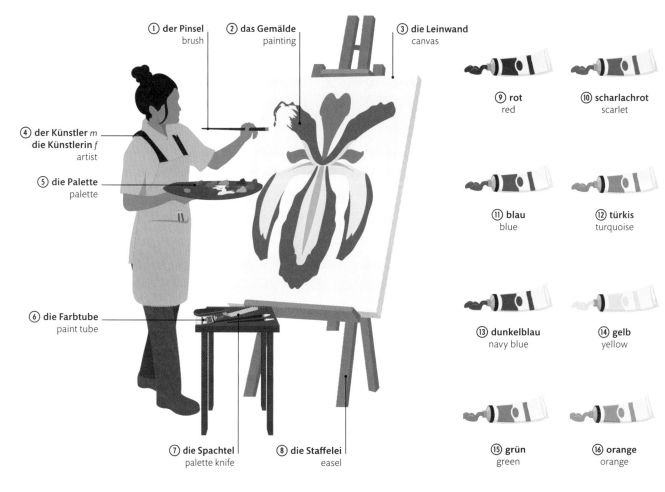

① **der Pinsel** brush

② **das Gemälde** painting

③ **die Leinwand** canvas

④ **der Künstler** m
die Künstlerin f
artist

⑤ **die Palette** palette

⑥ **die Farbtube** paint tube

⑦ **die Spachtel** palette knife

⑧ **die Staffelei** easel

⑨ **rot** red

⑩ **scharlachrot** scarlet

⑪ **blau** blue

⑫ **türkis** turquoise

⑬ **dunkelblau** navy blue

⑭ **gelb** yellow

⑮ **grün** green

⑯ **orange** orange

⑰ **violett** purple

⑱ **indigoblau** indigo

⑲ **pink** pink

⑳ **braun** brown

㉑ **grau** grey

㉒ **schwarz** black

㉓ **weiß** white

㉔ **die Ölfarbe** oil paints

㉕ **die Wasserfarbe** watercolour paints

㉖ **der Pastellstift** pastels

㉗ **die Acrylfarbe** acrylic paints

㉘ **die Plakatfarbe** poster paint

See also
37 Wohnraumverschönerung · Decorating **130** Museen und Kunstgalerien · Museums
and galleries **142** Kunst und Handwerk (Fortsetzung) · Arts and crafts continued

141.2 ANDERE KUNST- UND HANDWERKSARTEN · OTHER ARTS AND CRAFTS

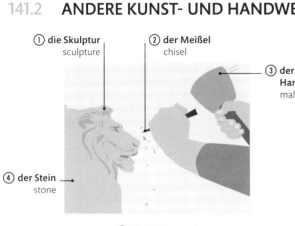

① **die Skulptur**
sculpture

② **der Meißel**
chisel

③ **der Hammer**
mallet

④ **der Stein**
stone

⑤ **die Bildhauerei**
sculpting

⑥ **das Zeichnen**
drawing

⑦ **die Skizze**
sketch

⑧ **die Zeichenkohle**
charcoal

⑨ **der Bleistift**
pencil

⑩ **der Zeichenblock**
sketch pad

⑪ **der Druck**
printing

⑫ **die Tinte**
ink

⑬ **die Gravur, der Stich**
engraving

⑮ **das Holz**
wood

⑭ **die Holzarbeit**
woodworking

⑯ **der Karton**
card

⑰ **die Collage**
collage

⑱ **der Kleber**
glue

⑲ **das Origami**
origami

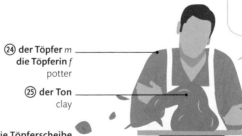

⑳ **der Modellbau**
model making

㉑ **das Pappmaché**
papier-mâché

㉒ **das Modellierwerkzeug**
modelling tool

㉓ **Schmuck herstellen**
making jewellery

㉘ **In meiner Freizeit mache ich Tontöpfe.**
I make pots in my spare time.

㉔ **der Töpfer** *m*
die Töpferin *f*
potter

㉕ **der Ton**
clay

㉖ **die Töpferscheibe**
potter's wheel

㉗ **die Tonware**
pottery

142.1 NÄHEN · SEWING

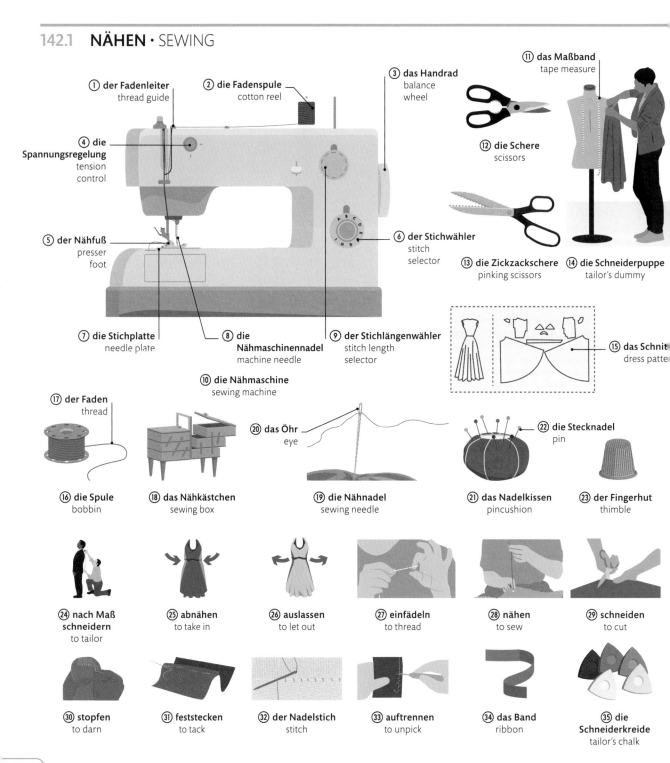

① **der Fadenleiter**
thread guide

② **die Fadenspule**
cotton reel

③ **das Handrad**
balance wheel

⑪ **das Maßband**
tape measure

④ **die Spannungsregelung**
tension control

⑫ **die Schere**
scissors

⑤ **der Nähfuß**
presser foot

⑥ **der Stichwähler**
stitch selector

⑬ **die Zickzackschere**
pinking scissors

⑭ **die Schneiderpuppe**
tailor's dummy

⑦ **die Stichplatte**
needle plate

⑧ **die Nähmaschinennadel**
machine needle

⑨ **der Stichlängenwähler**
stitch length selector

⑮ **das Schnit**
dress patte

⑩ **die Nähmaschine**
sewing machine

⑰ **der Faden**
thread

⑳ **das Öhr**
eye

㉒ **die Stecknadel**
pin

⑯ **die Spule**
bobbin

⑱ **das Nähkästchen**
sewing box

⑲ **die Nähnadel**
sewing needle

㉑ **das Nadelkissen**
pincushion

㉓ **der Fingerhut**
thimble

㉔ **nach Maß schneidern**
to tailor

㉕ **abnähen**
to take in

㉖ **auslassen**
to let out

㉗ **einfädeln**
to thread

㉘ **nähen**
to sew

㉙ **schneiden**
to cut

㉚ **stopfen**
to darn

㉛ **feststecken**
to tack

㉜ **der Nadelstich**
stitch

㉝ **auftrennen**
to unpick

㉞ **das Band**
ribbon

㉟ **die Schneiderkreide**
tailor's chalk

See also
11 Fähigkeiten und Handlungen • Abilities and actions **13-15** Kleidung • Clothes
37 Wohnraumverschönerung • Decorating **39** Gartenarbeit • Practical gardening

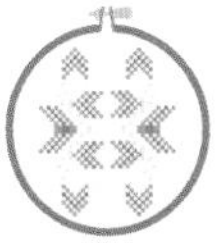

㊱ die Gobelinstickerei
needlepoint

㊲ die Stickerei
embroidery

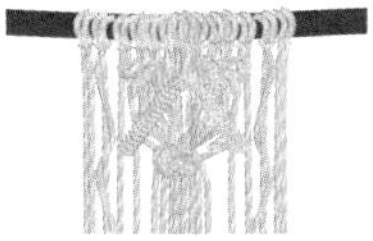

㊳ das Makramee
macramé

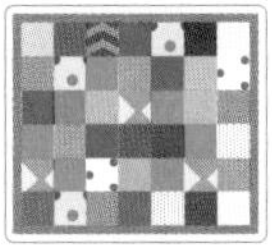

㊴ das Steppen
quilting

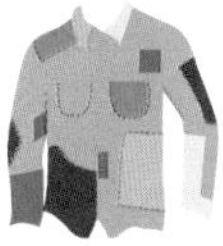

㊵ das Flickwerk
patchwork

㊶ der Stoff
fabric

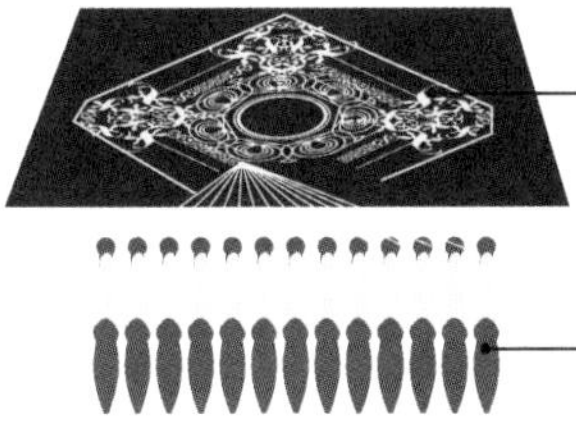

㊷ Spitze herstellen
lace-making

㊸ der Klöppel
lace bobbin

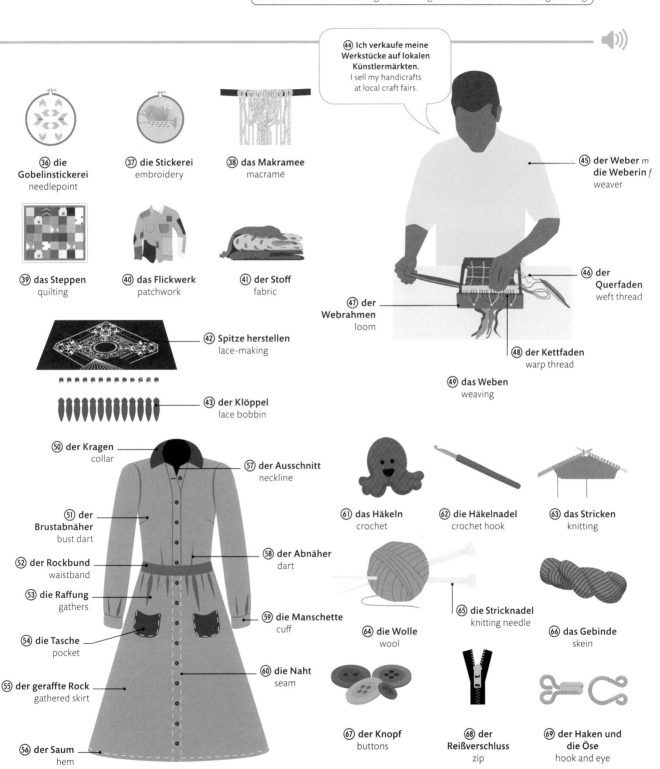

㊹ Ich verkaufe meine Werkstücke auf lokalen Künstlermärkten.
I sell my handicrafts at local craft fairs.

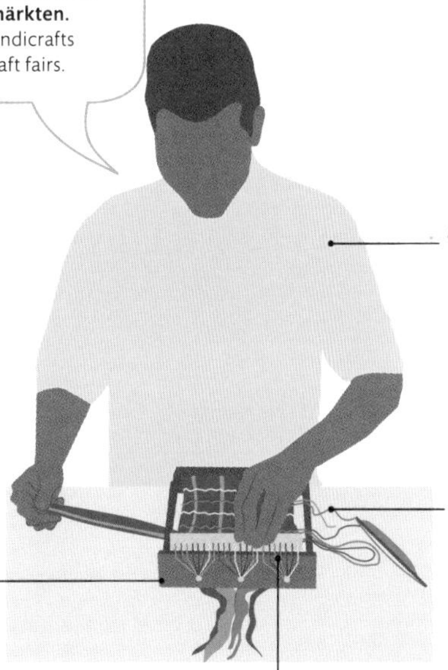

㊺ der Weber *m* **die Weberin** *f*
weaver

㊻ der Querfaden
weft thread

㊼ der Webrahmen
loom

㊽ der Kettfaden
warp thread

㊾ das Weben
weaving

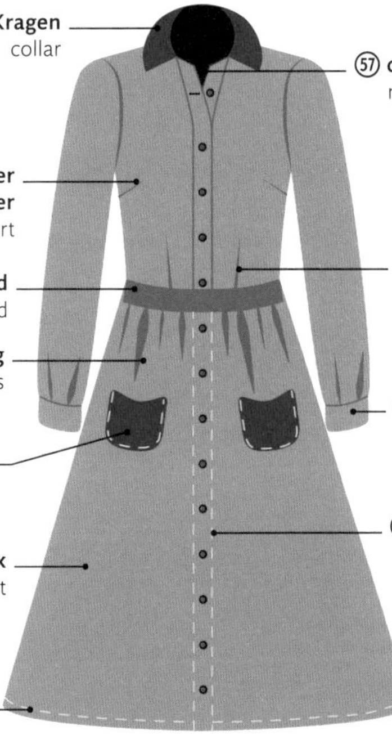

㊿ der Kragen
collar

(51) der Brustabnäher
bust dart

(52) der Rockbund
waistband

(53) die Raffung
gathers

(54) die Tasche
pocket

(55) der geraffte Rock
gathered skirt

(56) der Saum
hem

(57) der Ausschnitt
neckline

(58) der Abnäher
dart

(59) die Manschette
cuff

(60) die Naht
seam

(61) das Häkeln
crochet

(62) die Häkelnadel
crochet hook

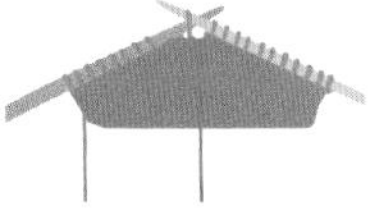

(63) das Stricken
knitting

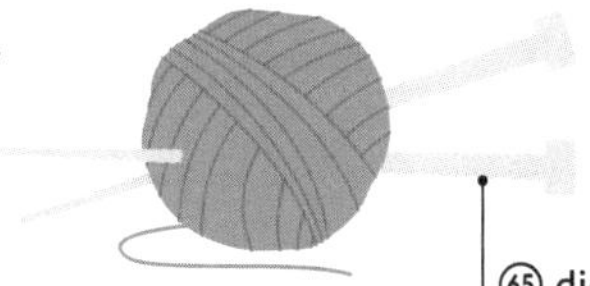

(64) die Wolle
wool

(65) die Stricknadel
knitting needle

(66) das Gebinde
skein

(67) der Knopf
buttons

(68) der Reißverschluss
zip

(69) der Haken und die Öse
hook and eye

143.1 DAS SONNENSYSTEM · THE SOLAR SYSTEM

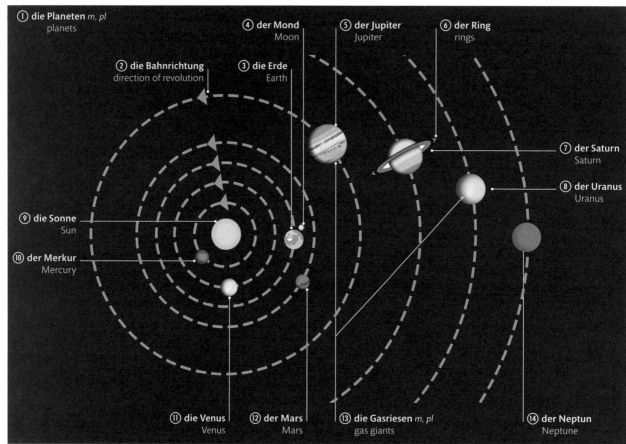

① **die Planeten** *m, pl*
planets

② **die Bahnrichtung**
direction of revolution

③ **die Erde**
Earth

④ **der Mond**
Moon

⑤ **der Jupiter**
Jupiter

⑥ **der Ring**
rings

⑦ **der Saturn**
Saturn

⑧ **der Uranus**
Uranus

⑨ **die Sonne**
Sun

⑩ **der Merkur**
Mercury

⑪ **die Venus**
Venus

⑫ **der Mars**
Mars

⑬ **die Gasriesen** *m, pl*
gas giants

⑭ **der Neptun**
Neptune

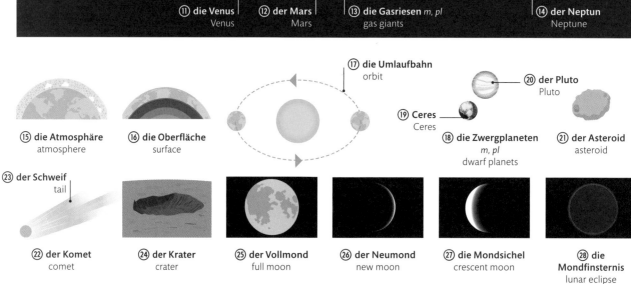

⑰ **die Umlaufbahn**
orbit

⑮ **die Atmosphäre**
atmosphere

⑯ **die Oberfläche**
surface

⑲ **Ceres**
Ceres

⑳ **der Pluto**
Pluto

⑱ **die Zwergplaneten**
m, pl
dwarf planets

㉑ **der Asteroid**
asteroid

㉓ **der Schweif**
tail

㉒ **der Komet**
comet

㉔ **der Krater**
crater

㉕ **der Vollmond**
full moon

㉖ **der Neumond**
new moon

㉗ **die Mondsichel**
crescent moon

㉘ **die Mondfinsternis**
lunar eclipse

See also
74 Mathematik · Mathematics **75** Physik · Physics **83** Computer und Technologie · Computers and technology **144** Der Weltraum (Fortsetzung) · Space continued **145** Der Planet Erde · Planet Earth **156** Gesteine und Mineralien · Rocks and minerals

143.2 DIE ERKUNDUNG DES WELTRAUMS · SPACE EXPLORATION

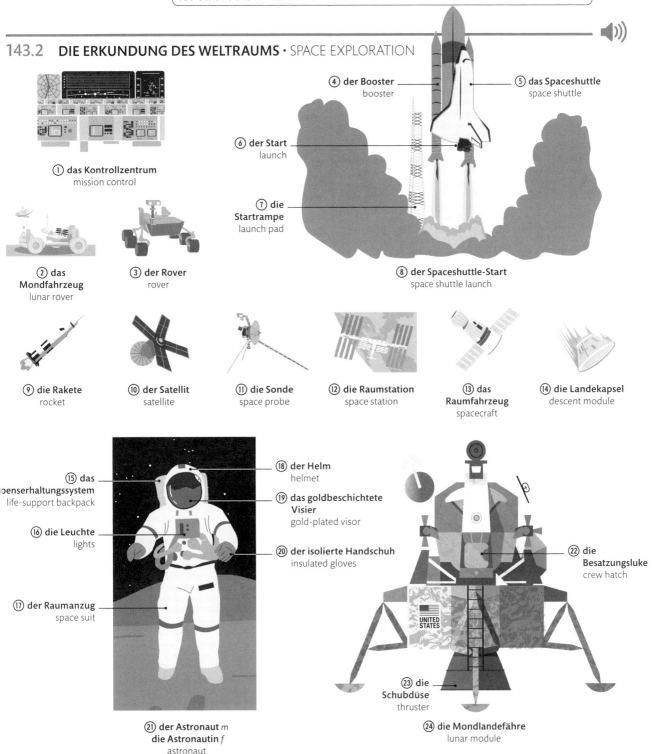

① **das Kontrollzentrum**
mission control

② **das Mondfahrzeug**
lunar rover

③ **der Rover**
rover

④ **der Booster**
booster

⑤ **das Spaceshuttle**
space shuttle

⑥ **der Start**
launch

⑦ **die Startrampe**
launch pad

⑧ **der Spaceshuttle-Start**
space shuttle launch

⑨ **die Rakete**
rocket

⑩ **der Satellit**
satellite

⑪ **die Sonde**
space probe

⑫ **die Raumstation**
space station

⑬ **das Raumfahrzeug**
spacecraft

⑭ **die Landekapsel**
descent module

⑮ **das Lebenserhaltungssystem**
life-support backpack

⑯ **die Leuchte**
lights

⑰ **der Raumanzug**
space suit

⑱ **der Helm**
helmet

⑲ **das goldbeschichtete Visier**
gold-plated visor

⑳ **der isolierte Handschuh**
insulated gloves

㉑ **der Astronaut** m
die Astronautin f
astronaut

㉒ **die Besatzungsluke**
crew hatch

㉓ **die Schubdüse**
thruster

㉔ **die Mondlandefähre**
lunar module

UNITED STATES

144.1 ASTRONOMIE · ASTRONOMY

① **das Fernglas**
binoculars

② **das Linsenteleskop (Fernrohr)**
refractor telescope

③ **das Spiegelteleskop**
reflector telescope

⑩ **das Okular**
eyepiece

⑫ **der Komet**
comet

⑪ **das Suchfernrohr**
finderscope

⑨ **Ich habe eben einen Kometen entdeckt!**
I've just spotted a comet.

⑬ **das Stativ**
tripod

⑭ **die Fokussierung**
focusing knob

⑮ **das Teleskop**
telescope

④ **das Radioteleskop**
radio telescope

⑤ **das Observatorium**
observatory

⑥ **das Weltraumteleskop**
space telescope

⑦ **das Sternbild**
constellation

⑧ **die Sternkarte**
star chart

144.2 STERNE UND STERNBILDER · STARS AND CONSTELLATIONS

① **die Schwerkraft**
gravity

② **das Polarlicht**
aurora

③ **der Stern**
star

④ **die Sonneneruption**
flare

⑤ **der Doppelstern**
double star

⑥ **der Neutronenstern**
neutron star

⑬ **der Polarstern / Polaris**
the Pole Star / Polaris

⑭ **der Große Wagen**
the Plough

⑮ **das Kreuz des Südens**
the Southern Cross

⑯ **der Orion**
Orion

⑰ **der rote Riese**
red giant

⑱ **der weiße Zwerg**
white dwarf

See also
74 Mathematik · Mathematics **75** Physik · Physics **83** Computer und Technologie · Computers and technology **145** Der Planet Erde · Planet Earth **156** Gesteine und Mineralien · Rocks and minerals

144.3 **DER TIERKREIS** · THE ZODIAC

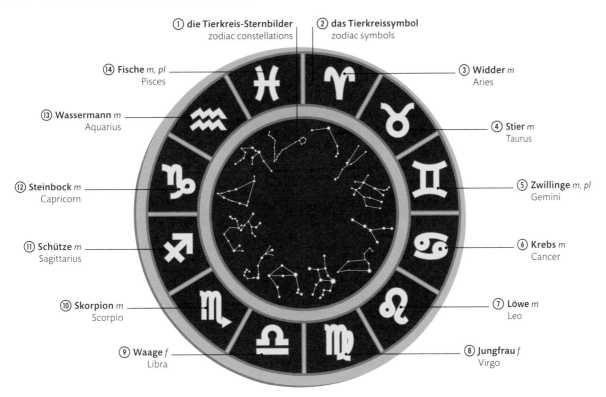

① **die Tierkreis-Sternbilder**
zodiac constellations

② **das Tierkreissymbol**
zodiac symbols

③ **Widder** *m*
Aries

④ **Stier** *m*
Taurus

⑤ **Zwillinge** *m, pl*
Gemini

⑥ **Krebs** *m*
Cancer

⑦ **Löwe** *m*
Leo

⑧ **Jungfrau** *f*
Virgo

⑨ **Waage** *f*
Libra

⑩ **Skorpion** *m*
Scorpio

⑪ **Schütze** *m*
Sagittarius

⑫ **Steinbock** *m*
Capricorn

⑬ **Wassermann** *m*
Aquarius

⑭ **Fische** *m, pl*
Pisces

⑦ **die Supernova**
supernova

⑧ **der Nebel**
nebula

⑨ **der Urknall**
the Big Bang

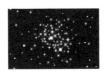

⑩ **der Sternhaufen**
star cluster

⑪ **die elliptische Galaxie**
elliptical galaxy

⑫ **die Spiralgalaxie**
spiral galaxy

⑲ **das Schwarze Loch**
black hole

⑳ **der Meteor**
meteor

㉑ **der Meteorschauer**
meteor shower

㉒ **die Milchstraße**
the Milky Way

㉓ **das Universum**
the universe

145.1 DIE ERDE · THE EARTH

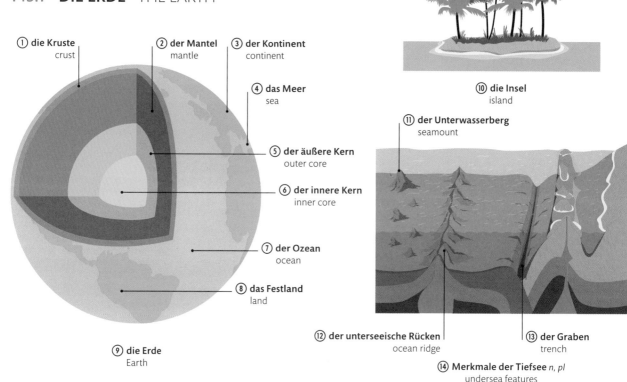

① die Kruste
crust

② der Mantel
mantle

③ der Kontinent
continent

④ das Meer
sea

⑤ der äußere Kern
outer core

⑥ der innere Kern
inner core

⑦ der Ozean
ocean

⑧ das Festland
land

⑨ die Erde
Earth

⑩ die Insel
island

⑪ der Unterwasserberg
seamount

⑫ der unterseeische Rücken
ocean ridge

⑬ der Graben
trench

⑭ Merkmale der Tiefsee n, pl
undersea features

145.2 DIE PLATTENTEKTONIK · PLATE TECTONICS

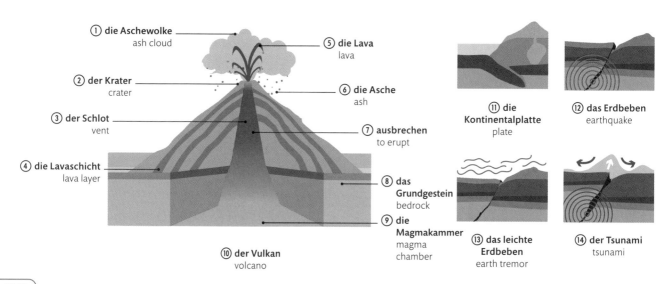

① die Aschewolke
ash cloud

② der Krater
crater

③ der Schlot
vent

④ die Lavaschicht
lava layer

⑤ die Lava
lava

⑥ die Asche
ash

⑦ ausbrechen
to erupt

⑧ das Grundgestein
bedrock

⑨ die Magmakammer
magma chamber

⑩ der Vulkan
volcano

⑪ die Kontinentalplatte
plate

⑫ das Erdbeben
earthquake

⑬ das leichte Erdbeben
earth tremor

⑭ der Tsunami
tsunami

See also
143-144 Der Weltraum · Space **146-147** Geografie · Geography **148** Karten und Richtungsangaben · Maps and directions **149-151** Länder · Countries

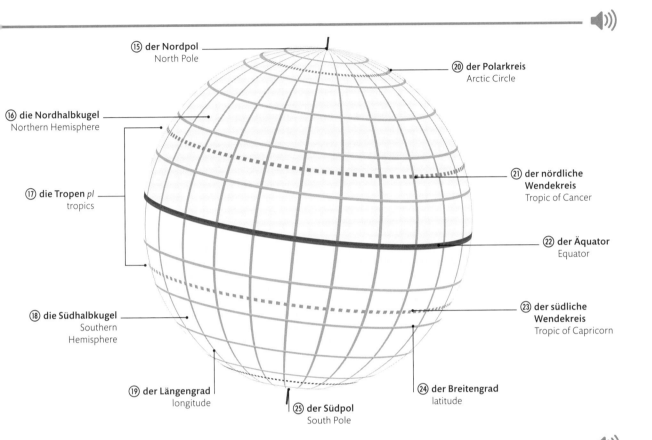

(15) **der Nordpol**
North Pole

(20) **der Polarkreis**
Arctic Circle

(16) **die Nordhalbkugel**
Northern Hemisphere

(21) **der nördliche Wendekreis**
Tropic of Cancer

(17) **die Tropen** *pl*
tropics

(22) **der Äquator**
Equator

(18) **die Südhalbkugel**
Southern Hemisphere

(23) **der südliche Wendekreis**
Tropic of Capricorn

(19) **der Längengrad**
longitude

(24) **der Breitengrad**
latitude

(25) **der Südpol**
South Pole

145.3   GEWÄSSER UND WASSERPHÄNOMENE · WATER FEATURES AND PHENOMENA

(1) **die Viktoriafälle**
Victoria Falls

(2) **die Hang-Son-Doong-Höhle**
Hang Son Doong

(3) **der Amazonas**
the Amazon

(4) **das Tote Meer**
the Dead Sea

(5) **der Cano Cristales**
Caño Cristales

(6) **Pamukkale**
Pamukkale

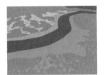

(7) **das Great Barrier Reef**
the Barrier Reef

(8) **der Ganges**
the Ganges

(9) **der Salto Angel**
Angel Falls

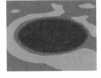

(10) **das Great Blue Hole**
the Great Blue Hole

(11) **der Natronsee**
Lake Natron

(12) **der Spotted Lake**
Spotted Lake

146.1 GEOGRAFISCHE MERKMALE UND LANDSCHAFTEN · GEOGRAPHICAL FEATURES AND LANDSCAP

① **der Wald**
wood

② **der Regenwald**
rain forest

③ **der Nadelwald**
coniferous forest

④ **der Laubwald**
deciduous forest

⑨ **der Wasserfall**
waterfall

⑤ **die Stromschnelle**
rapids

② **die Landschaft**
countryside

⑦ **der See**
lake

⑧ **der Sumpf**
swamp

⑩ **das Feld**
field

⑪ **die Hecke**
hedge

⑫ **das Tal**
valley

⑬ **das Ackerland**
farmland

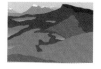

⑭ **das Feuchtgebiet**
wetlands

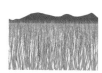

⑮ **das Grasland**
grassland

⑯ **die Prärie**
prairie

⑰ **die Steppe**
steppe

⑱ **der Tafelberg**
mesa

⑲ **das Hochland**
highland

⑳ **der Grat**
ridge

㉑ **das Gebirge**
mountain range

㉒ **die Savanne**
savannah

㉓ **die Gebirgskette**
chain

㉔ **der Geysir**
geyser

㉕ **die Ebene**
plain

㉖ **die Oase**
oasis

㉗ **die Wüste**
desert

㉘ **die Sanddüne**
sand dune

See also
133 Aktivitäten im Freien • Outdoor activites **145** Der Planet Erde • Planet Earth **147** Geografie (Fortsetzung) • Geography continued **148** Karten und Richtungsangaben • Maps and directions **149-151** Länder • Countries

㉙ **der Canyon**
canyon

㉚ **der Eisberg**
iceberg

㉛ **die Schlammlawine**
mudslide

㉜ **der Erdrutsch**
landslide

㊱ **der Gletscher**
glacier

㉝ **die Hochebene**
plateau

㉞ **die Polarregion**
polar region

㉟ **die Tundra**
tundra

146.2 HÖHLEN UND HÖHLENWANDERN · CAVES AND CAVING

① **der Eiszapfen**
icicle

② **die Stirnlampe**
headlamp

③ **die Säule**
column

④ **der unterirdische Flusslauf**
subterranean stream

⑤ **Helm und Stirnlampe sind in Höhlen unverzichtbar.**
A helmet and headlamp are essential when caving.

⑥ **der Stalaktit**
stalactite

⑦ **der Helm**
helmet

⑧ **der Höhlenwanderer** *m*
die Höhlenwanderin *f*
caver

⑨ **der Stalagmit**
stalagmite

147.1 KÜSTENMERKMALE · COASTAL FEATURES

① **der Ozean**
ocean

② **die Welle**
wave

③ **die Düne**
dune

④ **die Insel**
island

⑤ **die Meerenge**
strait

⑥ **der Kanal**
channel

⑦ **die Flut**
high tide

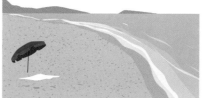

⑧ **die Ebbe**
low tide

⑨ **das Riff**
reef

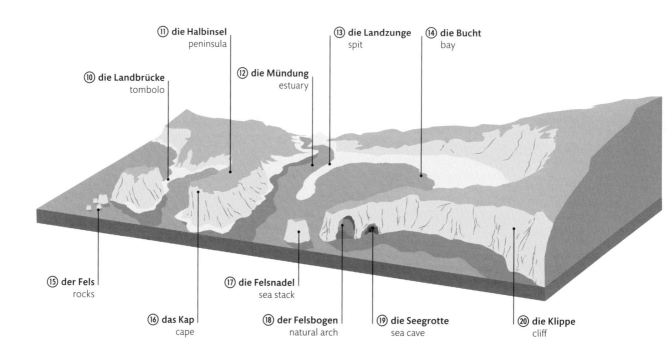

⑪ **die Halbinsel**
peninsula

⑬ **die Landzunge**
spit

⑭ **die Bucht**
bay

⑩ **die Landbrücke**
tombolo

⑫ **die Mündung**
estuary

⑮ **der Fels**
rocks

⑰ **die Felsnadel**
sea stack

⑯ **das Kap**
cape

⑱ **der Felsbogen**
natural arch

⑲ **die Seegrotte**
sea cave

⑳ **die Klippe**
cliff

See also
133 Aktivitäten im Freien • Outdoor activities **145** Der Planet Erde • Planet Earth
148 Karten und Richtungsangaben • Maps and directions **149-151** Länder • Countries

㉑ **das Sumpfland**
marsh

㉒ **das Delta**
delta

㉓ **der Golf**
gulf

㉔ **der Fjord**
fjord

㉕ **der Archipel**
archipelago

㉖ **die Landenge**
isthmus

㉗ **das Atoll**
atoll

㉘ **die Lagune**
lagoon

147.2 **MERKMALE VON FLÜSSEN** · RIVER FEATURES

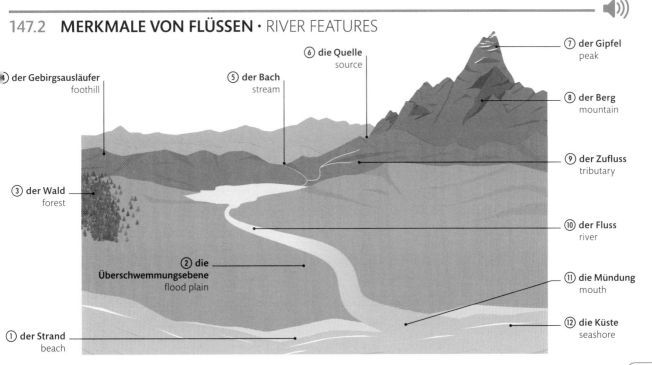

④ **der Gebirgsausläufer**
foothill

⑤ **der Bach**
stream

⑥ **die Quelle**
source

⑦ **der Gipfel**
peak

③ **der Wald**
forest

⑧ **der Berg**
mountain

⑨ **der Zufluss**
tributary

② **die Überschwemmungsebene**
flood plain

⑩ **der Fluss**
river

⑪ **die Mündung**
mouth

① **der Strand**
beach

⑫ **die Küste**
seashore

148.1 KARTEN LESEN · READING A MAP

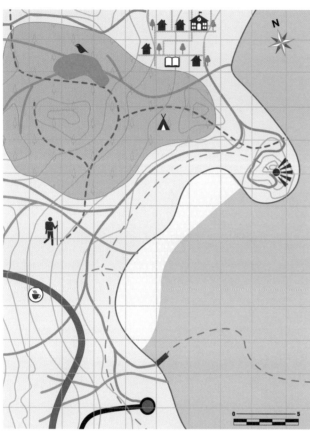

① die Landkarte
map

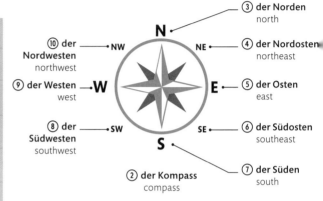

③ der Norden
north

④ der Nordosten
northeast

⑤ der Osten
east

⑥ der Südosten
southeast

⑦ der Süden
south

⑧ der Südwesten
southwest

⑨ der Westen
west

⑩ der Nordwesten
northwest

② der Kompass
compass

⑪ die Hauptverkehrsstraße
main road

⑫ die Nebenstraße
secondary road

⑬ der öffentliche Fußweg
public footpath

⑭ die Bahnlinie
railway

⑮ der Bahnhof
train station

⑯ der Campingplatz
campsite

⑰ der Rastplatz
service station

⑱ die Gitternetzlinien f, pl
grid lines

⑲ das Naturschutzgebiet
nature reserve

⑳ der Aussichtspunkt
viewpoint

㉑ der Wanderweg
walking trail

㉒ die Stadt
town

㉓ das Haus / das Gebäude
house / building

㉔ die Schule
school

㉕ die Bibliothek
library

㉖ die Fährverbindung
ferry route

㉗ die Höhenlinie
contours

㉘ der Fluss
river

㉙ der See
lake

㉚ der Wald
forest

㉛ der Strand
beach

See also
96 Straßen · Roads **133** Aktivitäten im Freien · Outdoor activities **145** Der Planet Erde · Planet Earth **146-147** Geografie · Geography **149-151** Länder · Countries

㉜ **im Uhrzeigersinn**
clockwise

㉝ **gegen den Uhrzeigersinn**
anticlockwise

㉞ **die Koordinaten** *f, pl*
coordinates

㉟ **der Orientierungslauf**
orienteering

㊱ **der Breitengrad**
latitude

㊲ **der Längengrad**
longitude

0   1 km

0   1 mile

㊳ **der Maßstab**
scale

㊴ **der Kartograf** *m*
die Kartografin *f*
cartographer

㊵ **die Online-Karte**
online map

㊶ **die Wanderkarte**
hiking map

㊷ **die Straßenkarte**
streetmap

148.2 ORTSANGABEN · PREPOSITIONS OF PLACE

① **neben**
next to / beside

② **gegenüber**
opposite

③ **zwischen**
between

④ **an der Kreuzung**
on the corner

⑤ **vor**
in front of

⑥ **hinter**
behind

⑦ **links von**
on the left

⑧ **rechts von**
on the right

148.3 RICHTUNGSVERBEN · DIRECTION VERBS

① **links abbiegen**
to go left /
to turn left

② **rechts abbiegen**
to go right /
to turn right

③ **geradeaus gehen /
fahren**
to go straight
on

④ **umkehren**
to go back

⑤ **an (dem
Restaurant) vorbei
gehen / fahren**
to go past
(the restaurant)

⑥ **die erste
Abzweigung
links abbiegen**
to take the first left

⑦ **die zweite
Abzweigung
rechts abbiegen**
to take the second right

⑧ **(am Hotel)
halten**
to stop at
(the hotel)

⑨ **die Route planen**
to plan your route

⑩ **sich verlaufen**
to lose
your way

⑪ **die Landkarte
lesen**
to read a map

⑫ **nach dem Weg
fragen**
to ask
directions

149.1 AFRIKA · AFRICA

① **Marokko**
Morocco

② **Mauretanien**
Mauritania

③ **Kap Verde**
Cape Verde

④ **der Senegal**
Senegal

⑤ **Gambia**
Gambia

⑥ **Guinea-Bissau**
Guinea-Bissau

⑦ **Guinea**
Guinea

⑧ **Sierra Leone**
Sierra Leone

⑨ **Liberia**
Liberia

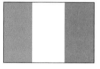
⑩ **die Elfenbeinküste**
Ivory Coast

⑪ **Burkina Faso**
Burkina Faso

⑫ **Mali**
Mali

⑬ **Algerien**
Algeria

⑭ **Tunesien**
Tunisia

⑮ **Libyen**
Libya

⑯ **der Niger**
Niger

⑰ **Ghana**
Ghana

⑱ **Togo**
Togo

⑲ **Benin**
Benin

⑳ **Nigeria**
Nigeria

㉑ **São Tomé und Príncipe**
São Tomé and Príncipe

㉒ **Äquatorialguinea**
Equatorial Guinea

㉓ **Gabun**
Gabon

㉔ **Kamerun**
Cameroon

㉕ **der Tschad**
Chad

㉖ **Ruanda**
Rwanda

㉗ **Burundi**
Burundi

㉘ **Tansania**
Tanzania

㉙ **Mosambik**
Mozambique

㉚ **Malawi**
Malawi

㉛ **die Republik Kongo**
Republic of the Congo

㉜ **die Demokratische Republik Kongo**
Democratic Republic of the Congo

㉝ **Sambia**
Zambia

㉞ **Angola**
Angola

㉟ **Namibia**
Namibia

㊱ **Botsuana**
Botswana

See also
145 Der Planet Erde • Planet Earth **146-147** Geografie • Geography **148** Karten und Richtungsangaben • Maps and directions **150-151** Länder (Fortsetzung) • Countries continued **152-153** Staatsangehörigkeiten • Nationalities

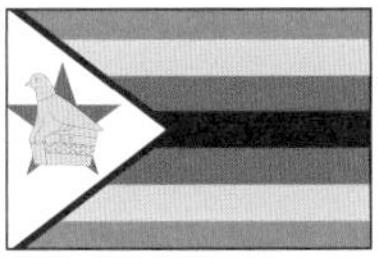

㊲ Simbabwe
Zimbabwe

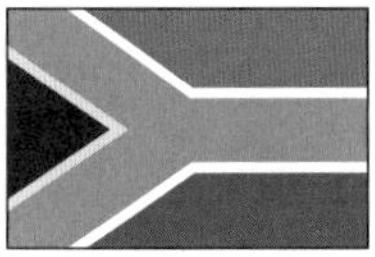

㊳ Südafrika
South Africa

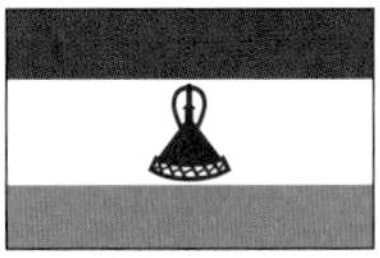

㊴ Lesotho
Lesotho

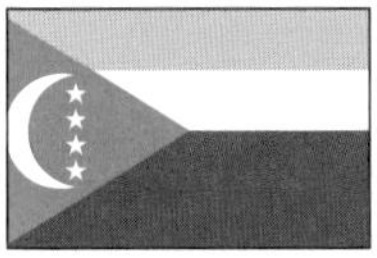

㊵ die Komoren *pl*
Comoros

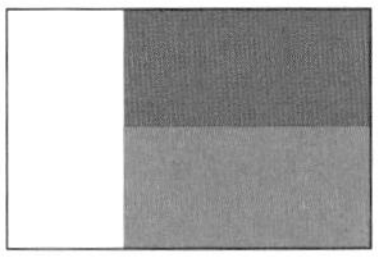

㊶ Madagaskar
Madagascar

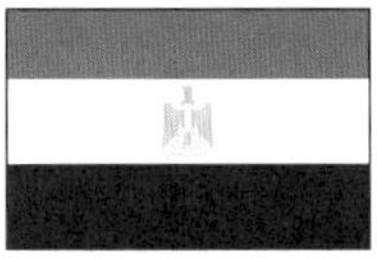

㊷ Ägypten
Egypt

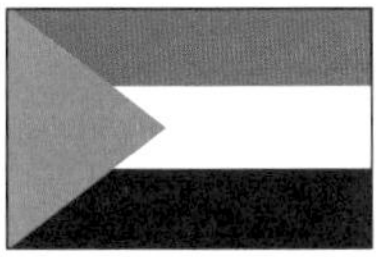

㊸ der Sudan
Sudan

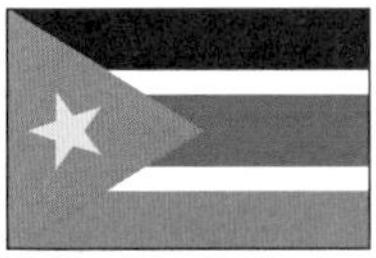

㊹ der Südsudan
South Sudan

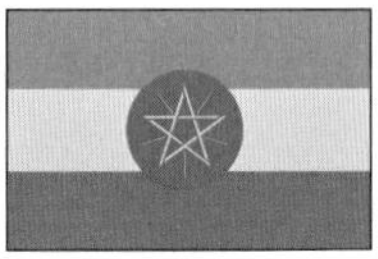

㊺ Äthiopien
Ethiopia

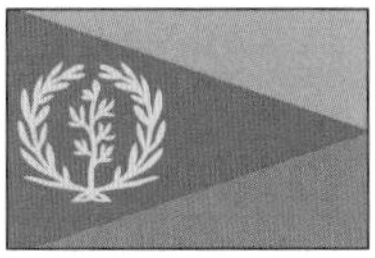

㊻ Eritrea
Eritrea

㊼ Somalia
Somalia

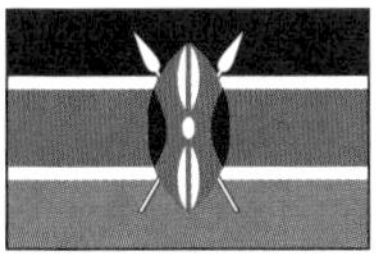

㊽ Kenia
Kenya

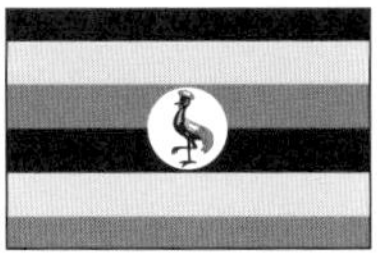

㊾ Uganda
Uganda

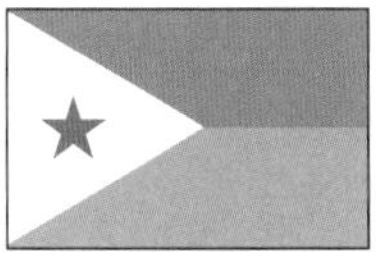

㊿ Dschibuti
Djibouti

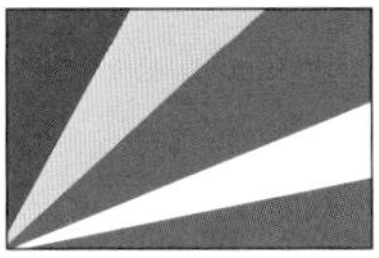

(51) die Seychellen *pl*
Seychelles

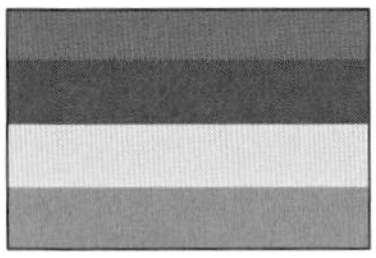

(52) Mauritius
Mauritius

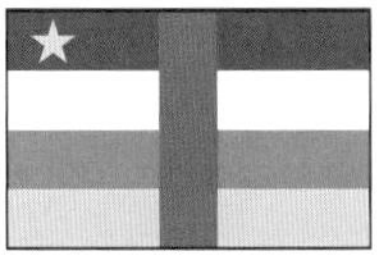

(53) die Zentralafrikanische Republik
Central African Republic

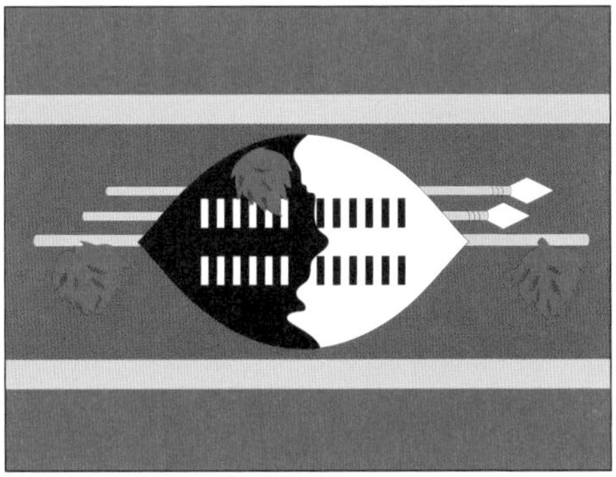

(54) Eswatini
Eswatini

149.2 SÜDAMERIKA
SOUTH AMERICA

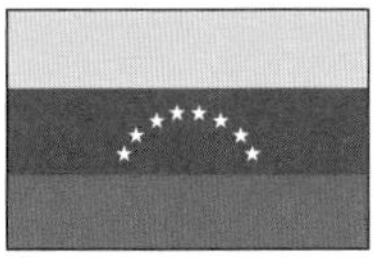

① Venezuela
Venezuela

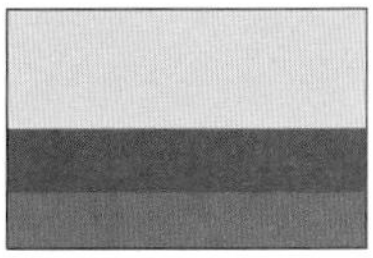

② Kolumbien
Colombia

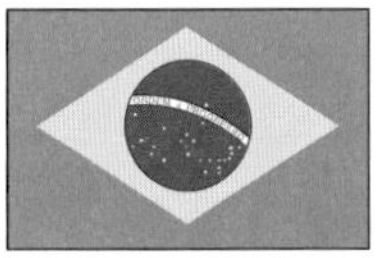

③ Brasilien
Brazil

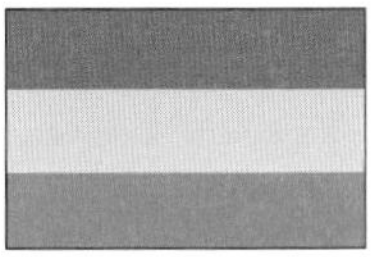

④ Bolivien
Bolivia

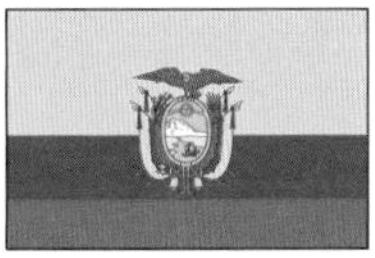

⑤ Ecuador
Ecuador

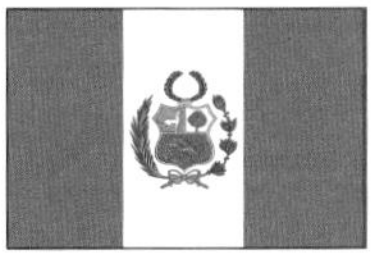

⑥ Peru
Peru

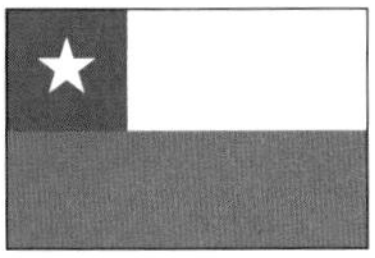

⑦ Chile
Chile

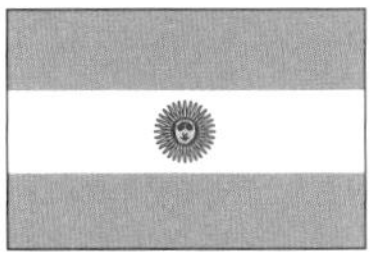

⑧ Argentinien
Argentina

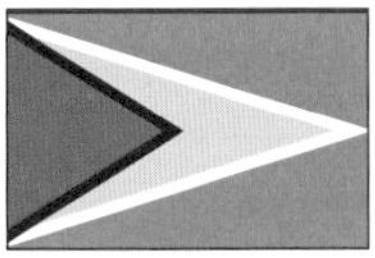

⑨ Guyana
Guyana

⑩ Suriname
Suriname

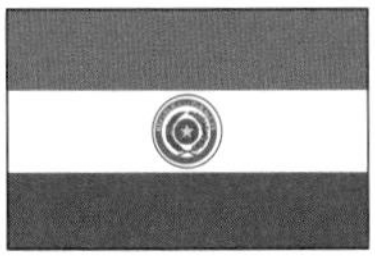

⑪ Paraguay
Paraguay

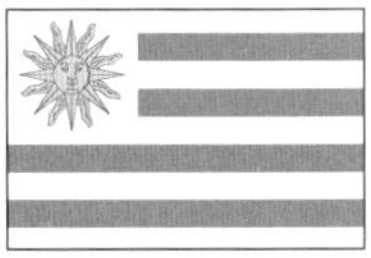

⑫ Uruguay
Uruguay

150.1 NORD- UND MITTELAMERIKA UND DIE KARIBIK
NORTH AND CENTRAL AMERICA AND THE CARIBBEAN

① **Kanada**
Canada

② **die USA** *pl*
United States of America

③ **Mexiko**
Mexico

④ **Guatemala**
Guatemala

⑤ **Belize**
Belize

⑥ **El Salvador**
El Salvador

⑧ **Honduras**
Honduras

⑨ **Nicaragua**
Nicaragua

⑩ **Costa Rica**
Costa Rica

⑪ **Panama**
Panama

⑫ **Kuba**
Cuba

⑬ **die Bahamas** *pl*
Bahamas

⑮ **Jamaika**
Jamaica

⑯ **Haiti**
Haiti

⑰ **die Dominikanische Republik**
Dominican Republic

⑱ **Barbados**
Barbados

⑲ **Trinidad und Tobago**
Trinidad and Tobago

⑳ **St. Kitts und Nevis**
St. Kitts and Nevis

㉒ **Dominica**
Dominica

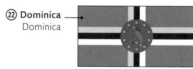

㉓ **Antigua und Barbuda**
Antigua and Barbuda

150.2 OZEANIEN · OCEANIA

① **Papua-Neuguinea**
Papua New Guinea

② **Australien**
Australia

③ **Neuseeland**
New Zealand

④ **die Marshallinseln** *pl*
Marshall Islands

⑤ **Palau**
Palau

⑥ **Mikronesien**
Micronesia

⑧ **Nauru**
Nauru

⑨ **Kiribati**
Kiribati

⑩ **Tuvalu**
Tuvalu

⑪ **Samoa**
Samoa

⑫ **Tonga**
Tonga

⑬ **Vanuatu**
Vanuatu

See also
145 Der Planet Erde · Planet Earth **146-147** Geografie · Geography
148 Karten und Richtungsangaben · Maps and directions
151 Länder (Fortsetzung) · Countries continued

150.3 **ASIEN** · ASIA

⑦ **Grenada**
Grenada

① **die Türkei**
Türkiye

② **Russland**
Russian Federation

③ **Georgien**
Georgia

④ **Armenien**
Armenia

⑤ **Aserbaidschan**
Azerbaijan

⑭ **St. Lucia**
St. Lucia

⑥ **der Irak**
Iraq

⑦ **Syrien**
Syria

⑧ **der Libanon**
Lebanon

⑨ **Israel**
Israel

⑩ **Jordanien**
Jordan

㉑ **St. Vincent und die Grenadinen** *pl*
St. Vincent and The Grenadines

⑪ **Pakistan**
Pakistan

⑫ **Indien**
India

⑬ **die Malediven** *pl*
Maldives

⑭ **Sri Lanka**
Sri Lanka

⑮ **China**
China

⑯ **die Mongolei**
Mongolia

⑰ **Nordkorea**
North Korea

⑱ **Südkorea**
South Korea

⑲ **Japan**
Japan

⑳ **Bangladesch**
Bangladesh

⑦ **die Salomonen** *pl*
Solomon Islands

㉑ **Bhutan**
Bhutan

㉒ **Myanmar (Burma)**
Myanmar (Burma)

㉓ **Thailand**
Thailand

㉗ **Nepal**
Nepal

⑭ **Fidschi**
Fiji

㉔ **Laos**
Laos

㉕ **Vietnam**
Vietnam

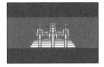
㉖ **Kambodscha**
Cambodia

151.1 ASIEN (FORTSETZUNG) · ASIA CONTINUED

① **Singapur**
Singapore

② **Indonesien**
Indonesia

③ **Brunei**
Brunei

④ **die Philippinen** *pl*
Philippines

⑤ **Osttimor**
East Timor

⑥ **Malaysia**
Malaysia

⑦ **die Vereinigten Arabischen Emirate** *pl*
United Arab Emirates

⑧ **der Oman**
Oman

⑨ **Bahrain**
Bahrain

⑩ **Katar**
Qatar

⑪ **Kuwait**
Kuwait

⑫ **der Iran**
Iran

⑬ **der Jemen**
Yemen

⑭ **Saudi-Arabien**
Saudi Arabia

⑮ **Usbekistan**
Uzbekistan

⑯ **Turkmenistan**
Turkmenistan

⑰ **Afghanistan**
Afghanistan

⑱ **Tadschikistan**
Tajikistan

⑲ **Kirgisistan**
Kyrgyzstan

⑳ **Kasachstan**
Kazakhstan

151.2 EUROPA · EUROPE

① **Irland**
Ireland

② **das Vereinigte Königreich**
United Kingdom

⑨ **Belgien**
Belgium

⑩ **die Niederlande** *pl*
Netherlands

⑰ **Portugal**
Portugal

⑱ **Spanien**
Spain

㉕ **Luxemburg**
Luxembourg

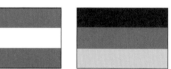

㉖ **Deutschland**
Germany

㉝ **Andorra**
Andorra

㉞ **Frankreich**
France

㊶ **Dänemark**
Denmark

㊷ **Norwegen**
Norway

See also
145 Der Planet Erde · Planet Earth **146-147** Geografie · Geography **148** Karten und Richtungsangaben · Maps and directions **152-153** Staatsangehörigkeiten · Nationalities

③ **Schweden**
Sweden

④ **Finnland**
Finland

⑤ **Estland**
Estonia

⑥ **Lettland**
Latvia

⑦ **Litauen**
Lithuania

⑧ **Polen**
Poland

⑪ **die Tschechische Republik**
Czech Republic

⑫ **Österreich**
Austria

⑬ **Liechtenstein**
Liechtenstein

⑭ **Italien**
Italy

⑮ **Monaco**
Monaco

⑯ **San Marino**
San Marino

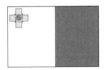
⑲ **Malta**
Malta

⑳ **Slowenien**
Slovenia

㉑ **Kroatien**
Croatia

㉒ **Ungarn**
Hungary

㉓ **die Slowakei**
Slovakia

㉔ **die Ukraine**
Ukraine

㉗ **Belarus**
Belarus

㉘ **Moldawien**
Moldova

㉙ **Rumänien**
Romania

㉚ **Serbien**
Serbia

㉛ **Bulgarien**
Bulgaria

㉜ **Albanien**
Albania

㉟ **Griechenland**
Greece

㊱ **Island**
Iceland

㊲ **Zypern**
Cyprus

㊳ **Montenegro**
Montenegro

㊴ **der Vatikanstaat**
Vatican City

㊵ **die Türkei**
Türkiye

㊸ **Bosnien und Herzegowina**
Bosnia and Herzegovina

㊹ **Nordmazedonien**
North Macedonia

㊺ **die Schweiz**
Switzerland

㊻ **Russland**
Russian Federation

152.1 AFRIKA · AFRICA

Country	Adjective	English Adjective	Country	Adjective	English Adjective
① Afrika Africa	afrikanisch	African	㉚ Dschibuti Djibouti	dschibutisch	Djiboutian
② Marokko Morocco	marokkanisch	Moroccan	㉛ Äthiopien Ethiopia	äthiopisch	Ethiopian
③ Mauretanien Mauritania	mauretanisch	Mauritanian	㉜ Somalia Somalia	somalisch	Somalian
④ Kap Verde Cape Verde	kapverdisch	Cape Verdean	㉝ Kenia Kenya	kenianisch	Kenyan
⑤ Senegal Senegal	senegalesisch	Senegalese	㉞ Uganda Uganda	ugandisch	Ugandan
⑥ Gambia Gambia	gambisch	Gambian	㉟ die Zentralafrikanische Republik Central African Republic	zentralafrikanisch	Central African
⑦ Guinea-Bissau Guinea-Bissau	guinea-bissauisch	Bissau-Guinean	㊱ Gabun Gabon	gabunisch	Gabonese
⑧ Guinea Guinea	guineisch	Guinean	㊲ Republik Kongo Republic of the Congo	kongolesisch	Congolese
⑨ Sierra Leone Sierra Leone	sierra-leonisch	Sierra Leonean	㊳ die Demokratische Republik Kongo Democratic Republic of the Congo	kongolesisch	Congolese
⑩ Liberia Liberia	liberianisch	Liberian	㊴ Ruanda Rwanda	ruandisch	Rwandan
⑪ die Elfenbeinküste Ivory Coast	ivorisch	Ivorian	㊵ Burundi Burundi	burundisch	Burundian
⑫ Burkina Faso Burkina Faso	burkinisch	Burkinabe	㊶ Tansania Tanzania	tansanisch	Tanzanian
⑬ Mali Mali	malisch	Malian	㊷ Mosambik Mozambique	mosambikisch	Mozambican
⑭ Algerien Algeria	algerisch	Algerian	㊸ Malawi Malawi	malaiisch	Malawian
⑮ Tunesien Tunisia	tunesisch	Tunisian	㊹ Sambia Zambia	sambisch	Zambian
⑯ Libyen Libya	libysch	Libyan	㊺ Angola Angola	angolanisch	Angolan
⑰ Niger Niger	nigrisch	Nigerien	㊻ Namibia Namibia	namibisch	Namibian
⑱ Ghana Ghana	ghanaisch	Ghanaian	㊼ Botsuana Botswana	botswanisch	Botswanan
⑲ Togo Togo	togoisch	Togolese	㊽ Simbabwe Zimbabwe	simbabwisch	Zimbabwean
⑳ Benin Benin	beninisch	Beninese	㊾ Südafrika South Africa	südafrikanisch	South African
㉑ Nigeria Nigeria	nigerianisch	Nigerian	㊿ Lesotho Lesotho	lesothisch	Basotho
㉒ São Tomé und Príncipe São Tomé and Príncipe	sao-tomeisch	São Toméan	51 Eswatini Eswatini	eswatinisch	Swazi
㉓ Äquatorialguinea Equatorial Guinea	äquatorialguineisch	Equatorial Guinean	52 die Komoren Comoros	komorisch	Comoran
㉔ Kamerun Cameroon	kamerunisch	Cameroonian	53 Madagaskar Madagascar	madagassisch	Madagascan
㉕ Tschad Chad	tschadisch	Chadian	54 die Seychellen Seychelles	seychellisch	Seychellois
㉖ Ägypten Egypt	ägyptisch	Egyptian	55 Mauritius Mauritius	mauritisch	Mauritian
㉗ Sudan Sudan	sudanesisch	Sudanese			
㉘ Südsudan South Sudan	südsudanesisch	South Sudanese			
㉙ Eritrea Eritrea	eritreisch	Eritrean			

See also
145 Der Planet Erde · Planet Earth **146-147** Geografie · Geography
148 Karten und Richtungsangaben · Maps and directions **149-151** Länder
Countries **153** Staatsangehörigkeiten (Fortsetzung) · Nationalities continued

152.2 SÜDAMERIKA · SOUTH AMERICA

Country	Adjective	English Adjective	Country	Adjective	English Adjective
① **Südamerika** South America	südamerikanisch	South American	⑧ **Brasilien** Brazil	brasilianisch	Brazilian
② **Venezuela** Venezuela	venezolanisch	Venezuelan	⑨ **Bolivien** Bolivia	bolivianisch	Bolivian
③ **Kolumbien** Colombia	kolumbisch	Colombian	⑩ **Chile** Chile	chilenisch	Chilean
④ **Ecuador** Ecuador	ecuadorianisch	Ecuadorian	⑪ **Argentinien** Argentina	argentinisch	Argentinian
⑤ **Peru** Peru	peruanisch	Peruvian	⑫ **Paraguay** Paraguay	paraguayisch	Paraguayan
⑥ **Guyana** Guyana	guyanisch	Guyanese	⑬ **Uruguay** Uruguay	uruguayisch	Uruguayan
⑦ **Suriname** Suriname	surinamisch	Surinamese			

152.3 NORD- UND MITTELAMERIKA UND DIE KARIBIK
NORTH AND CENTRAL AMERICA AND THE CARIBBEAN

Country	Adjective	English Adjective	Country	Adjective	English Adjective
① **Nord- und Mittelamerika und die Karibik** North and Central America and the Caribbean	nordamerikanisch, mittelamerikanisch und karibisch	North American, Central American, and Caribbean	⑭ **Jamaika** Jamaica	jamaikanisch	Jamaican
② **Kanada** Canada	kanadisch	Canadian	⑮ **Haiti** Haiti	haitianisch	Haitian
③ **die USA** United States of America	US-amerikanisch	American	⑯ **die Dominikanische Republik** Dominican Republic	dominikanisch	Dominican
④ **Mexiko** Mexico	mexikanisch	Mexican	⑰ **Barbados** Barbados	barbadisch	Barbadian
⑤ **Guatemala** Guatemala	guatemaltekisch	Guatemalan	⑱ **Trinidad und Tobago** Trinidad and Tobago	trinidadisch	Trinidadian or Tobagonian
⑥ **Belize** Belize	belizisch	Belizean	⑲ **St. Kitts und Nevis** St. Kitts and Nevis	kittisch oder nevisisch	Kittian or Nevisian
⑦ **El Salvador** El Salvador	salvadorianisch	Salvadoran	⑳ **Antigua und Barbuda** Antigua and Barbuda	antiguanisch	Antiguan or Barbudan
⑧ **Honduras** Honduras	honduranisch	Honduran	㉑ **Dominica** Dominica	dominicanisch	Dominican
⑨ **Nicaragua** Nicaragua	nicaraguanisch	Nicaraguan	㉒ **St. Lucia** St. Lucia	lucianisch	St. Lucian
⑩ **Costa Rica** Costa Rica	costa-ricanisch	Costa Rican	㉓ **St. Vincent und die Grenadinen** St. Vincent and The Grenadines	vincentisch	Vincentian
⑪ **Panama** Panama	costa-ricanisch	Panamanian	㉔ **Grenada** Grenada	grenadisch	Grenadian
⑫ **Kuba** Cuba	kubanisch	Cuban			
⑬ **die Bahamas** Bahamas	bahamaisch	Bahamian			

153.1 OZEANIEN · OCEANIA

Country	Adjective	English Adjective	Country	Adjective	English Adjective
① Ozeanien Oceania	ozeanisch	Oceanian	⑧ Nauru Nauru	nauruisch	Nauruan
② Papua-Neuguinea Papua New Guinea	papua-neuguinesisch	Papua New Guinean	⑨ Kiribati Kiribati	kiribatisch	Kiribati
③ Australien Australia	australisch	Australian	⑩ Tuvalu Tuvalu	tuvaluisch	Tuvaluan
④ Neuseeland New Zealand	neuseeländisch	New Zealand	⑪ Samoa Samoa	samoisch	Samoan
⑤ die Marshallinseln Marshall Islands	marshallisch	Marshallese	⑫ Tonga Tonga	tongaisch	Tongan
⑥ Palau Palau	palauisch	Palauan	⑬ Vanuatu Vanuatu	vanuatuisch	Vanuatuan
⑦ Mikronesien Micronesia	mikronesisch	Micronesian	⑭ die Salomonen Solomon Islands	salomonisch	Solomon Island
			⑮ Fidschi Fiji	fidschianisch	Fijian

153.2 ASIEN · ASIA

Country	Adjective	English Adjective	Country	Adjective	English Adjective
① Asien · Asia	aslatisch	Asian	⑳ Kasachstan Kazakhstan	kasachisch	Kazakh
② die Türkei Türkiye	türkisch	Turkish	㉑ Usbekistan Uzbekistan	usbekisch	Uzbek
③ Russland Russian Federation	russisch	Russian	㉒ Turkmenistan Turkmenistan	turkmenisch	Turkmen
④ Georgien Georgia	georgisch	Georgian	㉓ Afghanistan Afghanistan	afghanisch	Afghan
⑤ Armenien Armenia	armenisch	Armenian	㉔ Tadschikistan Tajikistan	tadschikisch	Tajikistani
⑥ Aserbaidschan Azerbaijan	aserbaidschanisch	Azerbaijani	㉕ Kirgisistan Kyrgyzstan	kirgisisch	Kyrgyz
⑦ der Iran Iran	iranisch	Iranian	㉖ Pakistan Pakistan	pakistanisch	Pakistani
⑧ der Irak Iraq	irakisch	Iraqi	㉗ Indien India	indisch	Indian
⑨ Syrien Syria	syrisch	Syrian	㉘ die Malediven Maldives	maledivisch	Maldivian
⑩ der Libanon Lebanon	libanesisch	Lebanese	㉙ Sri Lanka Sri Lanka	sri-lankisch	Sri Lankan
⑪ Israel Israel	israelisch	Israeli	㉚ China China	chinesisch	Chinese
⑫ Jordanien Jordan	jordanisch	Jordanian	㉛ die Mongolei Mongolia	mongolisch	Mongolian
⑬ Saudi-Arabien Saudi Arabia	saudi-arabisch	Saudi	㉜ Nordkorea North Korea	nordkoreanisch	North Korean
⑭ Kuwait Kuwait	kuwaitisch	Kuwaiti	㉝ Südkorea South Korea	südkoreanisch	South Korean
⑮ Bahrain Bahrain	bahrainisch	Bahraini	㉞ Japan Japan	japanisch	Japanese
⑯ Katar Qatar	katarisch	Qatari	㉟ Nepal Nepal	nepalesisch	Nepalese
⑰ die Vereinigten Arabischen Emirate United Arab Emirates	emiratisch	Emirati	㊱ Butan Bhutan	bhutanisch	Bhutanese
⑱ der Oman Oman	omanisch	Omani	㊲ Bangladesch Bangladesh	bangladeschisch	Bangladeshi
⑲ der Jemen Yemen	jemenitisch	Yemeni	㊳ Myanmar (Burma) Myanmar (Burma)	myanmarisch	Burmese
			㊴ Thailand Thailand	thailändisch	Thai

See also
145 Der Planet Erde · Planet Earth **146-147** Geografie · Geography **148** Karten und Richtungsangaben · Maps and directions **149-151** Länder · Countries

153.2 ASIEN (FORTSETZUNG) · ASIA CONTINUED

Country	Adjective	English Adjective	Country	Adjective	English Adjective
㊵ **Laos** Laos	laotisch	Laotian	㊹ **Singapur** Singapore	singapurisch	Singaporean
㊶ **Vietnam** Vietnam	vietnamesisch	Vietnamese	㊺ **Indonesien** Indonesia	indonesisch	Indonesian
㊷ **Kambodscha** Cambodia	kambodschanisch	Cambodian	㊻ **Brunei** Brunei	bruneiisch	Bruneian
㊸ **Malaysia** Malaysia	malaysisch	Malaysian	㊼ **die Philippinen** Philippines	philippinisch	Filipino
			㊽ **Osttimor** East Timor	timorisch	Timorese

153.3 EUROPA · EUROPE

Country	Adjective	English Adjective	Country	Adjective	English Adjective
① **Europa** · Europe	europäisch	European	㉕ **Monaco** Monaco	monegassisch	Monacan
② **Irland** Ireland	irisch	Irish	㉖ **San Marino** San Marino	san-marinesisch	Sammarinese
③ **das Vereinigte Königreich** United Kingdom	britisch	British	㉗ **Malta** Malta	maltesisch	Maltese
④ **Portugal** Portugal	portugiesisch	Portuguese	㉘ **Slowenien** Slovenia	slowenisch	Slovenian
⑤ **Spanien** Spain	spanisch	Spanish	㉙ **Kroatien** Croatia	kroatisch	Croatian
⑥ **Andorra** Andorra	andorranisch	Andorran	㉚ **Ungarn** Hungary	ungarisch	Hungarian
⑦ **Frankreich** France	französisch	French	㉛ **die Slowakei** Slovakia	slowakisch	Slovakian
⑧ **Belgien** Belgium	belgisch	Belgian	㉜ **die Ukraine** Ukraine	ukrainisch	Ukrainian
⑨ **die Niederlande** Netherlands	niederländisch	Dutch	㉝ **Belarus** Belarus	belarussisch	Belarusian
⑩ **Luxemburg** Luxembourg	luxemburgisch	Luxembourg	㉞ **Moldawien** Moldova	moldawisch	Moldovan
⑪ **Deutschland** Germany	deutsch	German	㉟ **Rumänien** Romania	rumänisch	Romanian
⑫ **Dänemark** Denmark	dänisch	Danish	㊱ **Serbien** Serbia	serbisch	Serbian
⑬ **Norwegen** Norway	norwegisch	Norwegian	㊲ **Bosnien und Herzegowina** Bosnia and Herzegovina	bosnisch und herzegowinisch	Bosnian or Herzegovinia
⑭ **Schweden** Sweden	schwedisch	Swedish	㊳ **Albanien** Albania	albanisch	Albanian
⑮ **Finnland** Finland	finnisch	Finnish	㊴ **Nordmazedonien** North Macedonia	nordmazedonisch	North Macedonian
⑯ **Estland** Estonia	estnisch	Estonian	㊵ **Bulgarien** Bulgaria	bulgarisch	Bulgarian
⑰ **Lettland** Latvia	lettisch	Latvian	㊶ **Griechenland** Greece	griechisch	Greek
⑱ **Litauen** Lithuania	litauisch	Lithuanian	㊷ **Montenegro** Montenegro	montenegrinisch	Montenegrin
⑲ **Polen** Poland	polnisch	Polish	㊸ **Island** Iceland	isländisch	Icelandic
⑳ **die Tschechische Republik** Czech Republic	tschechisch	Czech	㊹ **Zypern** Cyprus	zyprisch	Cypriot
㉑ **Österreich** Austria	österreichisch	Austrian	㊺ **die Türkei** Türkiye	türkisch	Turkish
㉒ **Liechtenstein** Liechtenstein	liechtensteinisch	Liechtensteiner	㊻ **Russland** Russian Federation	russisch	Russian
㉓ **die Schweiz** Switzerland	schweizerisch	Swiss			
㉔ **Italien** Italy	italienisch	Italian			

315

154 Das Wetter
Weather

154.1 DAS WETTER · WEATHER

① die Luftfeuchtigkeit
humidity

② die Hitzewelle
heatwave

③ die Dürre
drought

④ trocken
dry

⑤ nass
wet

⑥ bewölkt
overcast

⑦ der Smog
smog

⑧ der Regentropfen
raindrop

⑨ der leichte Schauer
light shower

⑩ der Nieselregen
drizzle

⑪ der Wolkenbruch
downpour

⑫ die Überschwemmung
flood

⑬ der Sandsturm
sandstorm

⑭ der Sturm
gale

⑮ das Gewitter
storm

⑯ der Donner
thunder

⑰ der Blitz
lightning

⑱ der Regenbogen
rainbow

⑲ der Schneeregen
sleet

⑳ die Schneeflocke
snowflake

㉑ die Schneeverwehung
snowdrift

㉒ der Blizzard
blizzard

㉓ der Schneesturm
snowstorm

㉔ der Hagel
hailstone

㉕ der Hurrikan
hurricane

㉖ der Tornado
tornado

㉘ Heute gießt es wie aus Eimern.
It's raining cats and dogs today.

㉗ die Pfütze
puddle

See also
145 Der Planet Erde · Planet Earth **146-147** Geografie · Geography
155 Klima und Umwelt · Climate and the environment

154.2 DIE TEMPERATUR · TEMPERATURE

① **eiskalt**
freezing

② **kalt**
cold

③ **kühl**
chilly

④ **warm**
warm

⑤ **heiß**
hot

⑥ **stickig**
stifling

⑦ **der Gefrierpunkt**
freezing point

⑧ **der Siedepunkt**
boiling point

⑨ **minus 10 Grad**
minus 10

⑩ **25 Grad**
25 degrees

⑯ **Es ist kochend heiß. Ich muss unbedingt in den Schatten!**
It's boiling! I need to find some shade

⑪ **Celsius**
Celsius

⑫ **Fahrenheit**
Fahrenheit

⑬ **kühl**
cool

⑭ **mild**
mild

⑮ **kochend heiß**
boiling

154.3 WETTERADJEKTIVE · WEATHER ADJECTIVES

① **die Sonne →
sonnig**
sun -› sunny

② **die Wolke → wolkig**
cloud -› cloudy

③ **der Nebel →
neblig**
fog -› foggy

④ **der Regen →
regnerisch**
rain -› rainy

⑤ **der Schnee →
verschneit**
snow -› snowy

⑥ **das Eis → eisig**
ice -› icy

⑦ **der Frost →
frostig**
frost -› frosty

⑧ **der Wind →
windig**
wind -› windy

⑨ **der Sturm →
stürmisch**
storm -› stormy

⑩ **der Donner →
gewittrig**
thunder -› thundery

⑪ **der Nebel →
neblig**
mist -› misty

⑫ **die Brise →
windig**
breeze -› breezy

155.1 DIE ATMOSPHÄRE · ATMOSPHERE

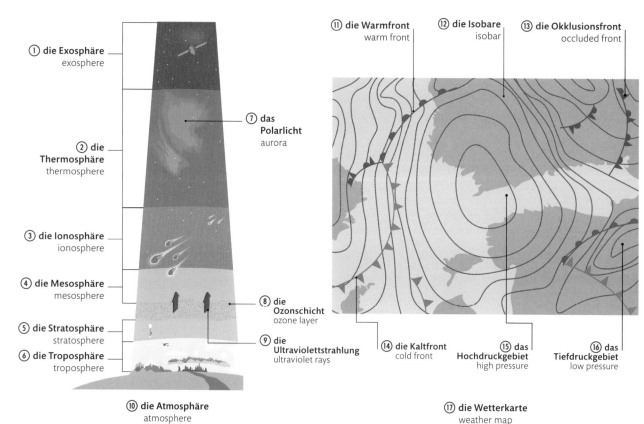

① die Exosphäre
exosphere

⑦ das Polarlicht
aurora

② die Thermosphäre
thermosphere

③ die Ionosphäre
ionosphere

④ die Mesosphäre
mesosphere

⑧ die Ozonschicht
ozone layer

⑤ die Stratosphäre
stratosphere

⑨ die Ultraviolettstrahlung
ultraviolet rays

⑥ die Troposphäre
troposphere

⑩ die Atmosphäre
atmosphere

⑪ die Warmfront
warm front

⑫ die Isobare
isobar

⑬ die Okklusionsfront
occluded front

⑭ die Kaltfront
cold front

⑮ das Hochdruckgebiet
high pressure

⑯ das Tiefdruckgebiet
low pressure

⑰ die Wetterkarte
weather map

155.2 UMWELTGEFÄHRDUNGEN · ENVIRONMENTAL ISSUES

② die Zerstörung von Lebensräumen
habitat loss

③ die gefährdete Art
endangered species

④ der Plastikmüll
plastic waste

⑤ die Überfischung
overfishing

① die Abholzung
deforestation

⑥ der Abbau der Ozonschicht
ozone depletion

⑦ die Verwüstung
desertification

⑧ der Ölteppich
oil slick

⑨ der saure Regen
acid rain

See also
145 Der Planet Erde · Planet Earth **146-147** Geografie Geography **154** Das Wetter · Weather

155.3 DER KLIMAWANDEL · CLIMATE CHANGE

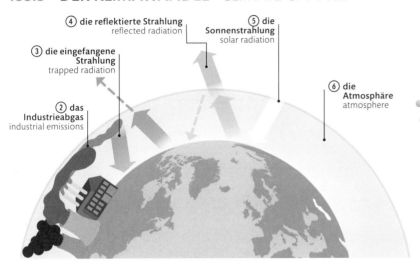

④ **die reflektierte Strahlung**
reflected radiation

⑤ **die Sonnenstrahlung**
solar radiation

③ **die eingefangene Strahlung**
trapped radiation

⑥ **die Atmosphäre**
atmosphere

② **das Industrieabgas**
industrial emissions

① **der Treibhauseffekt**
greenhouse effect

⑧ **das Kohlendioxid, CO_2**
carbon dioxide

⑨ **das Methan, CH_4**
methane

CH_4

CO_2

⑦ **das Treibhausgas**
greenhouse gases

⑩ **die fossilen Brennstoffe** *m, pl*
fossil fuels

⑪ **die Emissionen** *f, pl*
emissions

⑫ **die Umweltverschmutzung**
pollution

⑬ **das Ökosystem**
ecosystem

CO_2

⑭ **kohlenstofffrei**
zero carbon

⑮ **der abschmelzende Gletscher**
shrinking glaciers

⑯ **der abschmelzende Eisschild**
melting ice caps

155.4 ABFALL UND RECYCLING · WASTE AND RECYCLING

② **Ich versuche, so viel Kunststoff und Papier wie möglich zu recyceln.**
I try to recycle plastic and paper as much as possible.

③ **die Speisereste** *m, pl*
food waste

④ **das Papier**
paper

⑤ **der Kunststoff**
plastic

① **den Müll trennen**
to sort your rubbish

⑥ **das Glas**
glass

⑦ **das Metall**
metal

⑧ **der kompostierbare Müllbeutel**
compostable bags

⑨ **die Mülldeponie**
landfill

156 Gesteine und Mineralien
Rocks and minerals

156.1 GESTEINE · ROCKS

① das Sediment
sedimentary

② der Sandstein
sandstone

③ der Kalkstein
limestone

④ die Kreide
chalk

⑤ der Feuerstein
flint

⑥ das Konglomerat
conglomerate

⑦ das metamorphe
Gestein
metamorphic

⑧ der Schiefer
slate

⑨ der Schiefer
schist

⑩ der Gneis
gneiss

⑪ der Marmor
marble

⑫ der Quarzit
quartzite

⑬ das
Eruptivgestein
igneous

⑭ der Granit
granite

⑮ der Obsidian
obsidian

⑯ der Basalt
basalt

⑰ der Tuffstein
tuff

⑱ der Bimsstein
pumice

156.2 MINERALIEN · MINERALS

① der Quarz
quartz

② der Glimmer
mica

③ der Achat
agate

④ der Hämatit
hematite

⑤ der Kalzit
calcite

⑥ der Malachit
malachite

⑦ der Türkis
turquoise

⑧ der Onyx
onyx

⑨ der Schwefel
sulphur

⑩ der Grafit
graphite

⑪ die Geode
geode

⑫ die Sandrose
sand rose

See also
76 Chemie · Chemistry **78** Das Periodensystem · The periodic table
145 Der Planet Erde · Planet Earth **146-147** Geografie · Geography

156.3 **EDELSTEINE** · GEMS

① **der Diamant**
diamond

② **der Saphir**
sapphire

③ **der Smaragd**
emerald

④ **der Rubin**
ruby

⑤ **der Amethyst**
amethyst

⑥ **der Topas**
topaz

⑦ **der Aquamarin**
aquamarine

⑧ **der Mondstein**
moonstone

⑨ **der Opal**
opal

⑩ **der Turmalin**
tourmaline

⑪ **der Granat**
garnet

⑫ **der Zitrin**
citrine

⑬ **die Jade**
jade

⑭ **der Gagat**
jet

⑮ **der Lapislazuli**
lapis lazuli

⑯ **der Jaspis**
jasper

⑰ **das Tigerauge**
tiger's eye

⑱ **der Karneol**
carnelian

156.4 **METALLE** · METALS

① **das Gold**
gold

② **das Silber**
silver

③ **das Platin**
platinum

④ **das Magnesium**
magnesium

⑤ **das Eisen**
iron

⑥ **das Kupfer**
copper

⑦ **das Zinn**
tin

⑧ **das Aluminium**
aluminium

⑨ **das Quecksilber**
mercury

⑩ **das Nickel**
nickel

⑪ **das Zink**
zinc

⑫ **das Chrom**
chromium

157.1 GEOLOGISCHE ZEITALTER · GEOLOGICAL PERIODS

⑤ **der Trilobit**
trilobite

⑩ **die Cooksonia**
cooksonia

② **die Bakterien** *f, pl*
bacteria

④ **Marrella**
marrella

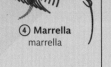

⑦ **der kieferlose Fisch**
jawless fish

⑨ **der Kiefermäuler**
jawed fish

① **das Präkambrium**
Precambrian

③ **das Kambrium**
Cambrian

⑥ **das Ordovizium**
Ordovician

⑧ **das Silur**
Silurian

㉖ **der Flugsaurier**
flying reptiles

㉗ **der Brachiosaurus**
brachiosaurus

㉘ **der Stegosaurus**
stegosaurus

㉚ **der Tyrannosaurus Rex**
tyrannosaurus rex

㉕ **der Jura**
Jurassic

㉛ **der Triceratops**
triceratops

㉜ **der Albertonectes**
albertonectes

㉝ **die Blütenpflanze**
flowering plants

㉟ **der Gastornis**
gastornis

㉙ **die Kreidezeit**
Cretaceous

㉞ **das Paläogen**
Paleogene

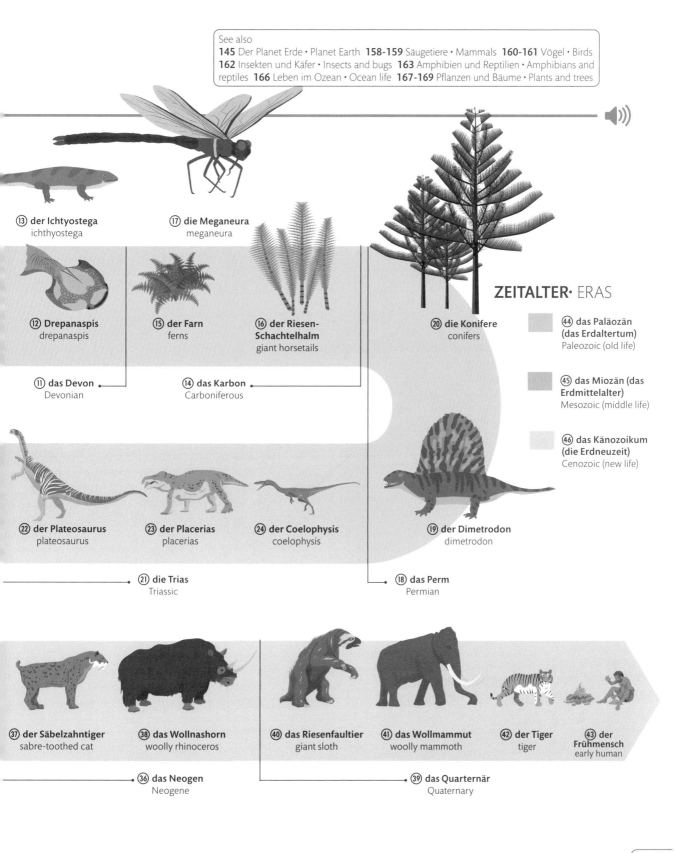

See also
145 Der Planet Erde · Planet Earth **158-159** Säugetiere · Mammals **160-161** Vögel · Birds
162 Insekten und Käfer · Insects and bugs **163** Amphibien und Reptilien · Amphibians and
reptiles **166** Leben im Ozean · Ocean life **167-169** Pflanzen und Bäume · Plants and trees

⑬ **der Ichtyostega**
ichthyostega

⑰ **die Meganeura**
meganeura

⑫ **Drepanaspis**
drepanaspis

⑮ **der Farn**
ferns

⑯ **der Riesen-Schachtelhalm**
giant horsetails

⑳ **die Konifere**
conifers

⑪ **das Devon**
Devonian

⑭ **das Karbon**
Carboniferous

ZEITALTER· ERAS

㊹ **das Paläozän (das Erdaltertum)**
Paleozoic (old life)

㊺ **das Miozän (das Erdmittelalter)**
Mesozoic (middle life)

㊻ **das Känozoikum (die Erdneuzeit)**
Cenozoic (new life)

㉒ **der Plateosaurus**
plateosaurus

㉓ **der Placerias**
placerias

㉔ **der Coelophysis**
coelophysis

⑲ **der Dimetrodon**
dimetrodon

㉑ **die Trias**
Triassic

⑱ **das Perm**
Permian

㊲ **der Säbelzahntiger**
sabre-toothed cat

㊳ **das Wollnashorn**
woolly rhinoceros

㊵ **das Riesenfaultier**
giant sloth

㊶ **das Wollmammut**
woolly mammoth

㊷ **der Tiger**
tiger

㊸ **der Frühmensch**
early human

㊱ **das Neogen**
Neogene

㊴ **das Quarternär**
Quaternary

158.1 SÄUGETIERARTEN · SPECIES OF MAMMALS

② **der Pavian**
baboon

③ **das Erdferkel**
aardvark

④ **das Nashorn**
rhinoceros

① **die Impala**
impala

⑧ **der Gepard**
cheetah

⑨ **der Löwe**
lion

⑩ **die Löwin**
lioness

⑪ **die Hyäne**
hyena

⑫ **die Savanne**
savannah

⑰ **das Schnabeltier**
platypus

⑱ **der Ameisenigel**
echidna

⑲ **der Tasmanische Teufel**
Tasmanian devil

⑳ **der Wombat**
wombat

㉓ **der Beutel**
pouch

㉒ **das Kängurujunge**
joey

㉑ **das Känguru**
kangaroo

㉔ **der Koala**
koala

㉕ **das Kaninchen**
rabbit

㉖ **der Hamster**
hamster

㉘ **die Schnurrhaare** *n, pl*
whiskers

㉗ **die Maus**
mouse

㉙ **die Ratte**
rat

㉚ **der Schwanz**
tail

㉛ **das Stachelschwein**
porcupine

㉜ **das Eichhörnchen**
squirrel

㉝ **der Igel**
hedgehog

㉞ **das Flughörnchen**
flying squirrel

㉟ **die Fledermaus**
bat

㊱ **der Flughund**
fruit bat

See also
157 Die Naturgeschichte • Natural history **159** Säugetiere (Fortsetzung) • Mammals continued
164 Haustiere • Pets **165** Bauernhoftiere • Farm animals **166** Leben im Ozean • Ocean life

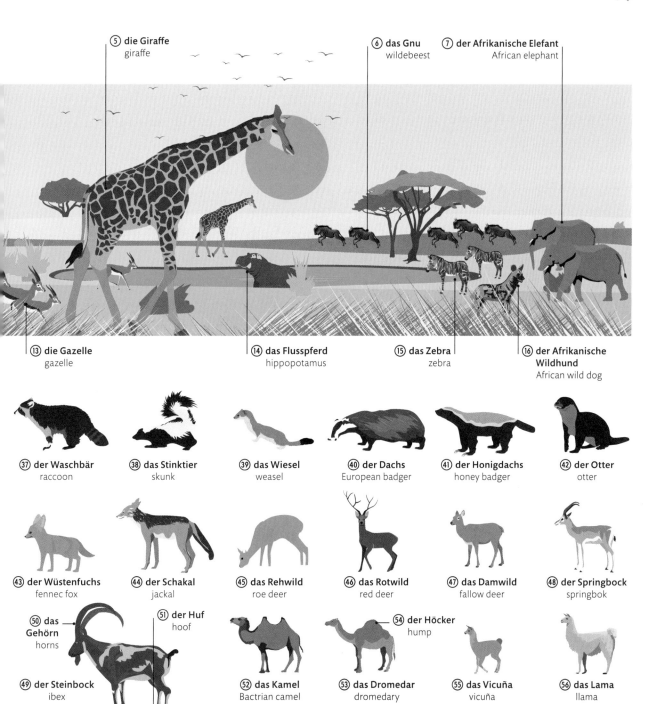

⑤ **die Giraffe**
giraffe

⑥ **das Gnu**
wildebeest

⑦ **der Afrikanische Elefant**
African elephant

⑬ **die Gazelle**
gazelle

⑭ **das Flusspferd**
hippopotamus

⑮ **das Zebra**
zebra

⑯ **der Afrikanische Wildhund**
African wild dog

㊲ **der Waschbär**
raccoon

㊳ **das Stinktier**
skunk

㊴ **das Wiesel**
weasel

㊵ **der Dachs**
European badger

㊶ **der Honigdachs**
honey badger

㊷ **der Otter**
otter

㊸ **der Wüstenfuchs**
fennec fox

㊹ **der Schakal**
jackal

㊺ **das Rehwild**
roe deer

㊻ **das Rotwild**
red deer

㊼ **das Damwild**
fallow deer

㊽ **der Springbock**
springbok

(50) **das Gehörn**
horns

(51) **der Huf**
hoof

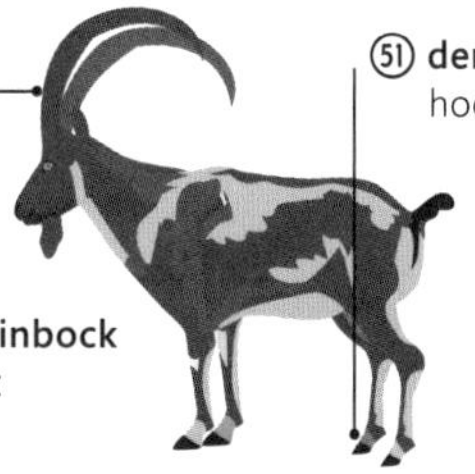
㊾ **der Steinbock**
ibex

(52) **das Kamel**
Bactrian camel

(54) **der Höcker**
hump

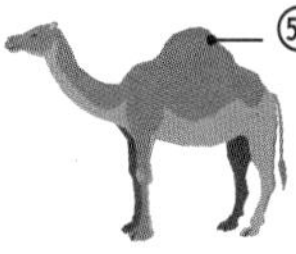
(53) **das Dromedar**
dromedary

(55) **das Vicuña**
vicuña

(56) **das Lama**
llama

159.1 SÄUGETIERARTEN · SPECIES OF MAMMALS

① **das Rentier**
reindeer

② **das Karibu**
caribou

③ **der Polarwolf**
Arctic wolf

④ **der Polarfuchs**
Arctic fox

⑤ **der Moschusochse**
musk ox

⑪ **der Fuchs**
red fox

⑩ **der Braunbär**
brown bear

⑧ **die Robbe**
seal

⑥ **der Eisbär**
polar bear

⑦ **der Schneehase**
Arctic hare

⑨ **die Arktis**
Arctic

⑮ **der Laubwald**
broadleaf forest

㉔ **der Rüssel**
trunk

㉓ **der Asiatische Elefant**
Asian elephant

㉕ **der Ameisenbär**
anteater

㉗ **das Junge**
cub

㉖ **der Tiger**
tiger

㉘ **der Leopard**
leopard

㉚ **der Rotluchs**
bobcat

㉙ **die Wildkatze**
wildcat

㉛ **der Schneeleopard**
snow leopard

㉜ **der Katta**
ring-tailed lemur

㉝ **das Kapuzineräffchen**
capuchin monkey

㉟ **der Schwanz**
tail

㉞ **der Klammeraffe**
spider monkey

㊲ **die gurkenförmige Nase**
pendulous nose

㊳ **der Makake**
macaque

㊴ **der Mandrill**
mandrill

㊵ **der Seidenaffe**
marmoset

㊶ **der Orang-Utan**
orangutan

㊱ **der Nasenaffe**
proboscis monkey

㊷ **der Schimpanse**
chimpanzee

㊸ **der Gibbon**
gibbon

㊹ **der Gorilla**
gorilla

㊺ **der Panda**
panda

See also
157 Die Naturgeschichte · Natural history **164** Haustiere · Pets
165 Bauernhoftiere · Farm animals **166** Leben im Ozean · Ocean life

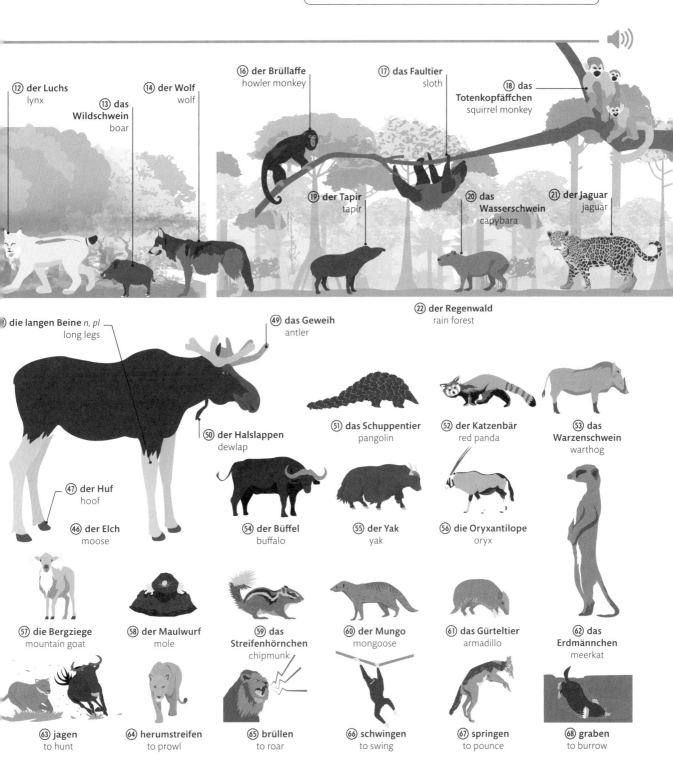

⑫ **der Luchs**
lynx

⑬ **das Wildschwein**
boar

⑭ **der Wolf**
wolf

⑯ **der Brüllaffe**
howler monkey

⑰ **das Faultier**
sloth

⑱ **das Totenkopfäffchen**
squirrel monkey

⑲ **der Tapir**
tapir

⑳ **das Wasserschwein**
capybara

㉑ **der Jaguar**
jaguar

㉒ **der Regenwald**
rain forest

⑱ **die langen Beine** *n, pl*
long legs

㊾ **das Geweih**
antler

㊿ **der Halslappen**
dewlap

㊼ **der Huf**
hoof

㊻ **der Elch**
moose

�51 **das Schuppentier**
pangolin

�52 **der Katzenbär**
red panda

�53 **das Warzenschwein**
warthog

�54 **der Büffel**
buffalo

�55 **der Yak**
yak

�56 **die Oryxantilope**
oryx

�57 **die Bergziege**
mountain goat

�58 **der Maulwurf**
mole

�59 **das Streifenhörnchen**
chipmunk

�60 **der Mungo**
mongoose

�61 **das Gürteltier**
armadillo

�62 **das Erdmännchen**
meerkat

�63 **jagen**
to hunt

�64 **herumstreifen**
to prowl

�65 **brüllen**
to roar

�66 **schwingen**
to swing

�67 **springen**
to pounce

�68 **graben**
to burrow

160.1 VOGELARTEN · SPECIES OF BIRDS

① der Grünspecht
green woodpecker

② der Schwarzspecht
black woodpecker

③ der Kolibri
hummingbird

④ die Mehlschwalbe
house martin

⑤ die Möwe
seagull

⑥ die Mauerschwalbe
swift

⑦ die Uferschwalbe
sand martin

⑧ die Küstenseeschwalbe
Arctic tern

⑨ der Helmspecht
pileated woodpecker

⑩ der Buntspecht
greater spotted woodpecker

⑪ der Schwanz
tail

⑫ die Schwalbe
swallow

⑬ der Kanarienvogel
canary

⑭ der Wellensittich
budgerigar

⑮ der Star
starling

⑯ die Nachtigall
nightingale

⑰ der Webervogel
weaverbird

⑱ der Rubintyrann
vermilion flycatcher

⑲ der Albatros
albatross

⑳ der Fregattvogel
frigate

㉑ der Steinadler
golden eagle

㉒ der Weißkopfseeadler
bald eagle

㉓ der Fischadler
osprey

㉔ der Kormoran
cormorant

㉕ der Tölpel
gannet

㉖ der Andenkondor
Andean condor

㉗ der Wanderfalke
peregrine falcon

㉘ der Geier
vulture

㉙ die Harpyie
harpy eagle

㉚ die Lumme
guillemot

㉛ der Papageitaucher
Atlantic puffin

See also
157 Die Naturgeschichte • Natural history **161** Vögel (Fortsetzung) Birds continued **165** Bauernhoftiere • Farm animals

㉜ der Laucharassari
emerald toucan
㉝ der Tukan
toco toucan
㉞ das Rotkehlchen
European robin
㉟ der Zaunkönig
wren
㊱ der Spatz
sparrow
㊲ das Nest
nest
㊳ der Rote Ibis
scarlet ibis
㊴ der Heilige Ibis
sacred ibis
㊵ der Fink
finch
㊶ die Taube
pigeon
㊷ die Amsel
blackbird
㊸ die Saatkrähe
rook
㊹ die Krähe
crow
㊺ die Drossel
thrush
㊻ der Rabe
raven
㊼ der Paradiesvogel
bird of paradise
㊽ der Pelikan
pelican
㊾ der Austerndieb
oystercatcher
㊿ der Eisvogel
kingfisher
(51) der Kookaburra
kookaburra
(52) der Storch
stork
(53) der Reiher
heron
(54) die Nilgans
Egyptian goose
(55) die Kanadagans
Canada goose
(56) die Schneegans
snow goose
(57) der Kranich
crane
(58) der Flamingo
flamingo
(59) der Strauß
ostrich
(60) der Kiwi
kiwi
(61) der Kasuar
cassowary
(62) der Emu
emu

161.1 VOGELARTEN · SPECIES OF BIRDS

① **der Rosakakadu**
galah

② **der Edelpapagei**
eclectus parrot

③ **der Sittich**
rose-ringed parakeet

④ **der Scharlachara**
scarlet macaw

⑤ **der Regenbogenlori**
lorikeet

⑮ **rufen**
to hoot

⑩ **die Schneeeule**
snowy owl

⑪ **der Uhu**
eagle owl

⑫ **der Bartkauz**
great grey owl

⑬ **der Haubenkauz**
crested owl

⑭ **die Schleiereule**
barn owl

㉒ **der Höckerschwan**
mute swan

㉓ **der Trauerschwan**
black swan

㉔ **der Singschwan**
whooper swan

㉕ **das Blässhuhn**
coot

㉖ **die Stockente**
mallard

㉗ **die Mandarinente**
mandarin duck

㉘ **der Haubentaucher**
grebe

㉙ **die Brautente**
wood duck

㉚ **die Wasserralle**
water rail

㉛ **der Brachvogel**
curlew

㉜ **der Fasan**
pheasant

㉝ **der Truthahn**
turkey

㉟ **ein Rad schlagen**
feathers displayed

㊱ **der Hals**
neck

㉞ **der Pfau**
peacock

See also
157 Die Naturgeschichte · Natural history
165 Bauernhoftiere · Farm animals

⑨ Ich habe gerade einen Steinadler entdeckt!
I've just spotted a golden eagle!

161.2 **VERBEN**
VERBS

⑥ **der Kakadu**
cockatoo

⑦ **der Graupapagei**
African grey parrot

⑧ **der Vogelbeobachter** *m*
die Vogelbeobachterin *f*
bird-watcher

① **schlüpfen**
to hatch

⑯ **der Waldkauz**
tawny owl

⑰ **der Elfenkauz**
elf owl

⑱ **das Küken**
hatchling

⑲ **die Eierschale**
eggshell

⑳ **der Jungvogel**
fledgling

㉑ **die weiche Daunenfeder**
soft down feathers

② **(in den Süden / Norden) ziehen**
to migrate

③ **(mit den Flügeln) schlagen**
to flap

㊵ **der Schopf**
crest

㊶ **der Schnabel**
bill / beak

㊴ **der Flügel**
wing

㊳ **die Schwanzfeder**
tail feathers

㊷ **die Klaue**
claw

㊲ **der Rotkardinal**
northern cardinal

④ **gleiten**
to glide

⑤ **einen Sturzflug machen**
to swoop

㊸ **der Kaiserpinguin**
emperor penguin

㊹ **der Felsenpinguin**
rockhopper penguin

㊺ **der Humboldtpinguin**
Humboldt penguin

㊻ **der Eselspinguin**
Gentoo penguin

㊼ **der Australische Zwergpinguin**
Australian little penguin

331

162.1 SCHMETTERLINGE UND FALTER · BUTTERFLIES AND MOTHS

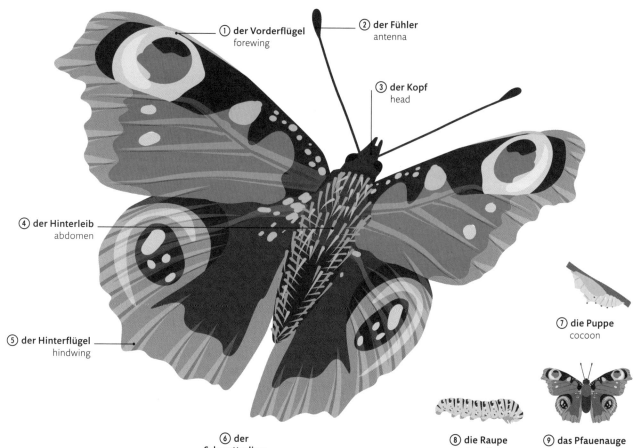

① **der Vorderflügel**
forewing

② **der Fühler**
antenna

③ **der Kopf**
head

④ **der Hinterleib**
abdomen

⑤ **der Hinterflügel**
hindwing

⑥ **der Schmetterling**
butterfly

⑦ **die Puppe**
cocoon

⑧ **die Raupe**
caterpillar

⑨ **das Pfauenauge**
peacock butterfly

⑩ **der Monarchfalter**
monarch butterfly

⑪ **der Distelfalter**
painted lady butterfly

⑫ **der Schwalbenschwanz**
swallowtail butterfly

⑬ **der Glasflügelfalter**
glasswing butterfly

⑭ **der Kohlweißling**
cabbage white butterfly

⑮ **der Birkenspanner**
peppered moth

⑯ **die Lunamotte**
luna moth

⑰ **das Karpfenschwänzchen**
hummingbird hawksmoth

⑱ **das Kleine Nachtpfauenauge**
emperor moth

⑲ **der Atlasspinner**
atlas moth

⑳ **die Kleidermotte**
clothes moth

㉑ **der Fledermausschwärmer**
hawk moth

See also
157 Die Naturgeschichte · Natural history **158-159** Säugetiere · Mammals
160-161 Vögel · Birds **163** Amphibien und Reptilien · Amphibians and reptiles

162.2 WEITERE KÄFER UND WIRBELLOSE · OTHER BUGS AND INVERTEBRATES

① der **Nashornkäfer**
rhinoceros beetle

② der **Hirschkäfer**
stag beetle

③ der **Rüsselkäfer**
weevil

④ die **Kakerlake**
cockroach

⑤ der **Marienkäfer**
ladybird

⑥ die **Fliege**
fly

⑦ der **Grashüpfer**
grasshopper

⑧ die **Heuschrecke**
locust

⑨ die **Gespenstschrecke**
leaf insect

⑩ die **Gottesanbeterin**
praying mantis

⑫ der **Stachel**
sting

⑪ der **Skorpion**
scorpion

⑬ die **Grille**
cricket

⑭ der **Hundertfüßer**
centipede

⑮ der **Tausendfüßer**
millipede

⑯ die **Libelle**
dragonfly

⑰ die **Mücke**
mosquito

⑱ der **Wurm**
worm

⑲ die **Tarantel**
tarantula

⑳ die **Schwarze Witwe**
black widow spider

㉑ die **Springspinne**
jumping spider

㉒ die **Sektorspinne**
orb weaver

㉓ die **Nacktschnecke**
slug

㉔ die **Schnecke**
snail

㉕ die **Termite**
termite

㉖ die **Ameise**
ant

㉗ die **Hummel**
bumble bee

㉘ die **Wespe**
wasp

㉙ die **Honigbiene**
honey bee

㉟ der **Schwarm**
swarm

㉚ **stechen**
to sting

㉛ **fliegen**
to fly

㉜ **brummen**
to buzz

㉝ das **Wespennest**
wasp nest

㉞ der **Bienenstock**
beehive

163.1 **AMPHIBIEN** · AMPHIBIANS

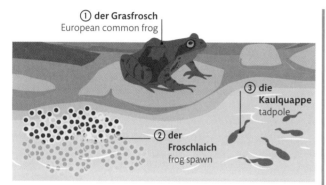

① **der Grasfrosch**
European common frog

③ **die Kaulquappe**
tadpole

② **der Froschlaich**
frog spawn

④ **der Wallace-Flugfrosch**
Wallace's flying frog

⑤ **der Pfeilgiftfrosch**
poison dart frog

⑥ **der Darwin-Nasenfrosch**
Darwin's frog

⑦ **der Rotaugenlaubfrosch**
red-eyed tree frog

⑧ **die Gemeine Kröte**
common toad

⑨ **der Afrikanische Ochsenfrosch**
African bullfrog

⑩ **die Chinesische Rotbauchunke**
Oriental fire-bellied toad

⑪ **die Präriekröte**
Great Plains toad

⑫ **der Feuersalamander**
fire salamander

⑬ **der Olm**
olm

⑭ **das Axolotl**
Mexican axolotl

⑮ **der Kammmolch**
great crested newt

⑯ **der Rotsalamander**
red salamander

163.2 **REPTILIEN** · REPTILES

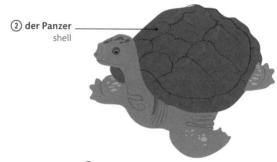

② **der Panzer**
shell

① **die Galapagosschildkröte**
Galápagos turtle

③ **die Strahlenschildkröte**
radiated tortoise

④ **die Matamata**
matamata

⑤ **die Diamantschildkröte**
diamond back terrapin

⑥ **die Australische Schlangenhalsschildkröte**
common snake-necked turtle

⑦ **die Grüne Meeresschildkröte**
green sea turtle

⑧ **die Lederschildkröte**
leatherback sea turtle

⑨ **das Parsons-Chamäleon**
parson's chameleon

⑩ **das Pantherchamäleon**
panther chameleon

⑪ **das Dreihornchamäleon**
Jackson's chameleon

⑫ **der Komodowaran**
Komodo dragon

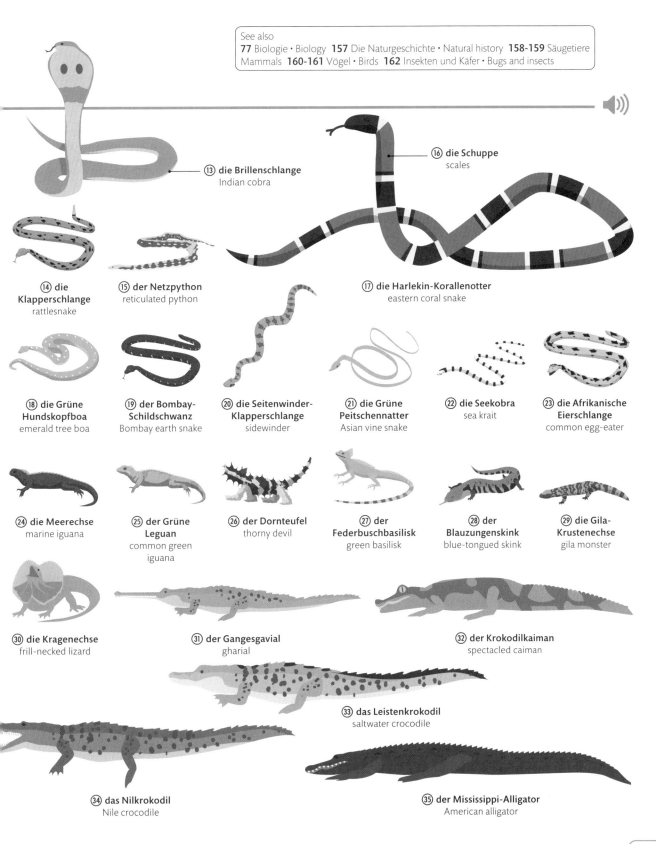

See also
77 Biologie · Biology **157** Die Naturgeschichte · Natural history **158-159** Säugetiere
Mammals **160-161** Vögel · Birds **162** Insekten und Käfer · Bugs and insects

⑬ **die Brillenschlange**
Indian cobra

⑯ **die Schuppe**
scales

⑭ **die Klapperschlange**
rattlesnake

⑮ **der Netzpython**
reticulated python

⑰ **die Harlekin-Korallenotter**
eastern coral snake

⑱ **die Grüne Hundskopfboa**
emerald tree boa

⑲ **der Bombay-Schildschwanz**
Bombay earth snake

⑳ **die Seitenwinder-Klapperschlange**
sidewinder

㉑ **die Grüne Peitschennatter**
Asian vine snake

㉒ **die Seekobra**
sea krait

㉓ **die Afrikanische Eierschlange**
common egg-eater

㉔ **die Meerechse**
marine iguana

㉕ **der Grüne Leguan**
common green iguana

㉖ **der Dornteufel**
thorny devil

㉗ **der Federbuschbasilisk**
green basilisk

㉘ **der Blauzungenskink**
blue-tongued skink

㉙ **die Gila-Krustenechse**
gila monster

㉚ **die Kragenechse**
frill-necked lizard

㉛ **der Gangesgavial**
gharial

㉜ **der Krokodilkaiman**
spectacled caiman

㉝ **das Leistenkrokodil**
saltwater crocodile

㉞ **das Nilkrokodil**
Nile crocodile

㉟ **der Mississippi-Alligator**
American alligator

164.1 KATZENRASSEN · CAT BREEDS

① die Britisch Kurzhaar
British shorthair

② die Ragdoll
Ragdoll

③ die Maine Coon
Maine coon

④ die Sphinx
sphinx

⑤ die Exotische Kurzhaarkatze
exotic shorthair

⑥ die Himalayan
Himalayan

⑦ die Perserkatze
Persian

⑧ die Burmakatze
Burmese

⑨ die Siamkatze
Siamese

⑩ die Bengalkatze
Bengal

⑪ die Bombaykatze
Bombay

⑫ die Japanische Stummelschwanzkatze
Japanese bobtail

⑬ die Angorakatze
Angora

⑭ die Abessinierkatze
Abyssinian

⑮ die American Curl
American curl

⑯ miauen
to meow

⑰ schnurren
to purr

⑱ sich verstecken
to hide

⑲ haaren
to moult

⑳ das Kätzchen
kitten

164.3 WEITERE HAUSTIERE · OTHER PETS

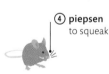

④ piepsen
to squeak

⑦ hüpfen
to hop

① der Hamster
hamster

② die Rennmaus
gerbil

③ die Maus
mouse

⑤ das Meerschweinchen
guinea pig

⑥ das Kaninchen
rabbit

⑧ das Frettchen
ferret

⑨ der Fisch
fish

⑩ die Eidechse
lizard

⑪ das Stabinsekt
stick insect

⑫ die Schildkröte
tortoise

⑬ der Wellensittich
budgerigar / budgie

⑭ der Nymphensittich
cockatiel

See also
158-159 Säugetiere · Mammals **160-161** Vögel · Birds **162** Insekten und Käfer
Insects and bugs **163** Amphibien und Reptilien · Amphibians and reptiles

164.2 HUNDERASSEN · DOG BREEDS

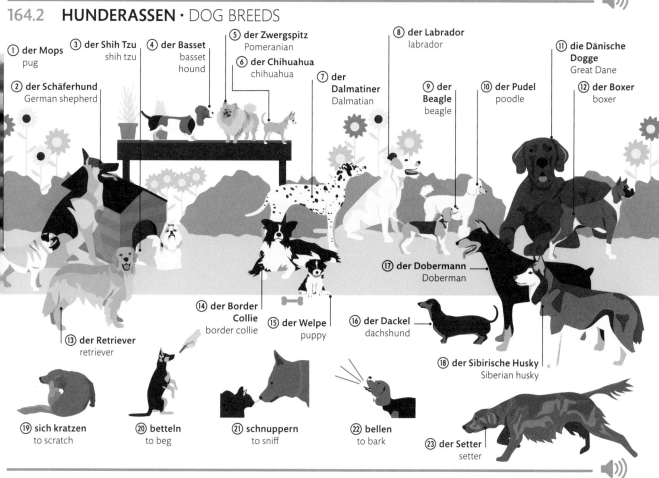

① der Mops
pug

② der Schäferhund
German shepherd

③ der Shih Tzu
shih tzu

④ der Basset
basset
hound

⑤ der Zwergspitz
Pomeranian

⑥ der Chihuahua
chihuahua

⑦ der Dalmatiner
Dalmatian

⑧ der Labrador
labrador

⑨ der Beagle
beagle

⑩ der Pudel
poodle

⑪ die Dänische Dogge
Great Dane

⑫ der Boxer
boxer

⑬ der Retriever
retriever

⑭ der Border Collie
border collie

⑮ der Welpe
puppy

⑯ der Dackel
dachshund

⑰ der Dobermann
Doberman

⑱ der Sibirische Husky
Siberian husky

⑲ sich kratzen
to scratch

⑳ betteln
to beg

㉑ schnuppern
to sniff

㉒ bellen
to bark

㉓ der Setter
setter

164.4 HAUSTIERBEDARF · PET SUPPLIES

① das Aquarium
fish tank /
aquarium

② der Korb
basket

③ die Hundehütte
kennel

④ der Käfig
cage

⑤ der Kaninchenstall
rabbit hutch

⑥ das Katzenklo
litter tray

⑦ die Leine
leash / lead

⑧ das Vivarium
vivarium

⑨ das Vogelfutter
birdseed

⑩ das Leckerli
treats

⑪ das Spielzeug
toys

165.1 AUF DEM BAUERNHOF · ON THE FARM

② **Ich füttere zweimal täglich die Hühner.**
I feed the chickens twice a day.

⑤ **die Kuh**
cow

① **das Huhn**
chicken

③ **das Schaf**
sheep

④ **das Küken**
chick

⑥ **das Lamm**
lamb

⑭ **der Hahn**
rooster / cockerel

⑮ **die Henne**
hen

⑯ **der Truthahn**
turkey

⑰ **das Geflügel**
poultry

② **die Biene**
bee

㉒ **die Schafsherde**
flock of sheep

⑱ **der Bock**
ram

⑲ **die Au**
ewe

⑳ **der Bienenstock**
hive

㉓ **die Kuhherde**
herd of cows

㉔ **der Bulle**
bull

㉕ **das Kalb**
calf

㉖ **die Rinder** *n, pl*
cattle

㉗ **der Esel**
donkey

See also
53 Fleisch · Meat **86** Landwirtschaft · Farming
158-159 Säugetiere · Mammals **164** Haustiere · Pets

⑦ **das Pferd**
horse

⑧ **die Gans**
goose

⑨ **das Küken**
gosling

⑩ **das Schwein**
pig

⑪ **das Ferkel**
piglet

⑫ **die Ente**
duck

⑬ **das Entlein**
duckling

㉘ **der Hengst**
stallion

㉙ **die Stute**
mare

㉚ **das Fohlen**
foal

㉛ **die Ziege**
goat

㉜ **das Zicklein**
kid

㉝ **der Strauß**
ostrich

㉞ **das Lama**
llama

㉟ **das Alpaka**
alpaca

㊱ **scheren**
to shear

㊲ **traben**
to trot

㊳ **galoppieren**
to gallop

㊴ **auf jemanden zulaufen**
to charge

㊵ **krähen**
to crow

㊶ **mähen**
to bleat

㊷ **schnauben**
to snort

㊸ **grunzen**
to grunt

㊹ **iahen**
to bray

㊺ **quaken**
to quack

166.1 MEERESTIERE · MARINE SPECIES

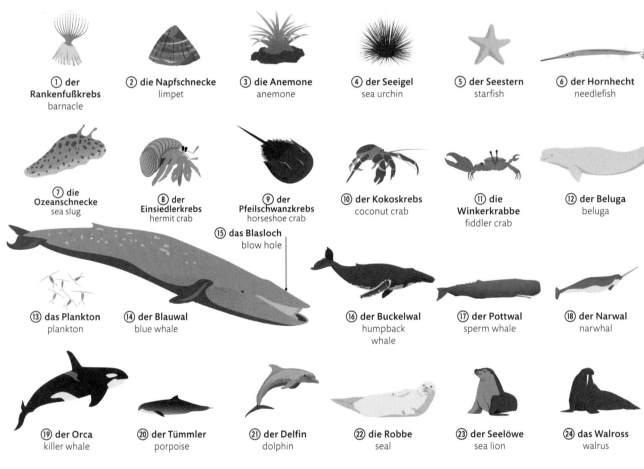

① **der Rankenfußkrebs** barnacle

② **die Napfschnecke** limpet

③ **die Anemone** anemone

④ **der Seeigel** sea urchin

⑤ **der Seestern** starfish

⑥ **der Hornhecht** needlefish

⑦ **die Ozeanschnecke** sea slug

⑧ **der Einsiedlerkrebs** hermit crab

⑨ **der Pfeilschwanzkrebs** horseshoe crab

⑩ **der Kokoskrebs** coconut crab

⑪ **die Winkerkrabbe** fiddler crab

⑫ **der Beluga** beluga

⑮ **das Blasloch** blow hole

⑬ **das Plankton** plankton

⑭ **der Blauwal** blue whale

⑯ **der Buckelwal** humpback whale

⑰ **der Pottwal** sperm whale

⑱ **der Narwal** narwhal

⑲ **der Orca** killer whale

⑳ **der Tümmler** porpoise

㉑ **der Delfin** dolphin

㉒ **die Robbe** seal

㉓ **der Seelöwe** sea lion

㉔ **das Walross** walrus

166.2 DAS KORALLENRIFF · CORAL REEF

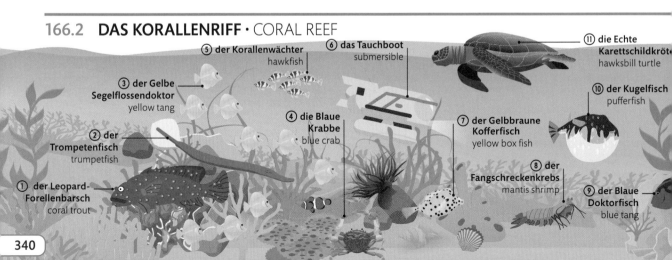

⑤ **der Korallenwächter** hawkfish

⑥ **das Tauchboot** submersible

⑪ **die Echte Karettschildkröte** hawksbill turtle

③ **der Gelbe Segelflossendoktor** yellow tang

④ **die Blaue Krabbe** blue crab

⑩ **der Kugelfisch** pufferfish

② **der Trompetenfisch** trumpetfish

⑦ **der Gelbbraune Kofferfisch** yellow box fish

① **der Leopard-Forellenbarsch** coral trout

⑧ **der Fangschreckenkrebs** mantis shrimp

⑨ **der Blaue Doktorfisch** blue tang

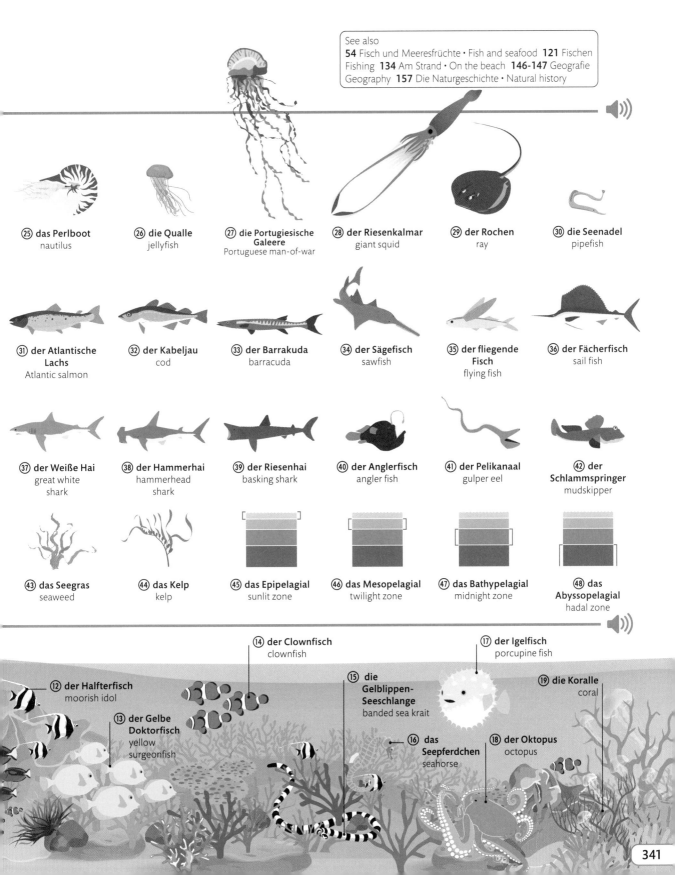

See also
54 Fisch und Meeresfrüchte • Fish and seafood **121** Fischen
Fishing **134** Am Strand • On the beach **146-147** Geografie
Geography **157** Die Naturgeschichte • Natural history

㉕ **das Perlboot**
nautilus

㉖ **die Qualle**
jellyfish

㉗ **die Portugiesische Galeere**
Portuguese man-of-war

㉘ **der Riesenkalmar**
giant squid

㉙ **der Rochen**
ray

㉚ **die Seenadel**
pipefish

㉛ **der Atlantische Lachs**
Atlantic salmon

㉜ **der Kabeljau**
cod

㉝ **der Barrakuda**
barracuda

㉞ **der Sägefisch**
sawfish

㉟ **der fliegende Fisch**
flying fish

㊱ **der Fächerfisch**
sail fish

㊲ **der Weiße Hai**
great white shark

㊳ **der Hammerhai**
hammerhead shark

㊴ **der Riesenhai**
basking shark

㊵ **der Anglerfisch**
angler fish

㊶ **der Pelikanaal**
gulper eel

㊷ **der Schlammspringer**
mudskipper

㊸ **das Seegras**
seaweed

㊹ **das Kelp**
kelp

㊺ **das Epipelagial**
sunlit zone

㊻ **das Mesopelagial**
twilight zone

㊼ **das Bathypelagial**
midnight zone

㊽ **das Abyssopelagial**
hadal zone

⑭ **der Clownfisch**
clownfish

⑰ **der Igelfisch**
porcupine fish

⑫ **der Halfterfisch**
moorish idol

⑬ **der Gelbe Doktorfisch**
yellow surgeonfish

⑮ **die Gelblippen-Seeschlange**
banded sea krait

⑯ **das Seepferdchen**
seahorse

⑱ **der Oktopus**
octopus

⑲ **die Koralle**
coral

167.1 PFLANZEN UND BÄUME · PLANTS AND TREES

① **das Lebermoos**
liverwort

② **das Moos**
moss

③ **der Schachtelhalm**
horsetail

④ **der Farn**
fern

⑤ **der Brotpalmfarn**
cycad

⑥ **der Ginkgo**
ginkgo

⑪ **der Nadelbaum**
conifers

⑦ **die Fichte**
spruce

⑧ **die Tanne**
fir

⑨ **die Andentanne**
monkey puzzle

⑩ **die Eibe**
yew

⑫ **die Lärche**
larch

⑬ **die Libanonzeder**
cedar of Lebanon

⑭ **die Pinie**
umbrella pine

⑳ **der Riesenmammutbaum**
giant sequoia

⑮ **die Seerose**
water lily

⑯ **die Magnolie**
magnolia

⑰ **der Avocadobaum**
avocado tree

⑱ **der Lorbeerbaum**
laurel

⑲ **die Calla**
arum lily

㉑ **der Josuabaum**
Joshua tree

㉒ **die Amaryllis**
amaryllis

㉓ **die Schusterpalme**
cast-iron plant

㉔ **der Drachenbaum**
dragon tree

㉕ **der Blaustern**
English bluebell

㉖ **das Schneeglöckchen**
snowdrop

㉗ **der Krokus**
crocus

See also
38 Gartenpflanzen und Zimmerpflanzen · Garden plants and houseplants **57** Obst · Fruit
58 Obst und Nüsse · Fruit and nuts **157** Die Naturgeschichte · Natural history
168-169 Pflanzen und Bäume (Fortsetzung) · Plants and trees continued **170** Pilze · Fungi

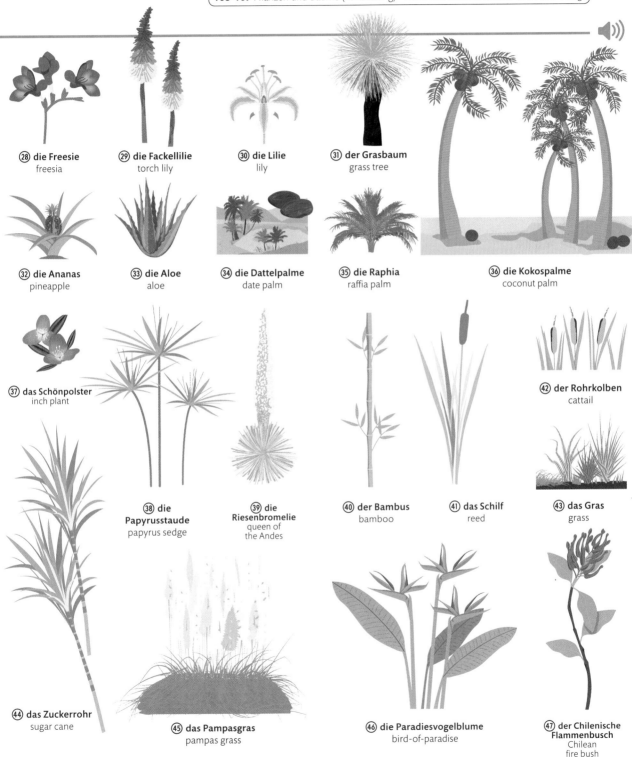

㉘ **die Freesie**
freesia

㉙ **die Fackellilie**
torch lily

㉚ **die Lilie**
lily

㉛ **der Grasbaum**
grass tree

㉜ **die Ananas**
pineapple

㉝ **die Aloe**
aloe

㉞ **die Dattelpalme**
date palm

㉟ **die Raphia**
raffia palm

㊱ **die Kokospalme**
coconut palm

㊲ **das Schönpolster**
inch plant

㊳ **die Papyrusstaude**
papyrus sedge

㊴ **die Riesenbromelie**
queen of the Andes

㊵ **der Bambus**
bamboo

㊶ **das Schilf**
reed

㊷ **der Rohrkolben**
cattail

㊸ **das Gras**
grass

㊹ **das Zuckerrohr**
sugar cane

㊺ **das Pampasgras**
pampas grass

㊻ **die Paradiesvogelblume**
bird-of-paradise

㊼ **der Chilenische Flammenbusch**
Chilean fire bush

168.1 PFLANZEN UND BÄUME · PLANTS AND TREES

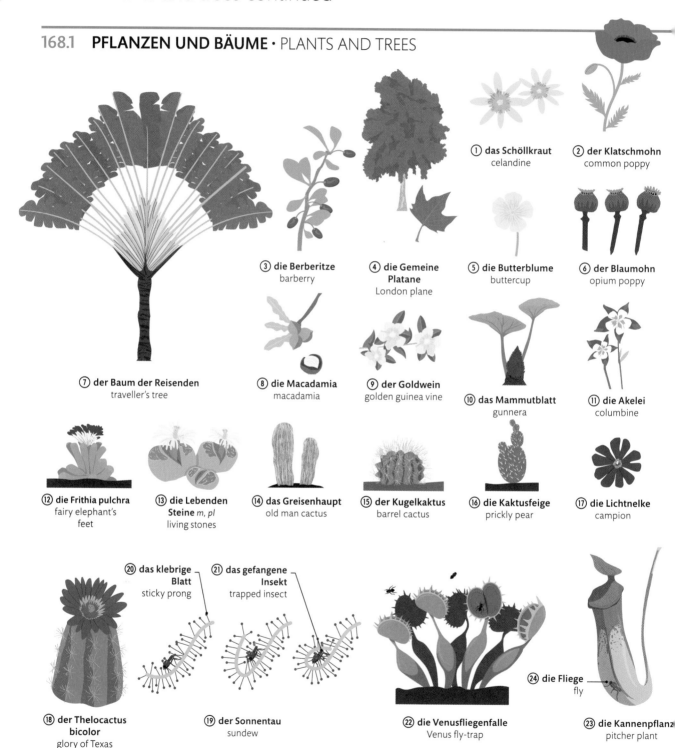

① das Schöllkraut
celandine

② der Klatschmohn
common poppy

③ die Berberitze
barberry

④ die Gemeine
Platane
London plane

⑤ die Butterblume
buttercup

⑥ der Blaumohn
opium poppy

⑦ der Baum der Reisenden
traveller's tree

⑧ die Macadamia
macadamia

⑨ der Goldwein
golden guinea vine

⑩ das Mammutblatt
gunnera

⑪ die Akelei
columbine

⑫ die Frithia pulchra
fairy elephant's
feet

⑬ die Lebenden
Steine m, pl
living stones

⑭ das Greisenhaupt
old man cactus

⑮ der Kugelkaktus
barrel cactus

⑯ die Kaktusfeige
prickly pear

⑰ die Lichtnelke
campion

⑳ das klebrige
Blatt
sticky prong

㉑ das gefangene
Insekt
trapped insect

㉔ die Fliege
fly

⑱ der Thelocactus
bicolor
glory of Texas

⑲ der Sonnentau
sundew

㉒ die Venusfliegenfalle
Venus fly-trap

㉓ die Kannenpflanz
pitcher plant

See also
38 Gartenpflanzen und Zimmerpflanzen • Garden plants and houseplants **57** Obst
Fruit **58** Obst und Nüsse • Fruit and nuts **157** Die Naturgeschichte • Natural history
169 Pflanzen und Bäume (Fortsetzung) • Plants and trees continued **170** Pilze • Fungi

㉕ **die Bougainville**
bougainvillea

㉖ **der Flammenbaum**
fire tree

㉗ **die Mistel**
mistletoe

㉘ **die Alpen-Hauswurz**
common houseleek

㉙ **der Wein**
grapevine

㉚ **das Brutblatt**
mother of thousands

㉛ **die Pfingstrose**
peony

㉜ **der Wilde Wein**
Virginia creeper

㉝ **die Myrte**
myrtle

㉞ **der Granatapfelbaum**
pomegranate

㉟ **der Braune Weiderich**
purple loosestrife

㊱ **die Henna**
henna

㊲ **der Zwergflaschenputzer**
Tonghi bottlebrush

㊳ **die Guave**
guava

㊴ **die Fuchsie**
fuchsia

㊵ **die Mimose**
mimosa

㊶ **die Seidenakazie**
silk tree

㊸ **die Hainbuche**
hornbeam

㊸ **die Haselnuss**
hazel

㊹ **der Samen**
seed

㊺ **der Walnussbaum**
walnut

㊻ **die Edelkastanie**
Spanish chestnut

㊼ **der Pekannussbaum**
pecan

㊽ **die Buche**
beech

㊾ **die Birke**
birch

㊿ **die Pappel**
poplar

169.1 PFLANZEN UND BÄUME · PLANTS AND TREES

② die Eichel
acorn

③ das Wüsteneisenholz
desert ironwood tree

④ der Wunderbaum
castor oil plant

⑤ die Weide
willow

⑥ der Mangrovenbaum
mangrove

① die Eiche
oak

⑦ der Gummibaum
rubber tree

⑧ die Passionsblume
passion flower

⑨ die Aschweide
grey willow

⑩ der Sanddorn
sea buckthorn

⑱ die Blüte
blossom

⑰ der Zweig
branch

⑯ die Kirsche
cherries

⑪ die Birne
pear

⑫ der Johannisapfel
crab apple

⑬ die Pflaume
plum

⑭ die Feige
fig

⑮ der Kirschbaum
cherry

⑲ die Ölweide
oleaster

⑳ der Hanf
hemp

㉑ der Hopfen
hop

㉒ die Hagebutte
dog rose

See also
38 Gartenpflanzen und Zimmerpflanzen • Garden plants and houseplants **57** Obst • Fruit
58 Obst und Nüsse • Fruit and nuts **157** Die Naturgeschichte • Natural history **170** Pilze • Fungi

㉓ **die Zwergmispel**
cotoneaster

㉔ **die Eberesche**
mountain ash

㉕ **die Mispel**
medlar

㉖ **der Weißdorn**
hawthorn

㉗ **die Ulme**
elm

㉘ **die Nessel**
nettle

㊸ **die Samara**
samara

㉙ **die Kapuzinerkresse**
nasturtium

㉚ **das Mauerblümchen**
wallflower

㉛ **der Hibiskus**
Chinese hibiscus

㉜ **der Kakaobaum**
cocoa

㉝ **die Linde**
lime / linden

㉞ **die Schlüsselblume**
cowslip

㉟ **der Chinesische Surenbaum**
Chinese mahogany

㊱ **der Affenbrotbaum**
baobab tree

㊷ **das Sommerblatt**
summer leaf

㊲ **der Ahorn**
maple

㊳ **die Rosskastanie**
horse chestnut

㊴ **der Oleander**
oleander

㊵ **die Olive**
olive

㊶ **der Bergahorn**
sycamore

㊸ **das Herbstblatt**
autumn leaf

㊺ **die Ackerwinde**
morning glory

㊻ **die Belladonna**
deadly nightshade

㊼ **der Schierling**
hemlock

㊽ **die Distel**
thistle

㊾ **der Efeu**
ivy

㊿ **die Lampionblume**
Chinese lantern

347

170.1 PILZARTEN · SPECIES OF FUNGI

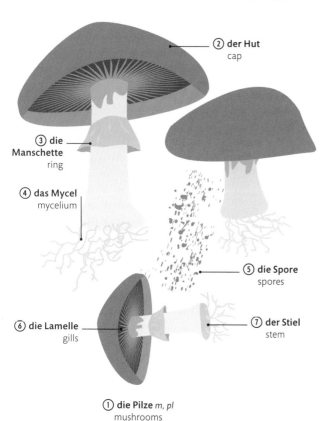

② **der Hut**
cap

③ **die Manschette**
ring

④ **das Mycel**
mycelium

⑤ **die Spore**
spores

⑥ **die Lamelle**
gills

⑦ **der Stiel**
stem

① **die Pilze** *m, pl*
mushrooms

⑧ **der Porling**
shaggy bracket fungus

⑨ **Pilze sammeln**
to forage / to pick mushrooms

⑭ **Manche Pilze sind giftig. Ich prüfe sie vor dem Sammeln immer.**
Some fungi are poisonous. I always check before picking.

⑬ **der Flaschenbovist**
common puffball

㉑ **die Zuchtpilze** *m, pl*
cultivated mushrooms

㉒ **die Giftpilze** *m, pl*
toadstools

㉓ **der Hexenring**
fairy ring

㉔ **der Austernpilz**
oyster mushroom

㉕ **die Laubwaldrotkappe**
orange-cap boletus

㉖ **der Schwefelporling**
chicken of the woods

㉗ **der Semmelstoppelpilz**
hedgehog mushroom

㉘ **der Igelstachelbart**
bear's head tooth

㉙ **die Totentrompete**
black trumpet

㉚ **der Spargelpilz**
shaggy mane mushroom

㉛ **der Kastanienschwamm**
hen of the wood

㉜ **der Schimmel**
mold

See also
55-56 Gemüse · Vegetables **133** Aktivitäten im Freien · Outdoor activities **167-169** Pflanzen und Bäume · Plants and trees

⑩ **der Enoki**
enoki mushroom

⑪ **der Shiitake**
shiitake mushroom

⑫ **der Saftling**
waxcap

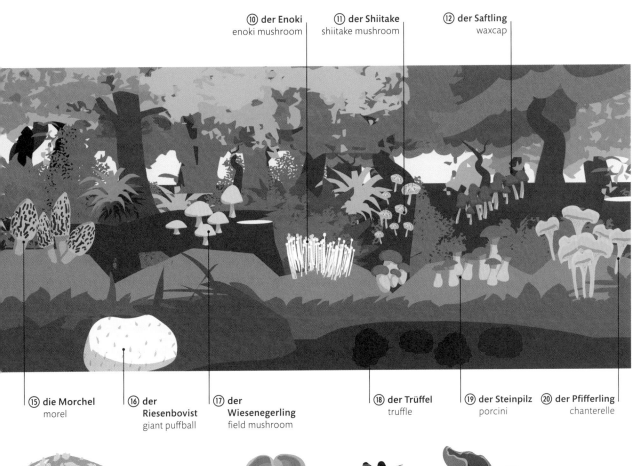

⑮ **die Morchel**
morel

⑯ **der Riesenbovist**
giant puffball

⑰ **der Wiesenegerling**
field mushroom

⑱ **der Trüffel**
truffle

⑲ **der Steinpilz**
porcini

⑳ **der Pfifferling**
chanterelle

③⑤ **der Orangerote Becherpilz**
orange peel fungus

③⑥ **die Stinkmorchel**
stinkhorn

③⑦ **das Hasenohr**
hare's ear

③③ **der Knollenblätterpilz**
death cap

③④ **Amanita ocreata**
death angel

③⑧ **der Dunkle Ölbaumtrichterling**
jack-o'-lantern

③⑨ **der Gemeine Kartoffelbovist**
common earthball

④⓪ **das Milchweiße Samthäuptchen**
milky conecap

④① **der Fliegenpilz**
fly agaric

171.1 DIE ZEIT ABLESEN · TELLING THE TIME

① Wie viel Uhr ist es?
What time is it?

② Es ist drei Uhr.
It's three o'clock.

③ ein Uhr
one o'clock

④ fünf nach eins
five past one

⑤ zehn nach eins
ten past one

⑥ Viertel nach eins
quarter past one

⑦ zwanzig nach eins
twenty past one

⑧ fünf vor halb zwei
twenty-five past one

⑨ halb zwei
one thirty / half past one

⑩ fünf nach halb zwei
twenty-five to two

⑪ zwanzig vor zwei
twenty to two

⑫ Viertel vor zwei
quarter to two

⑬ zehn vor zwei
ten to two

⑭ fünf vor zwei
five to two

⑮ zwei Uhr
two o'clock

⑯ die Sekunde
second

⑰ die Minute
minute

⑱ die Viertelstunde
quarter of an hour

171.2 DIE TAGESZEITEN · PARTS OF THE DAY

① die Morgendämmerung
dawn

② der Sonnenaufgang
sunrise

③ der Vormittag
morning

④ der Mittag
midday

⑤ der Nachmittag
afternoon

See also
172 Der Kalender • The calendar **173** Zahlen • Numbers
174 Gewichte und Maße • Weights and measures

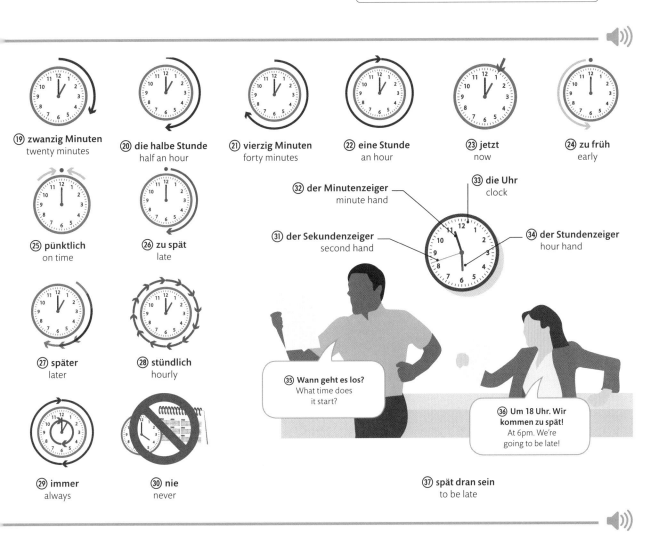

⑲ **zwanzig Minuten**
twenty minutes

⑳ **die halbe Stunde**
half an hour

㉑ **vierzig Minuten**
forty minutes

㉒ **eine Stunde**
an hour

㉓ **jetzt**
now

㉔ **zu früh**
early

㉕ **pünktlich**
on time

㉖ **zu spät**
late

㉗ **später**
later

㉘ **stündlich**
hourly

㉙ **immer**
always

㉚ **nie**
never

㉜ **der Minutenzeiger**
minute hand

㉝ **die Uhr**
clock

㉛ **der Sekundenzeiger**
second hand

㉞ **der Stundenzeiger**
hour hand

㉟ **Wann geht es los?**
What time does
it start?

㊱ **Um 18 Uhr. Wir
kommen zu spät!**
At 6pm. We're
going to be late!

㊲ **spät dran sein**
to be late

⑥ **der Abend**
evening

⑦ **der
Sonnenuntergang**
sunset

⑧ **die
Abenddämmerung**
dusk

⑨ **Mitternacht**
midnight

⑩ **die Nacht**
night

⑪ **der Tag**
day

172.1 KALENDER UND JAHRESZEITEN · CALENDAR AND SEASONS

① **der Tag**
day

② **die Woche**
week

③ **zwei Wochen** *f, pl*
two weeks / fortnight

④ **das Wochenende**
weekend

⑤ **der Monat**
month

⑥ **das Jahr**
year

⑦ **das Jahrzehnt**
decade

⑧ **das Jahrhundert**
century

⑨ **das Jahrtausend**
millennium

⑩ **Montag** *m*
Monday

⑪ **Dienstag** *m*
Tuesday

⑫ **Mittwoch** *m*
Wednesday

⑬ **Donnerstag** *m*
Thursday

⑭ **Freitag** *m*
Friday

⑮ **Samstag** *m*
Saturday

⑯ **Sonntag** *m*
Sunday

⑰ **Januar** *m*
January

⑱ **Februar** *m*
February

⑲ **März** *m*
March

⑳ **April** *m*
April

㉑ **Mai** *m*
May

㉒ **Juni** *m*
June

㉓ **Juli** *m*
July

㉔ **August** *m*
August

㉕ **September** *m*
September

㉖ **Oktober** *m*
October

㉗ **November** *m*
November

㉘ **Dezember** *m*
December

See also
171 Die Zeit • Time
173 Zahlen • Numbers

1900

㉙ **neunzehnhundert**
nineteen hundred

1901

㉚ **neunzehnhunderteins**
nineteen-oh-one

1910

㉛ **neunzehnhundertzehn**
nineteen ten

2000

㉜ **zweitausend**
two thousand

2001

㉝ **zweitausendeins**
two thousand and one

2033

㉞ **zweitausenddreiunddreißig**
twenty thirty-three

㉟ **einmal in der Woche**
once a week

㊱ **zweimal in der Woche**
twice a week

㊲ **dreimal in der Woche**
three times a week

㊳ **täglich**
every day

㊴ **alle zwei Tage**
every other day

㊵ **nur an Wochenenden**
only weekends

㊶ **stündlich**
hourly

㊷ **täglich**
daily

㊸ **wöchentlich**
weekly

㊹ **monatlich**
monthly

㊻ **das frische Laub**
new leaves

㊽ **das grüne Laub**
green foliage

㊺ **der Frühling**
spring

㊼ **der Sommer**
summer

㊾ **die Jahreszeiten** *f, pl*
seasons

㊼ **der kahle Baum**
bare branches

㊾ **das herabgefallene Laub**
leaf fall

㊿ **der Herbst**
autumn

52 **der Winter**
winter

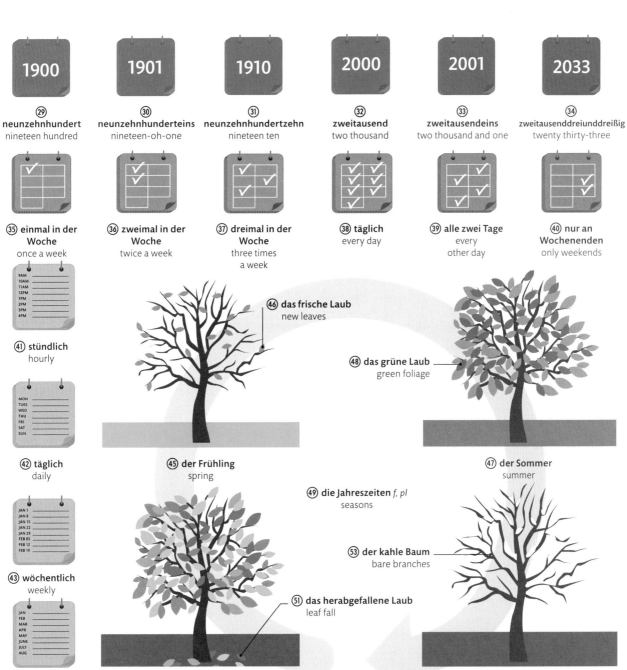

Zahlen
Numbers

173.1 GRUNDZAHLEN · CARDINAL NUMBERS

1	2	3	4	5	6
① eins one	② zwei two	③ drei three	④ vier four	⑤ fünf five	⑥ sechs six

7	8	9	10	11	12
⑦ sieben seven	⑧ acht eight	⑨ neun nine	⑩ zehn ten	⑪ elf eleven	⑫ zwölf twelve

13	14	15	16	17	18
⑬ dreizehn thirteen	⑭ vierzehn fourteen	⑮ fünfzehn fifteen	⑯ sechzehn sixteen	⑰ siebzehn seventeen	⑱ achtzehn eighteen

19	20	21	22	30	40
⑲ neunzehn nineteen	⑳ zwanzig twenty	㉑ einundzwanzig twenty-one	㉒ zweiundzwanzig twenty-two	㉓ dreißig thirty	㉔ vierzig forty

50	60	70	80	90	100	0
㉕ fünfzig fifty	㉖ sechzig sixty	㉗ siebzig seventy	㉘ achtzig eighty	㉙ neunzig ninety	㉚ hundert one hundred	㉛ null zero

173.2 ORDINALZAHLEN · ORDINAL NUMBERS

1st	2nd	3rd	4th	5th	6th
① erster / erste / erstes m / f / n first	② zweiter / zweite / zweites m / f / n second	③ dritter / dritte / drittes m / f / n third	④ vierter / vierte / viertes m / f / n fourth	⑤ fünfter / fünfte / fünftes m / f / n fifth	⑥ sechster / sechste / sechstes m / f / n sixth

7th	8th	9th	10th	20th	21st
⑦ siebter / siebte / siebtes m / f / n seventh	⑧ achter / achte / achtes m / f / n eighth	⑨ neunter / neunte / neuntes m / f / n ninth	⑩ zehnter / zehnte / zehntes m / f / n tenth	⑪ zwanzigster / zwanzigste / zwanzigste m / f / n twentieth	⑫ einundzwanzigster / einundzwanzigste / einundzwanzigste m / f / n twenty-first

See also
74 Mathematik · Mathematics **171** Die Zeit · Time **172** Der Kalender
The calendar **174** Gewichte und Maße · Weights and measures

173.3 GROSSE ZAHLEN · LARGE NUMBERS

200
① **zweihundert**
two hundred

250
② **zweihundertfünfzig**
two hundred and fifty

500
③ **fünfhundert**
five hundred

750
④ **siebenhundertfünfzig**
seven hundred and fifty

1,000
⑤ **eintausend**
one thousand

1,200
⑥
eintausendzweihundert
one thousand two hundred

10,000
⑦ **zehntausend**
ten thousand

100,000
⑧ **hunderttausend**
one hundred thousand

1,000,000
⑨ **eine Million**
one million

5,000,000
⑩ **fünf Millionen**
five million

500,000,000
⑪ **fünfhundert Millionen
eine halbe Milliarde**
five hundred million / half a billion

1,000,000,000
⑫ **eine Milliarde**
one billion

3,846
⑬
dreitausendachthundertsechsundvierzig
three thousand, eight hundred and forty-six

82,043
⑭ **zweiundachtzigtausenddreiundvierzig**
eighty-two thousand and forty-three

⑮ **Ich habe
mich verzählt!**
I've lost count!

234,407
⑯ **zweihundertvierunddreißigtausend-
vierhundertundsieben**
two hundred and thirty-four thousand,
four hundred and seven

3,089,342
⑰ **drei Millionen
neunundachtzigtausenddreihundertzweiundvierzig**
three million, eighty-nine thousand,
three hundred and forty-two

173.4 BRÜCHE, DEZIMALZAHLEN UND PROZENTANGABEN
FRACTIONS, DECIMALS, AND PERCENTAGES

⅛
① **ein Achtel** *n*
an eighth

¼
② **ein Viertel** *n*
a quarter

⅓
③ **ein Drittel** *n*
a third

½
④ **einhalb**
a half

⅗
⑤ **drei Fünftel** *n*
three-fifths

⅞
⑥ **sieben Achtel** *n*
seven-eighths

0.5
⑦ **null Komma fünf**
nought point five

1.7
⑧ **eins Komma
sieben**
one point seven

3.97
⑨ **drei Komma
neun sieben**
three point nine seven

1%
⑩ **ein Prozent** *n*
one percent

99%
⑪ **neunundneunzig
Prozent**
ninety-nine percent

100%
⑫ **hundert Prozent**
one hundred percent

174.1 GEWICHTE · WEIGHT

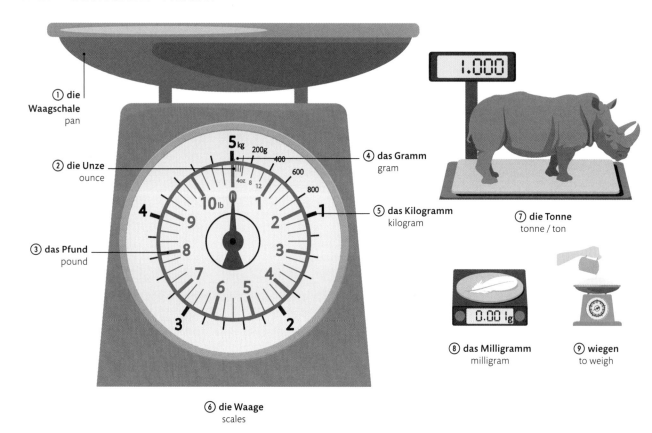

① **die Waagschale**
pan

② **die Unze**
ounce

③ **das Pfund**
pound

④ **das Gramm**
gram

⑤ **das Kilogramm**
kilogram

⑦ **die Tonne**
tonne / ton

⑧ **das Milligramm**
milligram

⑨ **wiegen**
to weigh

⑥ **die Waage**
scales

174.2 ENTFERNUNGEN, FLÄCHEN UND LÄNGEN · DISTANCE, AREA, AND LENGTH

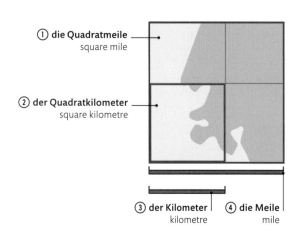

① **die Quadratmeile**
square mile

② **der Quadratkilometer**
square kilometre

③ **der Kilometer**
kilometre

④ **die Meile**
mile

100 Quadratmeter
100 metres (328 feet)

208,7 Quadratfuß
208.7 feet (63.5 m)

⑥ **der Acre**
acre

⑤ **der Hektar**
hectare

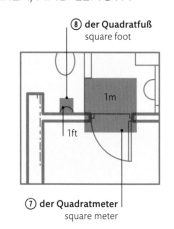

⑧ **der Quadratfuß**
square foot

1m

1ft

⑦ **der Quadratmeter**
square meter

See also
29 Kochen · Cooking **35** Heimwerken · Home improvements
74 Mathematik · Mathematics **173** Zahlen · Numbers

174.3 **DAS VOLUMEN** · LIQUID MEASUREMENTS / VOLUME

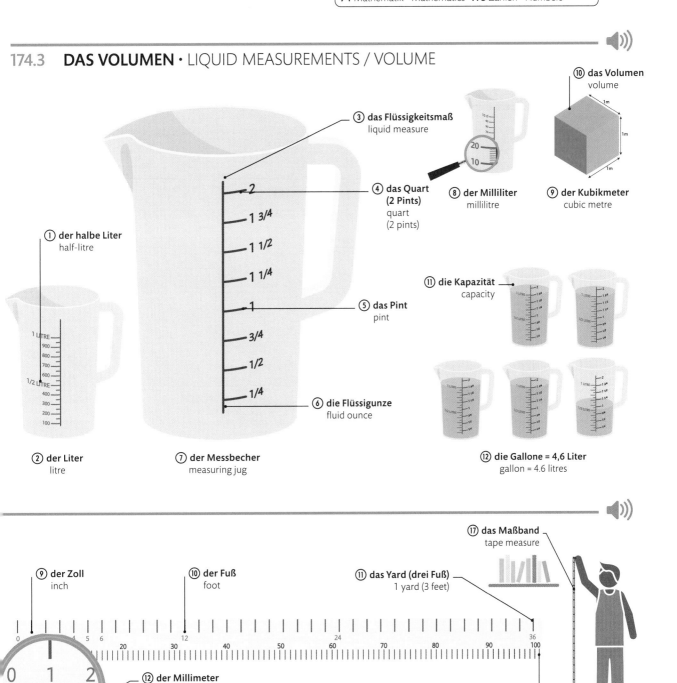

③ **das Flüssigkeitsmaß**
liquid measure

⑩ **das Volumen**
volume

④ **das Quart
(2 Pints)**
quart
(2 pints)

⑧ **der Milliliter**
millilitre

⑨ **der Kubikmeter**
cubic metre

① **der halbe Liter**
half-litre

⑤ **das Pint**
pint

⑪ **die Kapazität**
capacity

⑥ **die Flüssigunze**
fluid ounce

② **der Liter**
litre

⑦ **der Messbecher**
measuring jug

⑫ **die Gallone = 4,6 Liter**
gallon = 4.6 litres

⑰ **das Maßband**
tape measure

⑨ **der Zoll**
inch

⑩ **der Fuß**
foot

⑪ **das Yard (drei Fuß)**
1 yard (3 feet)

⑫ **der Millimeter**
millimetre

⑭ **das Lineal**
ruler

⑮ **der Meter**
metre

⑬ **der Zentimeter**
centimetre

⑯ **messen**
to measure

175.1 SCHREIBEN UND SCHREIBUTENSILIEN · WRITING AND WRITING EQUIPMENT

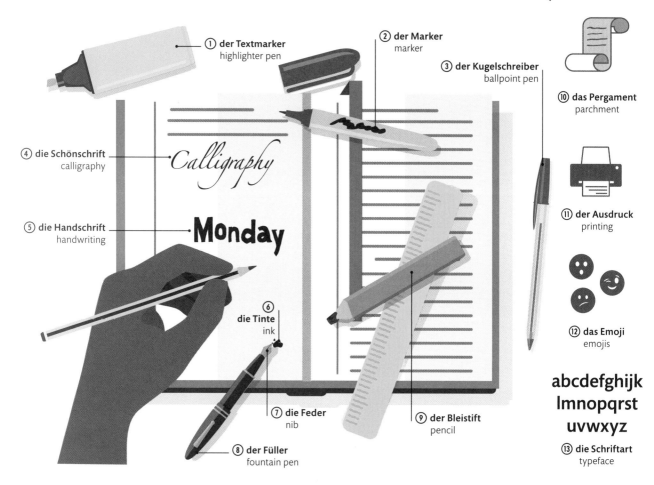

① der Textmarker
highlighter pen

② der Marker
marker

③ der Kugelschreiber
ballpoint pen

④ die Schönschrift
calligraphy

⑤ die Handschrift
handwriting

⑥ die Tinte
ink

⑦ die Feder
nib

⑧ der Füller
fountain pen

⑨ der Bleistift
pencil

⑩ das Pergament
parchment

⑪ der Ausdruck
printing

⑫ das Emoji
emojis

⑬ die Schriftart
typeface

Aa ⑭ der Buchstabe
letters

ABC ⑮ der Großbuchstabe
uppercase / capital letters

abc ⑯ der Kleinbuchstabe
lowercase

abc ⑰ fett
bold

abc ⑱ kursiv
italic

123 ⑲ die Ziffer
numerals

ft ⑳ der Buchstabenverbund
ligature

�21 der Punkt
full stop

�22 der Bindestrich
hyphen

�23 der Gedankenstrich
dash

�24 der Unterstrich
underscore

�25 das Komma
comma

See also
73 In der Schule • At school
138 Bücher und Lesen • Books and reading

;
㉖ **der Strichpunkt**
semicolon

:
㉗ **der Doppelpunkt**
colon

...
㉘ **das Auslassungszeichen**
ellipsis

!
㉙ **das Ausrufezeichen**
exclamation mark

?
㉚ **das Fragezeichen**
question mark

’
㉛ **der Apostroph**
apostrophe

‘
㉜ **das einfache Anführungszeichen**
single quotation mark

“
㉝ **das doppelte Anführungszeichen**
double quotation mark

*
㉞ **das Sternchen**
asterisk

@
㉟ **das At-Zeichen**
at sign / at symbol

&
㊱ **das Und-Zeichen**
ampersand

ũ
㊲ **die Tilde**
tilde

é
㊳ **der Accent aigu**
acute accent

è
㊴ **der Accent grave**
grave accent

ü
㊵ **der Umlaut**
umlaut

ĉ
㊶ **der Accent circonflexe**
circumflex

ç
㊷ **die Cedille**
cedilla

©
㊸ **das Copyright-Zeichen**
copyright

®
㊹ **das eingetragene Warenzeichen**
registered trademark

( )
㊺ **die Klammer**
brackets

#
㊻ **das Hashtag**
hashtag

cat
㊼ **das lateinische Alphabet**
Latin alphabet

Γάτα
㊽ **das griechische Alphabet**
Greek alphabet

кошка
㊾ **das kyrillische Alphabet**
Cyrillic alphabet

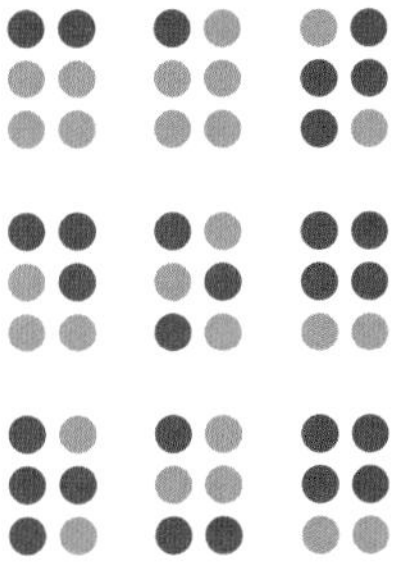
㊿ **die Blindenschrift**
Braille

قط
شجرة
ماء
(51) **die arabische Schrift**
Arabic script

市
車 両
道
(52) **die japanischen Schriftzeichen** *n, pl*
Japanese characters

桃
橘子
柠檬
(53) **die chinesischen Schriftzeichen** *n, pl*
Chinese characters

खेत
घोड़ा
नदी
(54) **Dewanagari** *f*
Devanagari script

(55) **die altägyptischen Hieroglyphen** *f, pl*
Ancient Egyptian hieroglyphs

176.1 MATERIALIEN · MATERIALS

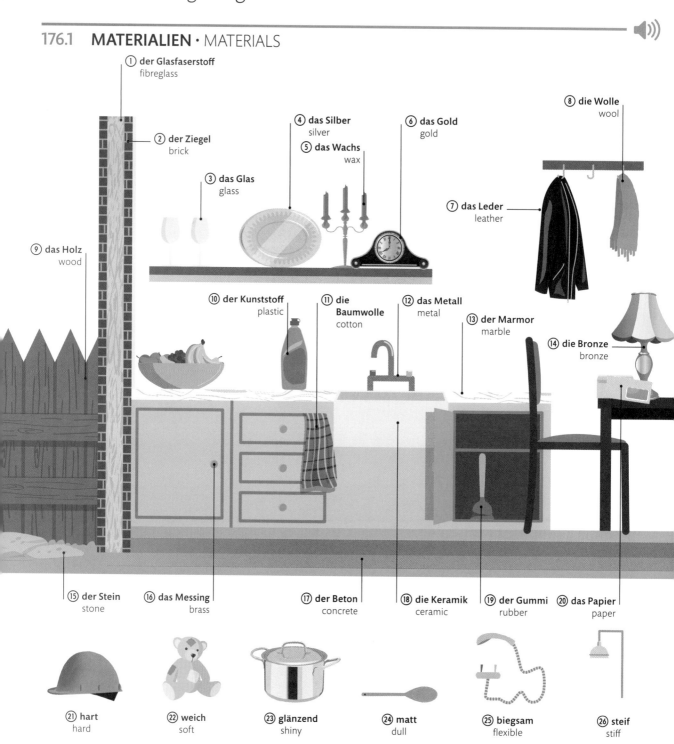

① der Glasfaserstoff
fibreglass

② der Ziegel
brick

③ das Glas
glass

④ das Silber
silver

⑤ das Wachs
wax

⑥ das Gold
gold

⑦ das Leder
leather

⑧ die Wolle
wool

⑨ das Holz
wood

⑩ der Kunststoff
plastic

⑪ die Baumwolle
cotton

⑫ das Metall
metal

⑬ der Marmor
marble

⑭ die Bronze
bronze

⑮ der Stein
stone

⑯ das Messing
brass

⑰ der Beton
concrete

⑱ die Keramik
ceramic

⑲ der Gummi
rubber

⑳ das Papier
paper

㉑ hart
hard

㉒ weich
soft

㉓ glänzend
shiny

㉔ matt
dull

㉕ biegsam
flexible

㉖ steif
stiff

See also
32 Haus und Heim • House and home **35** Heimwerken • Home improvements
37 Wohnraumverschönerung • Decorating **87** Der Bau • Construction
177 Dinge beschreiben (Fortsetzung) • Describing things continued

176.2 **ADJEKTIVE** · ADJECTIVES

① **groß**
big / large

② **klein**
small / little

③ **breit**
wide

④ **schmal / eng**
narrow

⑤ **tief**
deep

⑥ **seicht**
shallow

⑦ **hoch**
high

⑧ **niedrig**
low

⑨ **schwer**
heavy

⑩ **leicht**
light

⑪ **sauber**
clean

⑫ **schmutzig**
dirty

⑬ **heiß**
hot

⑭ **kalt**
cold

⑮ **lang**
long

⑯ **kurz**
short

⑰ **locker**
loose

⑱ **fest**
tight

⑲ **dünn**
thin

⑳ **dick**
thick

㉑ **nahe**
near

㉒ **fern**
far

㉓ **langsam**
slow

㉔ **schnell**
fast

㉕ **neu**
new

㉖ **alt**
old

㉗ **leer**
empty

㉘ **voll**
full

㉝ **hell**
light

㉞ **dunkel**
dark

㉙ **laut**
noisy

㉚ **leise**
quiet

㉛ **richtig**
correct

㉜ **falsch**
incorrect

177.1 ANSICHTEN · OPINIONS

② Was für eine atemberaubende Aussicht!
The view here is absolutely breathtaking.

① **atemberaubend**
breathtaking

③ **aufregend**
exciting

④ **schön**
beautiful

⑤ **spannend**
thrilling

⑥ **spaßig**
fun

⑦ **romantisch**
romantic

⑧ **beeindruckend**
stunning

⑨ **toll**
great

⑩ **unglaublich**
incredible

⑪ **wichtig**
important

⑫ **süß**
cute

⑬ **respektvoll**
respectful

⑭ **besonders**
special

⑮ **elegant**
graceful

⑯ **bemerkenswert**
remarkable

⑰ **herausragend**
outstanding

⑱ **urkomisch**
hilarious

⑲ **lustig**
funny

⑳ **außergewöhnlich**
extraordinary

㉑ **wundervoll**
wonderful

㉒ **harmlos**
harmless

㉓ **altmodisch**
old-fashioned

See also
06 Gefühle und Stimmung • Feelings and moods **10** Eigenschaften Personality traits **11** Fähigkeiten und Handlungen • Abilities and actions **93** Nützliche Fähigkeiten für den Arbeitsplatz • Workplace skills

㉔ **gut**
good

㉕ **schlecht**
bad

㉖ **fantastisch**
fantastic

㉗ **furchtbar**
terrible

㉘ **angenehm**
pleasant

㉙ **unangenehm**
unpleasant

㉚ **brillant**
brilliant

㉛ **schrecklich**
dreadful

㉜ **praktisch**
useful

㉝ **nutzlos**
useless

㉞ **wohlschmeckend**
delicious

㉟ **ekelerregend**
disgusting

㊱ **hübsch**
pretty

㊲ **hässlich**
ugly

㊳ **interessant**
interesting

㊴ **langweilig**
boring

㊵ **entspannend**
relaxing

㊶ **anstrengend**
exhausting

㊷ **hervorragend**
superb

㊸ **entsetzlich**
awful

㊹ **nett**
nice

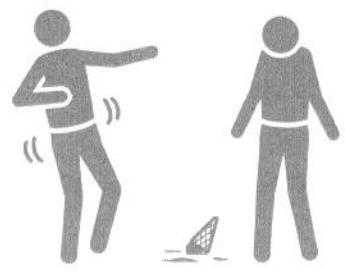
㊺ **gemein**
nasty

㊻ **verblüffend**
amazing

㊼ **durchschnittlich**
mediocre

㊽ **beängstigend**
frightening

㊾ **angsteinflößend**
terrifying

㊿ **seltsam**
strange / odd

(51) **schockierend**
shocking

(52) **ärgerlich**
annoying

(53) **fürchterlich**
horrible

(54) **ein Desaster**
disastrous

(55) **verwirrend**
confusing

(56) **ermüdend**
tiring

(57) **lästig**
irritating

(58) **grässlich**
dire

(59) **enttäuschend**
disappointing

178.1 ALLTAGSVERBEN · VERBS FOR DAILY LIFE

① **sich beruhigen**
to calm down

② **sich entspannen**
to chill out

③ **suchen**
to look for

④ **erwachsen werden**
to grow up

⑤ **jemanden anrufen**
to call up

⑥ **etwas anziehen**
to put on

⑦ **sich herausputzen**
to dress up

⑧ **angeben**
to show off

⑨ **anhäufen**
to pile up

⑩ **zurückgeben**
to give back

⑪ **einnicken**
to doze off

⑫ **ausschlafen**
to sleep in

⑬ **aufstehen**
to get up

⑭ **nach oben gehen**
to go up

⑮ **nach unten gehen**
to go down

⑯ **einholen**
to catch up

⑰ **Unsinn machen**
to mess around

⑱ **aufhängen**
to hang up

⑲ **hereinlassen**
to let in

⑳ **herausreißen**
to rip out

㉑ **etwas geht aus**
to run out (of)

㉒ **auslösen**
to set off

㉓ **über etwas stolpern**
to trip over

㉔ **abmessen**
to measure out

㉕ **zusammenbauen**
to put together

㉖ **renovieren**
to do up

㉗ **aufräumen**
to put away

㉙ Ich warte schon die ganze Nacht auf euch!
I've been waiting up all night!

㉘ **warten**
to wait up

㉚ **ausfüllen**
to fill out

㉛ **sich anmelden**
to log in

㉜ **sich abmelden**
to log out

See also
09 Die Alltagsroutine • Daily routines **11** Fähigkeiten und Handlungen
Abilities and actions **179-180** Nützliche Ausdrücke • Useful expressions

③③ aufwachen
to wake up

③④ abwiegen
to weigh out

③⑤ einschalten
to turn on

③⑥ ausschalten
to turn off

③⑦ lauter machen
to turn up

③⑧ leiser machen
to turn down

③⑨ eine Panne haben
to break down

④⓪ tanken
to fill up

④① einchecken
to check in

④② auschecken
to check out

④③ essen gehen
to eat out

④④ servieren
to wait on

④⑤ einsteigen
to get on

④⑥ aussteigen
to get off

④⑦ in Strömen regnen
to pour down

④⑧ wegfahren
to go away

④⑨ auf etwas hinweisen
to point out

⑤⓪ sich kümmern
to look after

⑤① beobachten
to look at

⑤② schenken
to give away

⑤③ verteilen
to give out

⑤④ aufgeben
to give up

**⑥⓪ Hallo! Schön, dass
ihr kommen konntet!**
Hi! So glad you could join us!

⑤⑤ sich trennen
to break up

⑤⑥ etwas absagen
to call off

⑤⑦ sich versöhnen
to make up

⑤⑧ sich treffen
to meet up

⑤⑨ sich treffen
to get together

⑥① austeilen
to hand out

⑥② aufputzen
to clean up

⑥③ aufheben
to pick up

⑥④ wegwerfen
to throw away

⑥⑤ weglaufen
to run away

⑥⑥ abfliegen
to take off

179.1 DIE BEGRÜSSUNG · GREETINGS

② **Hallo.**
Hi!

③ **Hi!**
Hello.

① **sich treffen**
to meet

⑥ **Guten Morgen.**
Good morning.

⑦ **Guten Tag.**
Good afternoon.

⑤ **Guten Abend.**
Good evening.

④ **sich (förmlich) begrüßen**
to greet (formal)

⑧ **Gute Nacht.**
Good night!

⑩ **Hey, wie geht's dir?**
Hi! How are you?

⑪ **Gut, danke.**
I'm fine, thanks.

⑫ **Nett dich zu sehen, Ed!**
Nice to see you, Ed.

⑨ **sich (informell) begrüßen**
to greet (informal)

⑭ **Auf Wiedersehen!**
Goodbye!

⑮ **Bis später!**
See you later!

⑬ **gehen**
to leave

179.2 JEMANDEN KENNENLERNEN · GETTING TO KNOW SOMEONE

① **Wie heißt du?**
What's your name?

② **Ich bin Sally.**
My name is Sally.

③ **Wie alt bist du?**
How old are you?

④ **Ich bin 25.**
I'm 25 years old.

⑤ **Wo wohnst du?**
Where do you live?

⑥ **Ich wohne in Edinburgh.**
I live in Edinburgh.

See also
07 Lebensereignisse • Life events **09** Die Alltagsroutine • Daily routines **46** Einkaufen • Shopping **180** Nützliche Ausdrücke (Fortsetzung) • Useful expressions continued

179.3 **EINKAUFEN** · SHOPPING

① **Wie viel kostet das?**
How much is this?

② **15 Dollar.**
It's 15 dollars

③ **Kann ich bei Ihnen zahlen?**
Can I pay here?

④ **Könnten Sie mir bitte die rote Tasse geben?**
Could you get the red cup for me, please?

⑤ **Kann ich Ihnen behilflich sein?**
Can I help you?

⑥ **Ich sehe mich nur um, danke.**
I'm just browsing, thanks.

⑦ **Verkaufen Sie auch Regenschirme?**
Do you sell umbrellas?

⑧ **Haben Sie das eine Größe kleiner?**
Do you have this in a smaller size?

⑨ **Lassen Sie mich kurz nachsehen.**
Let me check for you.

⑪ **Sprechen Sie Englisch?**
Do you speak English?

⑦ **Woher kommst du?**
Where are you from?

⑧ **Ich komme aus Italien.**
I'm from Italy.

⑨ **Was machen Sie beruflich?**
What do you do?

⑩ **Ich bin Diplomatin im Ruhestand.**
I'm a retired diplomat.

⑫ **Nur ein bisschen. Bitte sprechen Sie etwas langsamer.**
Only a little. Could you speak more slowly, please?

180.1 WEGBESCHREIBUNGEN · DIRECTIONS

① **Können Sie mir helfen?**
Can you help me, please?

② **Ja, natürlich!**
Yes, of course.

③ **Wo finde ich den Bahnhof?**
Where is the train station?

④ **Dahin brauchen Sie zu Fuß 15 Minuten. Biegen Sie am Supermarkt links ab.**
It's a 15-minute walk. Turn left at the supermarket.

⑤ **Wie weit ist es bis zum Hotel?**
How far is it to the hotel?

⑥ **Wir haben uns verlaufen!**
We've lost our way!

⑦ **Wir sollten nach dem Weg fragen.**
We should ask for help.

⑧ **Können Sie uns den Weg zum See zeigen?**
Can you show us the way to the lake?

⑨ **Wie kommen wir denn zum Strand?**
How do we get to the beach?

⑩ **Einfach geradeaus!**
It's straight ahead!

⑪ **Wo bekomme ich denn hier gutes Essen?**
Where can I find a good place to eat?

⑫ **Versuchen Sie es in dem Café neben der Post.**
Try the café next to the post office.

See also
42-43 In der Stadt · In town **148** Karten und
Richtungsangaben · Maps and directions

180.2 **PRÄPOSITIONEN** · PREPOSITIONS

① **innerhalb**
in

② **außerhalb**
out

③ **innen**
inside

④ **außen**
outside

⑤ **zwischen**
between

⑥ **unter**
under

⑦ **auf**
on

⑧ **neben**
next to / beside

⑨ **vor**
in front of

⑩ **hinter**
behind

⑪ **Wo ist die Katze?**
Where is
the cat?

⑫ **Sie sitzt auf
dem Regal!**
She's on the shelf!

English word list

The numbers after each word or phrase refer to the units in which they can be found.

KEY
adj – adjective
adv – adverb
n – noun
num – number
phr – phrase
prep – preposition
v – verb

A

à la carte menu *n* 69
A&E *n* 21, 50
aardvark *n* 158
abdomen *n* 01, 162
abdominals *n* 03
abilities *n* 11
ability to drive *n* 93
abseiling *n* 125
Abyssinian *n* 164
acacia *n* 47
accelerator *n* 99
access road *n* 106
accessories *n* 16
accident *n* 19
accident and
   emergency *n* 50
accommodation *n* 131
accordion *n* 129
account number *n* 45
accountant *n* 90, 94
accounts *n* 91
accurate *adj* 93
accused *n* 85
ace *n* 114, 140
ache *v* 20
Achilles tendon *n* 03
acid *n* 76
acid rain *n* 51, 155
acorn *n* 169
acoustic guitar *n* 129
acoustic guitarist *n* 129
acquaintance *n* 07

acquitted *adj* 85
acre *n* 174
acrylic paint *n* 141
act *v* 11
actinide series *n* 78
actinium *n* 78
action game *n* 136
action movie *n* 127
action points *n* 95
actions *n* 11
actor *n* 89, 126
acupressure *n* 24
acupuncture *n* 24
acute accent *n* 175
Adam's apple *n* 04
adaptable *adj* 93
add *v* 11, 29, 74
add to cart *v* 46
add to wishlist *v* 46
additives *n* 23
address *n* 45
adhesive tape *n* 20
administration *n* 91, 93
admiral *n* 88
admission fee *n* 130
admissions *n* 80
admit *v* 21
adrenal gland *n* 04
adult frog *n* 77
adult teeth *n* 03
adults *n* 05
advantage *n* 114
adventure game *n* 136
adventure
   playground *n* 133
adventurous *adj* 10
advertising *n* 91
adverts *n* 137
aerate *v* 39
aerial *n* 25, 97
aerobics *n* 124
aerobics step *n* 124
aerospace *n* 91
Afghan *adj* 153
Afghanistan *n* 151, 153
Africa *n* 149, 152
African *adj* 152
African bullfrog *n* 163
African daisy *n* 38
African elephant *n* 158
African grey
   parrot *n* 161
African wild dog *n* 158
Afro *n* 12
afternoon *n* 09, 171
aftershave *n* 18, 31
agate *n* 156
agbada *n* 15
agenda *n* 95
agriculture *n* 91
aikido *n* 117

aileron *n* 103
air ambulance *n* 50
air bed *n* 135
air cargo *n* 104
air conditioning *n* 33, 99
air control tower *n* 43
air cylinder *n* 118
air filter *n* 98, 100
air mattress *n* 135
air pump *n* 135
air vent *n* 103
airbag *n* 99
airball *n* 112
aircraft carrier *n* 88, 105
aircraft *n* 103
airforce *n* 88
airline *n* 104
airmail *n* 45
airman *n* 88
airport *n* 43, 104
airship *n* 103
airtight container *n* 52
aisle, aisles *n* 48, 80,
   103, 126
alarm *n* 50
alarm clock *n* 30
alarm goes off *phr* 09
Albania *n* 151, 153
Albanian *adj* 153
albatross *n* 160
albertonectes *n* 157
album *n* 129
alcohol-free beer *n* 68
ale *n* 68
alfalfa *n* 86
Algeria *n* 149, 152
Algerian *adj* 152
Alice band *n* 16
alien *n* 139
alkali *n* 76
alkali metals *n* 78
alkaline earth metals *n* 78
all-terrain vehicle *n* 100
Allen keys *n* 36
allergic *adj* 23
allergy *n* 19
alley *n* 42
alloy *n* 76
allspice *n* 59
almond milk *n* 61
almond oil *n* 60
almonds *n* 58, 68
aloe *n* 167
alpaca *n* 165
alpine plants *n* 41
alternating current *n* 33, 75
alto *n* 126
aluminium *n* 78, 156
always *adj* 171
amaryllis *n* 167
amazed *adj* 06

amazing *adj* 177
Amazon *n* 145
ambitious *adj* 10, 93
ambulance *n* 21, 50
ambulance stretcher *n* 50
American *adj* 152
American alligator *n* 163
American curl *n* 164
American
   football field *n* 107
American football *n* 107
American football positions
   n 107
americium *n* 78
amethyst *n* 156
amount *n* 45
amp *n* 33
ampersand *n* 175
amphibians *n* 163
amphibious vehicle *n* 88
amplifier *n* 129
amulet *n* 139
amused *adj* 06
anaesthetist *n* 90
analytics *n* 93
anchor *n* 105, 119
anchovies *n* 64
Ancient Egyptian
   hieroglyphs *n* 175
Ancient Greek temple *n* 44
ancient ruins *n* 44
Andean condor *n* 160
Andorra *n* 151, 153
Andorran *adj* 153
anemone *n* 134, 166
Angel Falls *n* 145
angle *n* 74
angler *n* 121
angler fish *n* 166
Angola *n* 149, 152
Angolan *adj* 152
Angora *n* 164
angry *adj* 06
animal cell *n* 77
animation *n* 127
anise *n* 59
ankle *n* 01-02
ankle boots *n* 17
ankle strap heels *n* 17
ankle weights *n* 124
anklet *n* 16
anniversary *n* 07
annoyed *adj* 06
annoying *adj* 177
annual *n* 41
annual general
   meeting (AGM) *n* 95
annual leave *n* 81
anorak *n* 15
answer *v* 73
ant *n* 162
anteater *n* 159
antenna *n* 162
anther *n* 38

anti-inflammatory *n* 49
antibiotics *n* 49
anticlockwise *adv* 148
antifreeze *n* 97
Antigua and
   Barbuda *n* 150, 152
Antiguan *adj* 152
antimony *n* 78
antiques shop *n* 46
antiseptic *n* 20
antiseptic wipes *n* 20
antler *n* 159
anxious *adj* 06
any other business
   phr 95
apartment *n* 131
apex *n* 74
apostrophe *n* 175
app developer *n* 89
appeal *n* 85
appearance *n* 12
appendicitis *n* 19
appendix *n* 04
applause *n* 126
apple *n* 58
apple corer *n* 28
apple juice *n* 65
applicant *n* 81
application form *n* 92
apply for a job *v* 92
applying for a job *n* 92
appointment *n* 20, 81
appreciative *adj* 06
apprentice *n* 81, 92
approachable *adj* 10
apricot *n* 57
April *n* 172
apron *n* 13, 29
aquamarine *n* 156
aquarium *n* 164
Aquarius *n* 144
Arabic script *n* 175
arable farm *n* 86
arbor knot *n* 121
arc *n* 74, 112
arch *n* 02, 41, 44
arch window *n* 32
archaeological
   site *n* 132
archaeology *n* 79
archaeologist *n* 79
archer *n* 125
archery *n* 125
archipelago *n* 147
architect *n* 90
architecture *n* 44
archive *n* 79
Arctic *n* 159
Arctic Circle *n* 145
Arctic fox *n* 159
Arctic hare *n* 159
Arctic tern *n* 160
Arctic wolf *n* 159
area *n* 74, 174

arena *n* 120
Argentina *n* 149, 152
Argentinian *adj* 152
argon *n* 78
Aries *n* 144
arm, arms *n* 01, 126
arm circles *n* 124
arm protection *n* 110
armadillo *n* 159
armband *n* 118
armchair *n* 26
armed drone *n* 88
armed forces *n* 88
Armenia *n* 150, 153
Armenian *adj* 153
armour *n* 79
armoured
   vehicle *n* 88
armpit *n* 01
armrest *n* 99, 103
army *n* 88
aromatherapy *n* 24
arrest *n* 50
arrival *n* 43
arrive *v* 09
arrive early *v* 09
arrive home *v* 09
arrive late *v* 09
arrive on time *v* 09
arrogant *adj* 10
arrow *n* 79, 125
arrow slit *n* 44
arsenic *n* 78
art, arts *n* 73, 91, 141-142
art college *n* 80
Art Deco *n* 130
art gallery *n* 43, 130, 132
Art Nouveau *n* 130
art school *n* 80
art shop *n* 46
art therapy *n* 24
artery *n* 04
artichoke *n* 56
artichoke heart *n* 56
article *n* 138
articulated bus *n* 99
artificial intelligence *n* 83
artisan *n* 79
artist *n* 90, 141
arum lily *n* 167
ash *n* 145
ash cloud *n* 145
Asia *n* 150, 153
Asian *adj* 153
Asian elephant *n* 159
Asian vine snake *n* 163
ask directions *v* 148
asparagus *n* 56
asparagus tip *n* 56
assertive *adj* 10, 93
astatine *n* 78
asterisk *n* 175
asteroid *n* 143
asthma *n* 19

astigmatism *n* 22
astronaut *n* 143
astronomy *n* 144
at sign *n* 83, 175
at symbol *n* 83, 175
athlete *n* 116
athletics *n* 116, 125
athletics track *n* 116
Atlantic puffin *n* 160
Atlantic salmon *n* 166
atlas moth *n* 162
atlas *n* 73
ATM *n* 45
atmosphere *n* 143, 155
atoll *n* 147
atom *n* 76
attachment *n* 83
attack helicopter *n* 88
attack zone *n* 110
attend a meeting *v* 95
attic *n* 25
attractions *n* 132
aubergine *n* 56
auburn hair *n* 12
audience *n* 126, 127
audio *n* 136
audio guide *n* 130
audition *n* 127
August *n* 172
aunt *n* 05
aurora *n* 144, 155
Australia *n* 150, 153
Australian *adj* 153
Australian
   little penguin *n* 161
Austria *n* 151, 153
Austrian *adj* 153
author *n* 138
autobiography *n* 138
autocue *n* 84
automatic *n* 99
automotive industry
   n 91
autumn *n* 57, 172
autumn leaf *n* 169
avalanche *n* 122
avatar *n* 84
avenue *n* 43
avocado *n* 56
avocado toast *n* 71
avocado tree *n* 167
awful *adj* 177
awning *n* 65
axe *n* 36, 50, 79
axle *n* 100
ayran *n* 61
ayurveda *n* 24
azalea *n* 38
Azerbaijan *n* 150, 153
Azerbaijani *adj* 153

B

babies' clothes *n* 13
baboon *n* 158
baby *n* 05
baby bath *n* 08
baby changing
   facilities *n* 47
baby formula *n* 08
baby monitor *n* 08, 30
baby products *n* 48
baby sweetcorn *n* 55
babygro *n* 13
back *adj* 03
back *n* 26
back bacon *n* 53
back brush *n* 31
back door *n* 97
back seat *n* 99
back up *v* 83
back-flip *n* 118
backache *n* 19
backboard *n* 112
backdrop *n* 126
backgammon *n* 140
backhand *n* 114
backing singers *n* 129
backpack *n* 16, 135
backpack sprayer *n* 40
backstay *n* 119
backstop net *n* 113
backstroke *n* 118
backswing *n* 115
bacon *n* 53, 71
bacteria *n* 77, 157
Bactrian camel *n* 158
bad *adj* 52, 177
bad robot *n* 139
badge *n* 50
badge *n* 16
badminton *n* 114
bag, bags *n* 16, 52
bag store *n* 47
bagel *n* 62, 71
baggage claim *n* 104
baggage trailer *n* 104
bagpipes *n* 129
baguette *n* 62
baggy *adj* 13, 176
Bahamas *n* 150, 162
Bahamian *adj* 152
Bahrain *n* 151, 153
Bahraini *adj* 153
bail *n* 85, 111
Baisakhi *n* 07
bait *n* 121
bait *v* 121
bake *v* 29, 62-63
baked *adj* 72

baked beans *n* 71
baker *n* 62
bakery *n* 46, 48, 62-63
baking *n* 29
baking tray *n* 29
baklava *n* 63
balance wheel *n* 142
balanced diet *n* 23
balcony *n* 25
bald *adj* 12
bald eagle *n* 160
ball *n* 02, 08, 109-110,
   112, 114
ball boy *n* 114
ball girl *n* 114
ballerina *n* 126
ballet *n* 126
ballet flats *n* 17
ballet leotard *n* 126
ballet shoes *n* 126
ballistic missile *n* 88
balloon *n* 08
ballpoint pen *n* 175
balsamic vinegar *n* 60
bamboo *n* 41, 55, 167
banana *n* 58
band *n* 129
bandage *n* 20, 49
banded sea krait *n* 166
Bangladesh *n* 150, 153
Bangladeshi *adj* 153
bangle *n* 16
banister *n* 25-26
banjo *n* 129
bank *n* 45, 94
bank loan *n* 45
bank statement *n* 45
banking *n* 91
banner *n* 109
baobab tree *n* 169
baptism *n* 07
bar, bars *n* 30, 68, 109, 124
bar chart *n* 95
bar counter *n* 68
bar mitzvah *n* 07
bar snacks *n* 68
bar stool *n* 68
bar tender *n* 69
barb *n* 121
Barbadian *adj* 152
Barbados *n* 150, 152
barbecue *n* 41
barbecue *n* 135
barbell *n* 124
barber *n* 89
barberry *n* 168
Barbudan *adj* 152
barcode *n* 48
bare branches *n* 172
bargain *n* 48
barista *n* 65, 89
baritone *n* 126
barium *n* 78
bark *v* 164

barley *n* 86
barn *n* 86
barn owl *n* 161
barnacle *n* 134, 166
barracuda *n* 166
barrel cactus *n* 168
Barrier Reef *n* 145
bartender *n* 68, 89
basa *n* 54
basalt *n* 156
base *n* 74, 76
baseball *n* 113
baseball cap *n* 16
baseball cleats *n* 17
baseball game *n* 113
baseline *n* 114
basement *n* 25, 47
basil *n* 59
basin *n* 22, 33
basket *n* 48, 101, 103,
   112, 164
basket of fruit *n* 57
basketball *n* 112
basketball player *n* 112
basking shark *n* 166
Basotho *adj* 152
basque *n* 14
bass *n* 126
bass clef *n* 128
bass drum *n* 128
bass guitarist *n* 129
basset hound *n* 164
bassoon *n* 128
bat *n* 111, 113-114, 158
bat *v* 111, 113
bat mitzvah *n* 07
bath towel *n* 31
bath toys *n* 31
bath tub *n* 31
bathmat *n* 31
bathroom *n* 31
bathroom extractor
   fan *n* 31
bathroom scales *n* 31
baton *n* 116
batsman *n* 111
Battenburg markings *n* 50
batter *n* 111, 113
battering ram *n* 79
battery *n* 75, 83, 98
battery pack *n* 35
batting glove *n* 113
battle *n* 79, 88
battlement *n* 44
battleship *n* 105
Bauhaus *n* 130
bay *n* 147
bay leaf *n* 59
bay tree *n* 38
bay window *n* 25
bayonet base *n* 33
be absent *v* 95
be born *v* 07
be delayed *v* 104

E

F

go on a holiday v 131
go on an excursion v 132
go on a tour v 132
go on Hajj v 07
go on maternity leave v 81
go out of business v 94
go out with friends v 09
go past
  (the restaurant) v 148
go straight
  on v 96, 148
go to a café v 09
go to bed v 09
go to nursery v 07
go to school v 09
go to sleep v 09
go to work v 09
go up v 178
go viral v 84
go-cart n 123
goal n 108-110
goal crease n 110
goal line n 107, 110
goal posts n 108
goalball n 125
goalie stick n 110
goalkeeper n 109-110
goalpost n 107-09
goat n 53, 165
goat's cheese n 61
goat's milk n 61
goatee n 12
goblin n 139
goggles n 15, 118, 122
goji berry n 57
gold adj 176
gold n 78, 116, 156, 176
gold-plated visor n 143
golden eagle n 160
golden guinea vine n 168
golf n 115
golf bag n 115
golf ball n 115
golf cap n 115
golf clubs n 115
golf course n 115
golf equipment n 115
golf shoe,
  golf shoes n 17, 115
golf trolley n 115
golfer n 115
gong n 128
good adj 177
good afternoon phr 179
good evening phr 179
good listener n 93
good morning phr 179
good night phr 179
goodbye phr 179
goose n 53, 165
goose egg n 61
gooseberry n 57
gorilla n 159
gosling n 165

gospel n 129
gossip magazine n 138
government building n 43
GPS n 99
grab bar n 31
graceful adj 177
grade n 73
grader n 87
graduate n 80
graduate v 07
graduation ceremony n 80
graffiti n 85
graft v 39
gram n 174
granary bread n 62
granddaughter n 05
grandfather n 05
grandmother n 05
grandparents n 05
grandson n 05
granite n 156
grapefruit n 57
grapes n 57
grapeseed oil n 60
grapevine n 168
graphite n 156
grass, grasses n 25, 41, 167
grass collector n 40
grass tree n 167
grasshopper n 162
grassland n 146
grate v 29
grated cheese n 61
grater n 28
grave accent n 175
gravel n 35, 40
gravity n 144
graze n 19
grease v 29
greasy hair n 12
great adj 177
Great Blue Hole n 145
great crested newt n 163
Great Dane n 164
great grey owl n 161
Great Mosque
  of Djenné n 44
Great Plains toad n 163
great white shark n 166
greater spotted
  woodpecker n 160
grebe n 161
Greece n 151, 153
Greek adj 153
Greek alphabet n 175
Greek mythology n 139
Greek salad n 72
green adj 01, 141
green n 115, 141
green basilisk n 163
green beans n 55
green energy n 51
green foliage n 172

green olives n 64
green sea turtle n 163
green tea n 66
green woodpecker n 160
greengrocer n 89
greengrocers n 46, 56
greenhouse n 39
greenhouse effect n 155
greenhouse gases n 155
greet v 179
greetings n 179
gremlin n 139
Grenada n 150, 152
grenade n 88
grenade launcher n 88
Grenadian adj 152
grey adj 01, 141
grey n 01, 141
grey hair n 12
grey willow n 169
grid lines n 148
griddle pan n 28
griffin n 139
grill v 29
grilled adj 72
grilled tomato n 71
grin v 02
grip n 115
groin n 01
groin protector n 117
groom n 07
groom v 120
groove n 115
ground chilli n 59
ground cinnamon n 59
ground cover n 41
ground floor n 25, 47
ground level n 47
ground maintenance n 89
ground mince n 53
ground sheet n 135
groundnut oil n 60
group therapy n 24
grout n 37
grow up v 178
grow your hair v 12
growing up n 05
grunt v 165
guarantee n 47
Guatemala n 150, 152
Guatemalan adj 152
guava n 58, 168
guest n 26
guest house n 131
guest speaker n 95
guests n 131
guidebook n 131-132, 138
guided tour n 132
guillemot n 160
guilty adj 06, 85
Guinea n 149, 152
guinea pig n 164
Guinea-Bissau n 149, 152
Guinean adj 152

gulf n 147
gull n 134
gully n 111
gulp v 52
gulper eel n 166
gum n 03
gun, guns n 88
gunfire n 88
gunnera n 168
gutter n 25, 43
guy rope n 135
Guyana n 149, 152
Guyanese adj 152
gym n 124, 131
gym equipment n 124
gym machines n 124
gymnastics n 125
gynaecology n 21
gypsophila n 47
gyrocopter n 103

H

habitat loss n 155
hacking n 85
hacksaw n 36
hadal zone n 166
haddock tail n 54
haemorrhage n 19
hafnium n 78
haggle v 46
hailstone n 154
hair n 01, 12
hair band n 16
hair curler n 12
hair dryer n 12
hair dye n 18
hair gel n 12
hair salon n 47
hair scissors n 12
hair spray n 12
hair straightener n 12
hair towel wrap n 18
hairbrush n 12
hairdresser n 89
hairpin turn n 123
Haiti n 150, 152
Haitian adj 152
hakama n 117
halal adj 72
half num 173
half an hour n 171
half moon pose n 24
half time n 109
half-court line n 112

half-litre n 174
half-way line n 109
halfback n 107
halfway line n 108
halibut n 54
halloumi n 64
Halloween n 07
halls of residence n 80
hallway n 25-26
halogens n 78
halter n 120
halter neck n 15
halva n 67
ham n 53, 71
hamburger n 70
hammer n 36, 116
hammer v 35
hammerhead
  shark n 166
hammock n 135
hamper n 133, 134
hamster n 158, 164
hamstrings n 03
hand, hands n 01-02
hand cream n 18
hand drill n 36
hand fork n 40
hand grips n 124
hand in
  your notice v 81
hand luggage n
  103-104
hand out v 178
hand towel n 31
handbag n 16
handball n 125
handbrake n 99
handcuffs n 50
handful n 29
handicap n 115
handkerchief n 16
handle n 16, 28, 40, 87,
  110, 113-114
handle with care phr 45
handlebar n 101
handouts n 95
handrail n 25, 99
handsaw n 36
handsome adj 12
handwriting n 175
hang v 37
hang glider n 125
hang out clothes v 34
Hang Son Doong n 145
hang up v 14, 178
hang-gliding n 125
hangar n 104
hanging basket n 41
hangman n 140
Hanukkah n 07
happy adj 06
harbour n 106
harbour master n 106
hard adj 57, 176

M

O

send v 83
send a parcel v 09
Senegal n 149, 152
Senegalese adj 152
sensitive adj 10, 18
sentence n 85
sepal n 38
September n 172
Serbia n 151, 153
Serbian adj 153
series n 137
serious adj 06, 10
serve v 65, 114
service charge n 69
service focused adj 93
service included phr 69
service line n 114
service not
   included phr 69
service station n 148
service the car v 98
service vehicle n 104
services n 131
serving spoon n 27
sesame allergy n 23
sesame seed oil n 60
set n 114, 126
set honey n 60
set menu n 69
set off v 98, 178
set sail v 106
set square n 73-74
set the alarm v 09
set the table v 26, 34
sets n 126
setter n 112, 164
seven num 173
seventeen num 173
seventh num 173
seventy num 173
sew v 142
sewing n 142
sewing box n 142
sewing machine n 142
sewing needle n 142
Seychelles n 149, 152
Seychellois adj 152
shade plants n 41
shaft n 115
shaggy bracket
   fungus n 170
shaggy mane
   mushroom n 170
shake v 11
shake hands v 92
shake your head v 02
shale n 51
shale gas n 51
shallot n 56
shallow adj 176
shallow end n 118
shaobing n 62
shapes n 74
share v 84

share price n 94
share your screen v 95
shares n 94
sharp adj 128
sharpening stone n 36
shave v 09, 12, 31
shaved head n 12
shaving foam n 31
shears n 40
shed n 25, 39
sheep n 165
sheep farm n 86
sheep's milk n 61
sheep's milk cheese n 61
sheer v 165
sheet n 30, 119
shelf n 26-27
shell n 58, 61, 163
shelter n 44
shelves n 27, 48
sherry n 68
shiatsu n 24
shield n 40, 79
shih tzu n 164
shiitake mushroom n
   56, 170
shin n 01
shin guard n 110
shiny adj 176
ship's captain n 89
shipping n 91
shipping container n 106
ships n 105
shipyard n 106
shirt n 15
shiver v 02
shocked adj 06
shocking adj 177
shoe accessories n 17
shoe brush n 17
shoe polish n 17
shoe shop n 46
shoe trees n 17
shoelaces n 17
shoes n 17
shoe accessories n 17
shoot v 112
shooting guard n 112
shop n 42
shop window n 25
shoplifting n 85
shopper n 47
shopping n 46, 179
shopping
   centre n 42, 47
shopping channel n 137
shopping list n 46
shopping mall n 42, 47
shopping spree n 46
short adj 12, 176
short corner n 112
short hair n 12
short-sighted adj 22
short-sleeved shirt n 14

shortbread n 63
shorts n 14
shot n 68
shot put n 116
shotgun n 88
shoulder n 01
shoulder bag n 16
shoulder blade n 03
shoulder pad n 15, 107,
   110
shoulder strap n 16
shoulder-launched
   missile n 88
shoulder-length hair n 12
shout v 11
shovel n 40, 87
show of hands n 95
show off v 178
shower n 31
shower block n 135
shower curtain n 31
shower door n 31
shower gel n 31
showjumping n 120
shredder n 82
shrinking glaciers n 155
shrubs n 41
shrug v 02
shuffle v 140
shutoff valve n 33
shutter n 25
shuttle bus n 99
shuttlecock n 114
shy adj 10
Siamese n 164
Siberian husky n 164
siblings n 05
side n 69, 74
side car n 100
side dishes n 72
side effects n 49
side order n 69
side parting n 12
side plate n 27
side shuffles n 124
side street n 42
side view n 97
side-saddle n 120
sideboard n 26
sideburns n 12
sidedeck n 119
sideline n 107, 112, 114
sidestroke n 118
sidewinder n 163
Sierra Leone n 149, 152
Sierra Leonean adj 152
sieve n 28
sieve v 39
sift v 62
sigh v 02
sightseeing n 99, 132
sign n 104
sign a contract v 92
signal n 102

signature n 45, 83
signet ring n 16
silencer n 98, 100
silicon n 78
silk n 13
silk tree n 168
silly adj 10
silo n 86
silt n 39
Silurian adj 157
Silurian n 157
silver adj 176
silver n 78, 116, 156, 176
sim card n 48
simmer v 29
simulation game n 136
sing v 11
Singapore n 151, 153
Singaporean adj 153
singer n 89
single adj 68
single bed n 30
single cream n 61
single parent n 05
single quotation
   mark n 175
single room n 131
single-burner
   camping stove n 135
singles n 114
sink n 27
sink n 33
sinus n 04
sip v 52
sirloin steak n 53
sister n 05
sister-in-law n 05
sit down v 11
sit-up n 124
sitar n 129
sitcom n 137
site manager n 89
site manager's office n 135
six num 173
sixteen num 173
sixth num 173
sixty num 173
skate n 54, 122
skate v 110
skate wing n 54
skateboard n 125
skateboarding n 125, 133
skein n 142
skeleton n 03, 122
sketch n 141
sketch pad n 141
skewer n 28
ski n 119, 122
ski boot n 17, 122
ski instructor n 89
ski jacket n 122
ski jump n 122
ski lodge n 122
ski pole n 122

ski resort n 122
ski run n 122
ski slope n 122
skier n 122
skiing n 122
skillet n 28
skimmed milk n 61
skin n 01, 58
skin care n 49
skin type n 18
skip v 124
skipping n 133
skipping
   rope n 08, 124
skirt n 14
skirting board n 30
skittles n 08
skull n 03
skunk n 158
skydiving n 125
skyscraper n 42
slalom n 122
slate n 156
sledgehammer n 87
sledging n 122
sleep in v 178
sleeping bag n 135
sleeping
   compartment n 102
sleeping mat n 135
sleeping pills n 49
sleepsuit n 13
sleet n 154
sleeve n 15
sleeveless adj 15
sleigh n 122
slice n 53, 114
slice v 29, 62
sliced bread n 62
slicer n 62
slide n 43, 77, 95
slide v 113
slides n 17
sling n 19-20
slingback heels n 17
slip n 14, 111
slip road n 96
slip-ons n 17
slippers n 14, 17
slit skirt n 15
sloth n 159
slotted spoon n 28
Slovakia n 151, 153
Slovakian adj 153
Slovenia n 151, 153
Slovenian adj 153
slow adj 176
slow down v 98
slug n 162
sluice gates n 51
small adj 176
small creatures n 162
small forward n 112
small intestine n 04

Z

XY

German word list

The numbers after each word or phrase refer to the units in which they can be found. The article precedes the word in cases where the suffix would change without it.

À-la-Carte-Menü 69
Aal 54
Ab Wheel 124
Abbau der Ozonschicht 155
abbeißen 52
Abbeizmittel 37
abbremsen 98
Abdecktuch 37
Abend 09, 171
Abenddämmerung 171
das Abendessen 26, 72
Abendessen kochen 09
Abendkarte 69
Abendkleid 15
abenteuerlustig 10
Abenteuerspiel 136
Abenteuerspielplatz 133
Abessinierkatze 164
Abfahrt 122
Abfahrtstafel 102
Abfall 33, 155
Abfalleimer 33, 82
Abfallsammelstelle 135
abfangen 113
abfliegen 178
Abflug 43, 104
Abflughalle 104
Abfluss 31, 33, 43
Abfluss (der Toilette) frei machen 35
Abfluss (des Waschbeckens) frei machen 35
Abflussrohr 33
Abführmittel 49
abgelenkt 06
Abholzung 155

Abisolierzange 36
Ablage 82
Ableger 39
abmessen 178
Abmessungen 74
abnähen 142
Abnäher 142
abnehmen 20, 23
Abpfiff 109
absagen 69
Absatz 17
abschlagen 115
Abschlagplatz 115
abschleppen 96
Abschleppwagen 98
Abschluss 80
Abschluss machen 07
Abschlussfeier 80
der abschmelzende Eisschild 155
der abschmelzende Gletscher 155
abschreiben 11
Abseilen 125
abseits der Piste 122
absetzen 98
Abspannleine 135
Absperrung 96
Absperrventil 33
abspielen 137
abspülen 09
abstauben 34
absteigen 100, 101
abstimmen 85
Abteil 102
Abteilungen 21, 91
Abtropfgestell 27
abwehren 112
abwesend sein 95
abwiegen 178
Abyssopelagial 166
Abzieher 34
Accent aigu 175
Accent circonflexe 175
Accent grave 175
Accessoires 16
Achat 156
Achillessehne 03
Achse 100
Achsel 01
acht 173
Achteck 74
Achtel 173
achter / achte 173
Achterbahn 133
Achterdeck 105

Achterstag 119
Achtsamkeit 24
achtzehn 173
achtzig 173
Ackerbaubetrieb 86
Ackerland 86, 146
Ackerwinde 169
Acre 174
Acrylfarbe 141
Actinoide 78
Actionfilm 127
Actionspiel 136
Adamsapfel 04
addieren 11, 74
Adel 79
Adelsherr 79
Adjektive 52, 176
Admiral / Admiralin 88
Adresse 45
Advantage 114
Aerobic 124
Aerobic-Stepper 124
Affenbrotbaum 169
afghanisch 153
Afghanistan 151, 153
Afrika 149, 152
afrikanisch 152
der Afrikanische Elefant 158
der Afrikanische Ochsenfrosch 163
der Afrikanische Wildhund 158
Afro 12
Aftershave 18, 31
Agbada 15
Ägypten 149, 152
ägyptisch 152
Ahorn 169
Ahornsirup 60
Aikido 117
Airbag 99
Airball 112
Akazie 47
Akelei 168
Akkord 128
Akkordeon 129
Akku 35, 83
Akkubohrer 35
akkurat 10
Aktenschrank 82
Aktentasche 16
Aktien 94
Aktienbroker / Aktienbrokerin 94
Aktienpreis 94

Aktinium 78
Aktionspunkt 95
Aktivitäten 09
Aktivitäten an der frischen Luft 133
Aktivitäten im Freien 133
aktuelle Geschehnisse 137
Akupressur 24
Akupunktur 24
Akustikgitarre 129
Akustikgitarrist / Akustikgitarristin 129
Alarmanlage 25, 50
Albanien 151, 153
albanisch 153
Albatros 160
albern 10
Albertonectes 157
Album 129
Ale 68
Alfalfa 86
Algerien 149, 152
algerisch 152
Alkali 76
Alkalimetalle 78
das alkoholfreie Bier 68
der alkoholfreie Cocktail 68
Alkoholtest 50
Alkoholwischtuch 20
alle Zimmer besetzt 131
alle zwei Tage 172
Allee 43
der / die Alleinerziehende 05
allen antworten 83
Allergie 19
allergisch 23
alles besetzt 135
allgemeines Aussehen 12
Allradfahrzeug 97
Alltagsroutine 09
Alltagsverben 178
Aloe 167
Alpaka 165
Alpen-Hauswurz 168
alt 12, 126, 176
altägyptische Hieroglyphen 175
alte Ruine 44
altgriechische Tempel 44
altmodisch 177
Aluminium 78, 156
am Spalier aufziehen 39
Amanita ocreata 170
Amaryllis 167
Amazonas 145
ambulant 21

Ameise 162
Ameisenbär 159
Ameisenigel 158
American Curl 164
American Football 107
Americium 78
Amethyst 156
Ampel 43, 96
Ampere 33
Amphibien 163
Amphibienfahrzeug 88
Amsel 160
Amulett 139
amüsiert 06
an Bord gehen 106
an der Kreuzung 148
an einer Besprechung teilnehmen 95
Analyse 93
Ananas 58, 167
Ananas-Guave 58
Ananassaft 65
Anästhesiologe / Anästhesiologin 90
anbeißen 121
anbrennen 29
Anchovi 64
Andenkirsche 57
Andenkondor 160
Andentanne 167
Andorra 151, 153
andorranisch 153
Anemone 134, 166
anfahren 148
anfangen 95
angeben 178
Angebot 82
angeekelt 06
angehen 148
der / die Angeklagte 85
Angel 121
Angel Falls 145
Angelausrüstung 121
Angelhaken 121
Angelkasten 121
Angeln 121
Angelschein 121
angenehm 177
das angeordnete Gedränge 108
Angler / Anglerin 121
Anglerfisch 166
Anglerweste 121
Angola 149, 152
angolanisch 152
Angorakatze 164
angreifen 107, 108
Angriff 107
Angriffszone 110

E

G

H

M

Acknowledgments

The publisher would like to thank:

Dr. Steven Snape for his assistance with hieroglyphs. Elizabeth Blakemore for editorial assistance; Mark Lloyd, Charlotte Johnson, and Anna Scully for design assistance; Simon Mumford for national flags; Sunita Gahir and Ali Jayne Scrivens for additional illustration; Adam Brackenbury for art colour correction; Claire Ashby and Romaine Werblow for images; William Collins for fonts; Lori Hand, Kayla Dugger, and Jane Perlmutter for Americanization; Justine Willis for proofreading; Elizabeth Blakemore for indexing; Helen Peters for the wordlists; Christine Stroyan for audio recording management and ID Audio for audio recording and production.

DK India

Senior Art Editors Vikas Sachdeva, Ira Sharma; **Art Editor** Anukriti Arora; **Assistant Art Editors** Ankita Das, Adhithi Priya; **Editors** Hina Jain, Saumya Agarwal; **DTP Designer** Manish Upreti

DK WHAT WILL YOU LEARN NEXT?

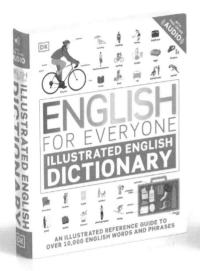

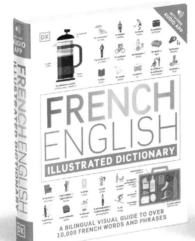

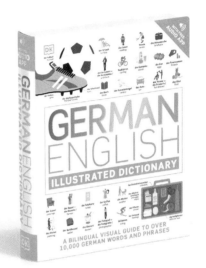

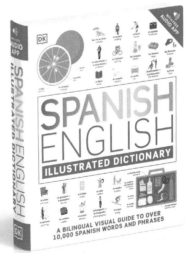